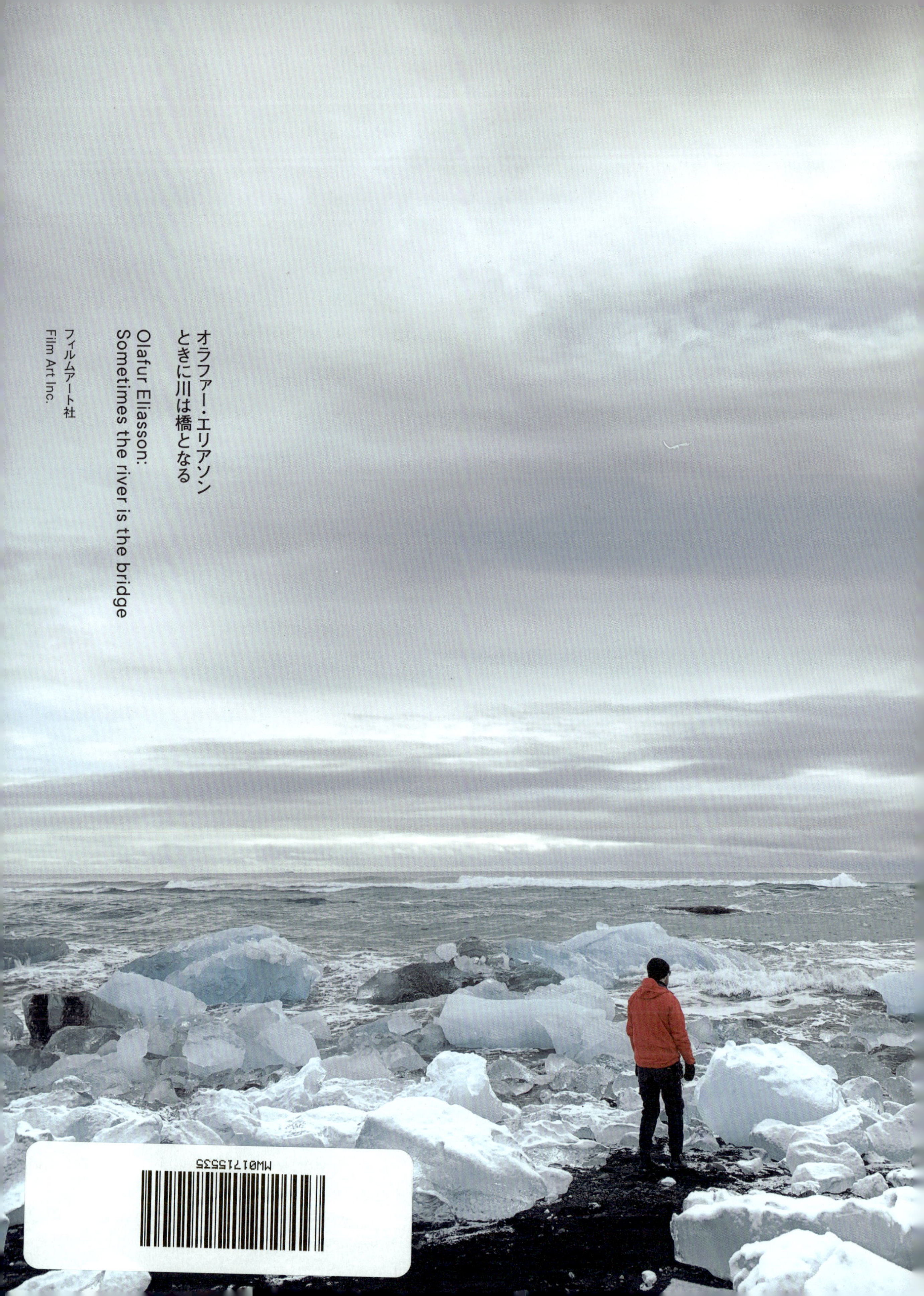

オラファー・エリアソン
ときに川は橋となる

Olafur Eliasson:
Sometimes the river is the bridge

フィルムアート社
Film Art Inc.

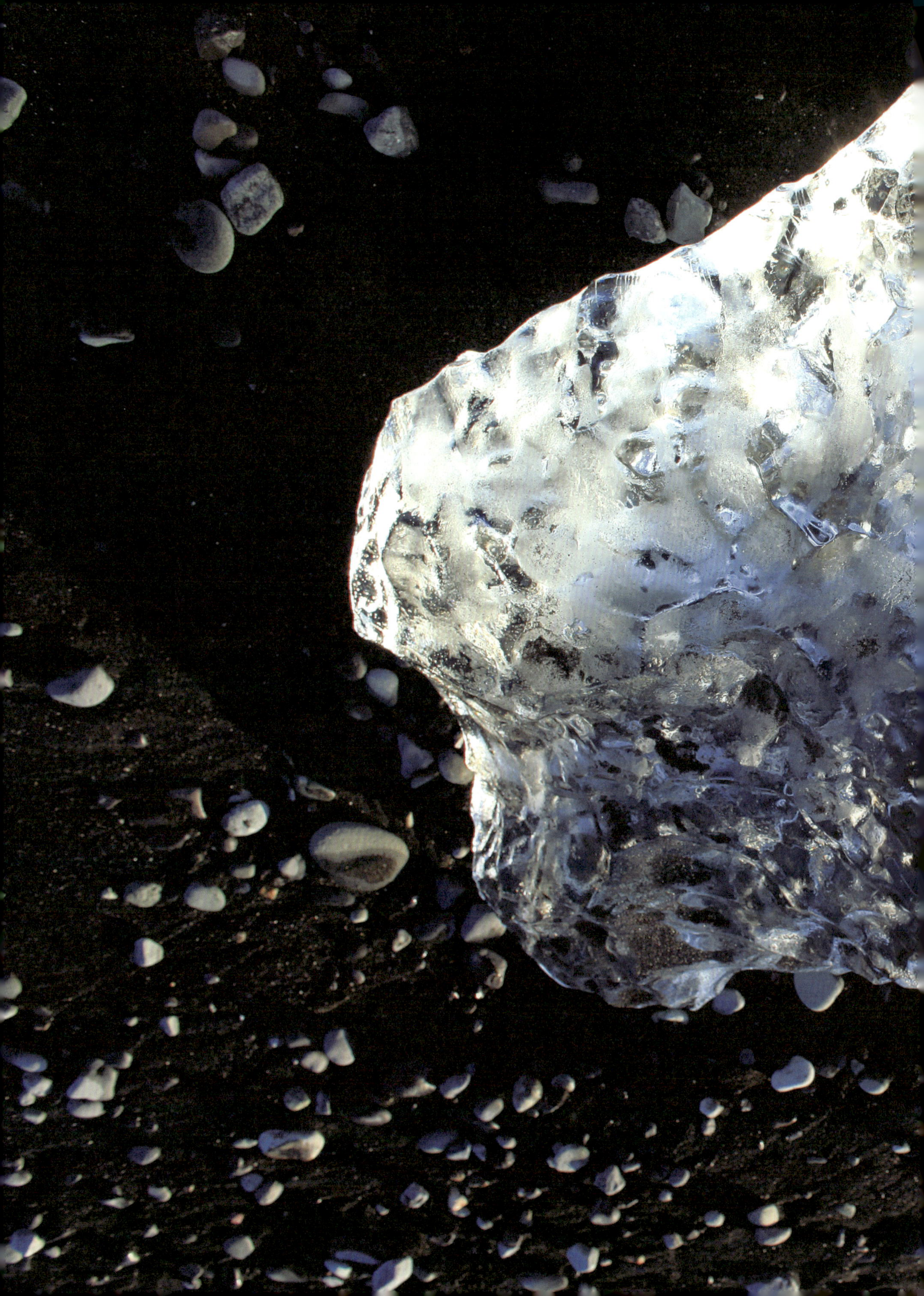

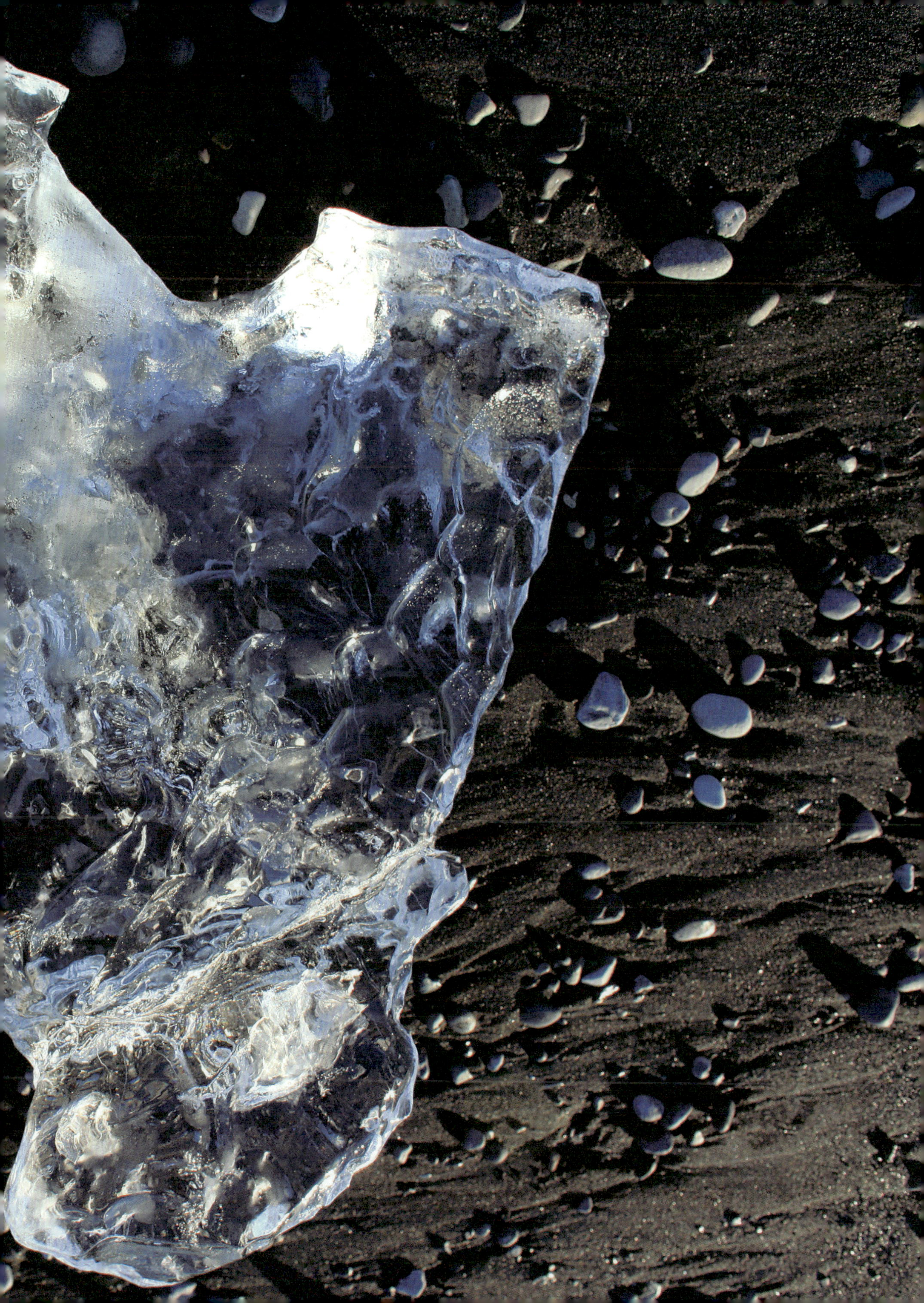

目次

図版

テキスト

付録

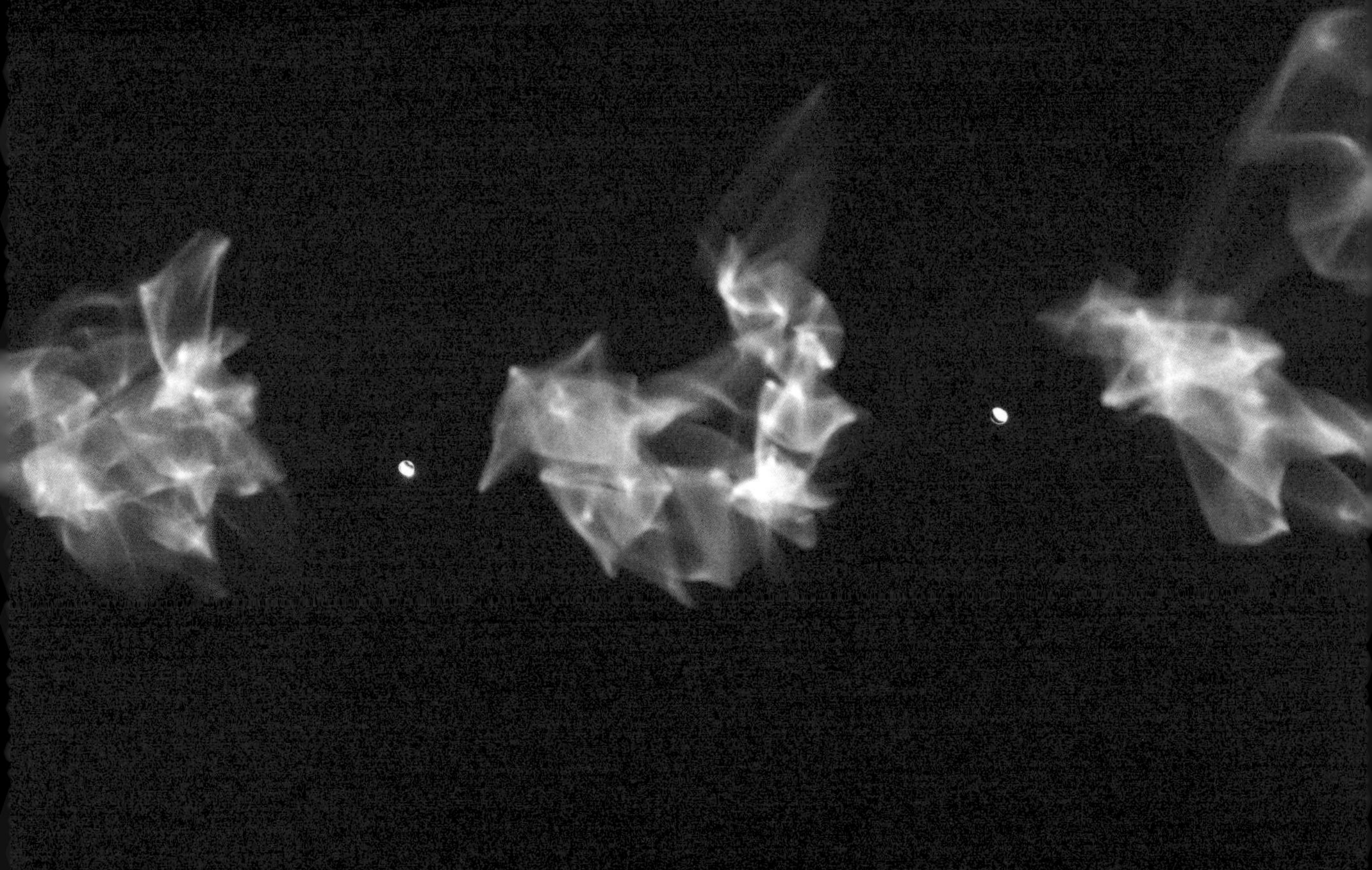

Contents

Plates

Essays

Appendices

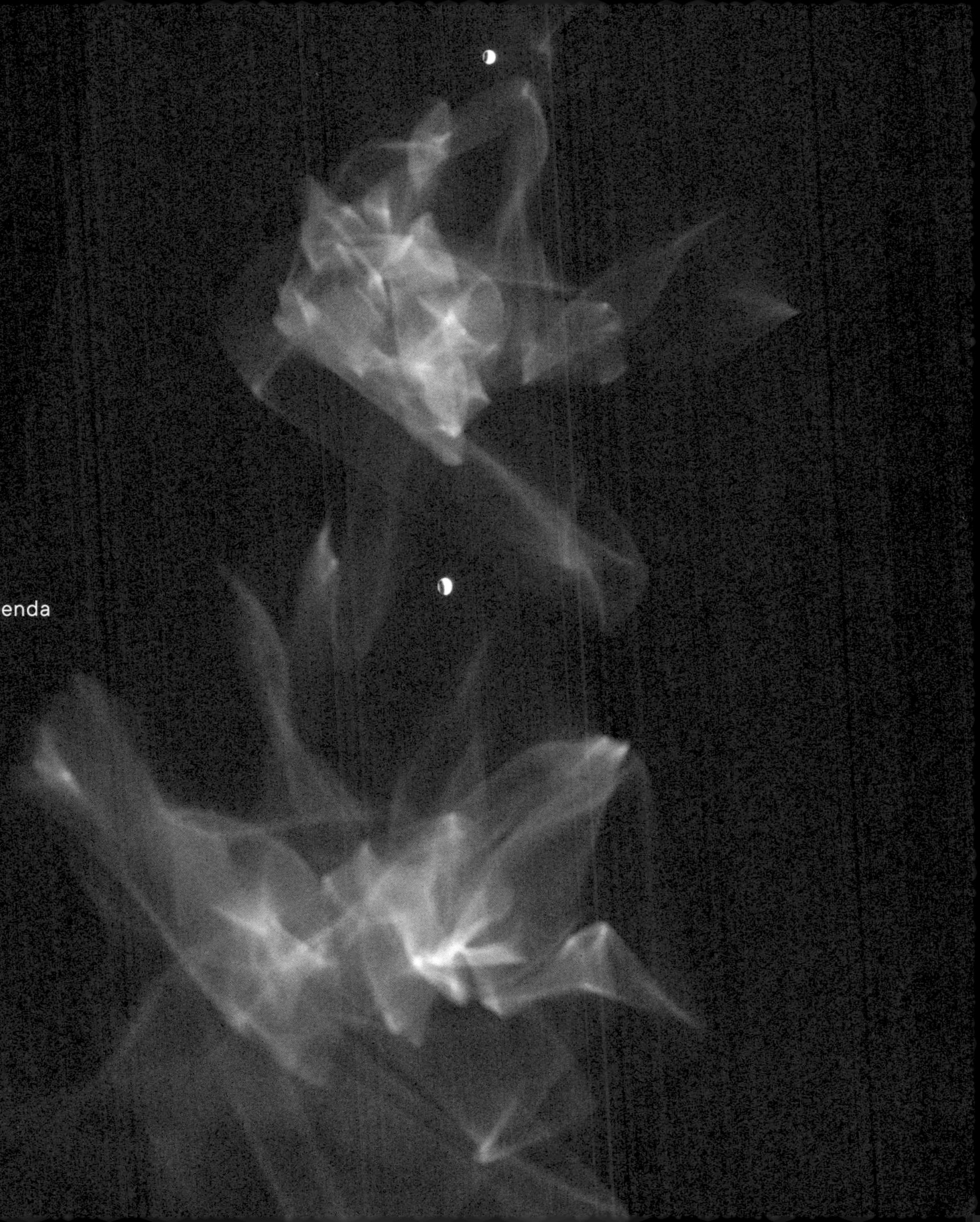

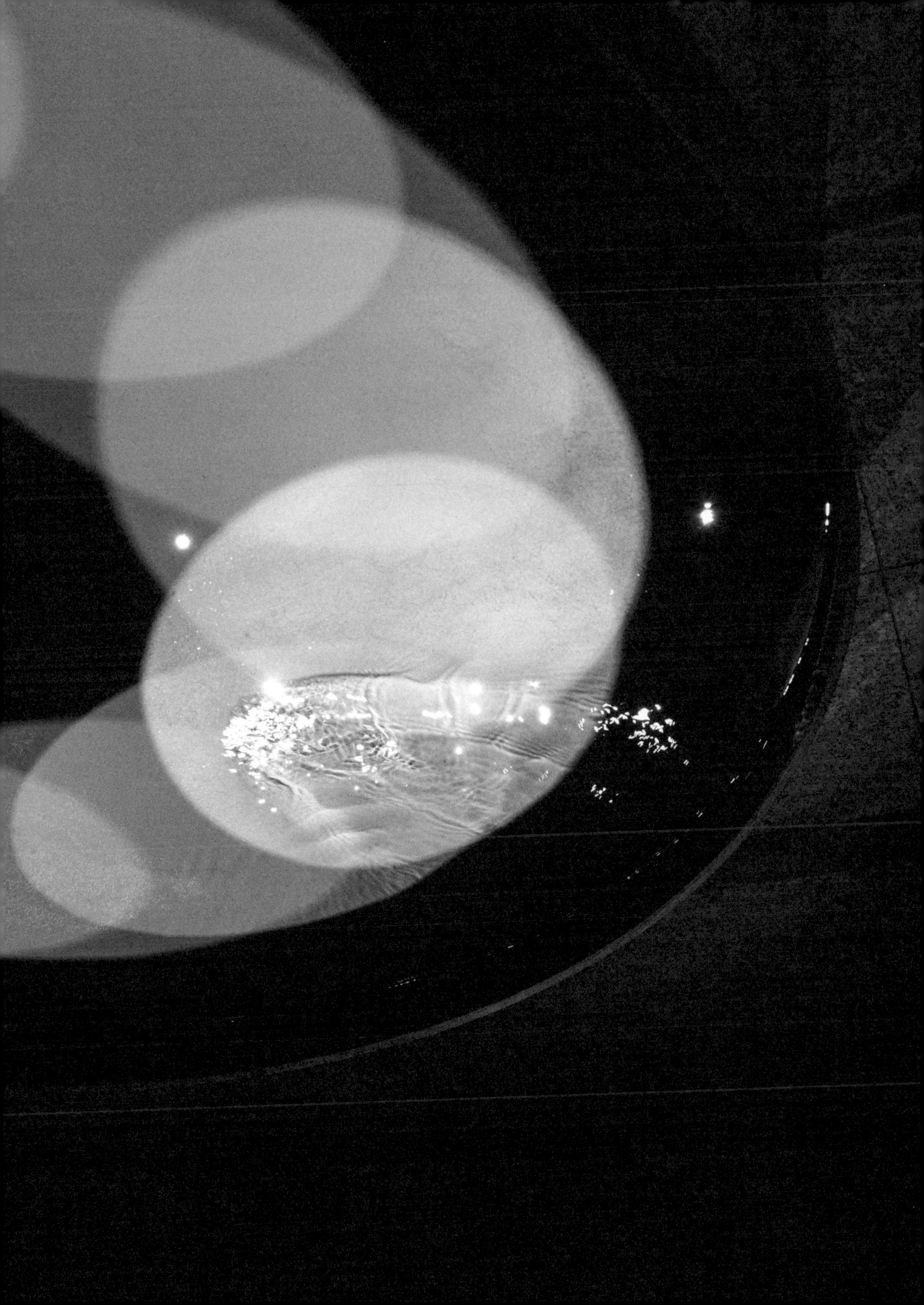

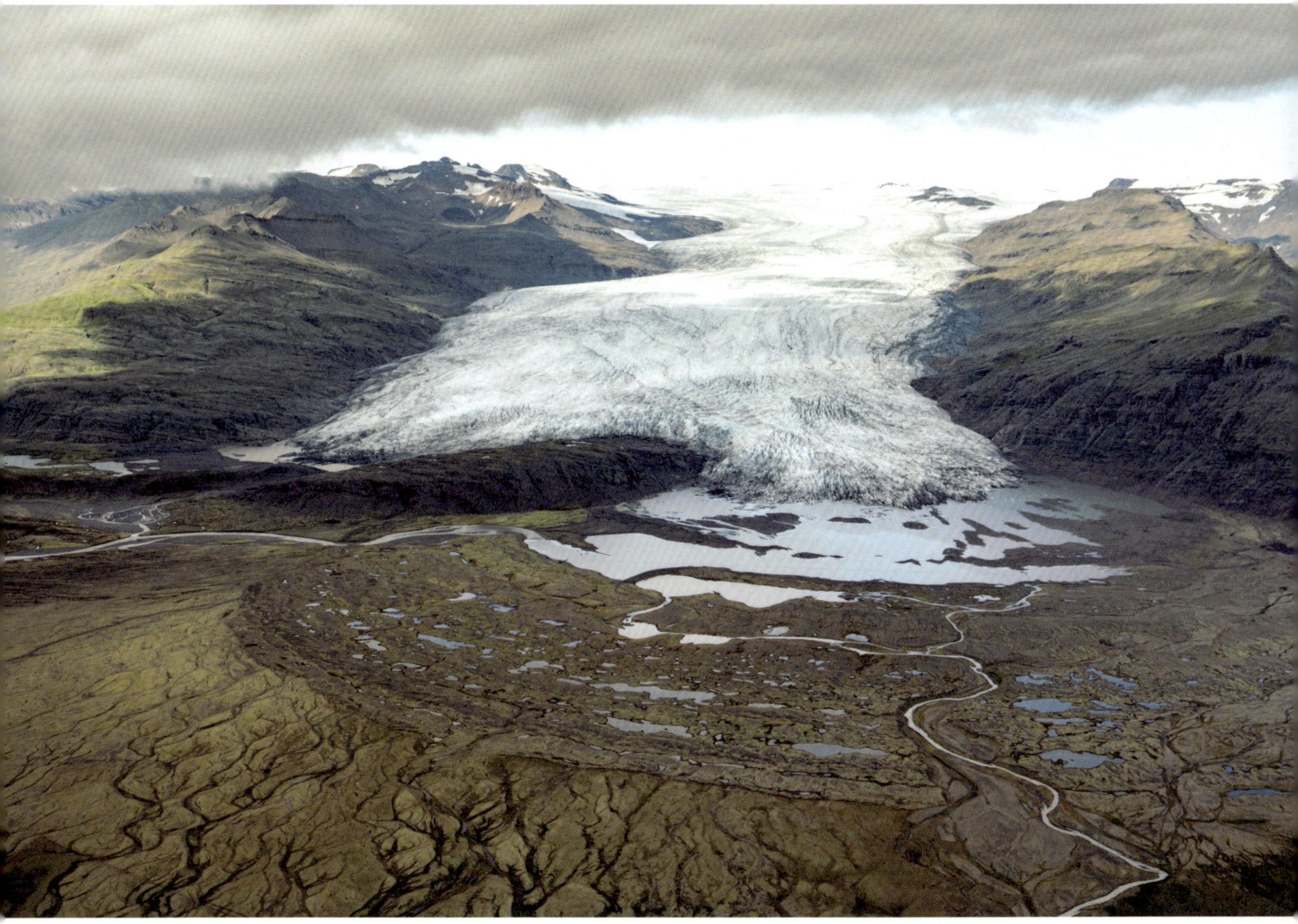

溶ける氷河のシリーズ 1999/2019［部分］
Details from *The glacier melt series 1999/2019*
2019

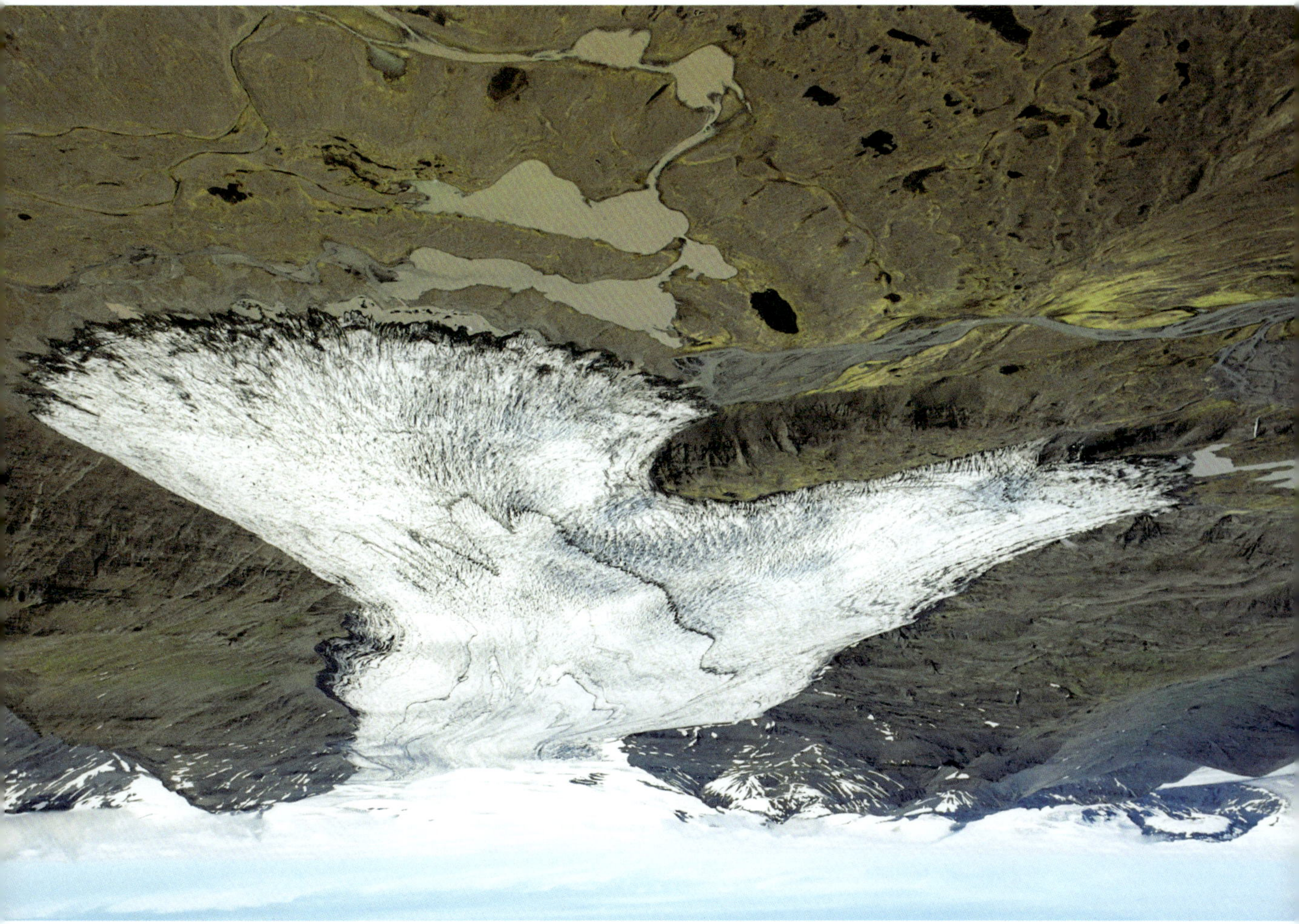

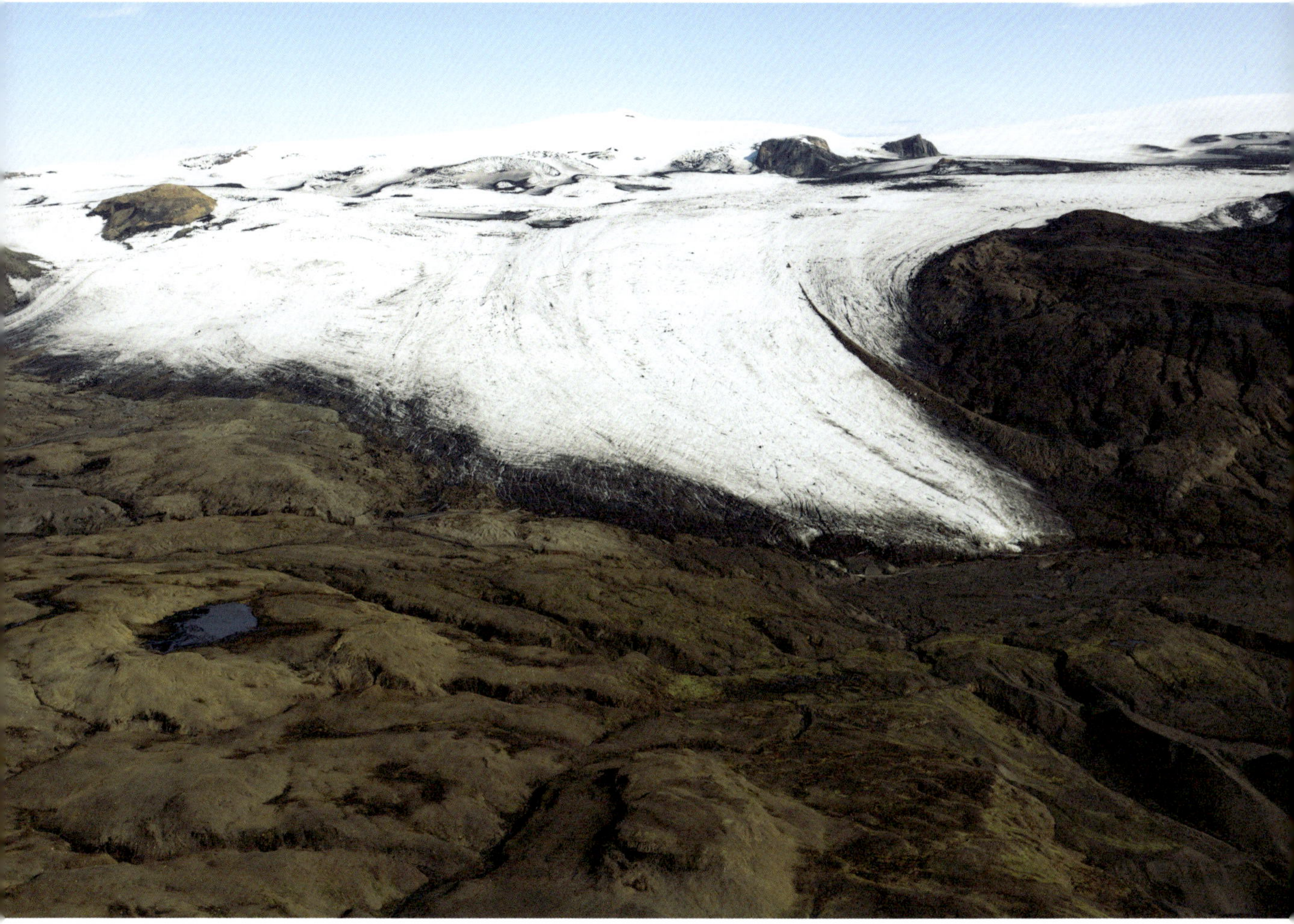

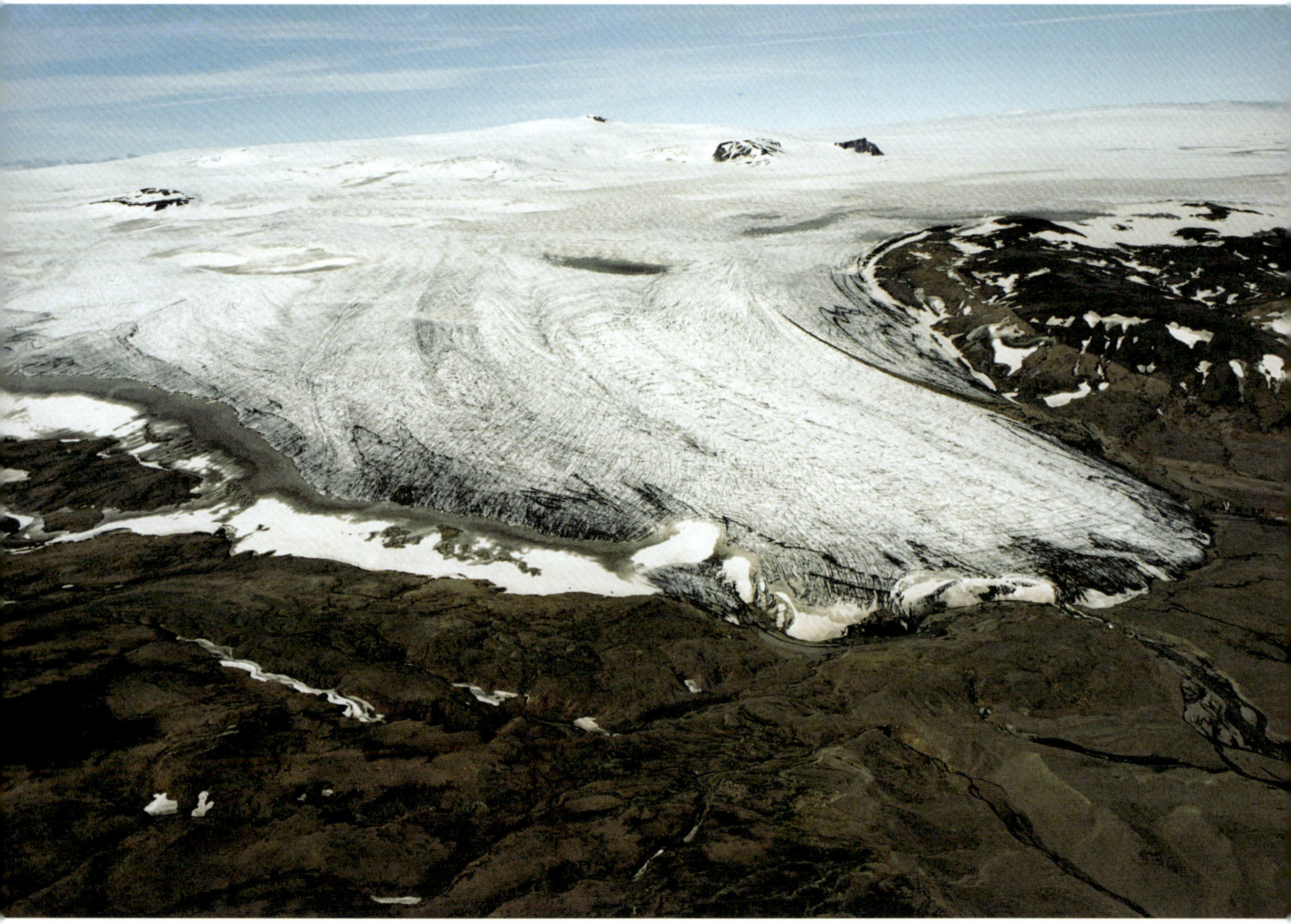

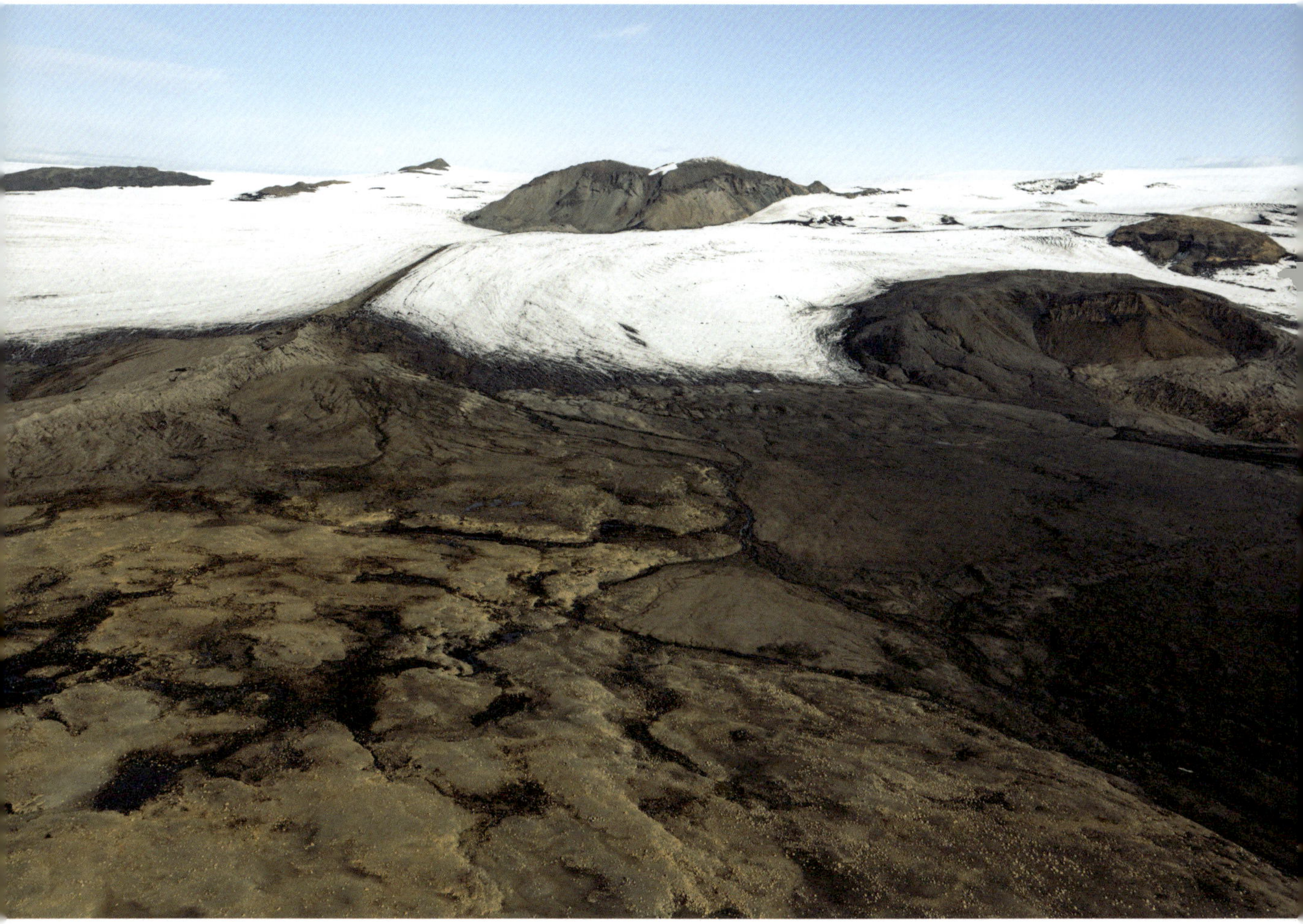

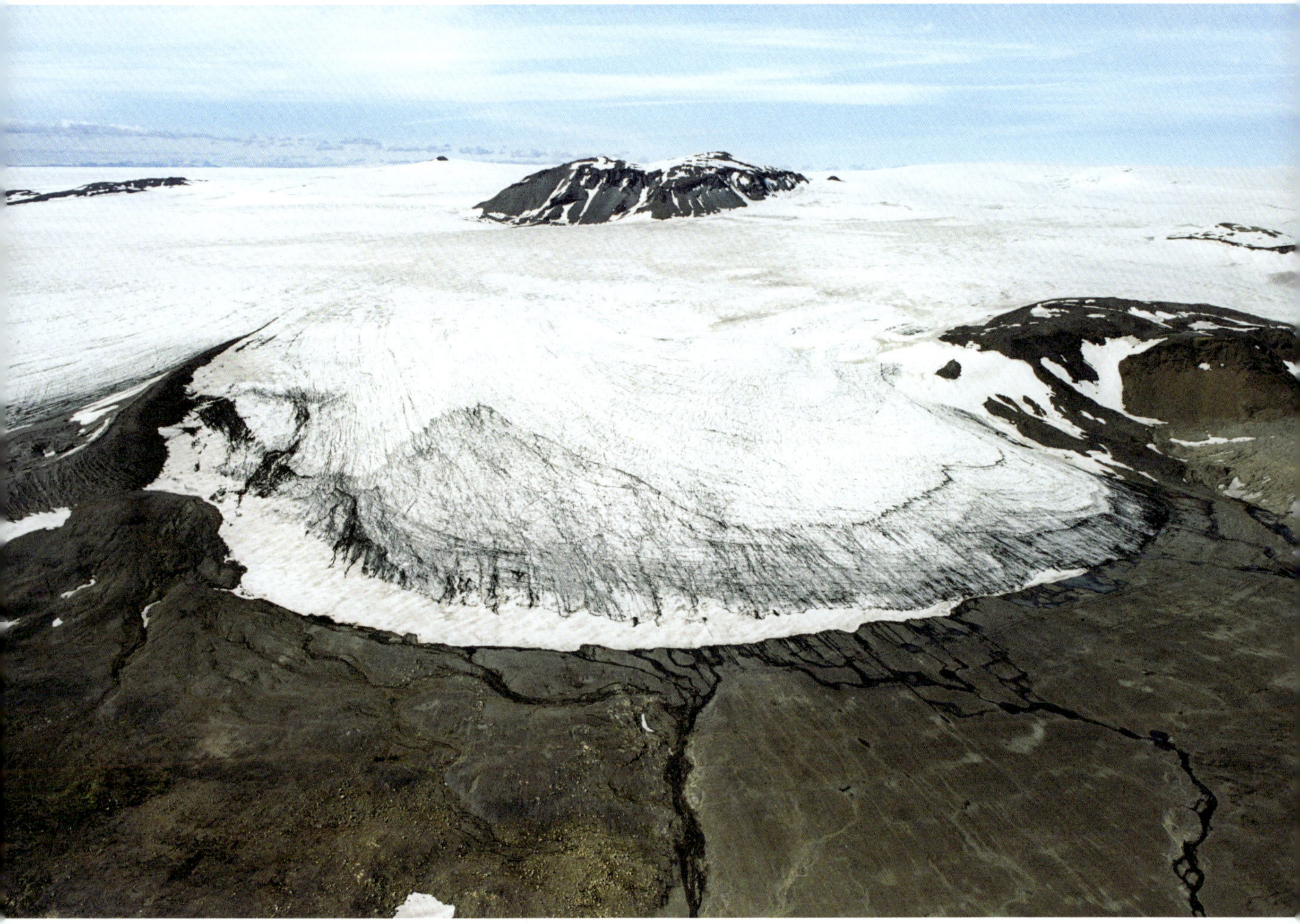

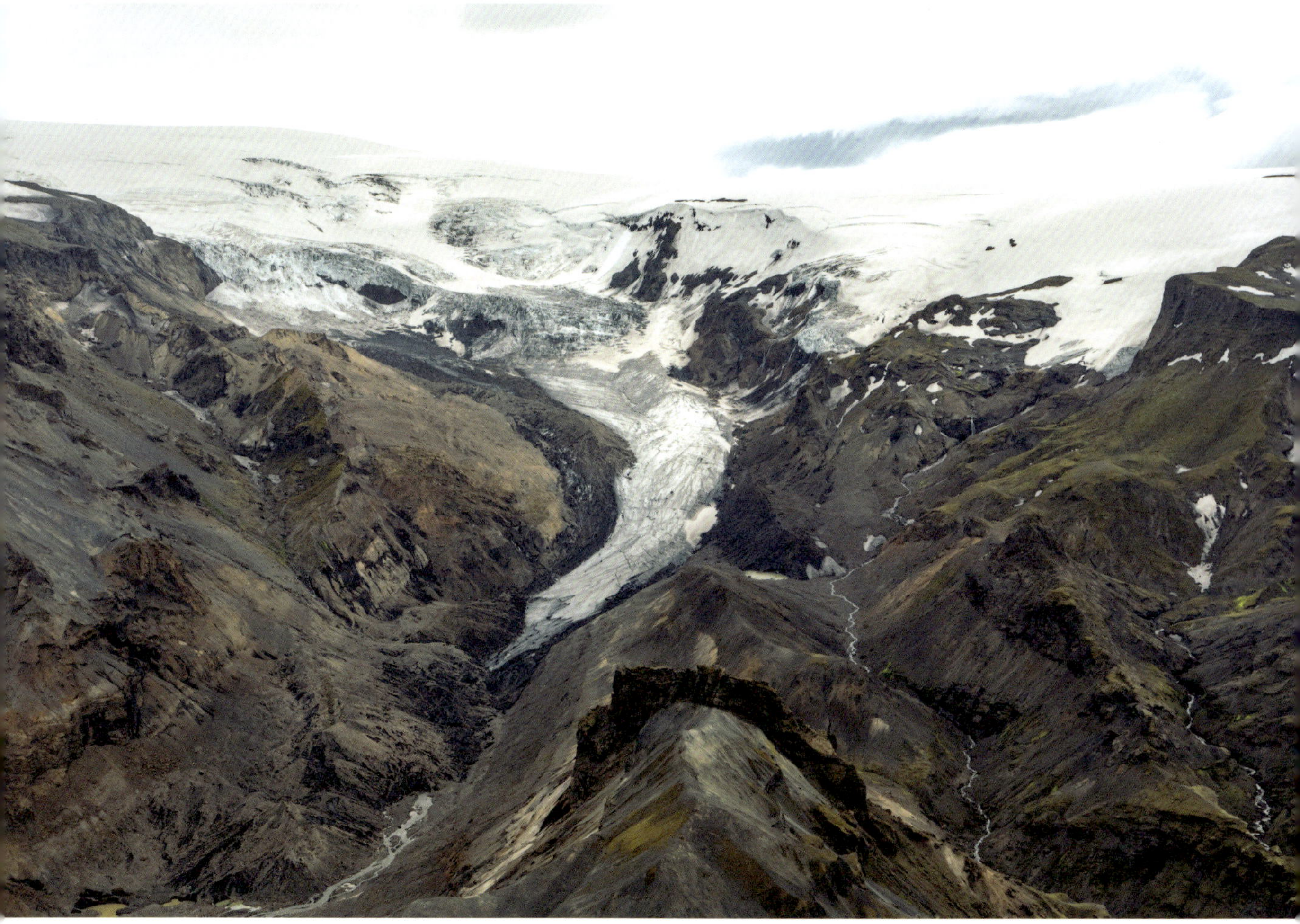

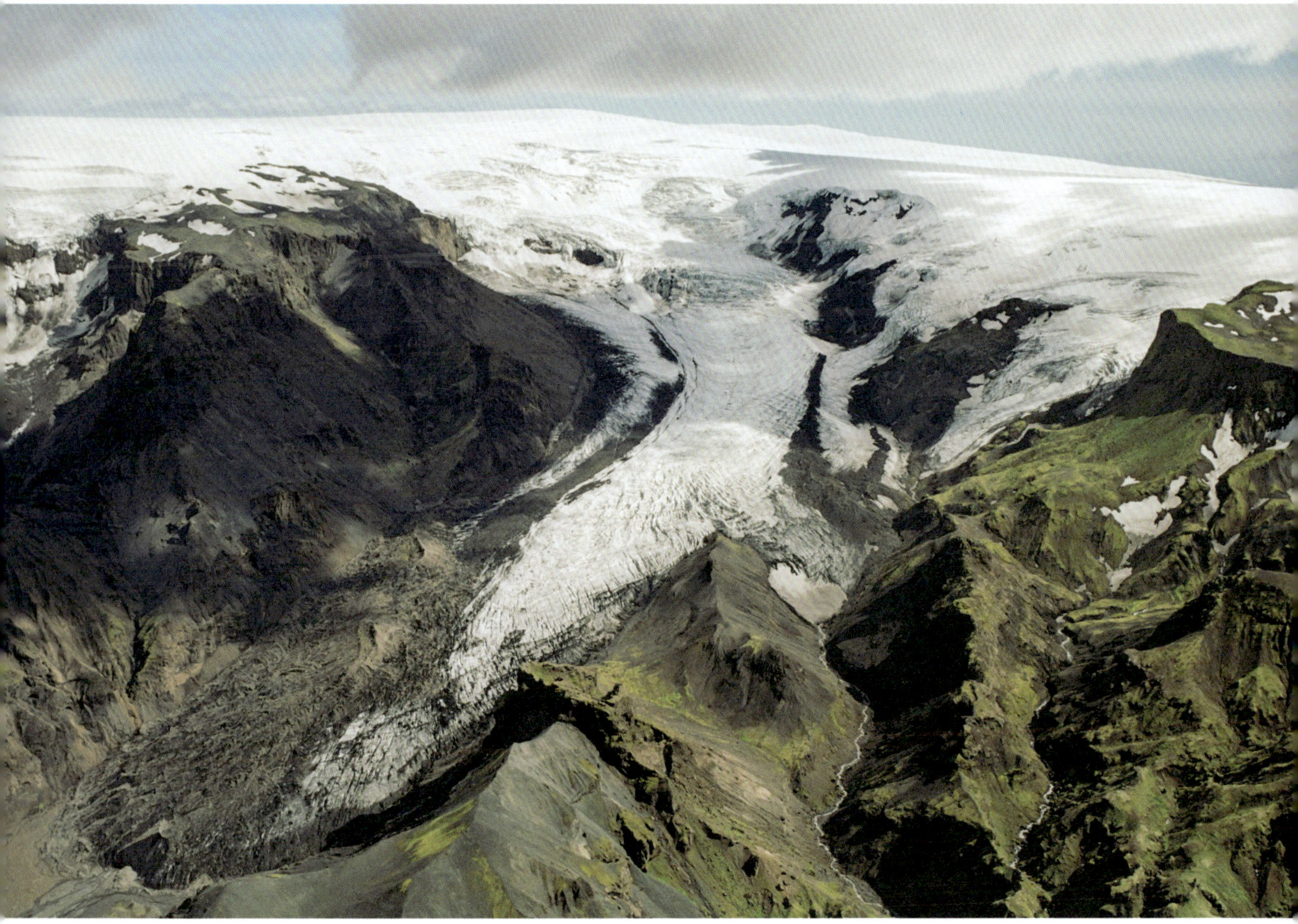

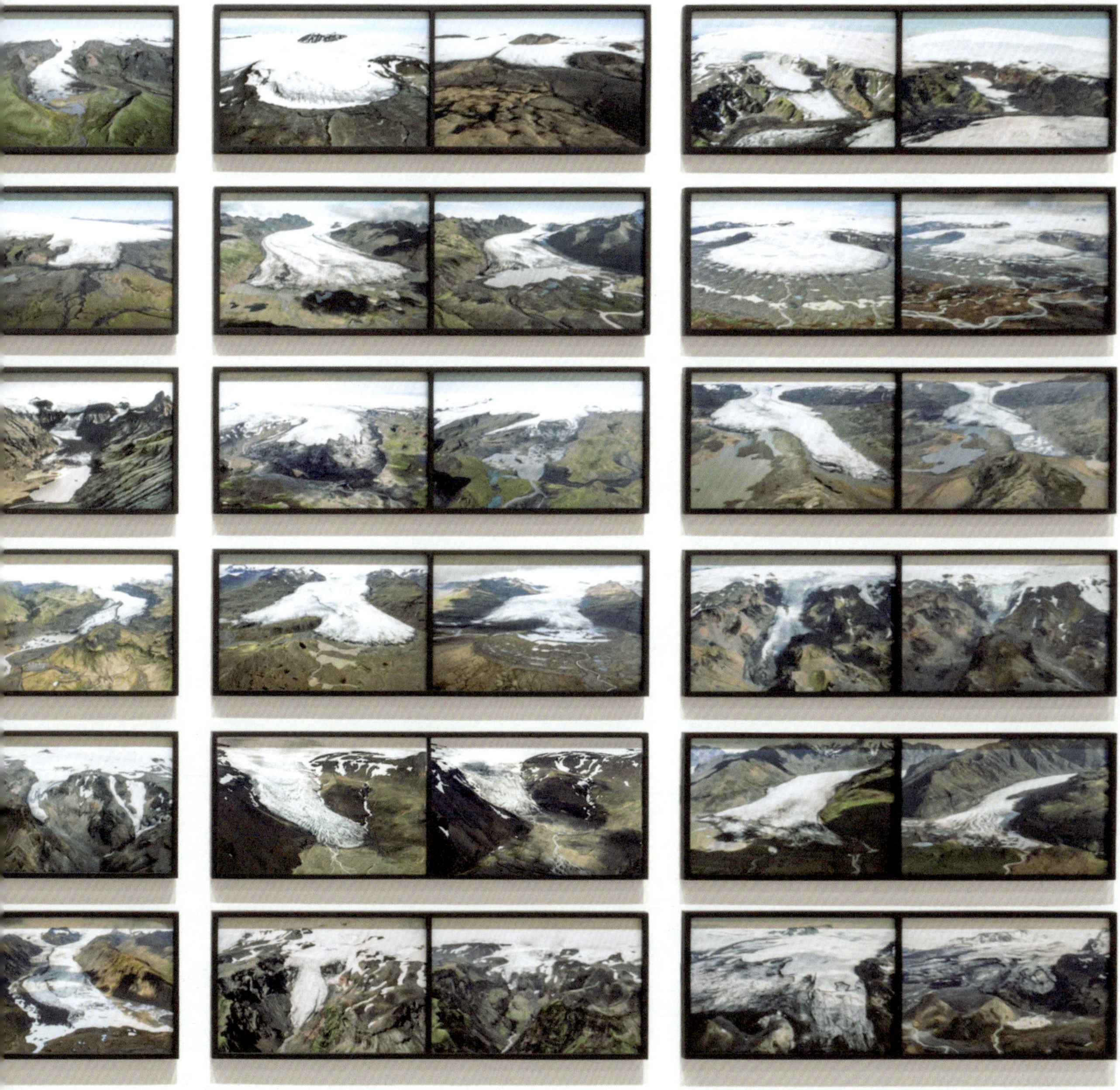

溶ける氷河のシリーズ 1999/2019
The glacier melt series 1999/2019
2019

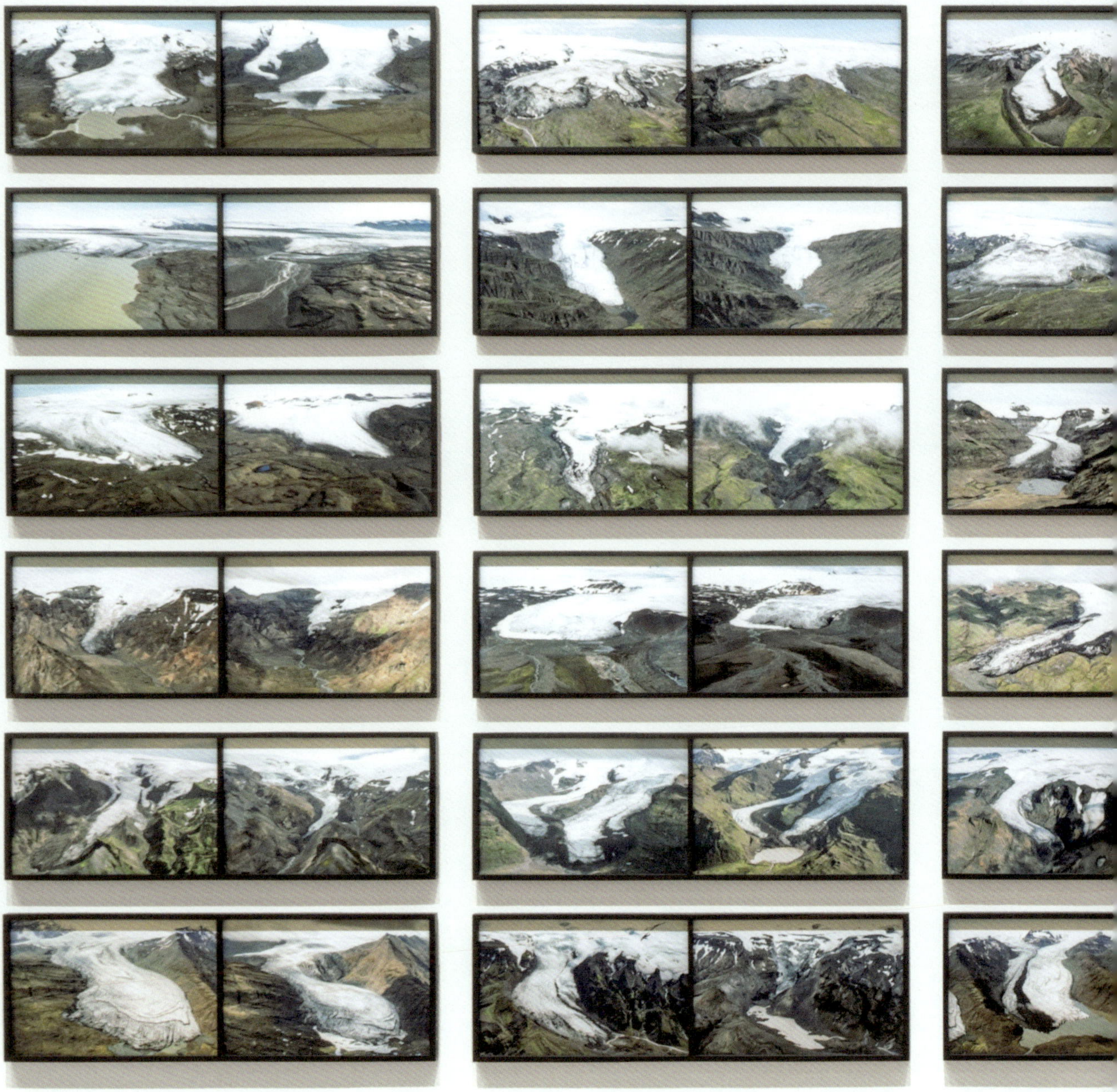

In 1999, Olafur Eliasson photographed several dozen glaciers in Iceland as part of his on-going project to document the natural phenomena of the country; this particular series of photographs formed a work called *The glacier series.* Twenty years later, Eliasson decided to return to Iceland to photograph the glaciers again. A new work, *The glacier melt series 1999/2019*, brings together thirty pairs of images from 1999 and 2019 to reveal the dramatic impact that global warming is having on our world.

エリアソンは最初期から氷河や火山、洞窟といったアイスランドの自然の数々を写真で記録してきた。この30点組の作品は1999年と2019年に撮影したまったく同じ地点の写真を併置することによって、気候変動による20年間の氷河の後退を目に見える形で示している。

昼と夜の溶岩
Day and night lava
2018

Eliasson's works often include natural objects from the Icelandic wilderness – which he spent his summers in while growing up and continues to visit regularly for inspiration – and optical devices like this concave mirror, which produce surprising spatial distortions and shifts in scale.

エリアソンの作品の中には氷河や溶岩石、流木といったアイスランドの自然物でできたものがある。この作品の溶岩石も作家本人が原野を歩きまわりながら拾い集めたものであり、そのときの記憶が作品には内在している。エリアソンの空間や自然現象に対する感覚はスカンジナビアで生まれ育ったことと深く関係しているといえるだろう。

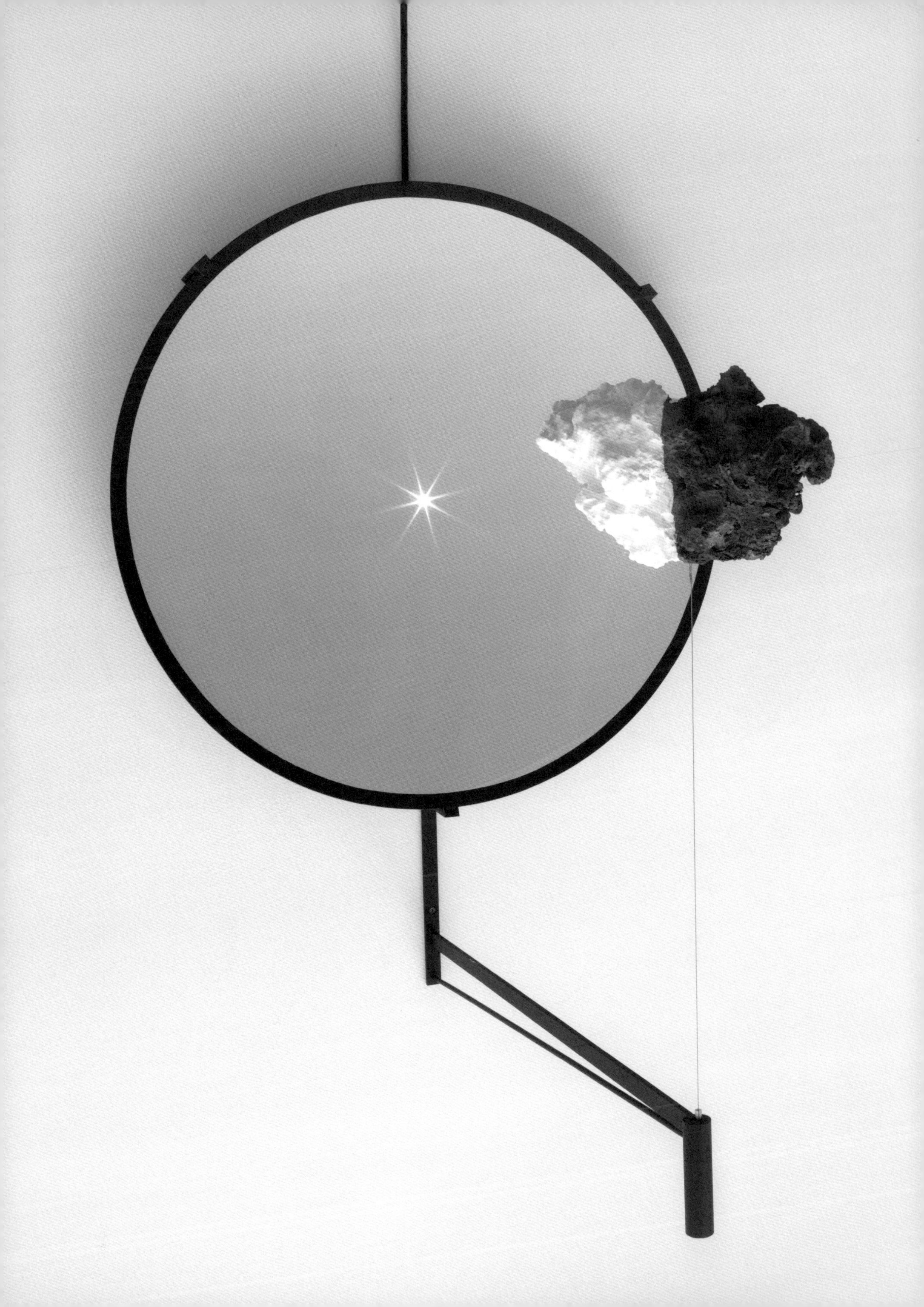

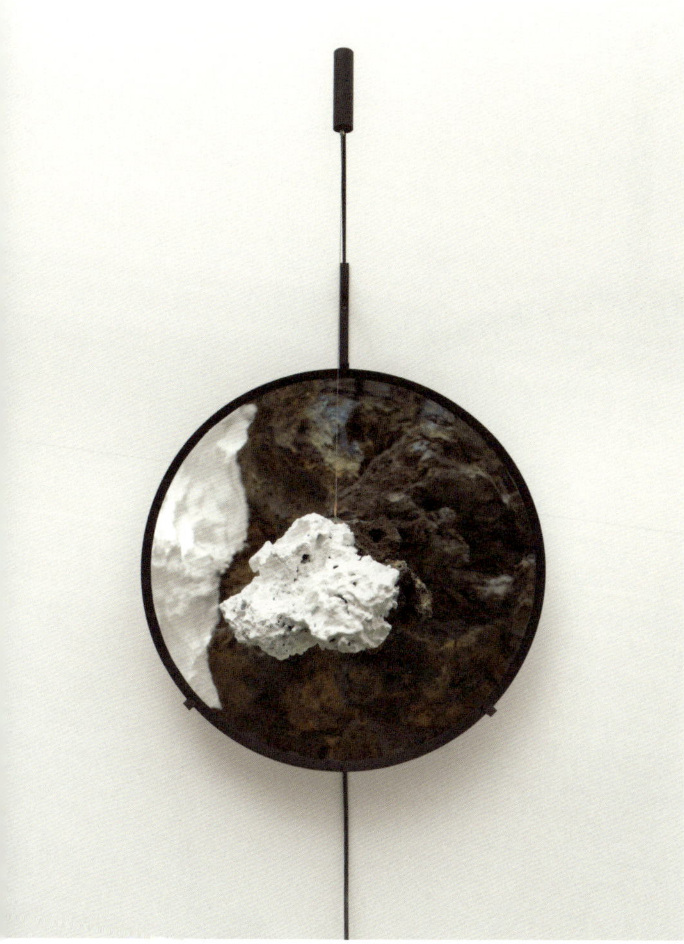

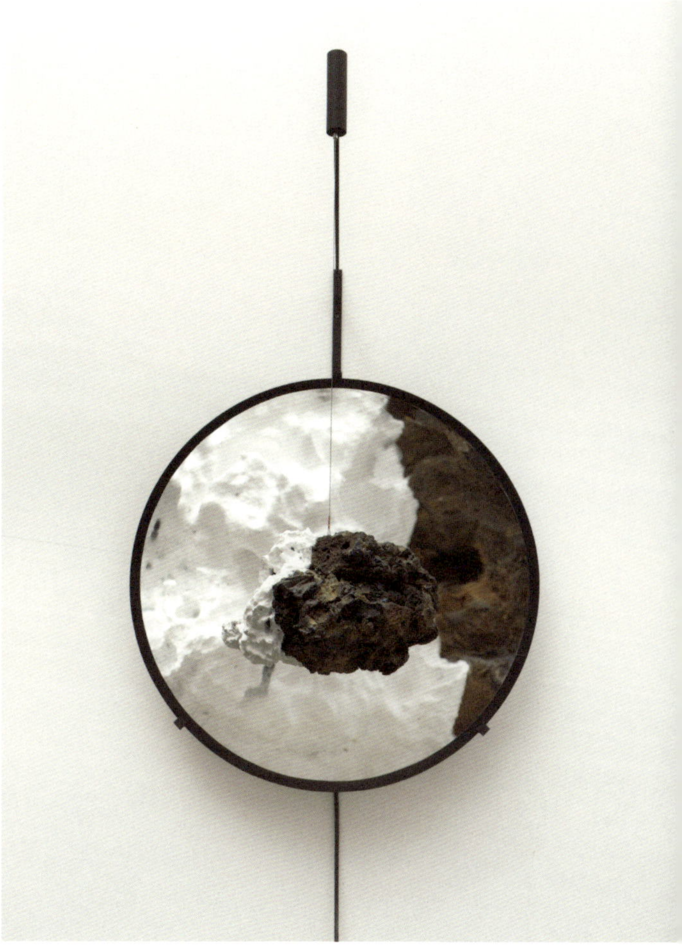

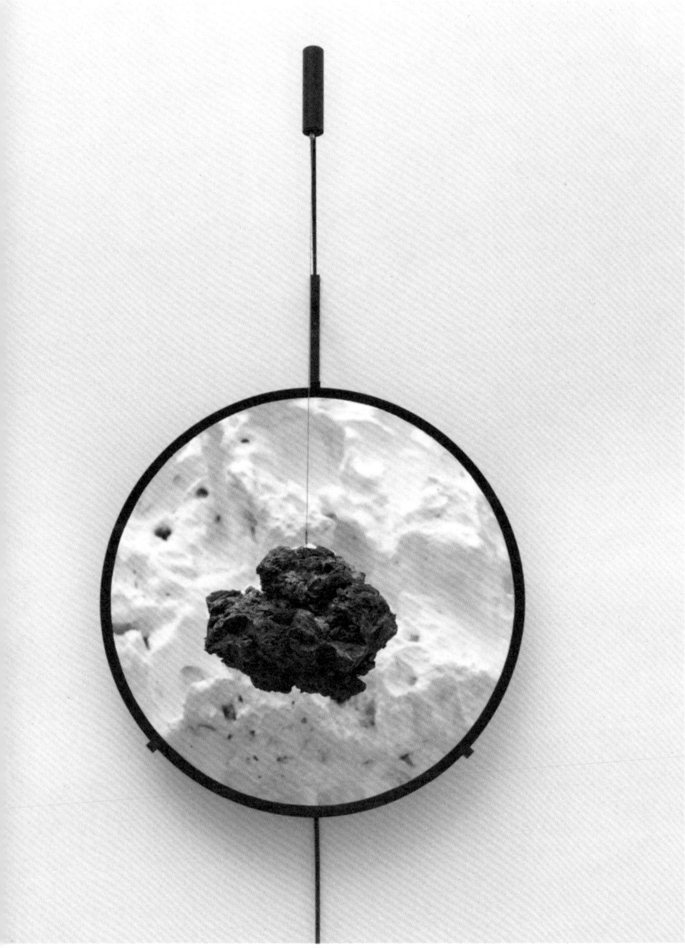

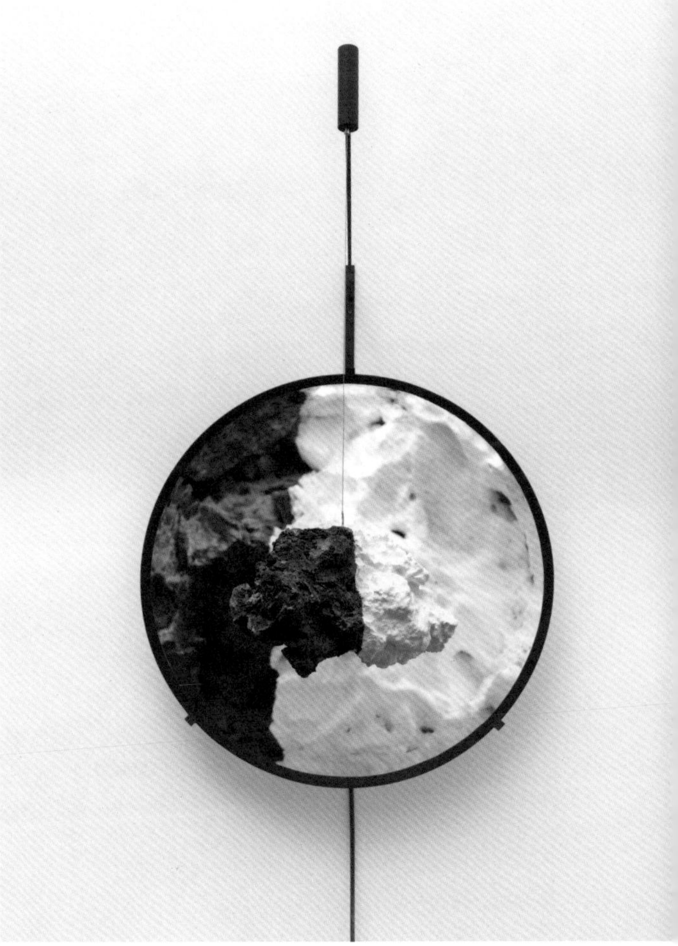

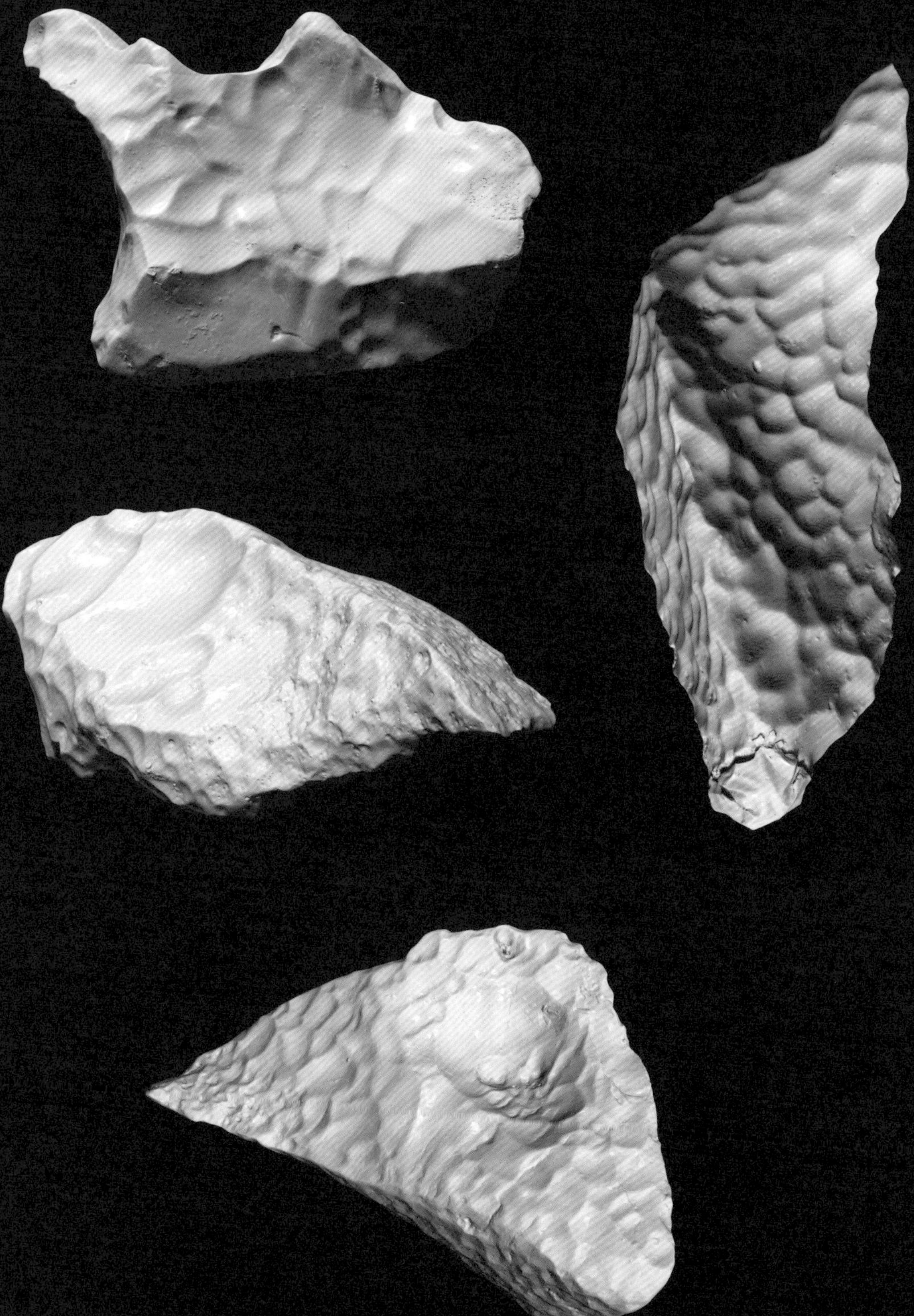

氷の研究室
Ice lab

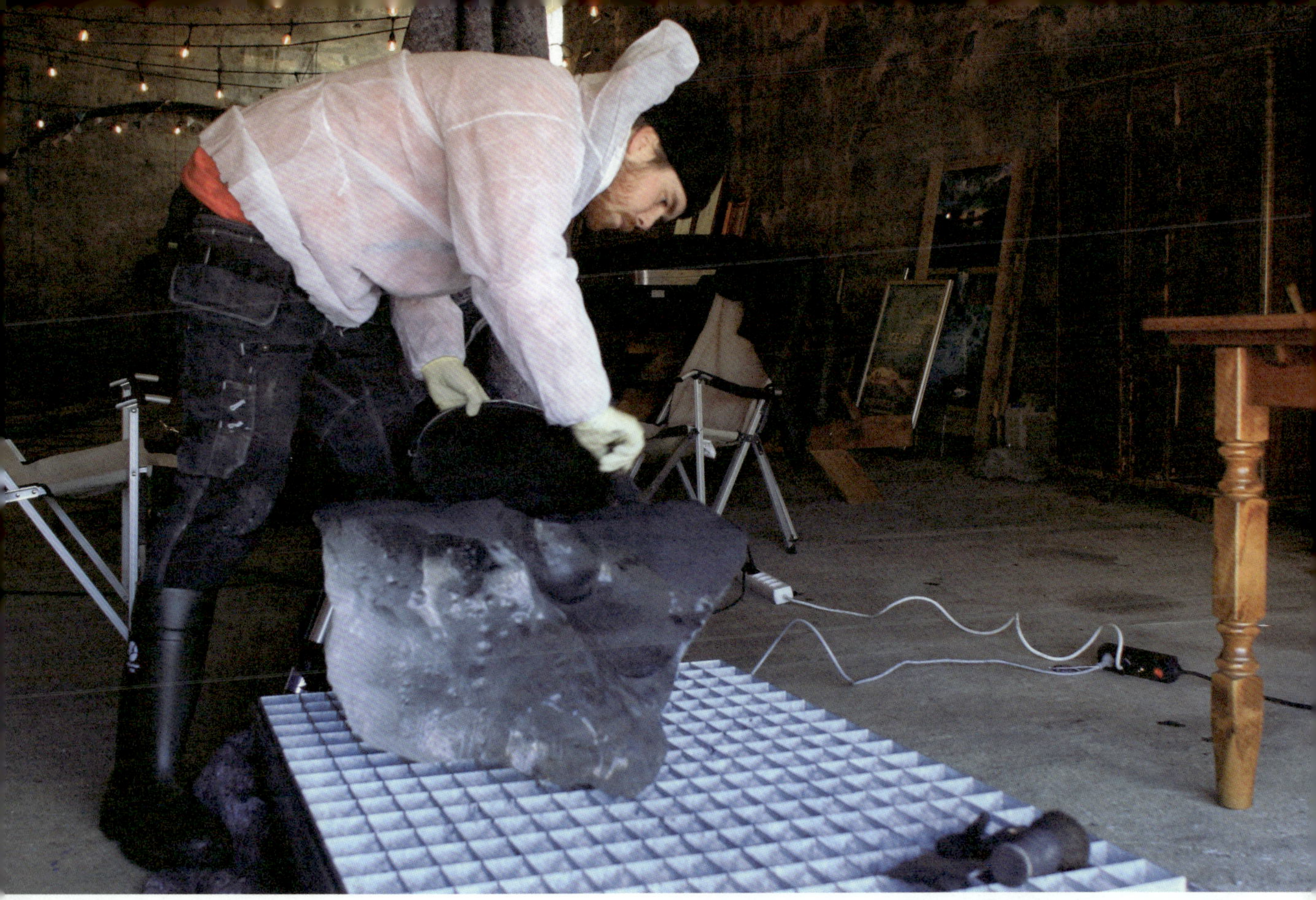

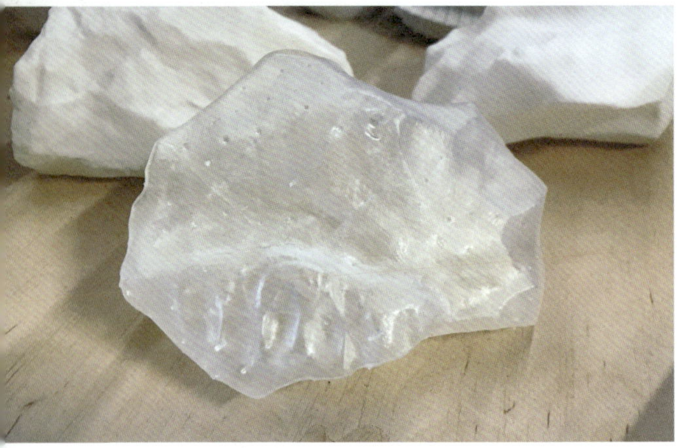

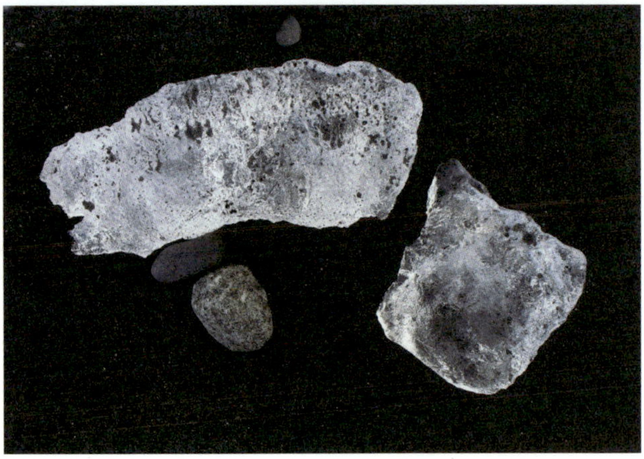

For many years Eliasson has travelled to the southern coast of Iceland, to a site called Diamond Beach. The beach gets its name from the glistening pieces of ice that wash up there; they are brought in by the tide and rest on the shore until they melt away. Eliasson first used ice from this location in an artwork in 2006, when he exhibited a number of the blocks unaltered in a refrigerated gallery for *Your waste of time*, at neugerriemschneider, Berlin. This winter, he and his team returned to the beach to observe the ice. Eliasson is interested in the seasonal change of water from liquid to solid and in the excessive melting taking place as a result of global warming. The disappearance of the ice has been the subject of a number of his artworks in recent years. As part of the current investigations, Eliasson and his team are making 3D scans of individual ice blocks; the data can be used to replicate the ice as 3D prints and may also form the basis for new artworks in the future.

アイスランド南部には流出した氷河が打ち上げられる海岸があり、日光に照らされて輝く透明な氷がダイヤモンドのように見えることから、そこはダイヤモンド・ビーチと称されている。 近年エリアソンとスタジオのチームは現地で氷塊を3Dスキャンし、記録しているという。 氷の3Dデータには氷河が形成され流出するまでの途方もない時間が内包されている一方で、その氷がすでに溶けて存在しないこともまた示唆されている。

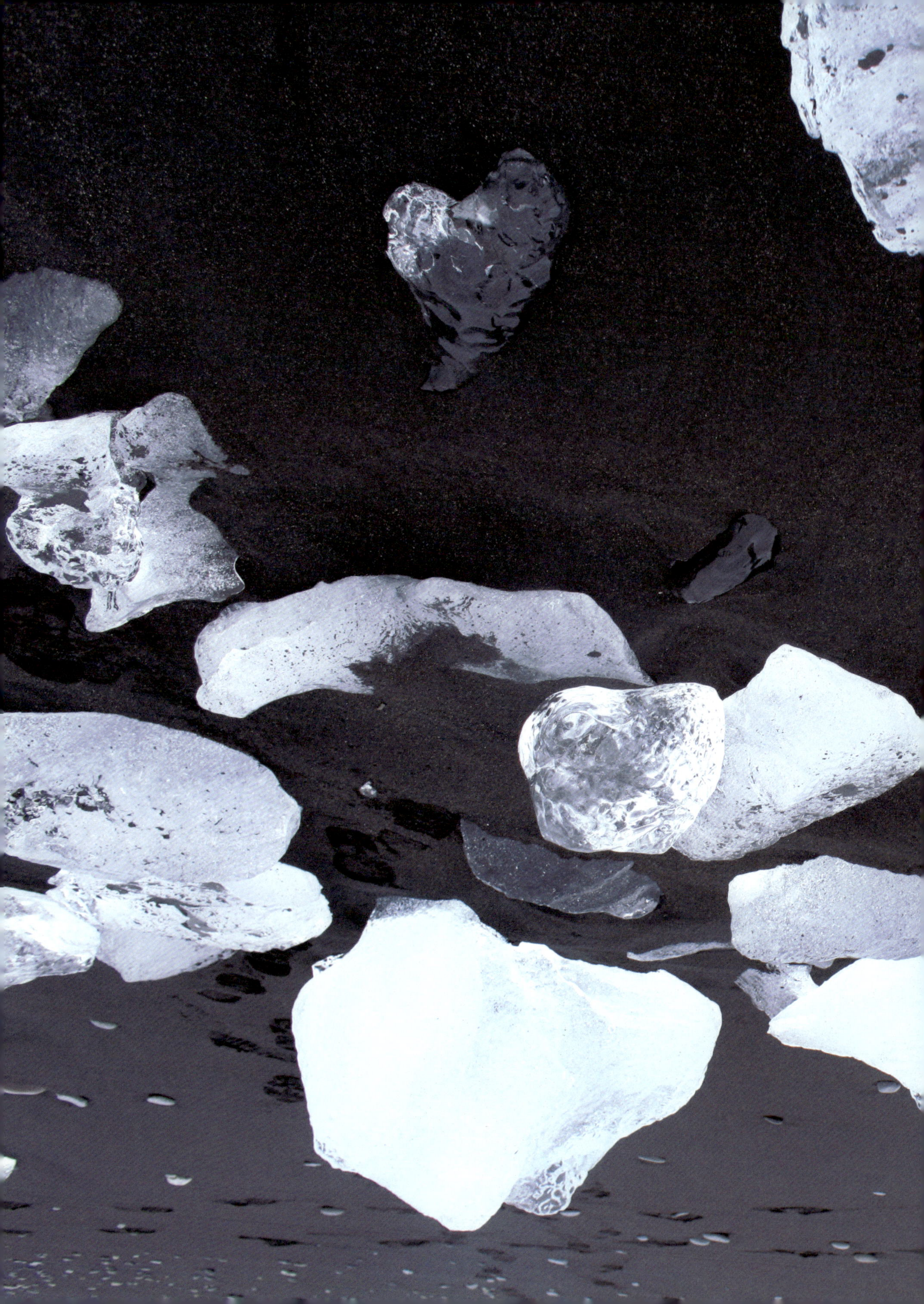

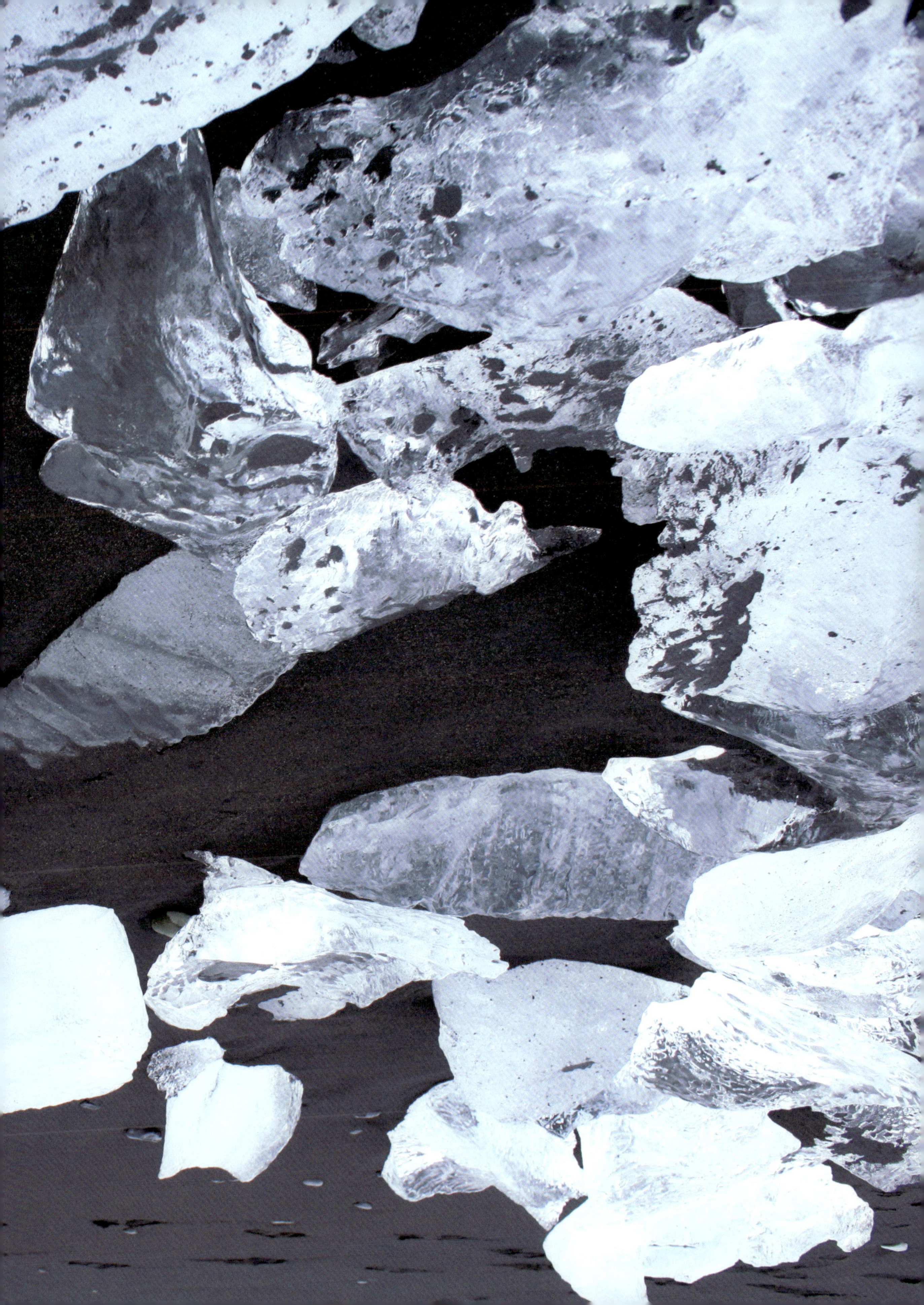

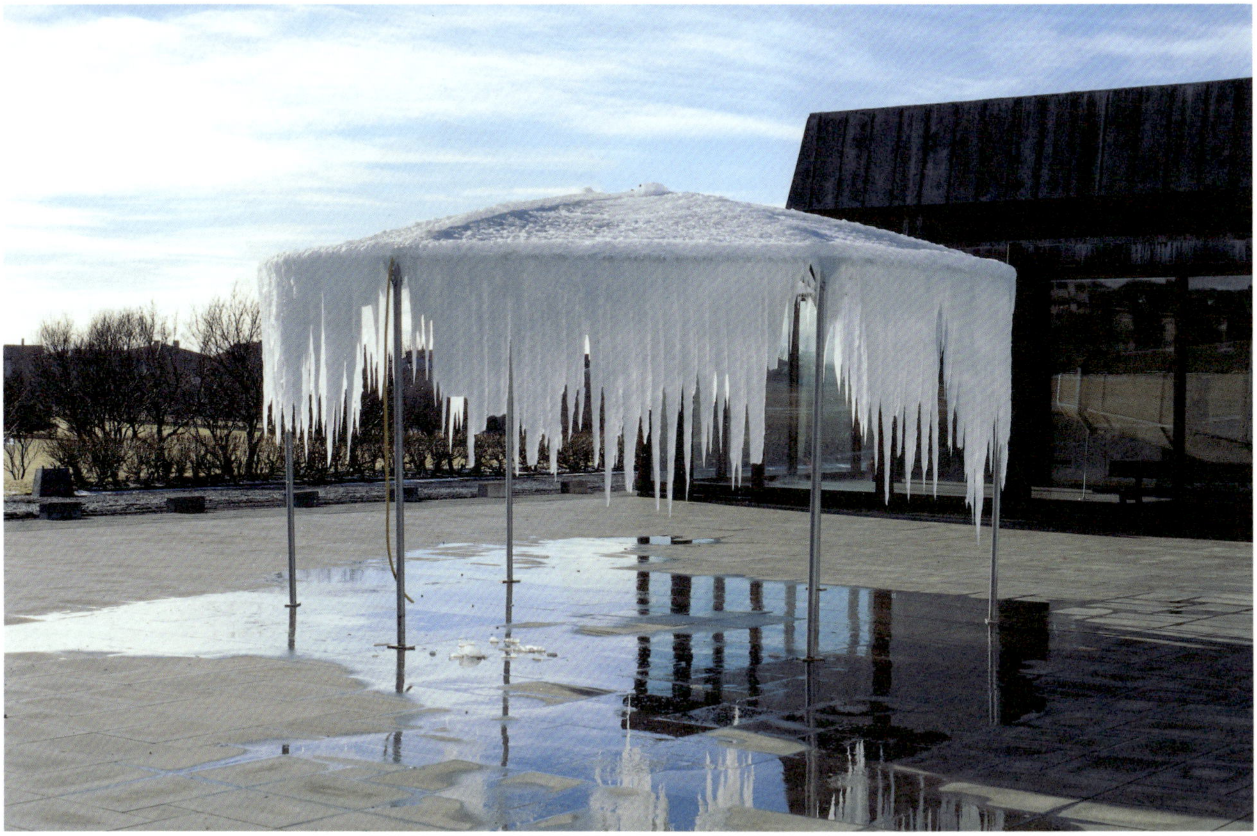

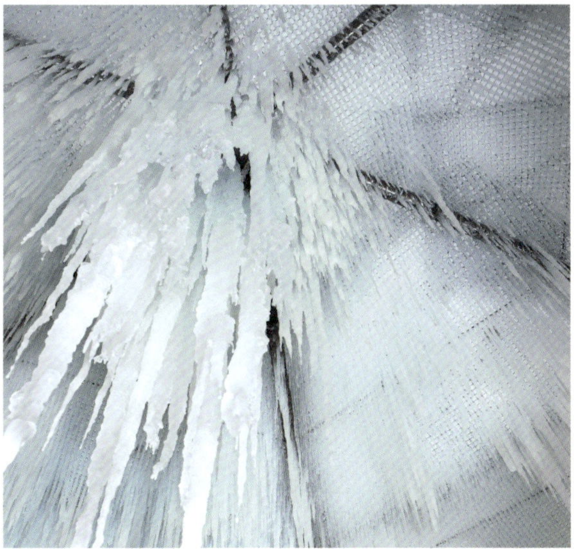

氷のパビリオン
Ice pavilion
1998

Eliasson's artworks using ice have taken a variety of forms over the years. They have been situated in landscapes both natural and urban, and also placed in galleries and museums. He exhibited ice as a readymade sculpture at his gallery in Berlin for *Your waste of time*, 2006. Eliasson has allowed ice to sculpt surprising abstract forms, as in *Ice pavilion*, 1998, and *Presence of absence pavilion*, 2019; and photographed the unique topographies of glaciers in photographic series like *The glacier mill series*, 2007. *Ice Watch*, 2014, for which blocks of drifting ice were harvested off the coast of Greenland and brought to public squares in Copenhagen (2014), Paris (2015), and London (2018) is a call for action to fight climate change (see pages 88–91).

氷はエリアソンの作品の中にさまざまな形で表れている。屋外に置かれた構造物にスプリンクラーを取り付けて氷柱を生成した《氷のパビリオン》(1998)、ベルリンのギャラリーに合計6トンの氷河の氷を展示した《あなたの時間の浪費》(2006)、《氷河おう穴のシリーズ》(2007)のようなアイスランドの氷河の写真、溶け去った氷の形を空白として示した彫刻《不在の存在パビリオン》(2019)など、多角的なアプローチを展開してきた。また、グリーンランドの巨大な氷を街なかに展示することによって気候変動を体感させるプロジェクト《アイス・ウォッチ》はこれまでコペンハーゲン(2014)、パリ(2015)、ロンドン(2018)でおこなわれた(88–91頁を参照)。

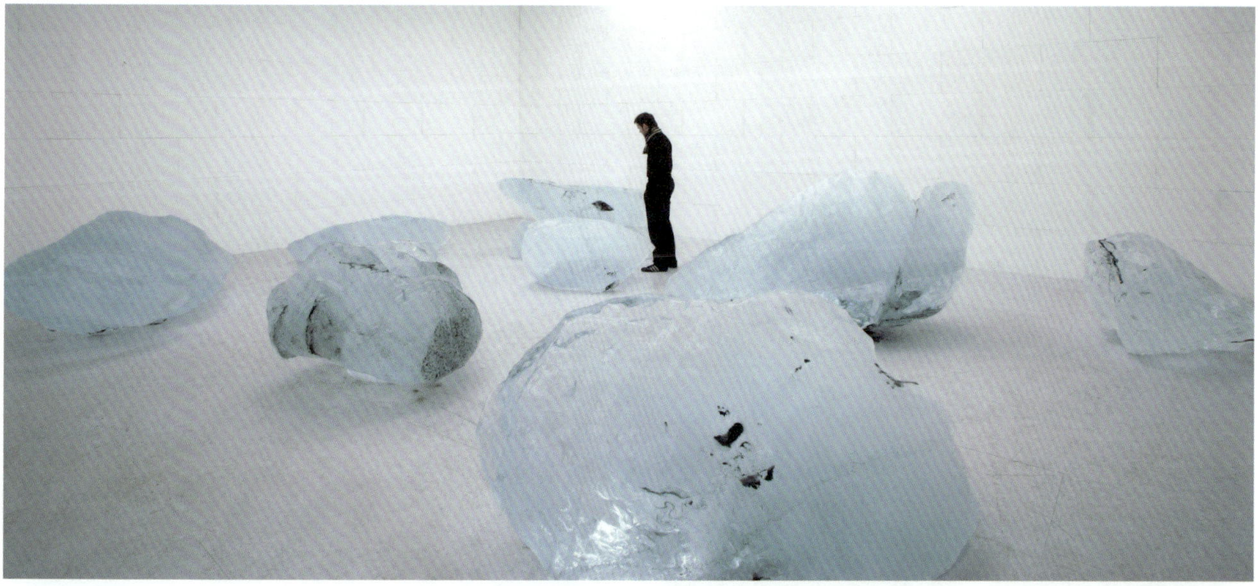

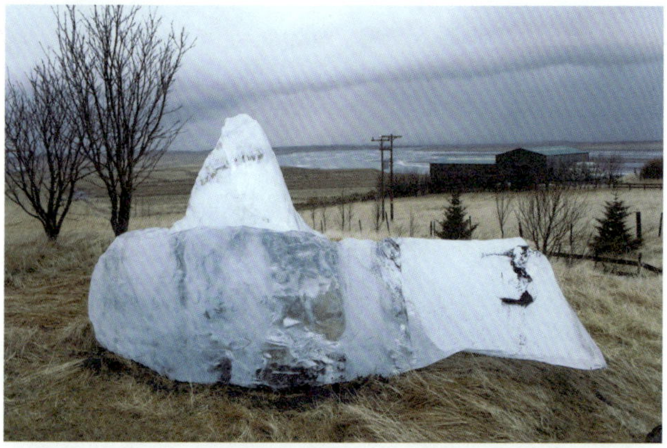

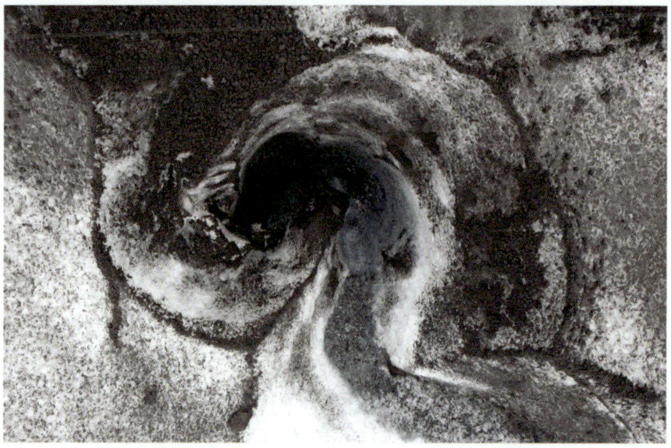

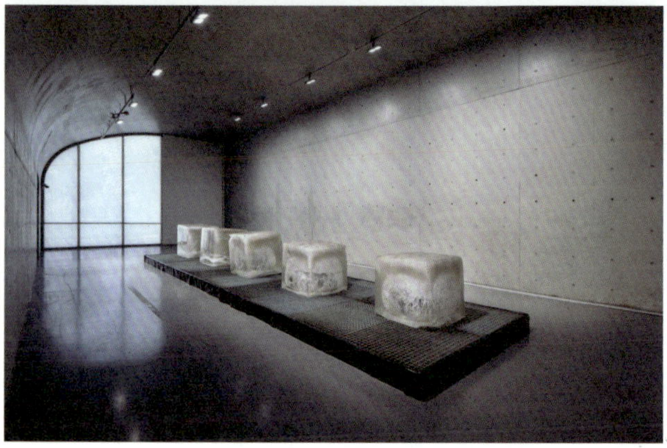

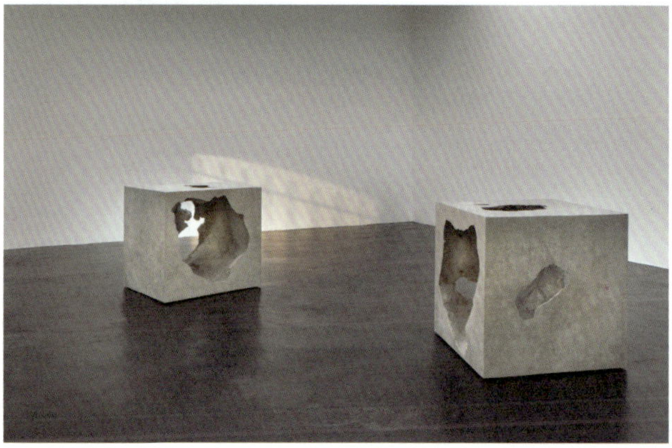

上段｜top
あなたの時間の浪費
Your waste of time
2006

中段左｜2nd row, left
グンナーの土地で溶ける氷［部分］
Detail from *Melting ice on Gunnar's land*
2008

中段右｜2nd row, right
氷河おう穴のシリーズ［部分］
Detail from *The glacier mill series*
2007

下段左｜3rd row left
静かなる川
Still river
2016

下段右｜3rd row right
不在の存在（ヌープ・カンゲルルア、2015年9月24日#1）
不在の存在（ヌープ・カンゲルルア、2015年9月24日#2）
The presence of absence (Nuup Kangerlua, 24 September 2015 #1)
The presence of absence (Nuup Kangerlua, 24 September 2015 #2)
2016

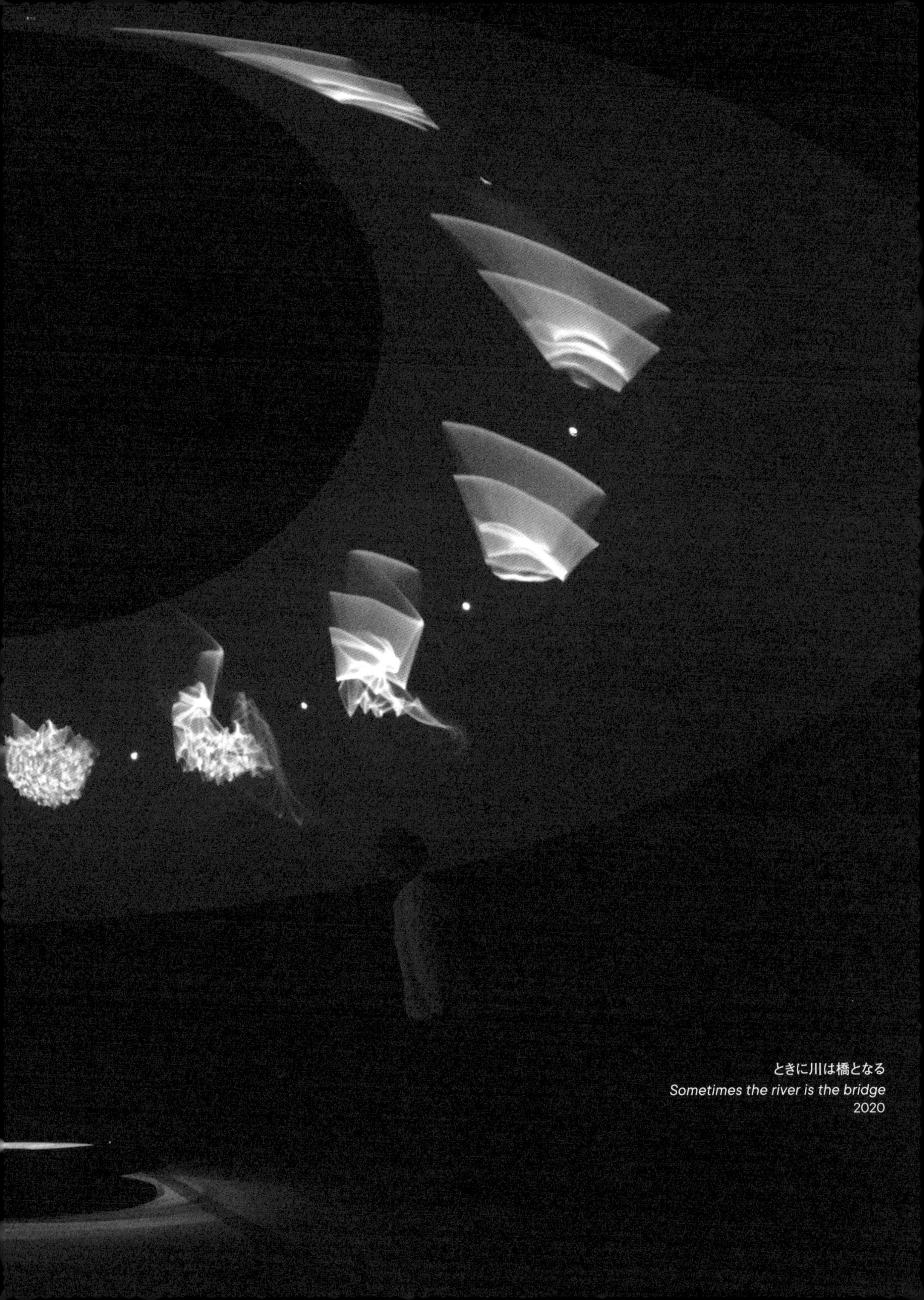

ときに川は橋となる
Sometimes the river is the bridge
2020

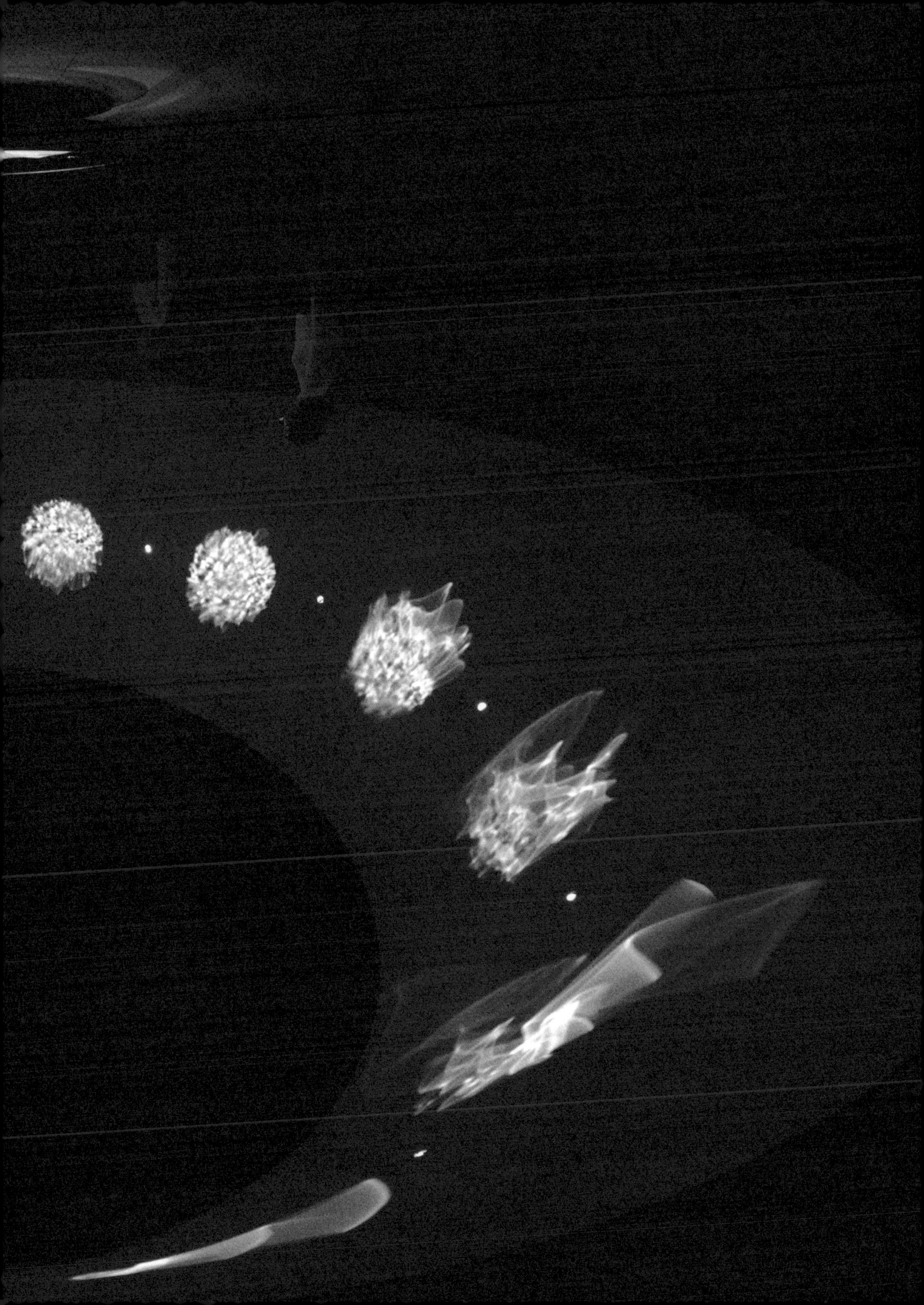

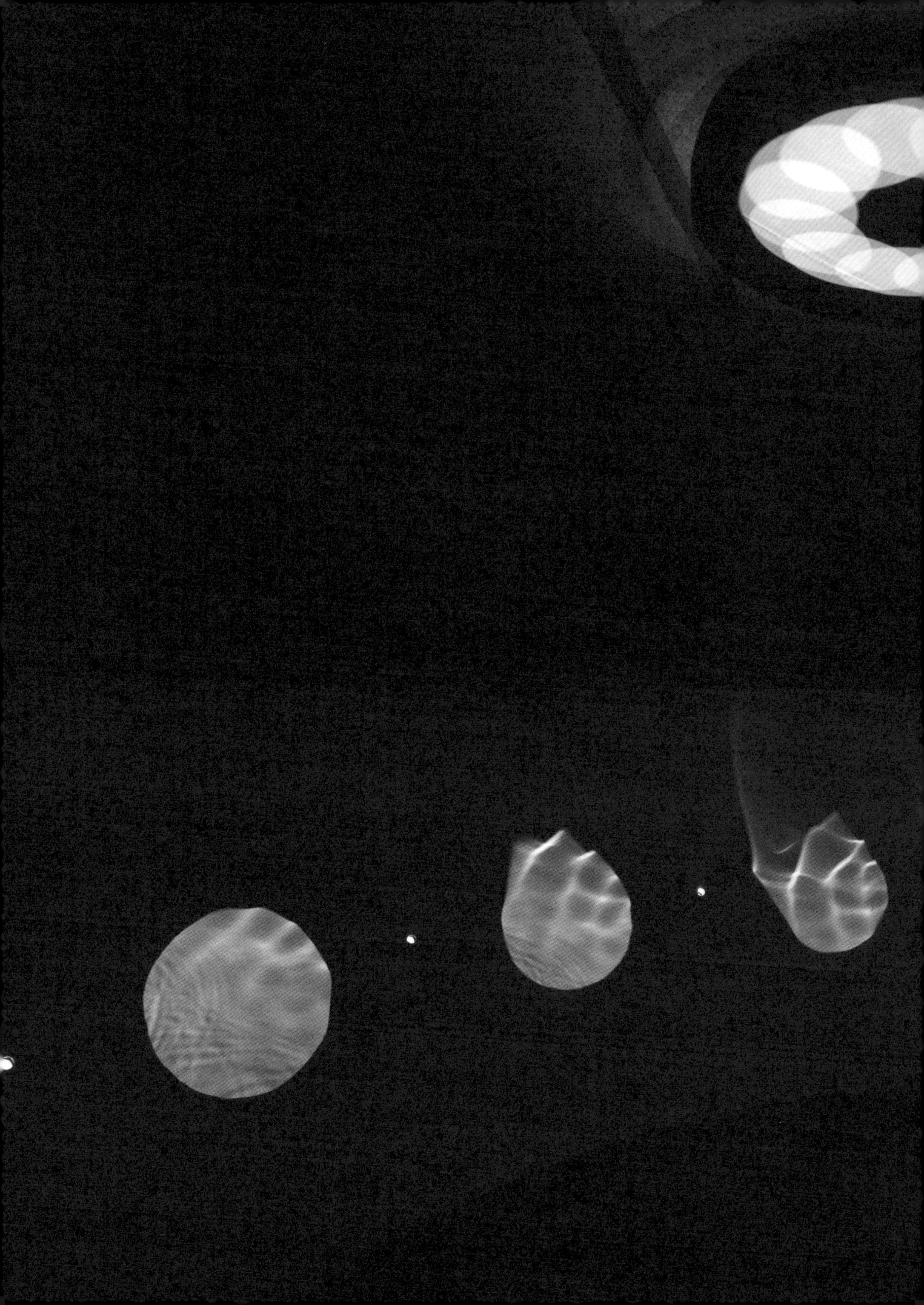

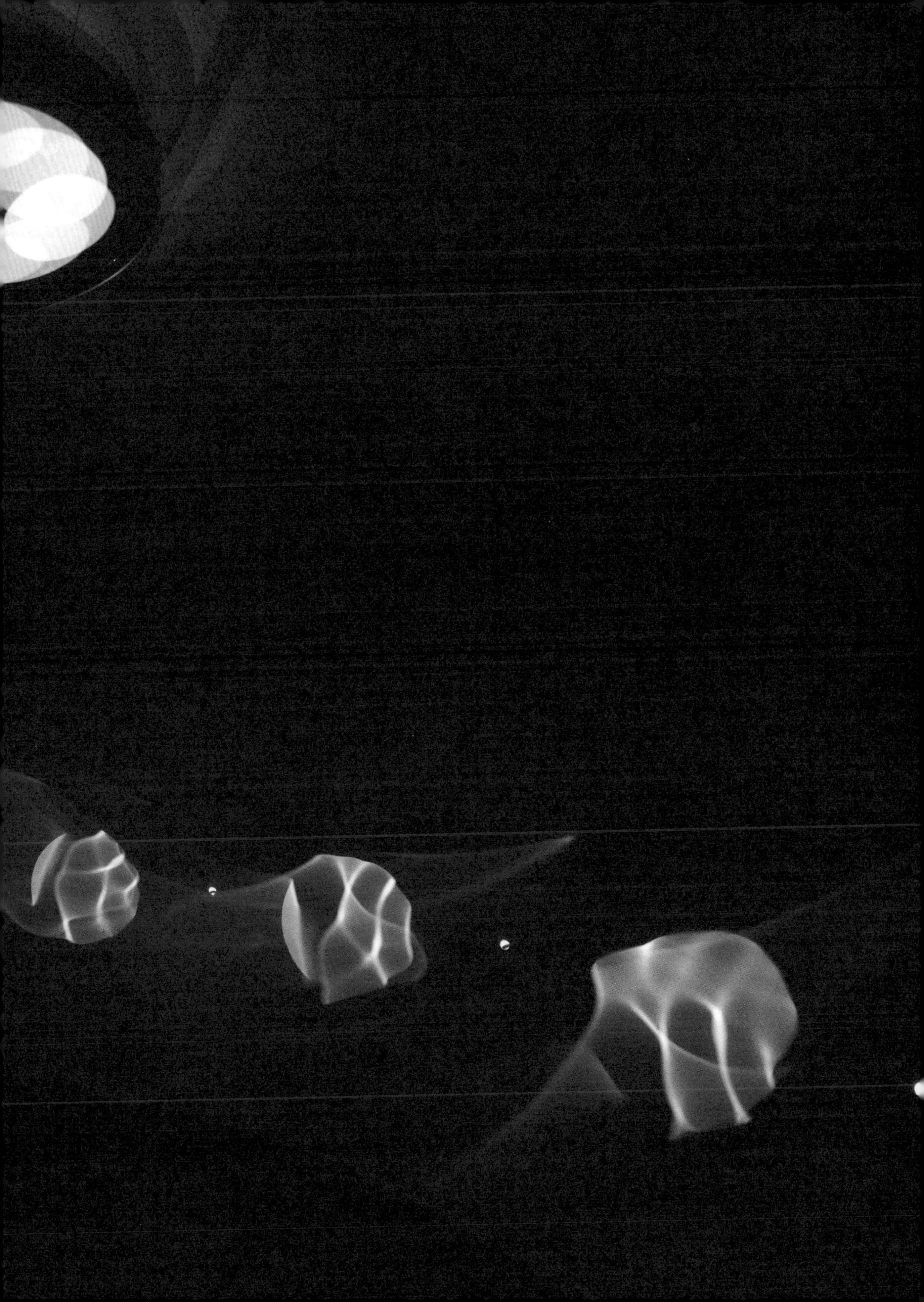

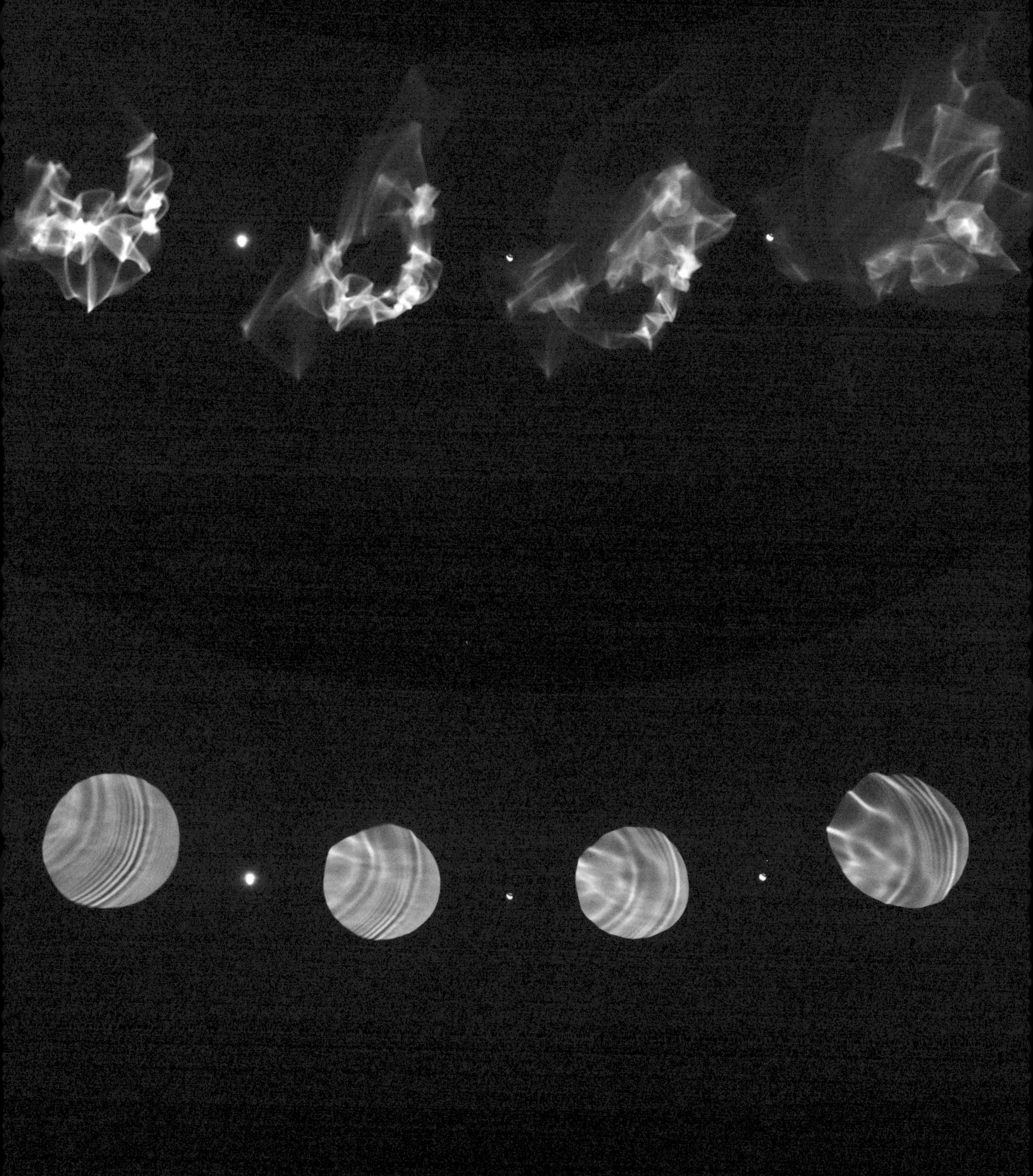

水が張られた大きなシャーレが空間の中心に置かれ、12のスポットライトで照らされている。 水面が揺れると頭上のスクリーンにはとらえがたいさざなみのイメージが映し出される。 絶えず変化しつつ徐々に広がるさざなみのような流動する状況を、エリアソンは限界を超えるための欠かせない要素ととらえている。 世界との新しい向き合い方を提示するこの作品は同名の展覧会のための新作である。

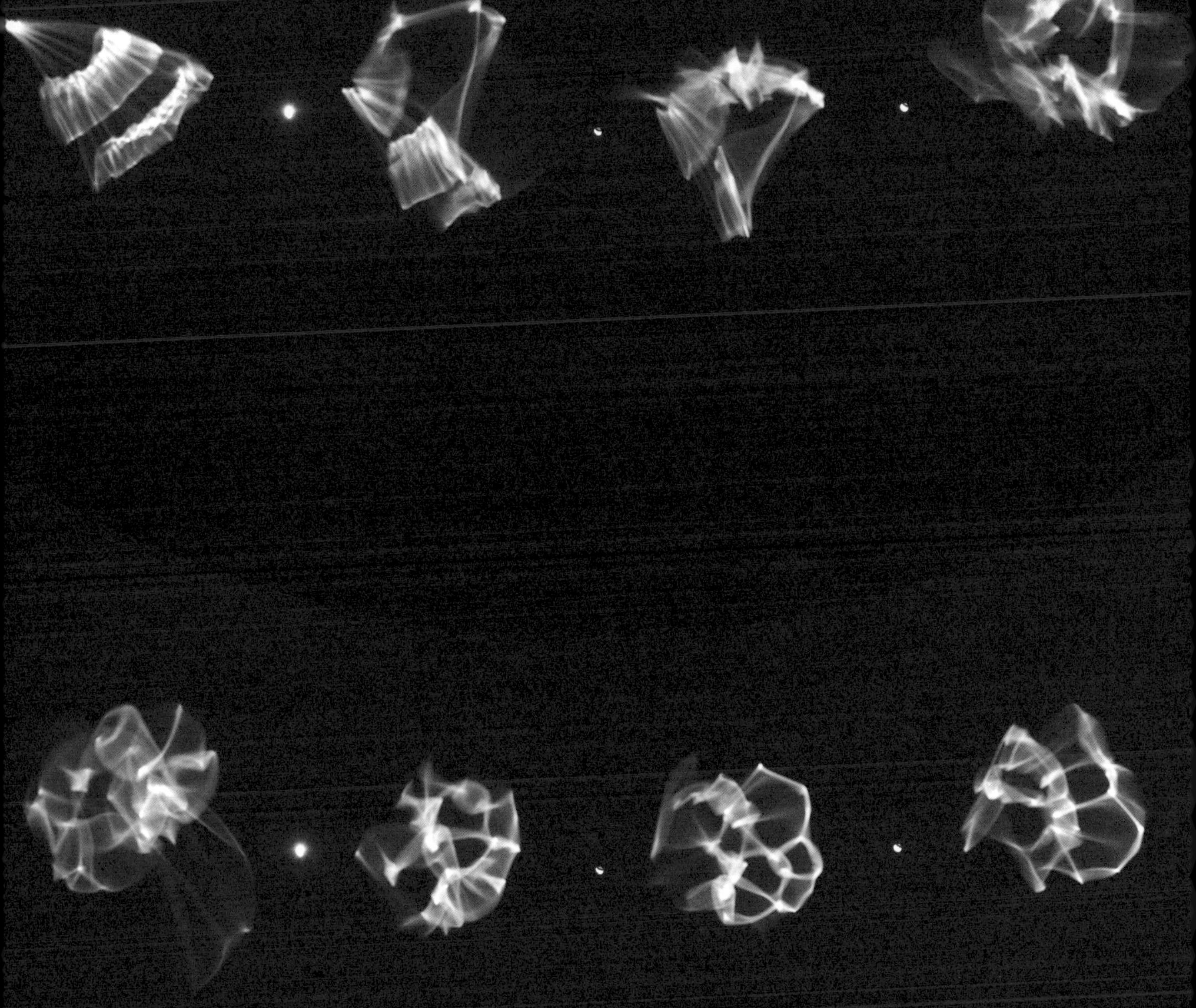

The shallow pool at the centre of this work is agitated by a small motor that fills the surface of the water with small waves. The drawing on the screen above the pool is an ephemeral phenomenon produced anew in each moment through the dynamic interplay of water, movement, and light.

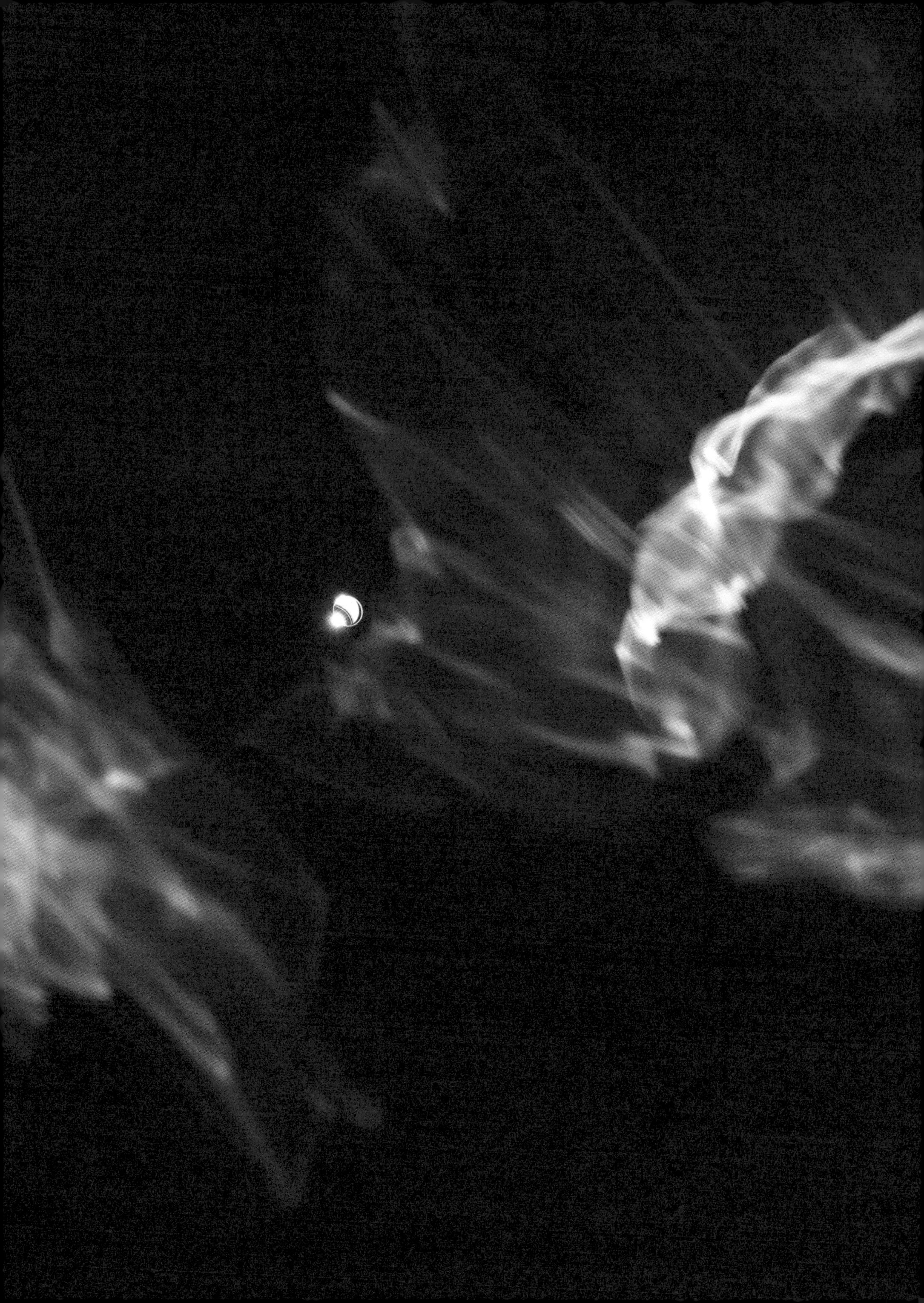

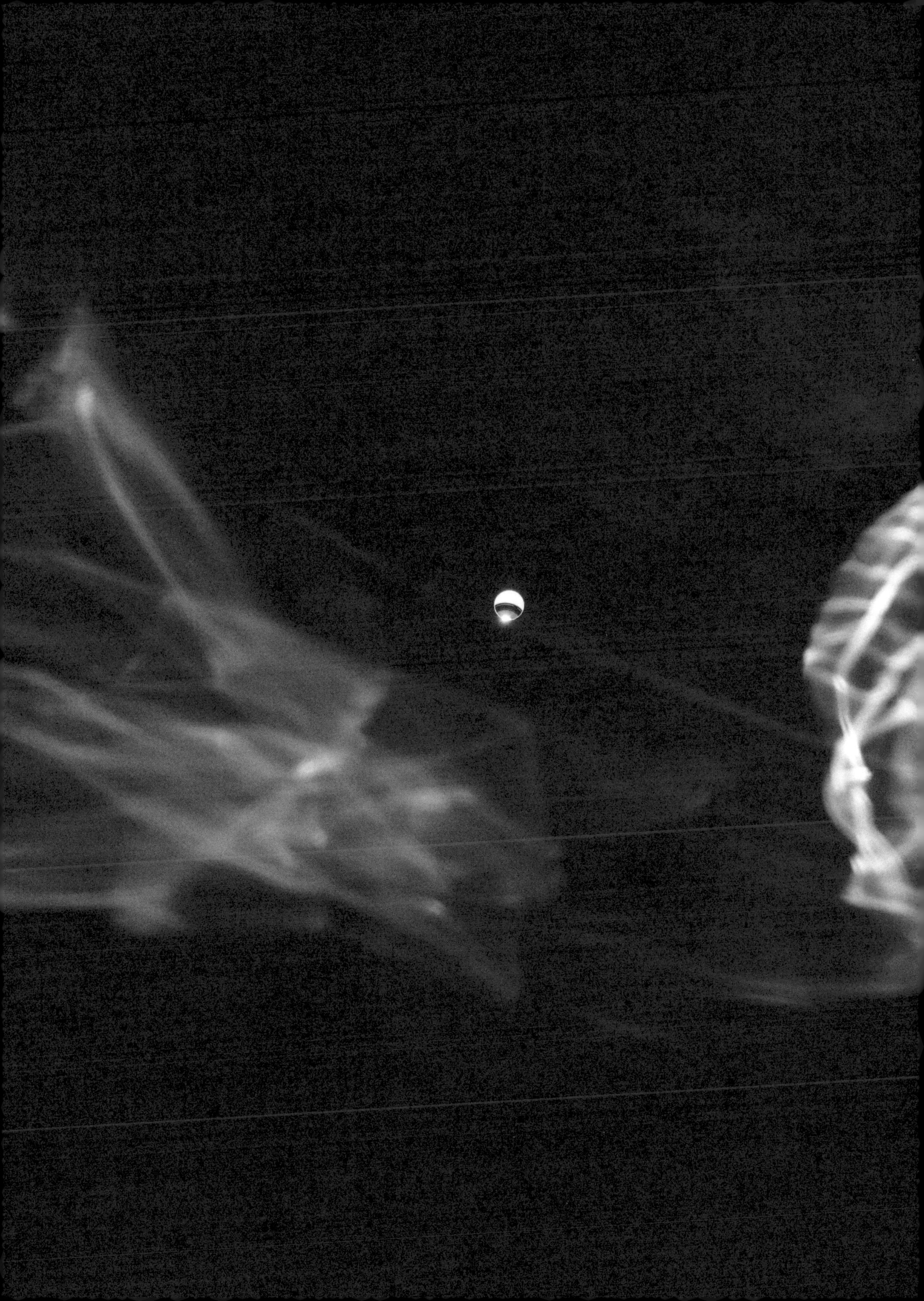

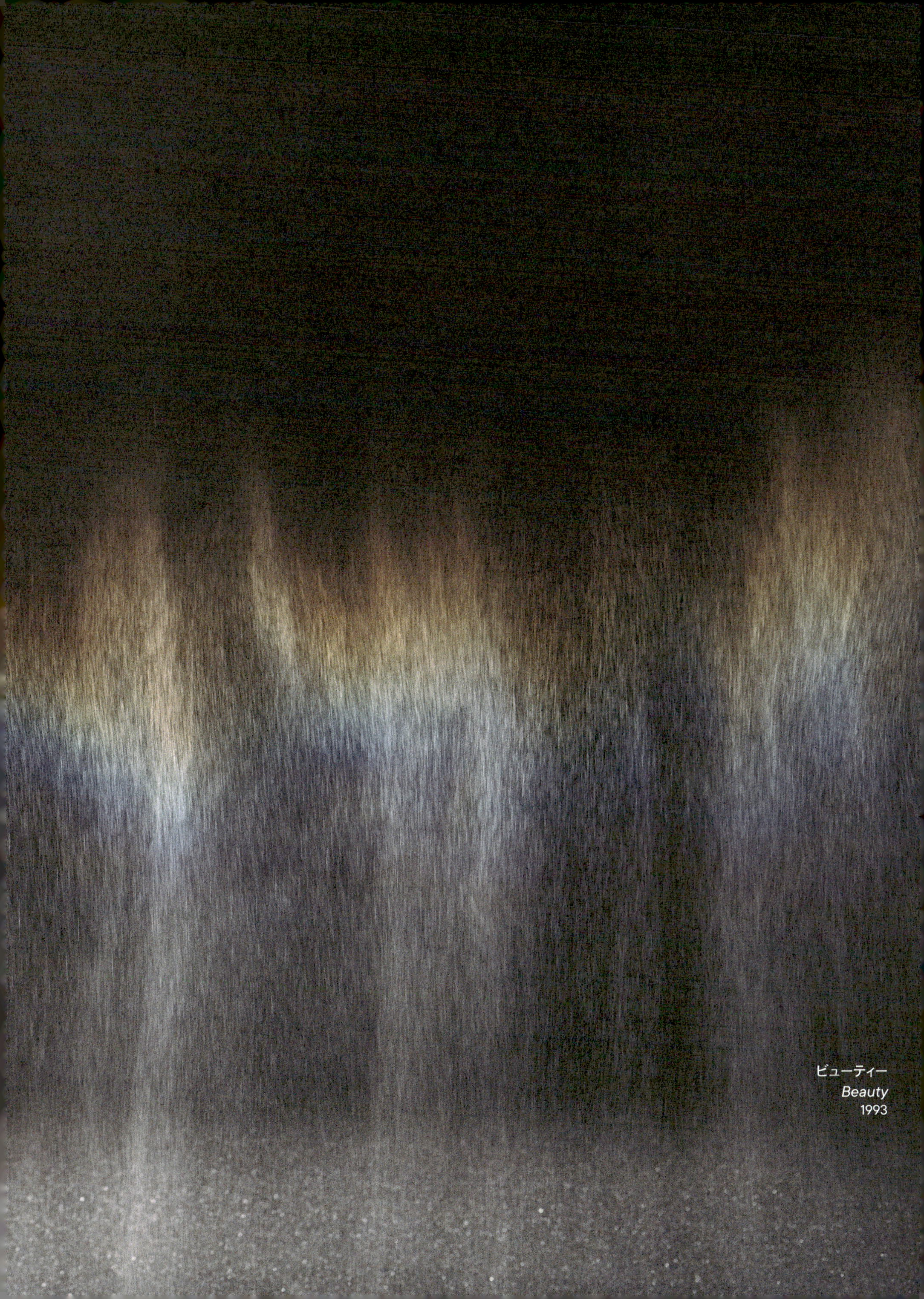
ビューティー
Beauty
1993

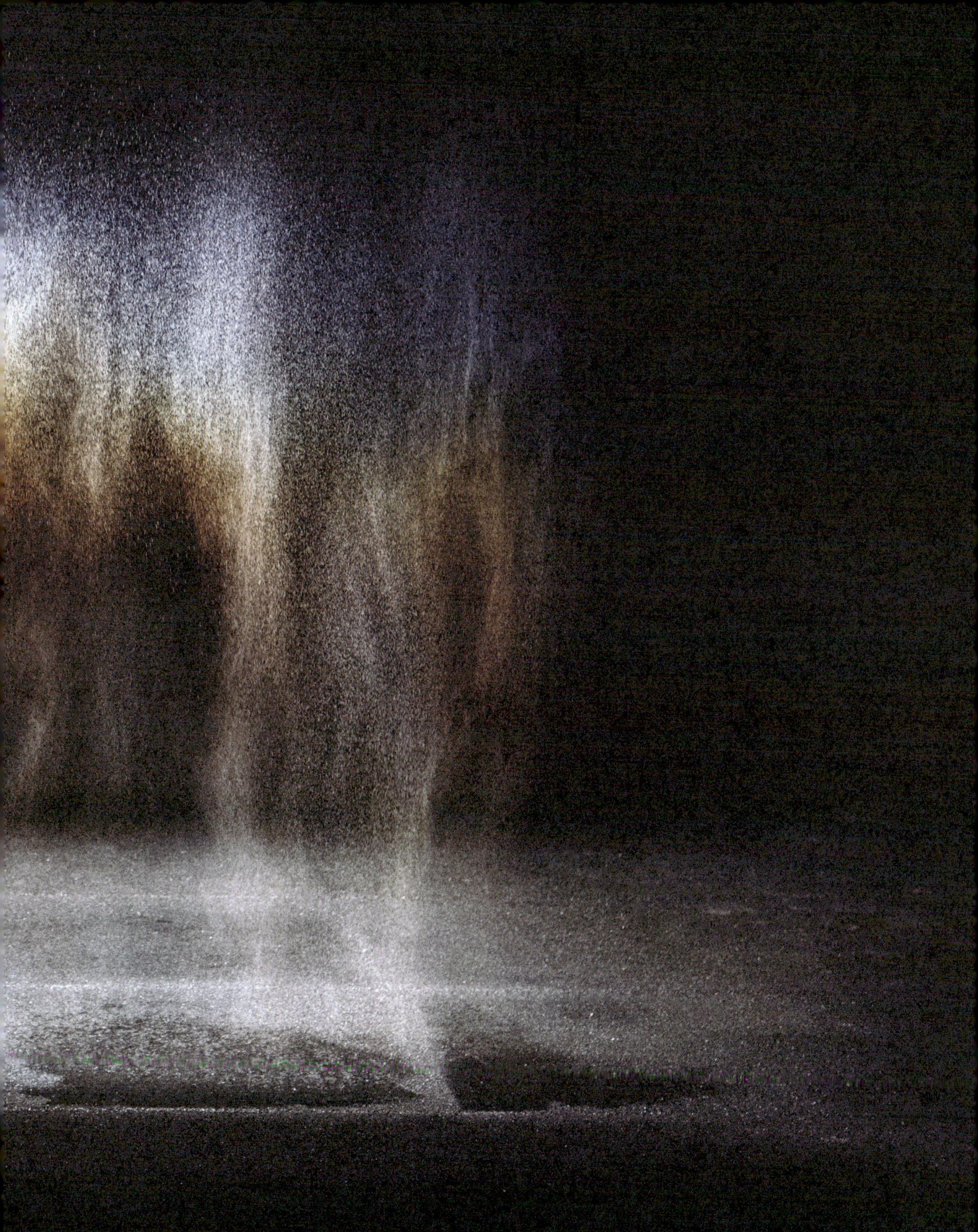

暗闇の中の霧状の水に光をあてることによって目の前に虹が現れる。虹の色や形は見る人の位置によって異なる。「光があなたの目に入らないかぎり虹はどこにもない」とエリアソンが言うように、虹を見るという私たちの体験こそがこの作品の本質にほかならない。自然現象を自らの手で再現したエリアソンの初期の代表作である。

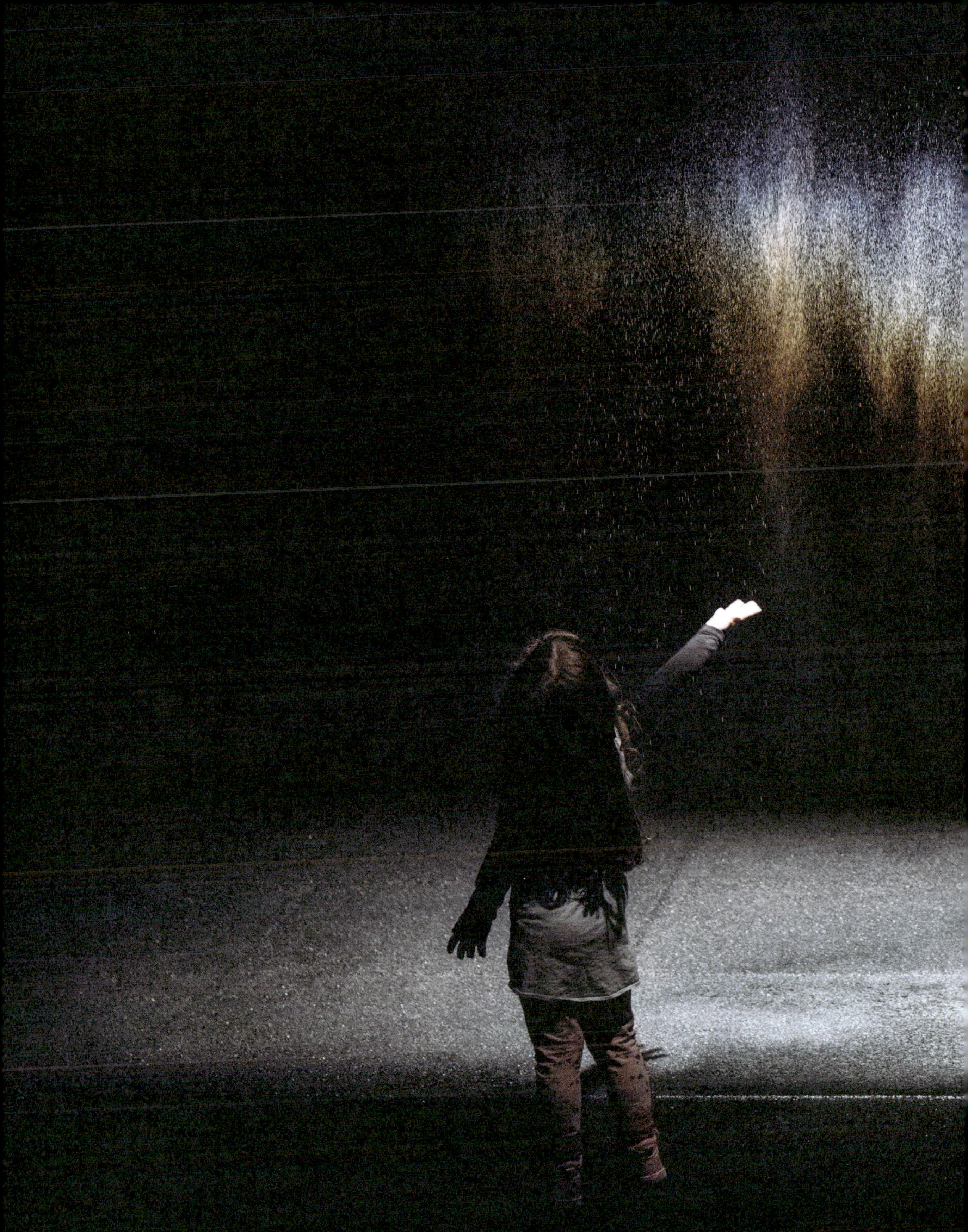

In this early work, a spotlight shines obliquely through a curtain of fine mist. Since the experience of the visual effects generated by the interplay of water and light changes in response to visitors' positions within the room, the artwork exists only in the coming together of eye and objects and is unique for each viewer.

あなたのオレンジ色の残像が現われる
Your orange afterimage exposed
2000

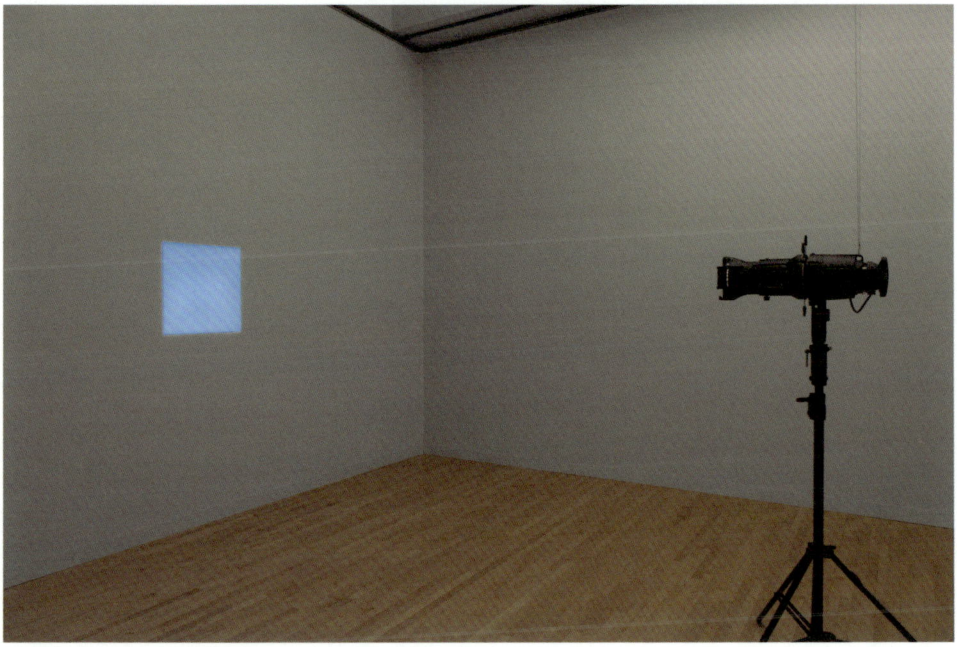

The bright blue square on the gallery wall flashes on and off at intervals – 15 seconds on, 10 seconds off. When the light is off, a vivid afterimage appears in the vision of each viewer to complete the work. A subtle version of this effect can be experienced by staring at the blue square on the opposite page for several seconds and then suddenly directing one's gaze to the white area above this text.

青い正方形のイメージが一定の間隔で現れては消えていく。青いイメージをしばらく見続けていると、それが消えたときに夕陽のようなオレンジ色の残像が立ち現れるだろう。青いイメージは作品のための装置にすぎず、作品そのものは私たちひとりひとりが知覚している間にだけ存在しているのである。

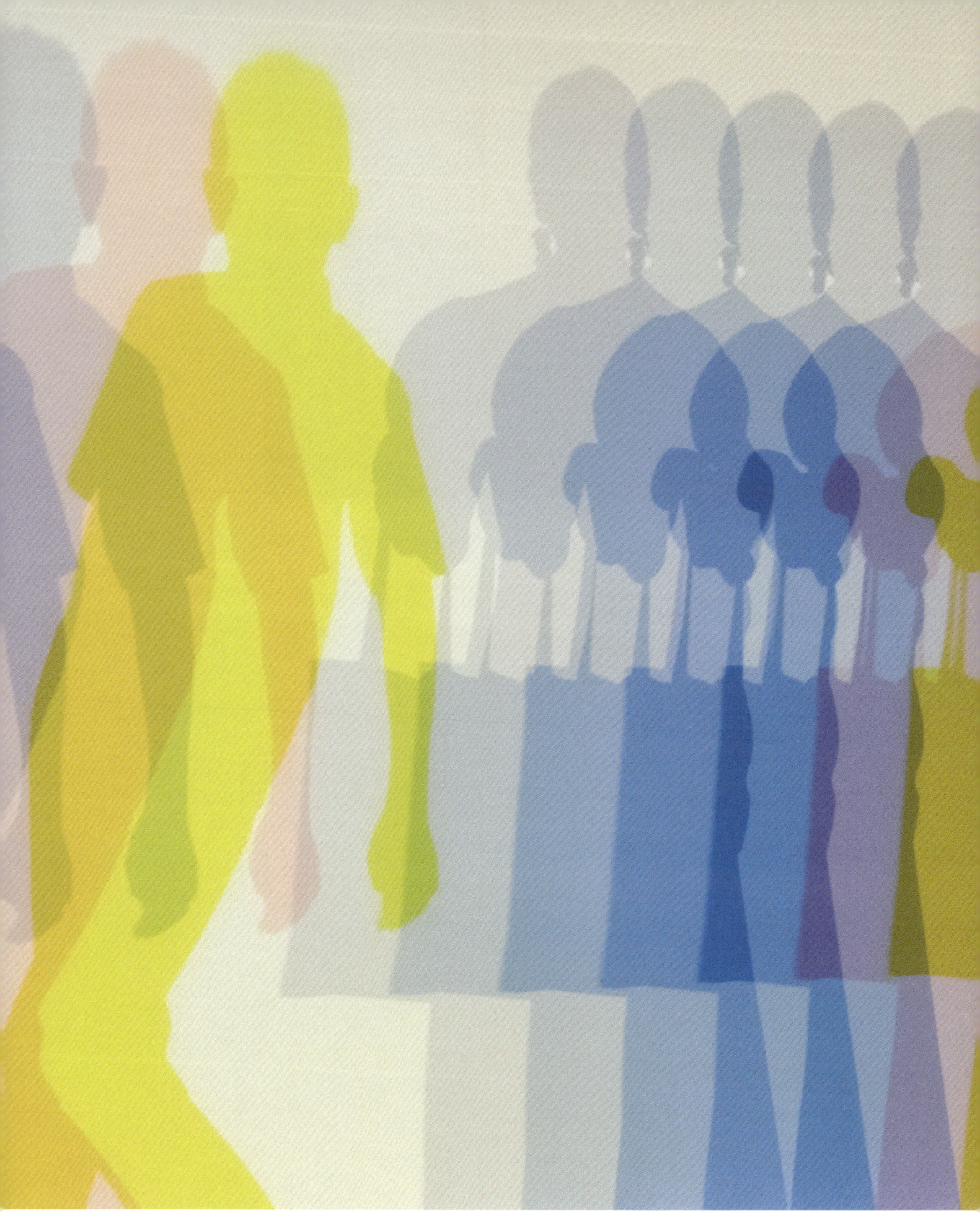

あなたに今起きていること、起きたこと、これから起きること
Your happening, has happened, will happen
2020

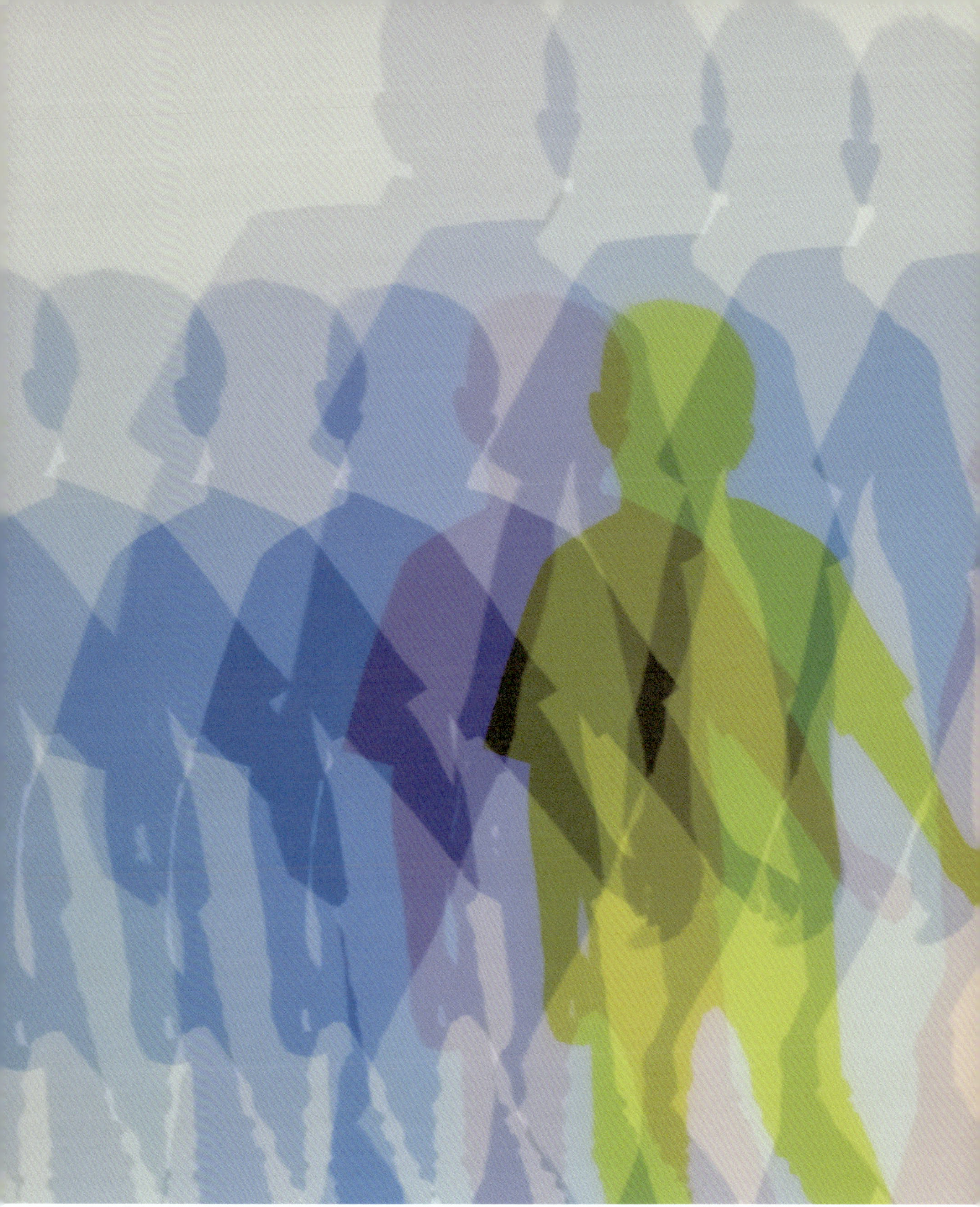

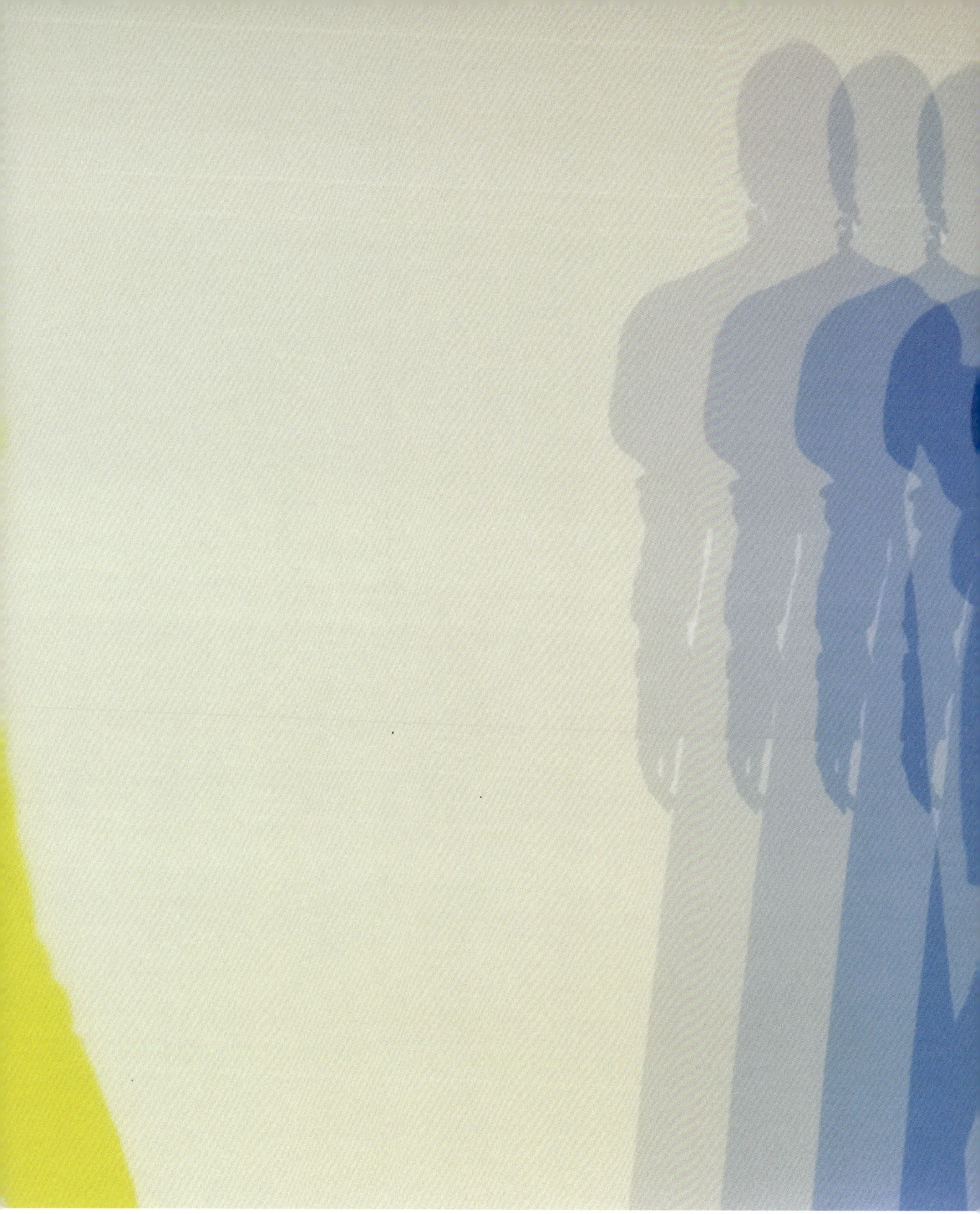

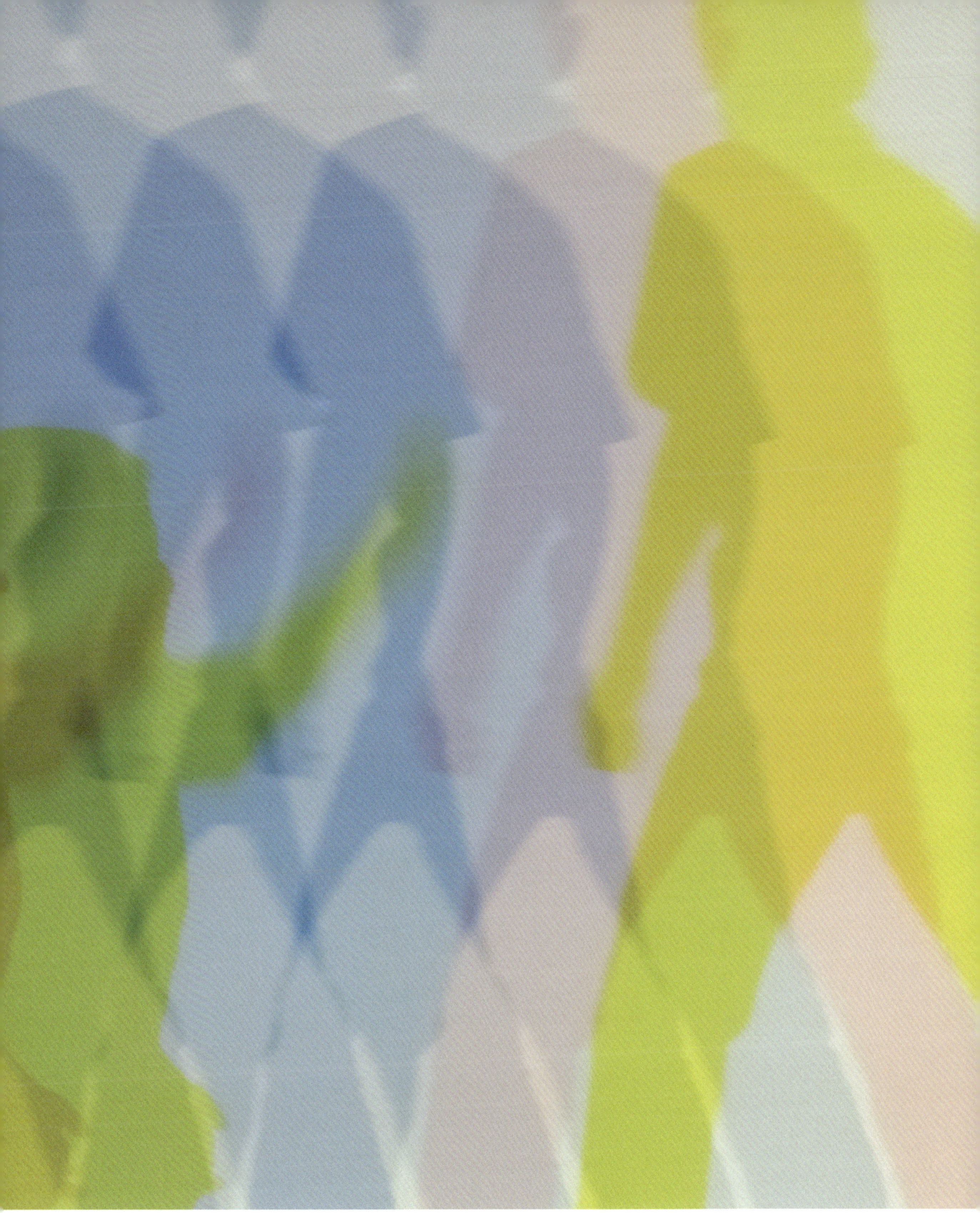

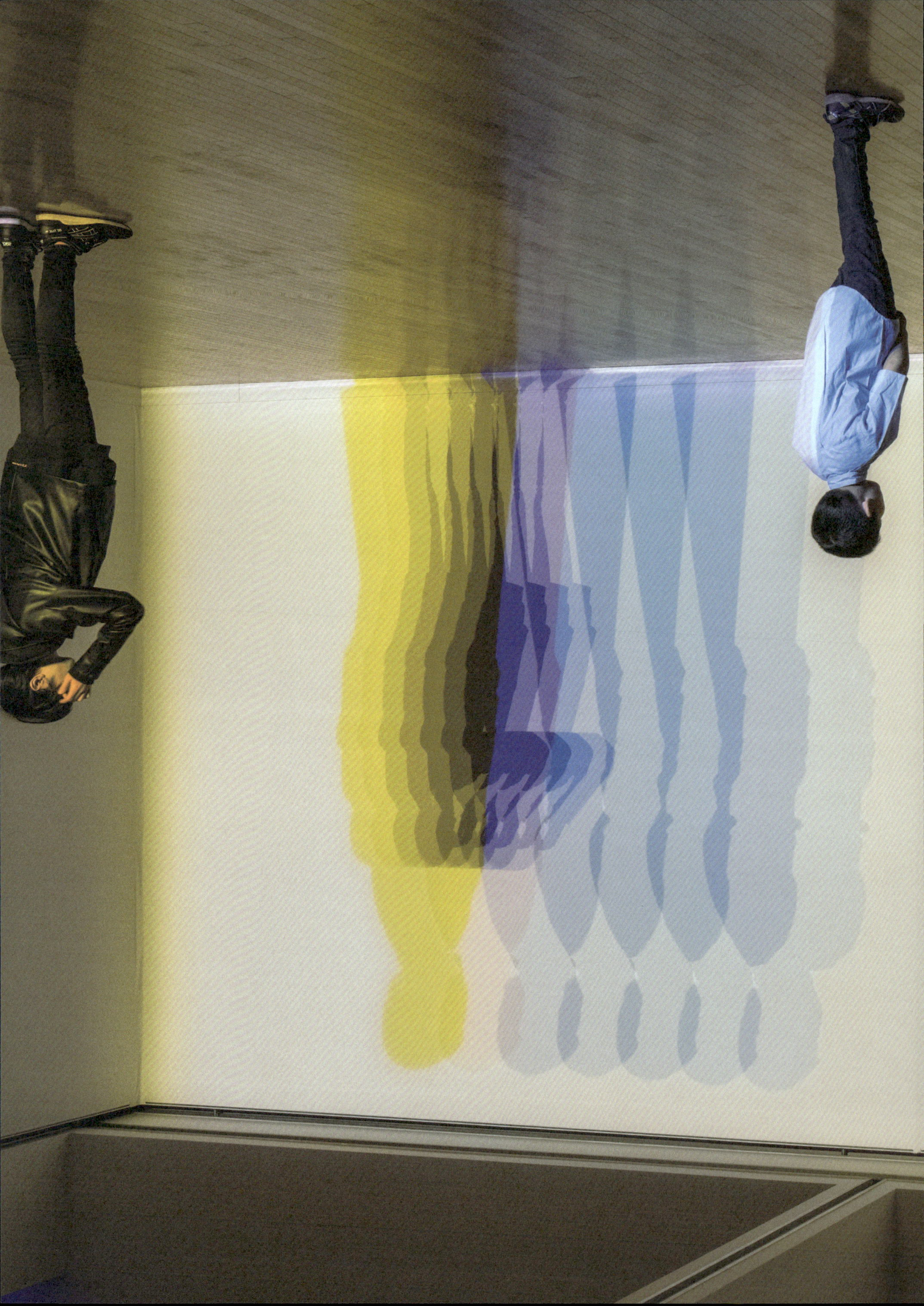

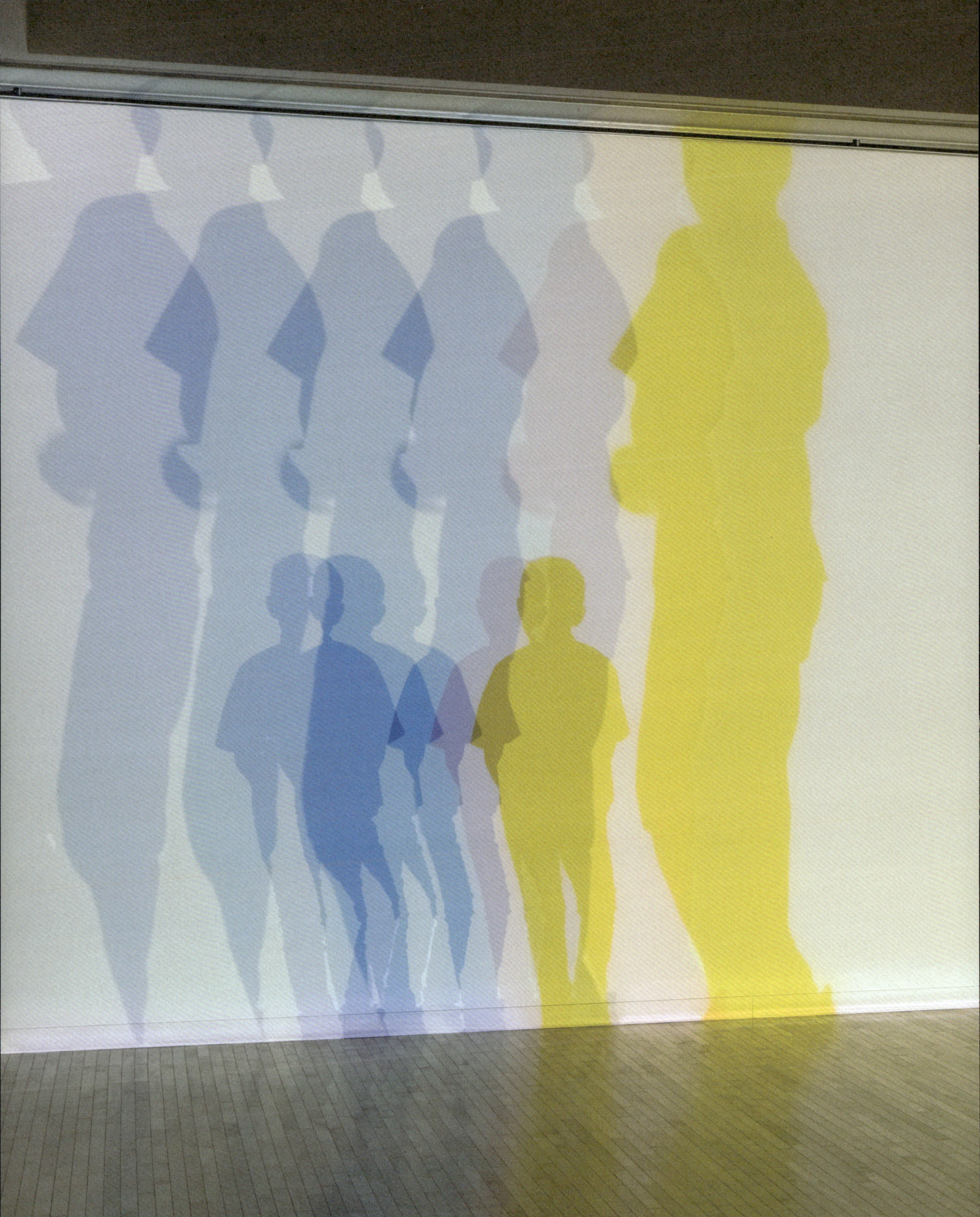

When visitors enter the space they discover a display that amplifies their movements, inviting their engagement and interaction.

この作品の展示室には床に置かれたライト以外に何もない。しかし誰かがライトの前を横切ると、重なり合う複数の影が壁に投じられる。「あなたが動いているときにだけ物事が見える」とエリアソンは言う。 行動や変化を起こすことが新たな発見やものの見方につながっているのかもしれない。

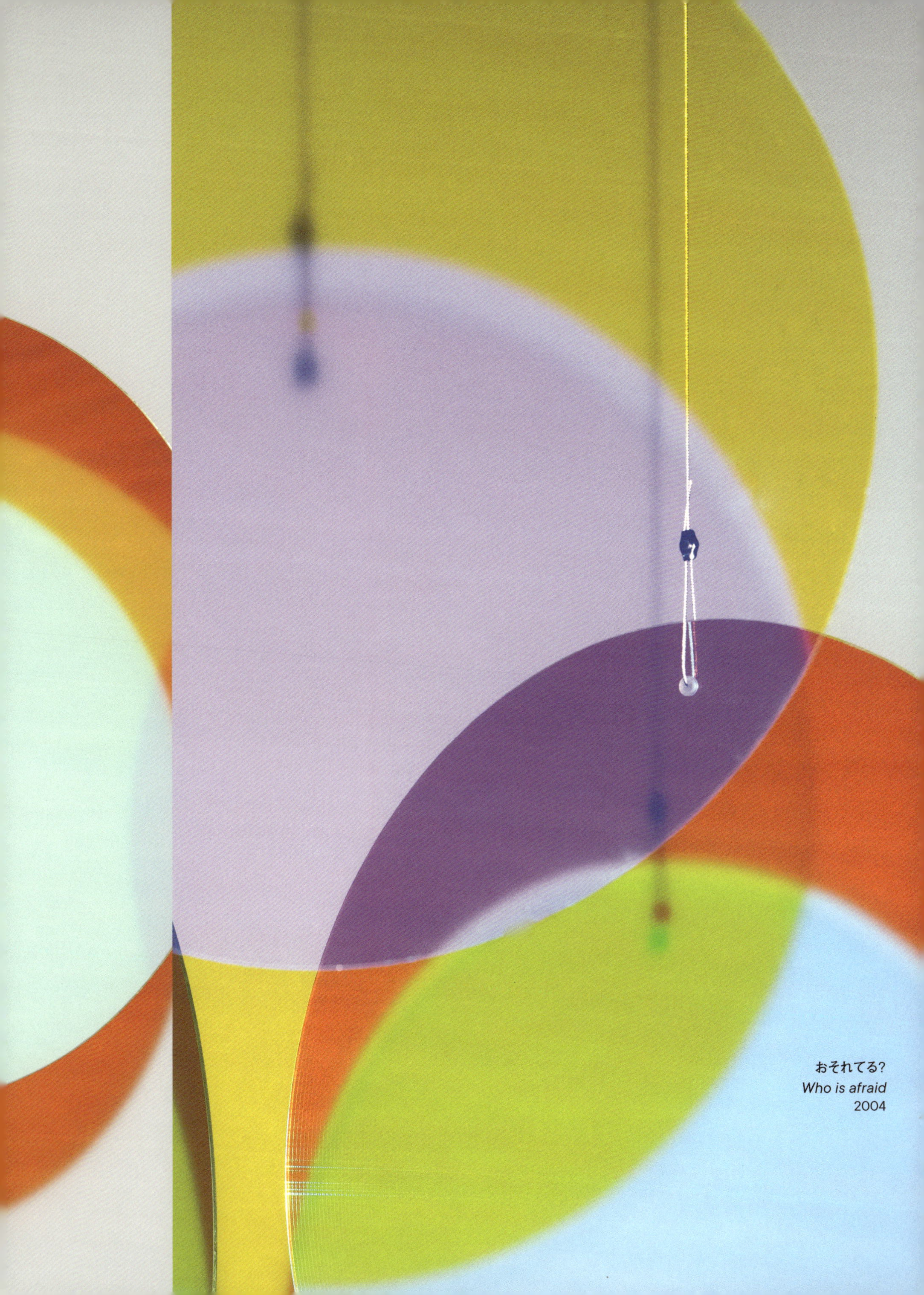

おそれてる?
Who is afraid
2004

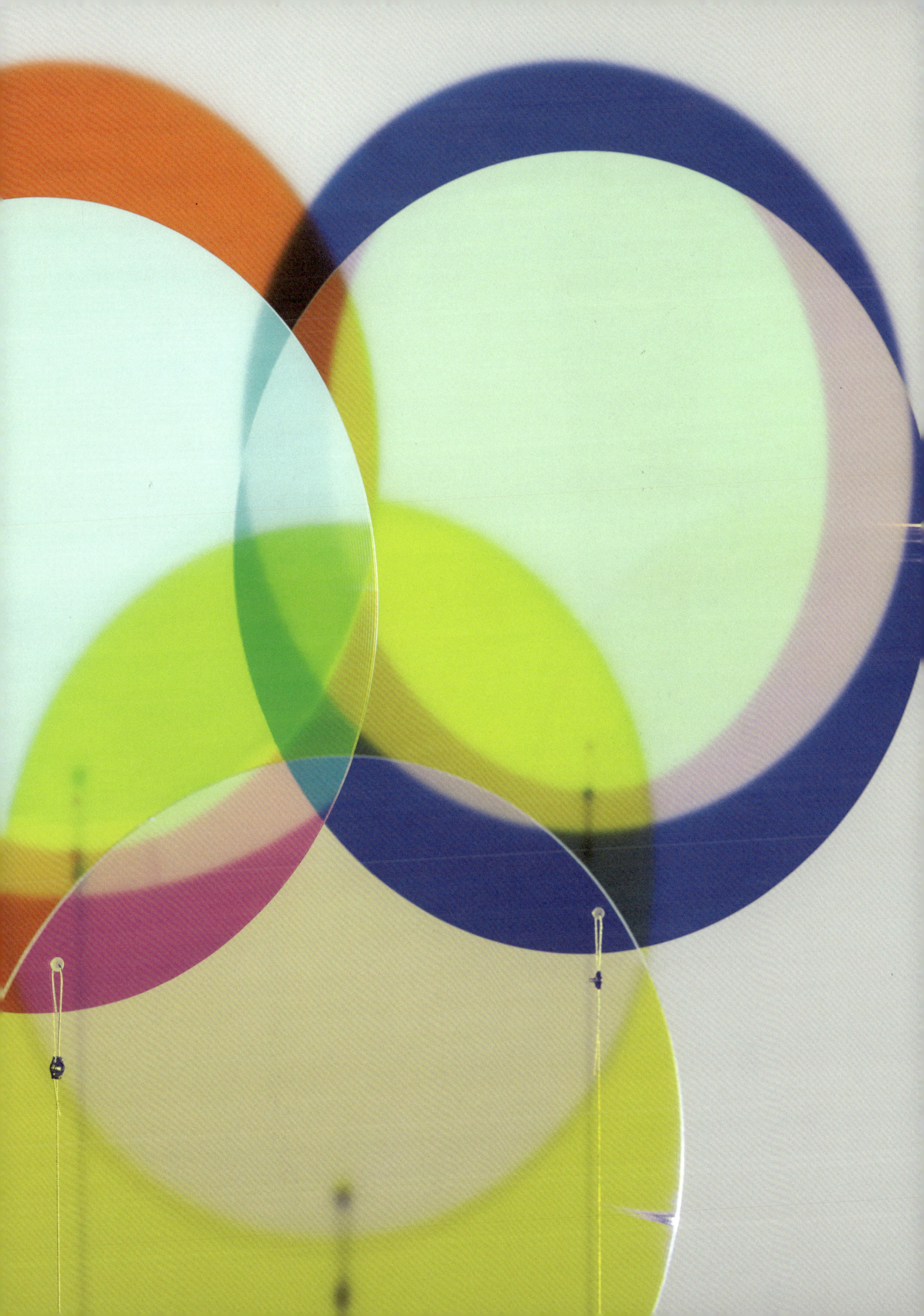

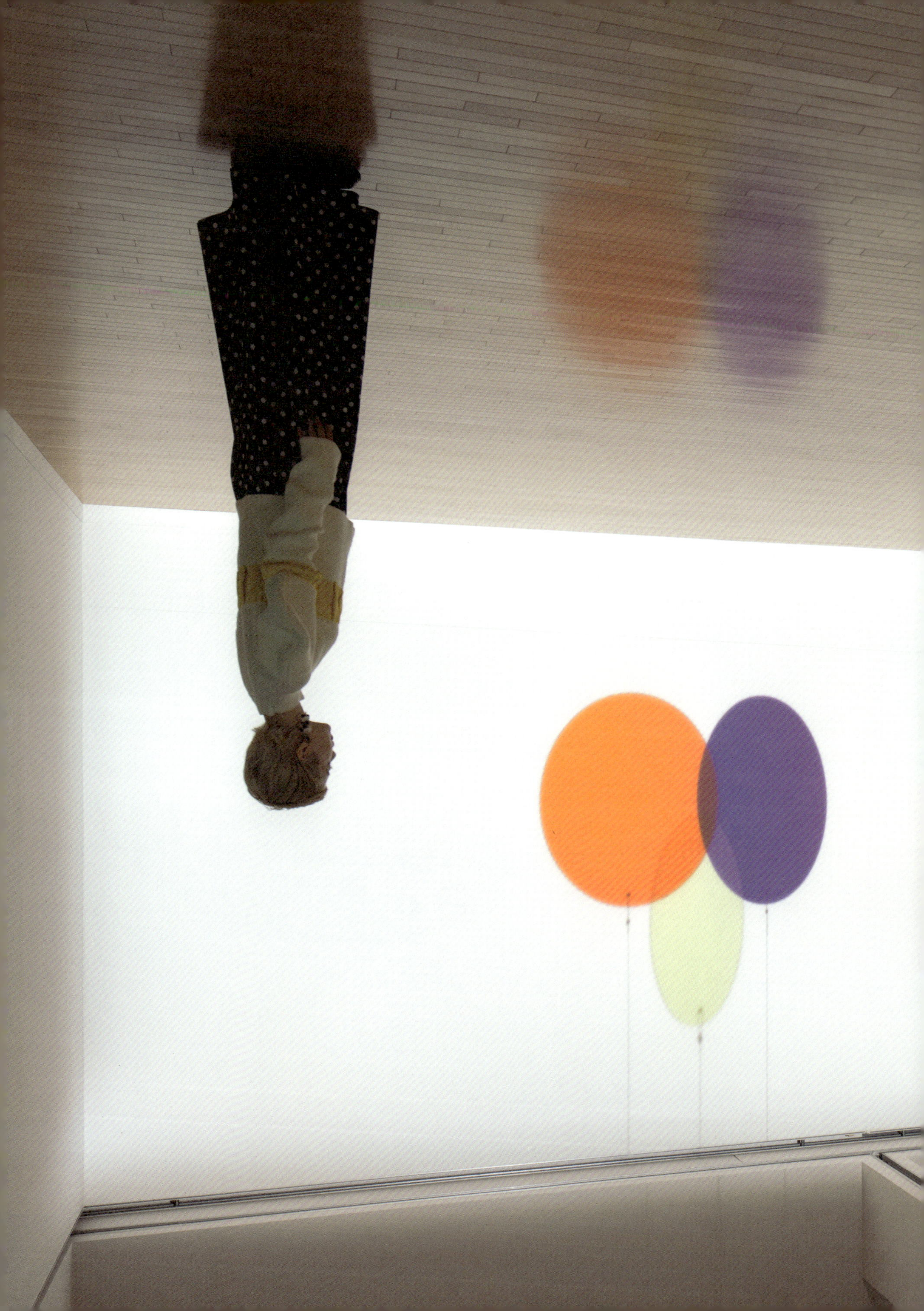

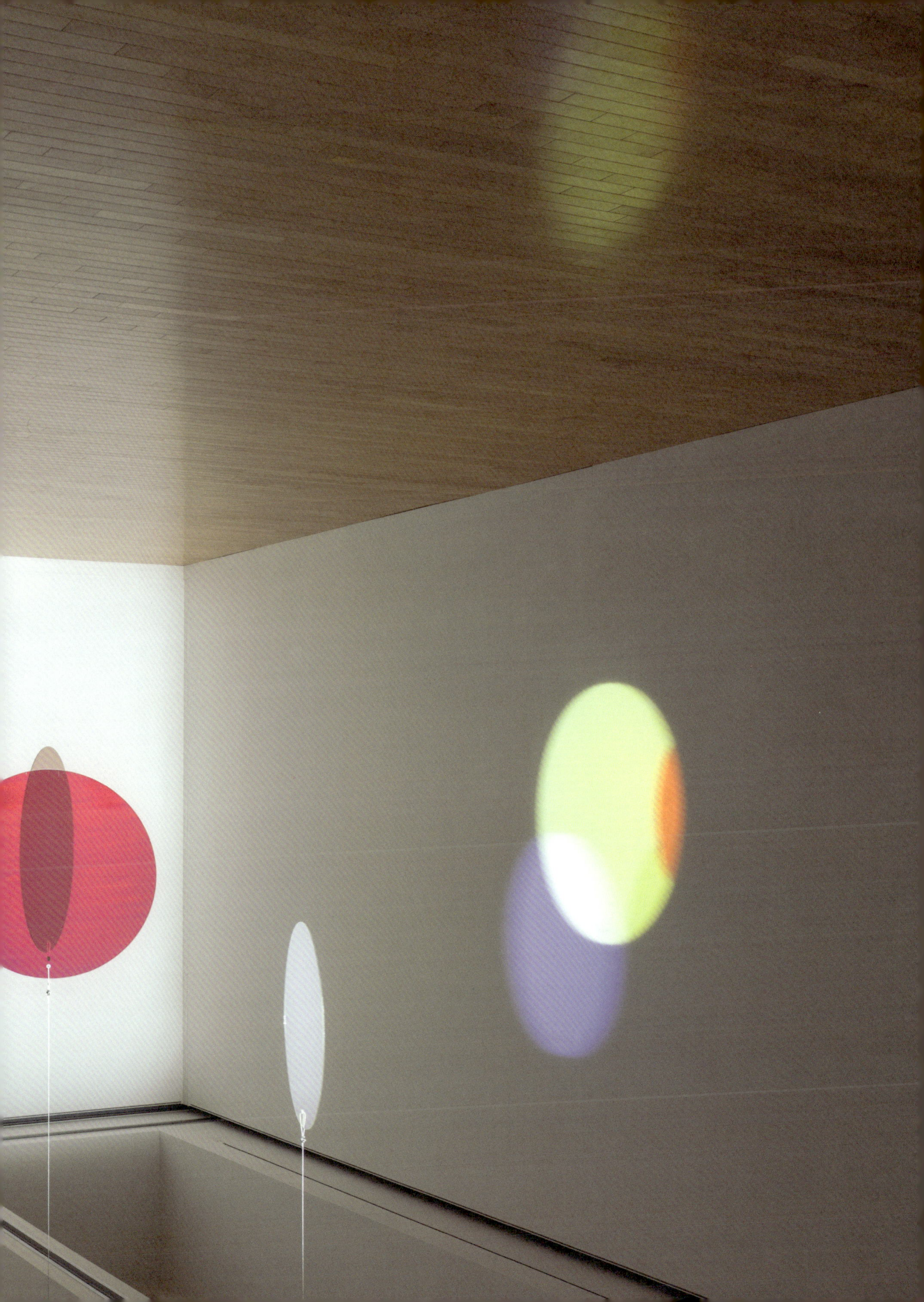

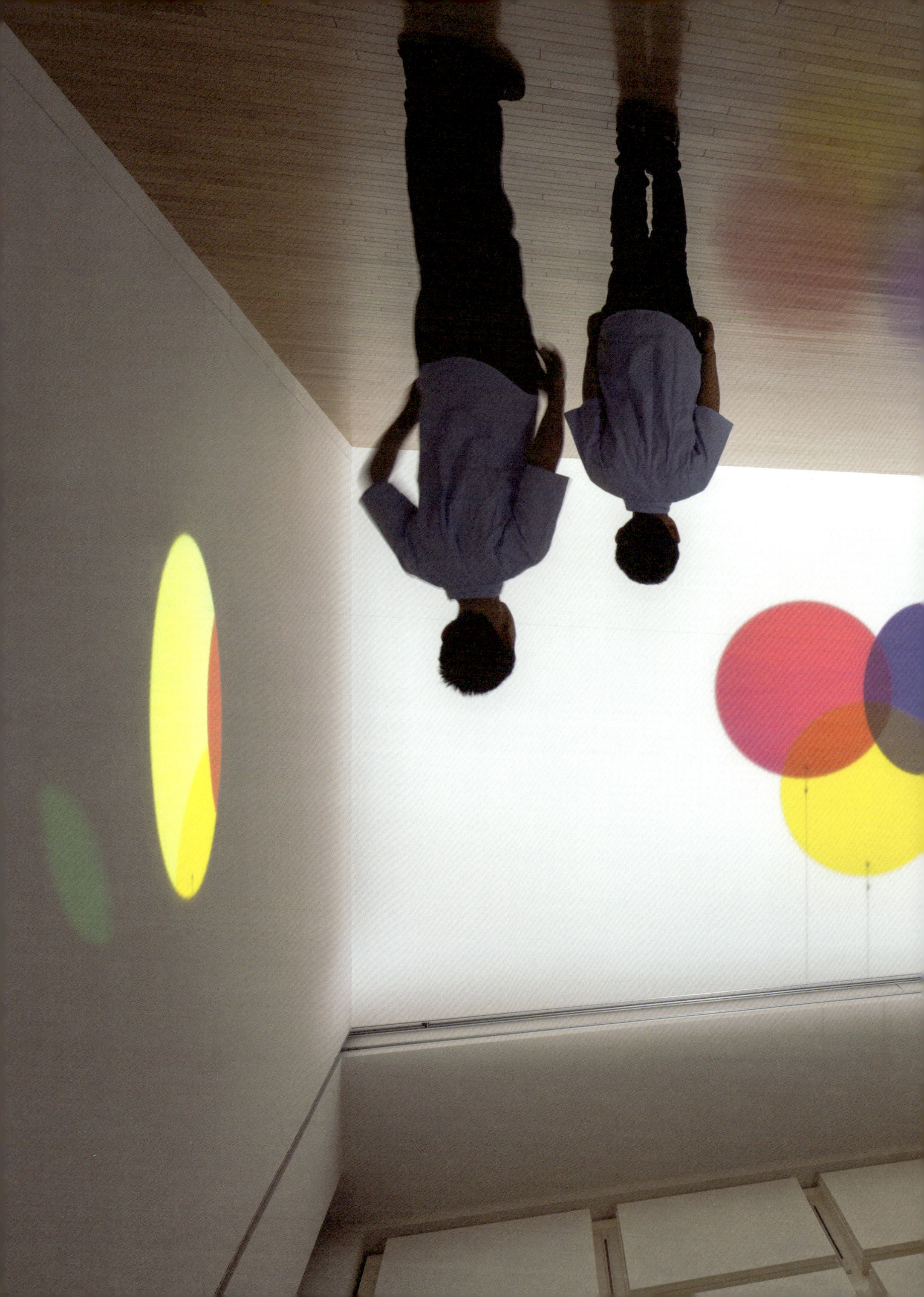

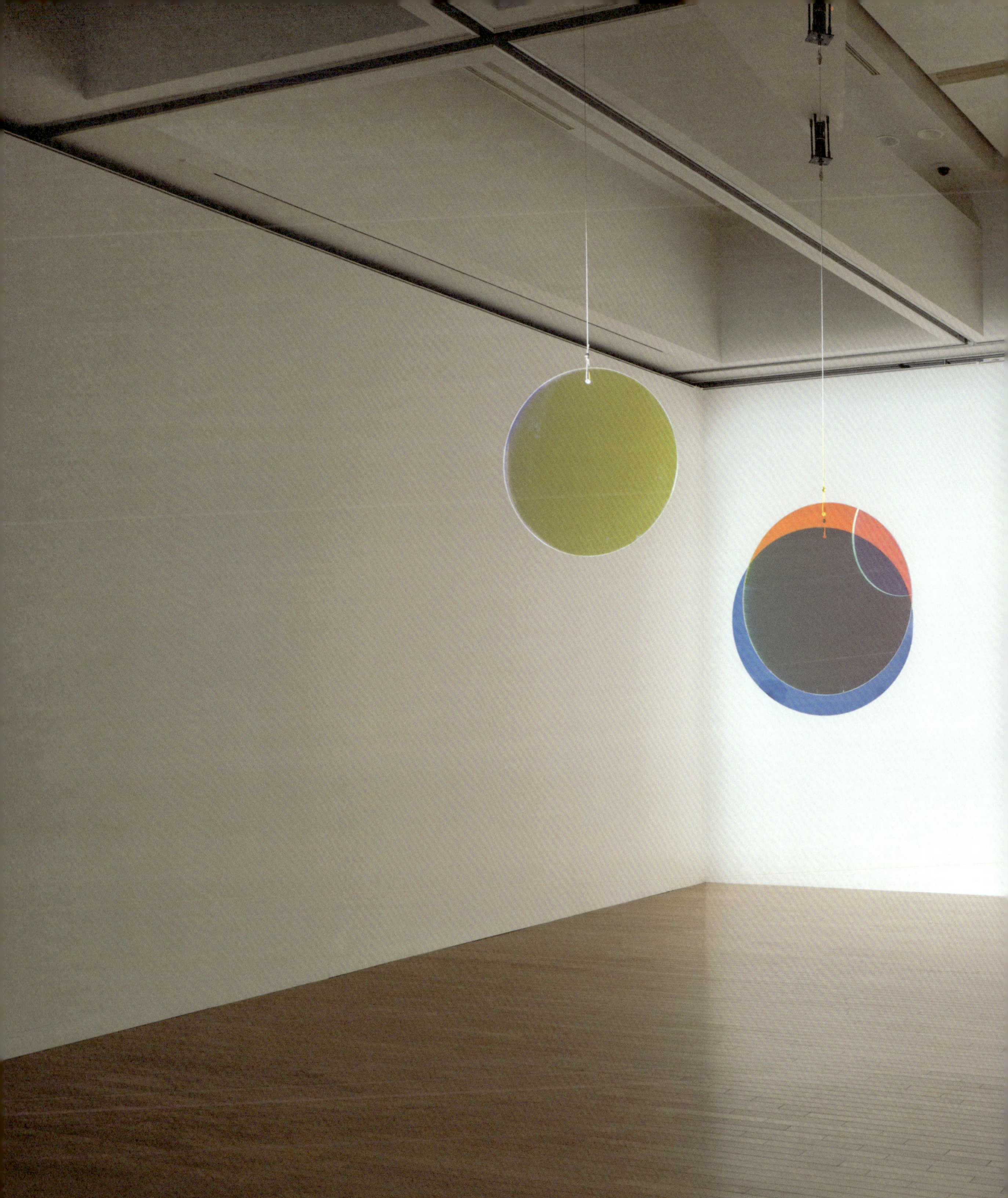

Works that explore colour theory are prominent in Eliasson's practice. The glass discs in this work each have a special coating that reflects light of one colour while allowing light of the opposite colour to pass through. When the continuously changing cyan, magenta, and yellow shapes on the wall overlap they mix to produce tones of red, green, or blue – the three primary colours.

ゆっくりと回転する3つの円形のガラス板を光が照らし、壁に複数の円が浮かび上がっている。大きさの異なるガラス板には特定の波長の光を反射し、補色の光を透過させる特殊な加工が施されている。壁に投影されたシアン、マゼンタ、イエローの円が等しく重なり合ったとき、その部分は黒色になる。エリアソンの色彩理論の探求から生まれた作品である。

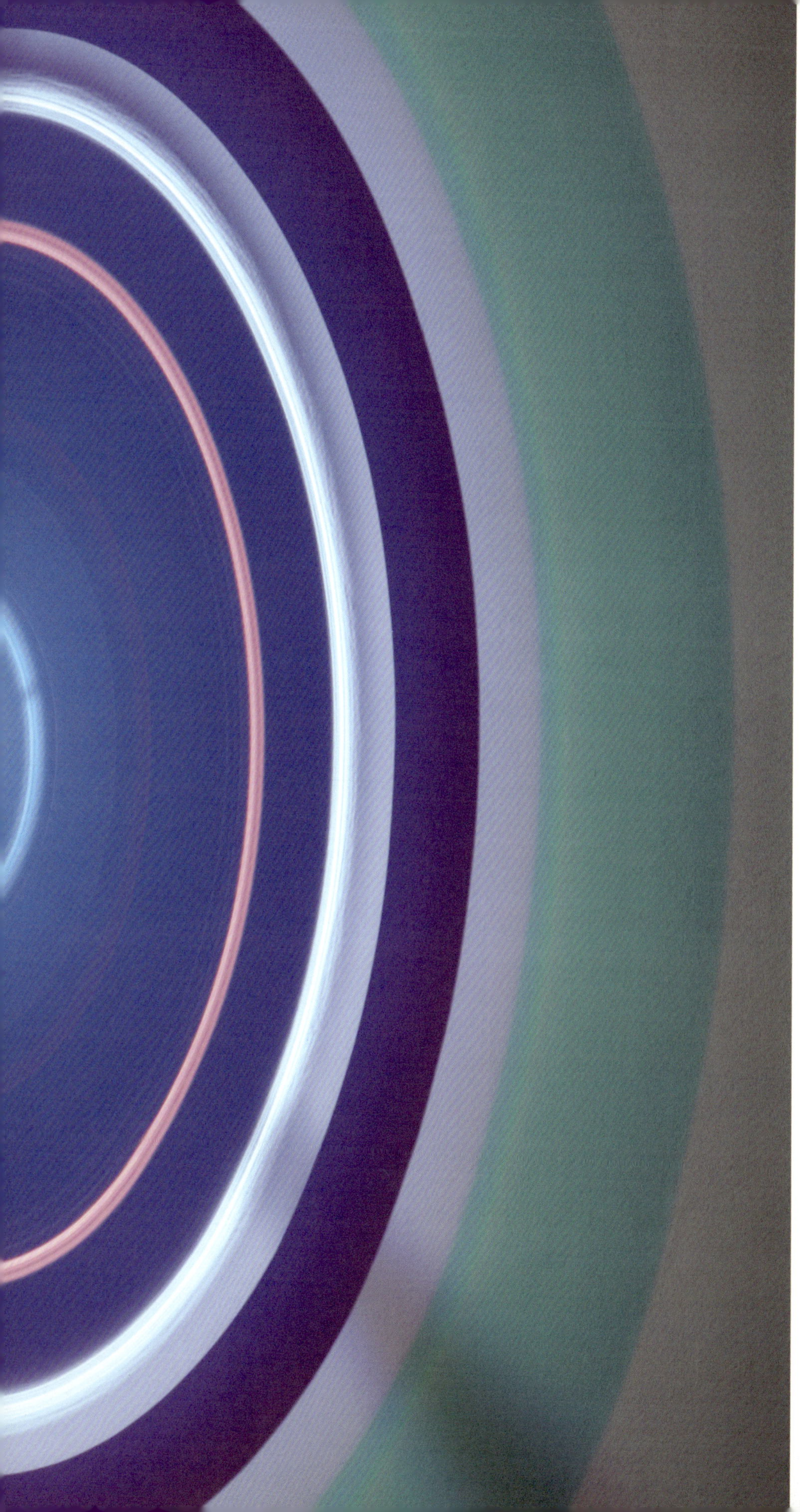

人間を超えたレゾネーター
Beyond-human resonator
2019

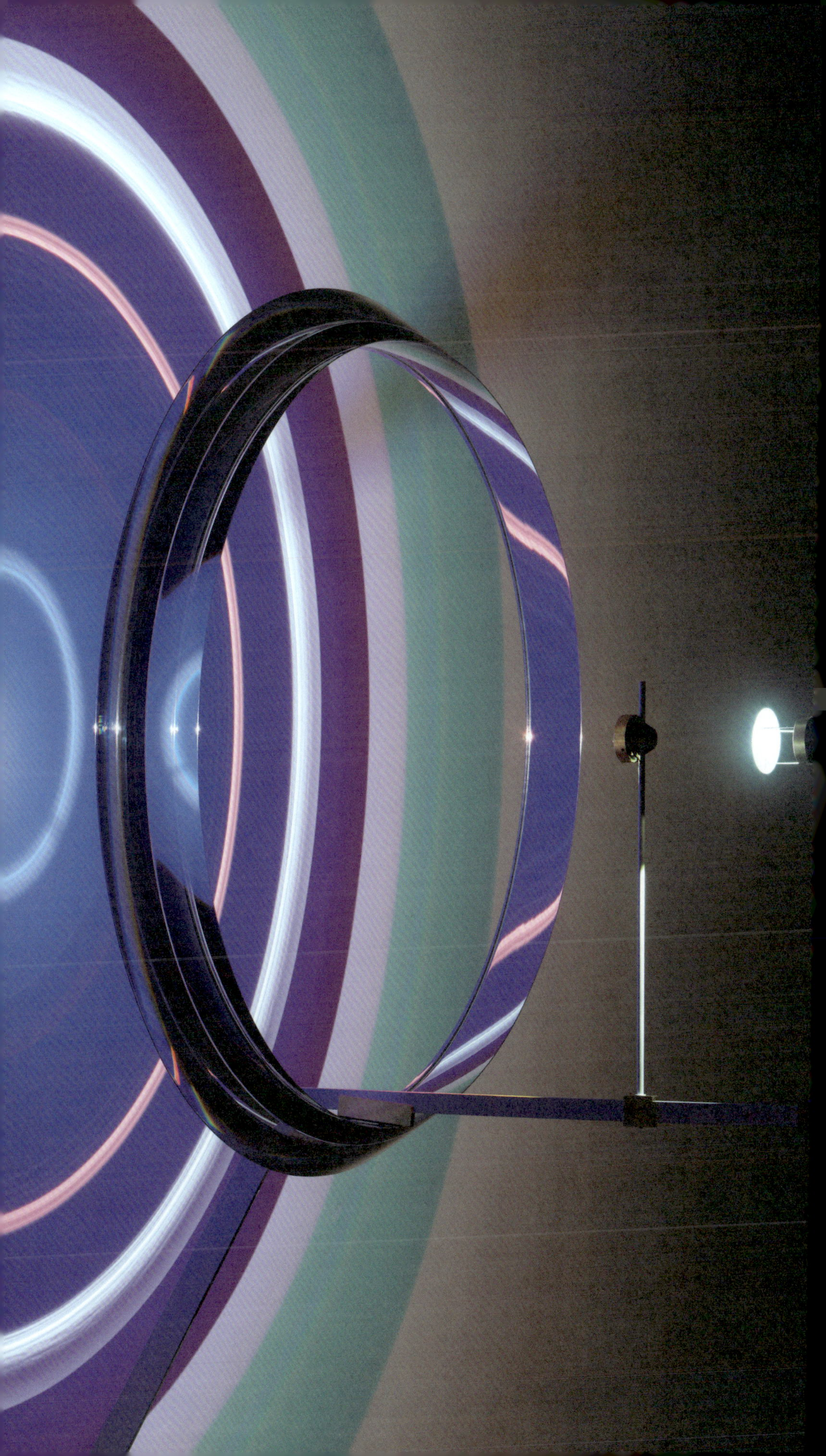

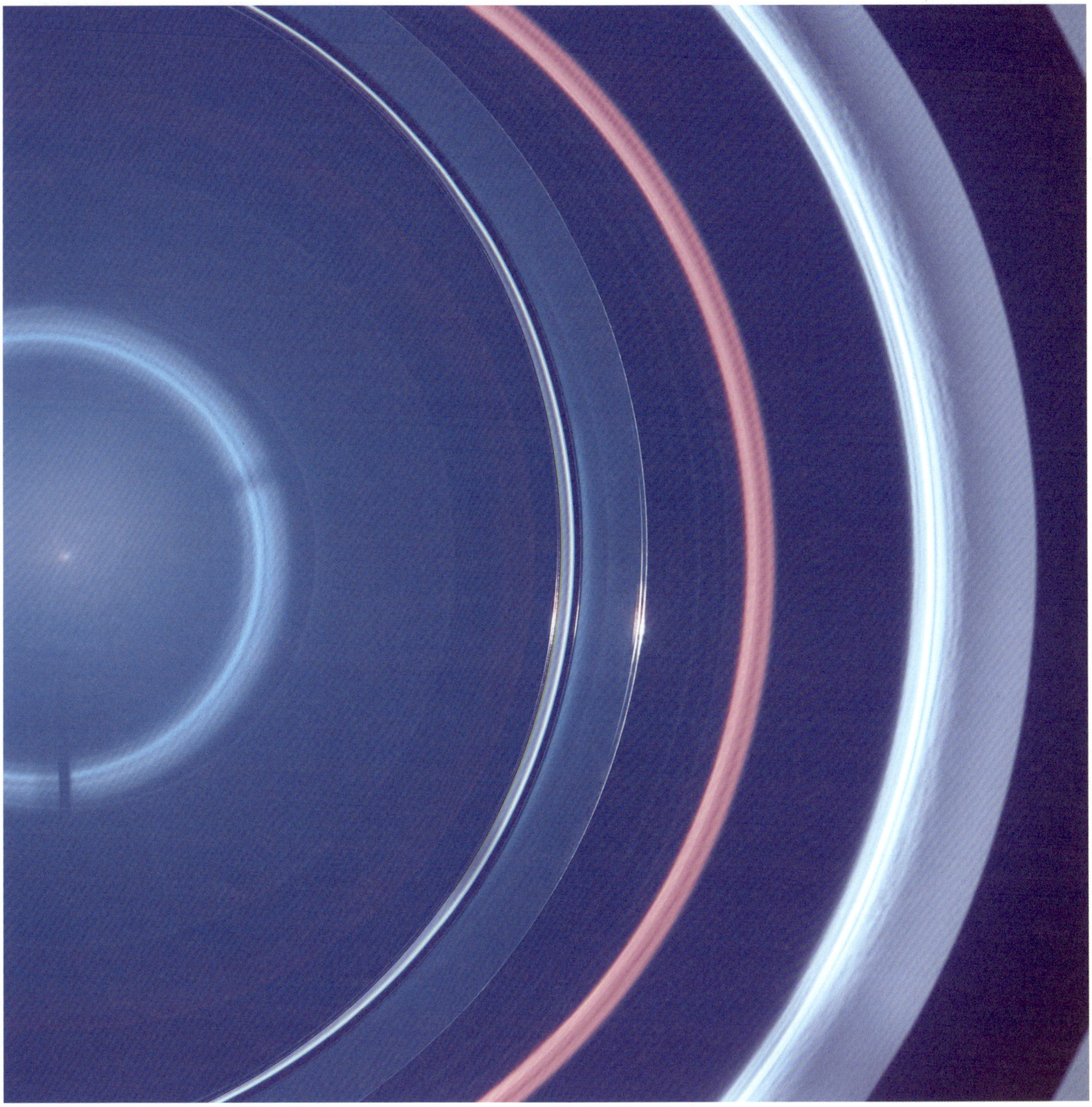

In this work, a large ring of bevelled glass is used to paint on a gallery wall with vividly coloured light. The ring acts as a prism, refracting and intensifying the light, which has been tinted by a glass colour-effect filter.

大きなガラスのリングによって分光した光が壁に同心円の絵画を描いている。この作品には暗い海を明るく遠くまで照らす灯台の光の仕組みが応用されている。単純な仕掛けによって見る人に大きな驚きを与えるというエリアソンの作品の特徴がよく表れている作品である。

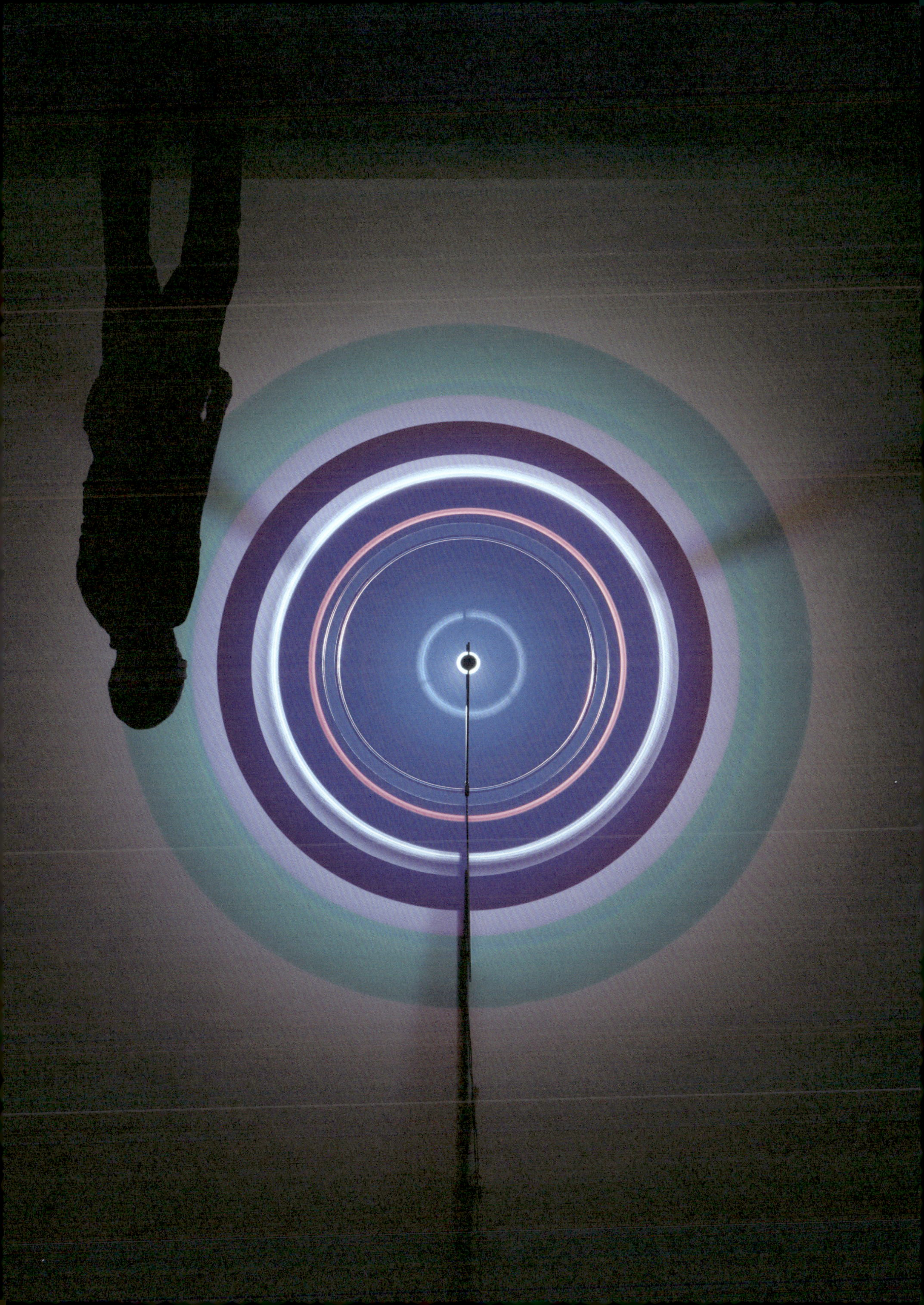

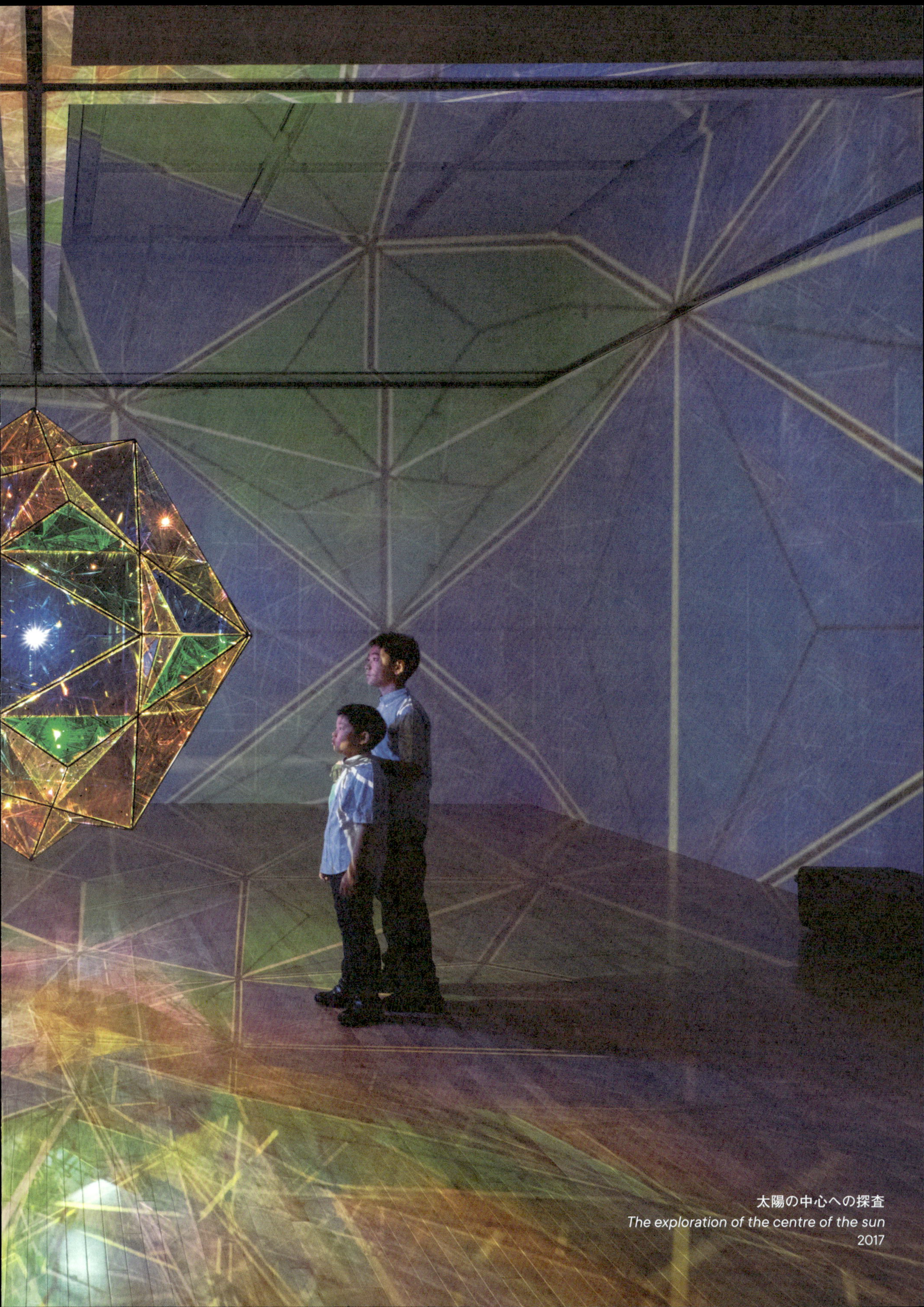

太陽の中心への探査
The exploration of the centre of the sun
2017

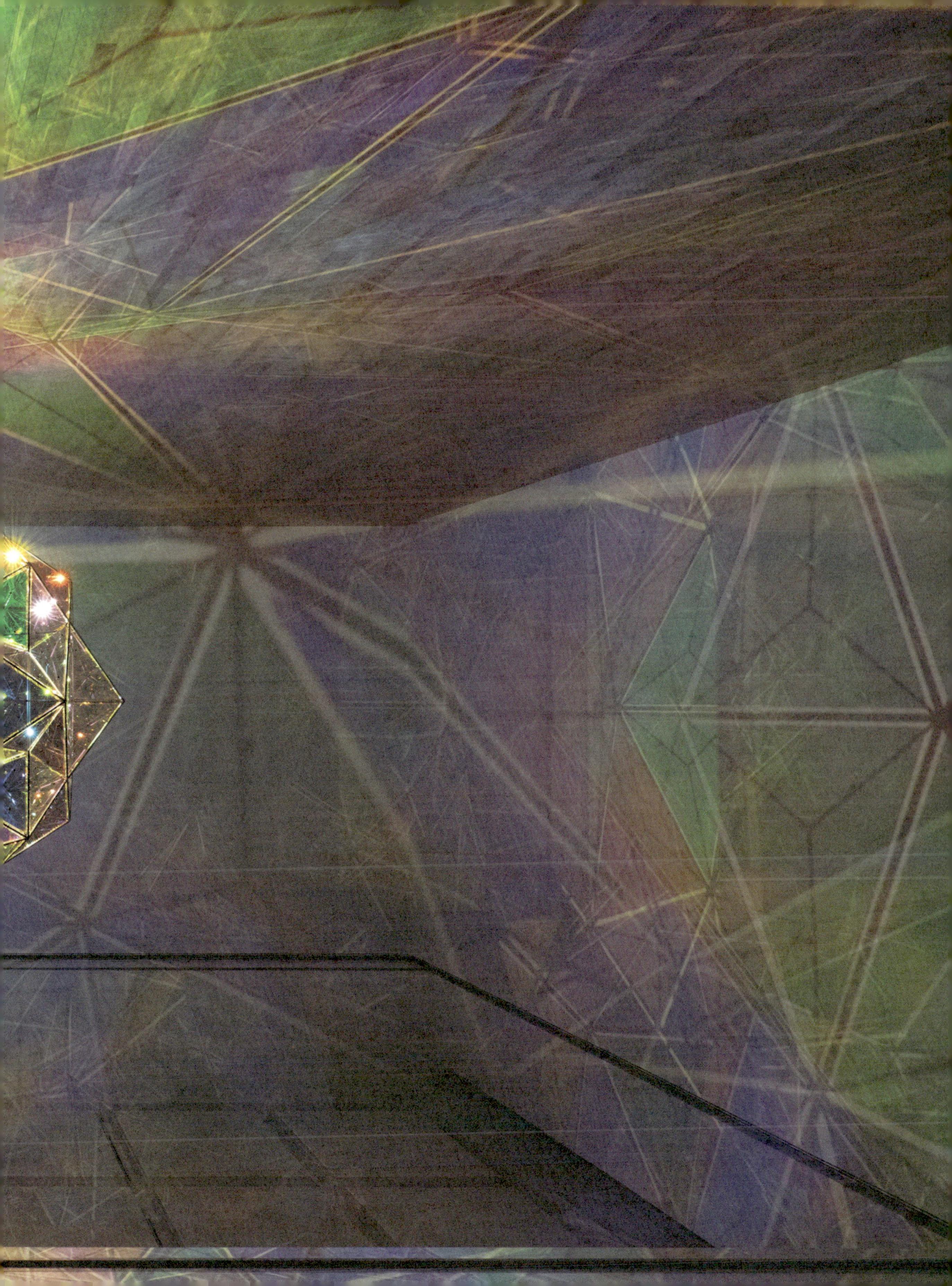

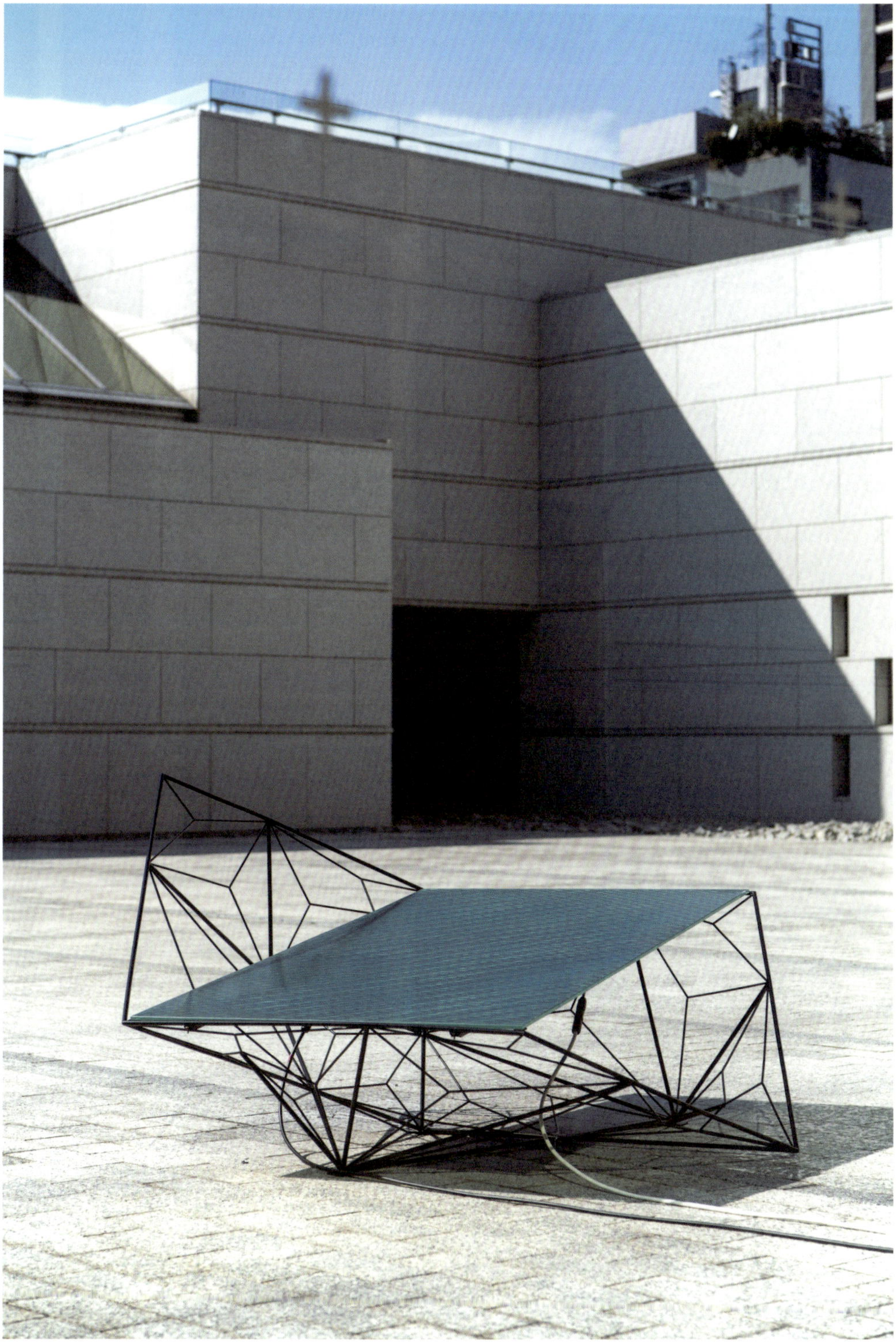

A solar panel in the museum's courtyard powers LEDs mounted on a slowly rotating armature suspended within an asymmetrical polyhedron. The highly reflective, colour-limiting panes of glass multiply the light countless times, producing a galaxy-like array of shifting stars in a variety of colours.

エリアソンは長年にわたりガラスでできた多面体の作品を制作してきた。本作品の光と動きはソーラーエネルギーが生み出している。こうした光の立体作品からはエリアソンの光と幾何学への関心、すなわち生きていくために不可欠な存在である太陽とこの世界を成り立たせている構造や法則への志向が見てとれる。

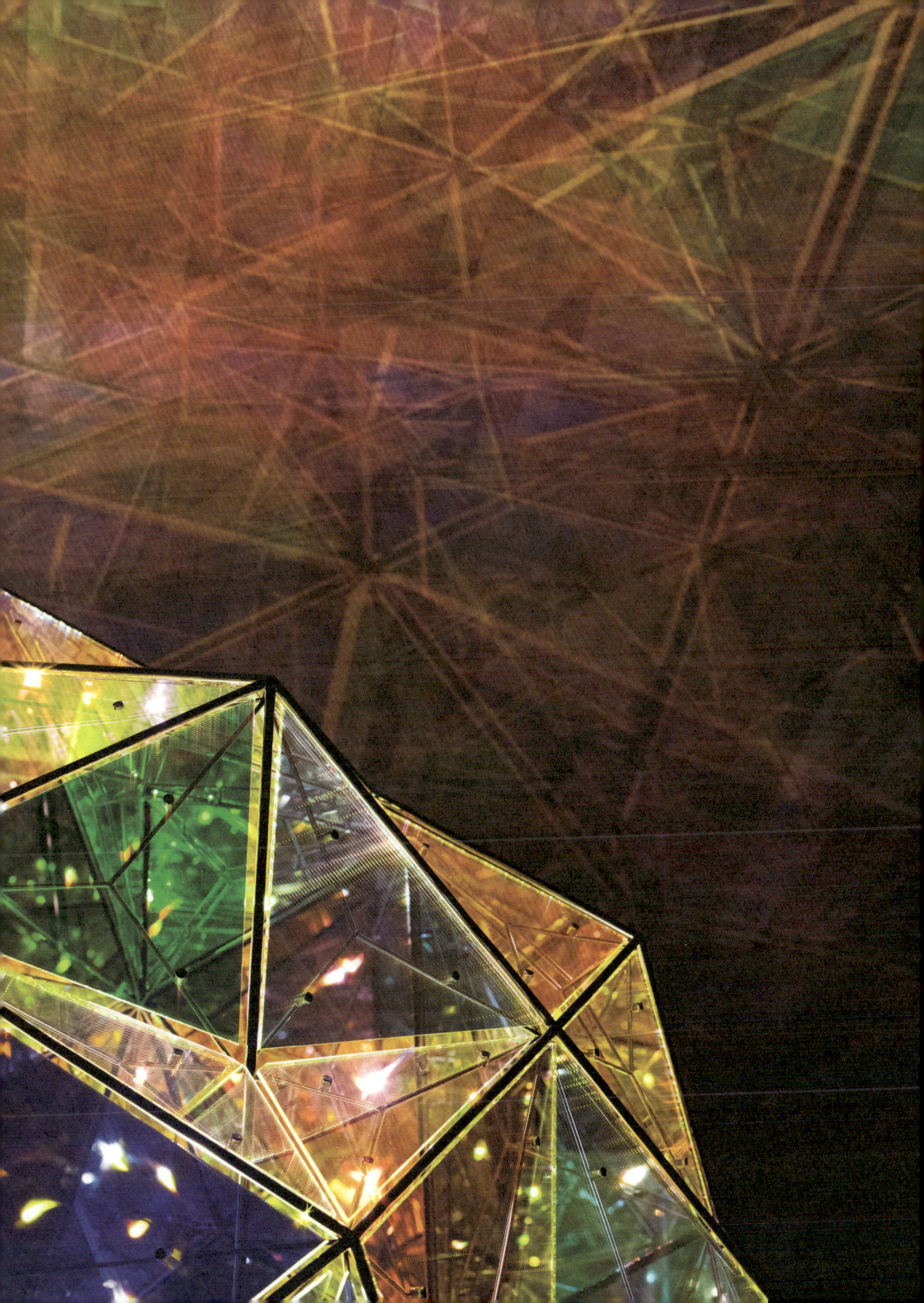

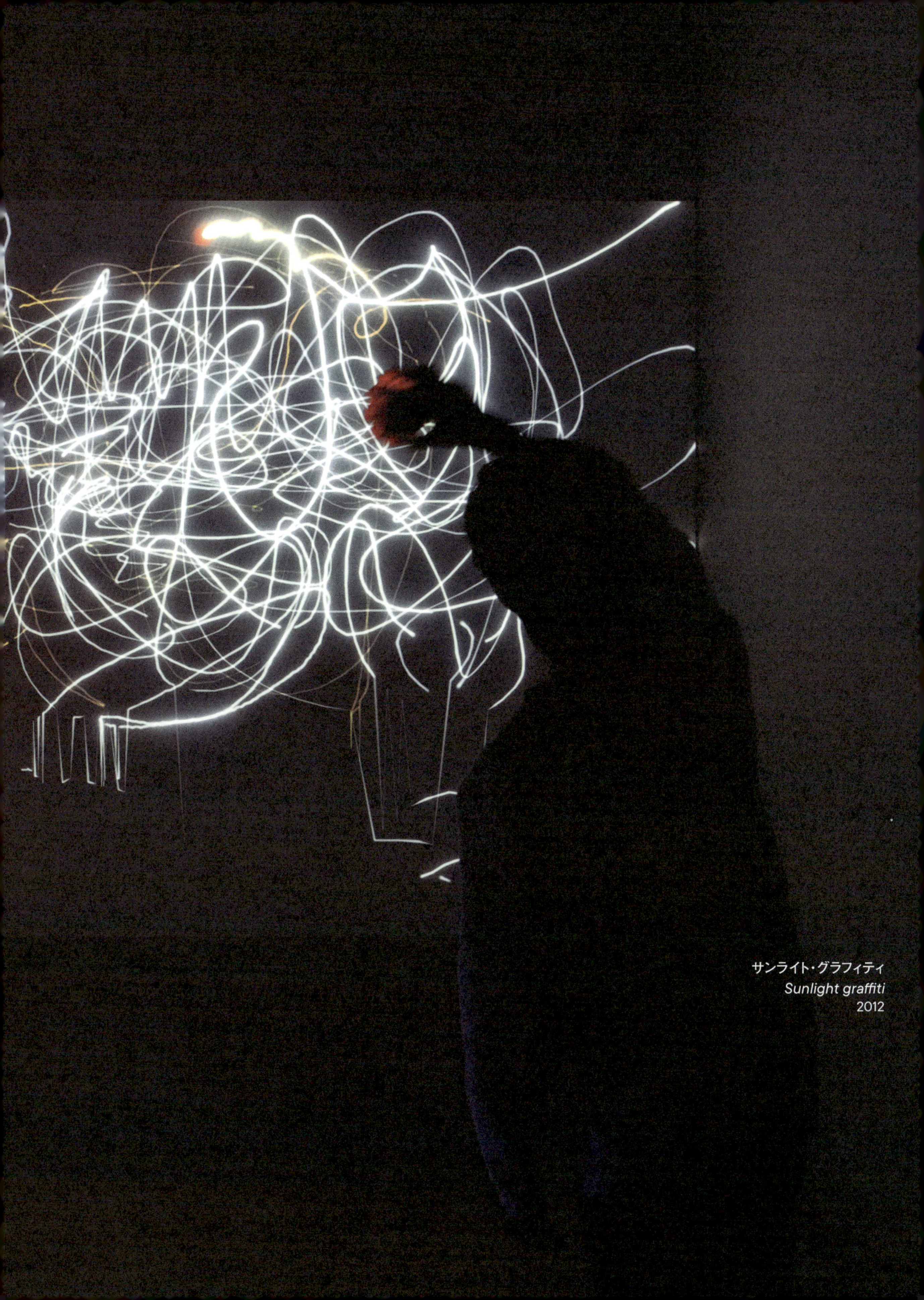

サンライト・グラフィティ
Sunlight graffiti
2012

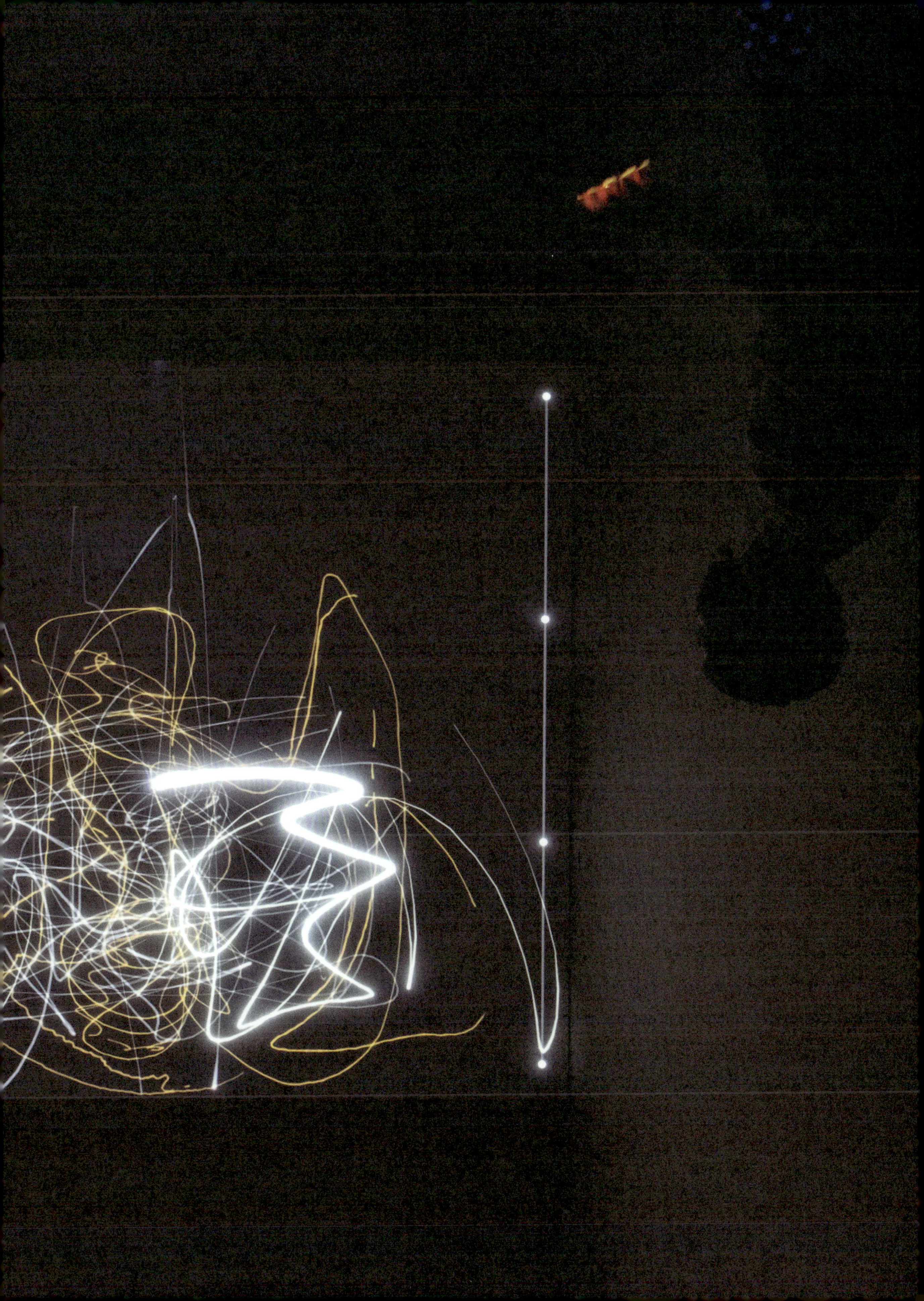

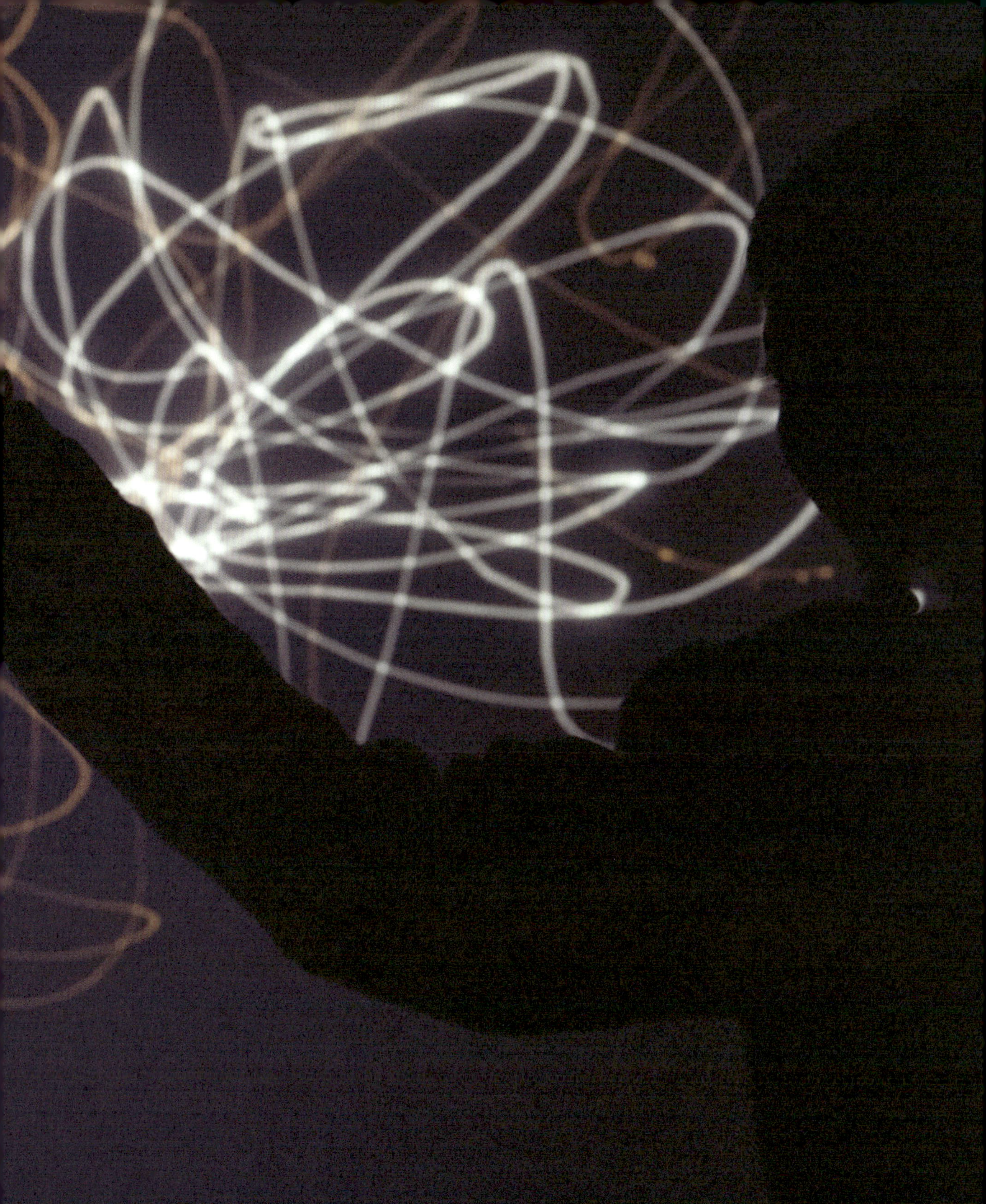

Sunlight graffiti was originally conceived as an opportunity for participants to create works of art through light and movement using Little Sun solar-powered handheld lamps. Here the installation functions as a scientific experiment that invites visitors to draw with light together.

2012年にエリアソンは携帯式のソーラーライト「リトルサン」をエンジニアのフレデリック・オッテセンと共同開発した。《サンライト・グラフィティ》ではリトルサンを手にした体験者が空間に自由に光のドローイングを描く。リトルサンを手にしたダンサーの身体表現とその光の軌跡が収められた映像作品《あなたの光の動き》もあわせて展示された。

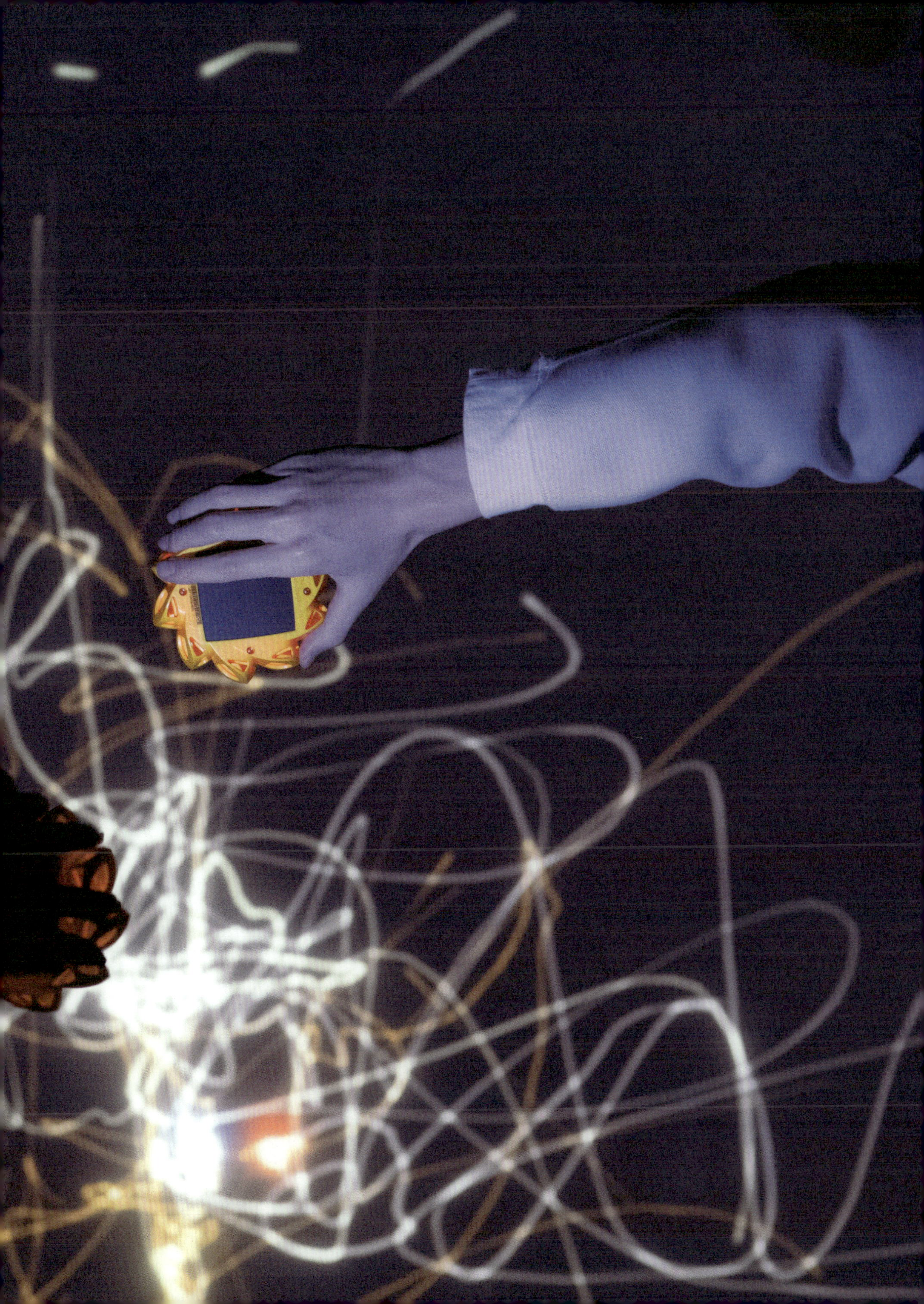

「リトルサン・サンライズ」カーネギーホール（ニューヨーク）でのコンサート・イベント「パリ協定への道」より
Little Sun sunrise at Carnegie Hall, New York City, Pathway to Paris
2017

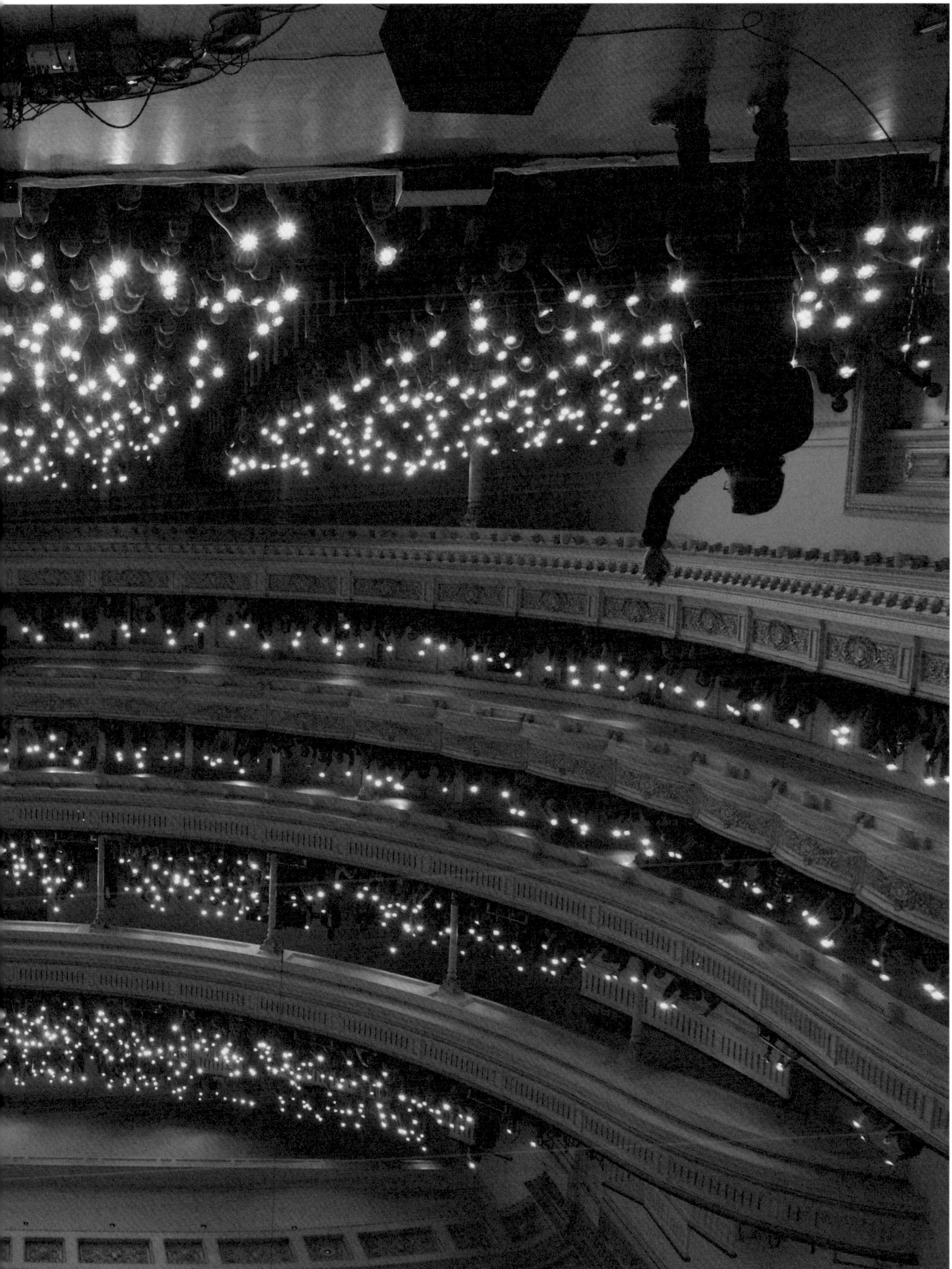

no. 7

クリティカルゾーンの記憶（ドイツ―ポーランド―ロシア―中国―日本）no. 1–12［部分］
Details from *Memories from the critical zone (Germany–Poland–Russia–China–Japan, nos. 1–12)*
2020

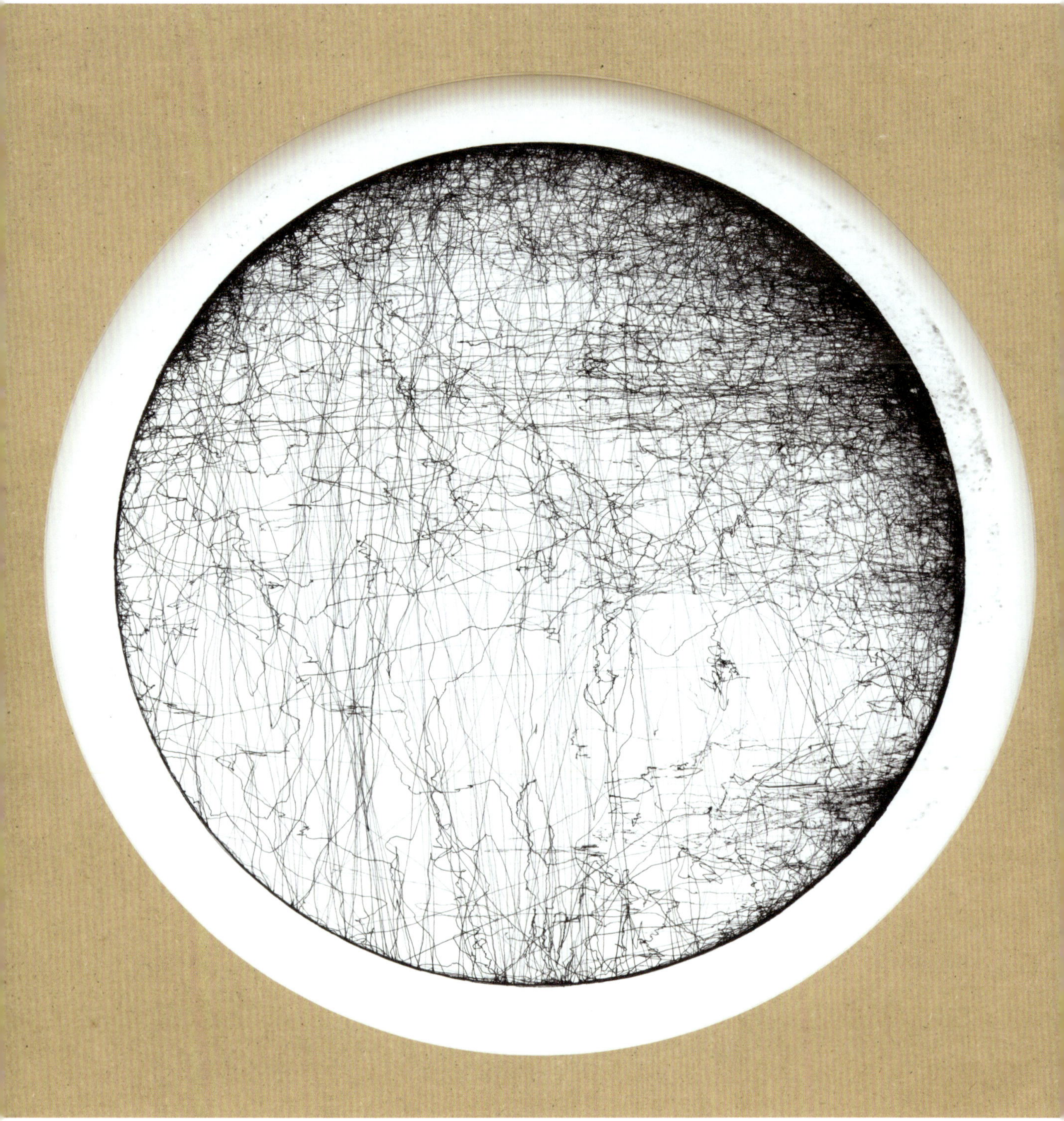

no. 10

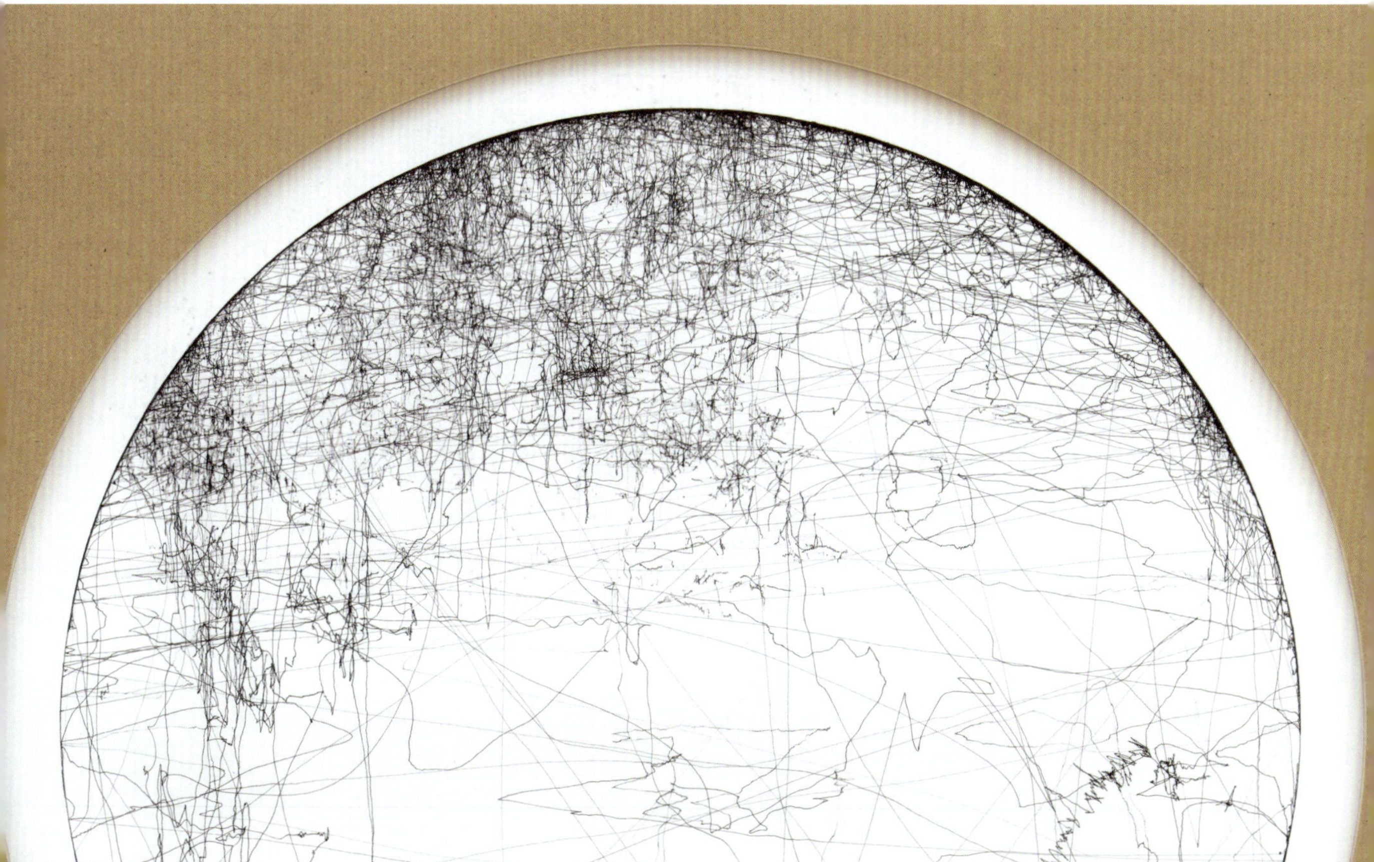

no. 1

展覧会「ときに川は橋となる」で展示されている作品の多くは、二酸化炭素を多く排出する航空機ではなく、ベルリンから東京まで鉄道と船で運ばれた。この12点の円形のドローイングは輸送中の動きや揺れを記録する装置によって描かれている。人の手では表現しえない無数の線描には、移動の過程で作品に起こった出来事がくまなく描き出されている。

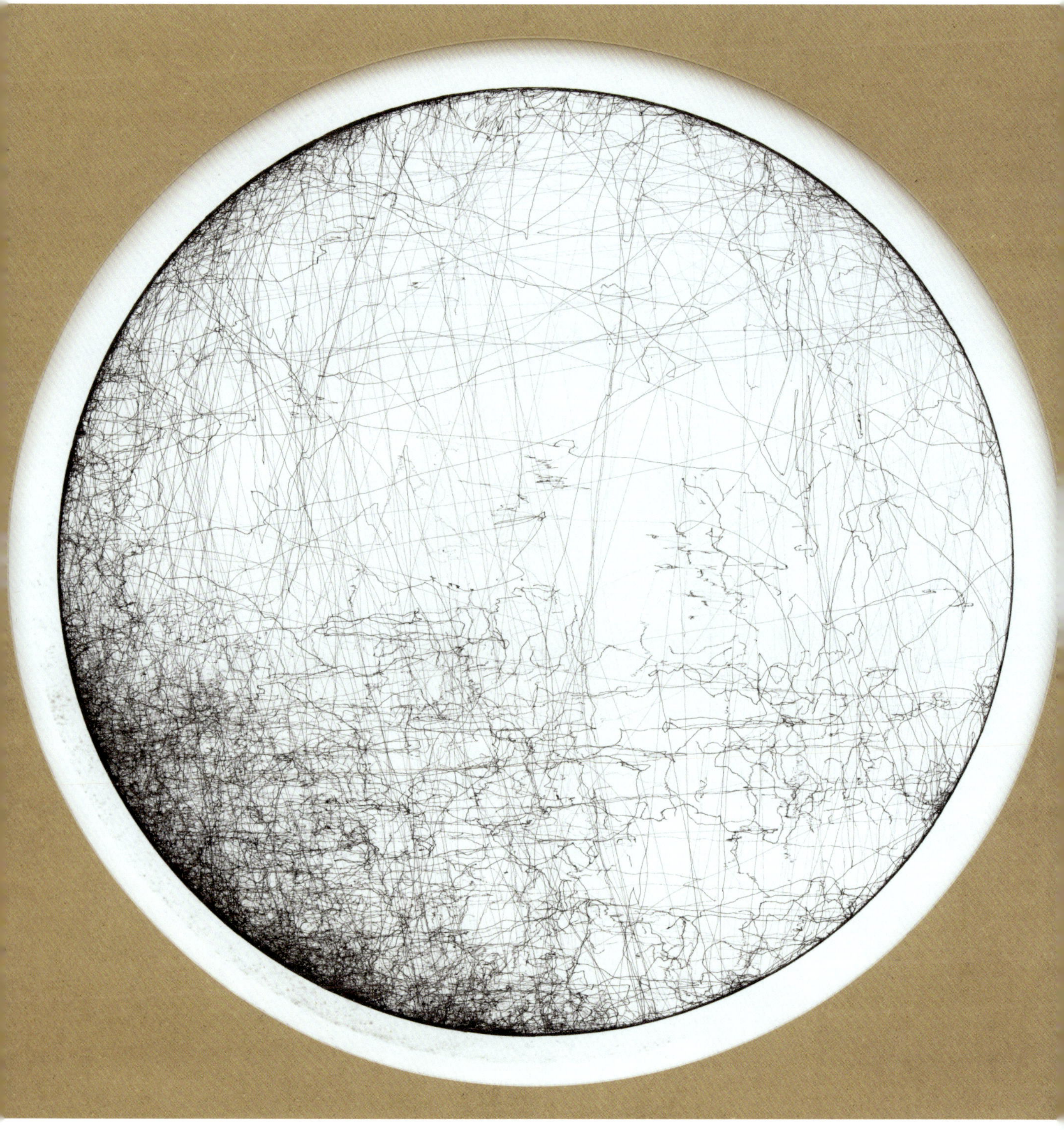

no. 2

Most of the artworks in *Sometimes the river is the bridge* were shipped by surface transport from Berlin to Tokyo to reduce the exhibition's carbon footprint. Drawings were produced by a chance process that unfolded while the artworks were travelling by truck, train, and boat along their route. In each set-up, a ballpoint pen was held by a mechanical arm so that it moved over the surface of the paper in response to the movements of the crate, producing a visual record of the terrain over which the artworks passed. 'Critical zone' is a term from geology that refers to the thin layer of the earth that supports living systems.

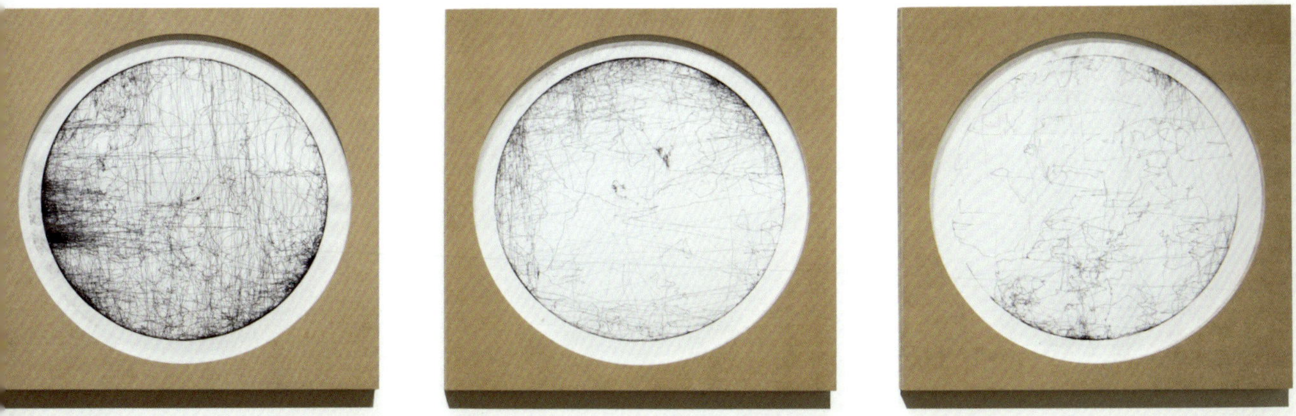

nos. 7–12

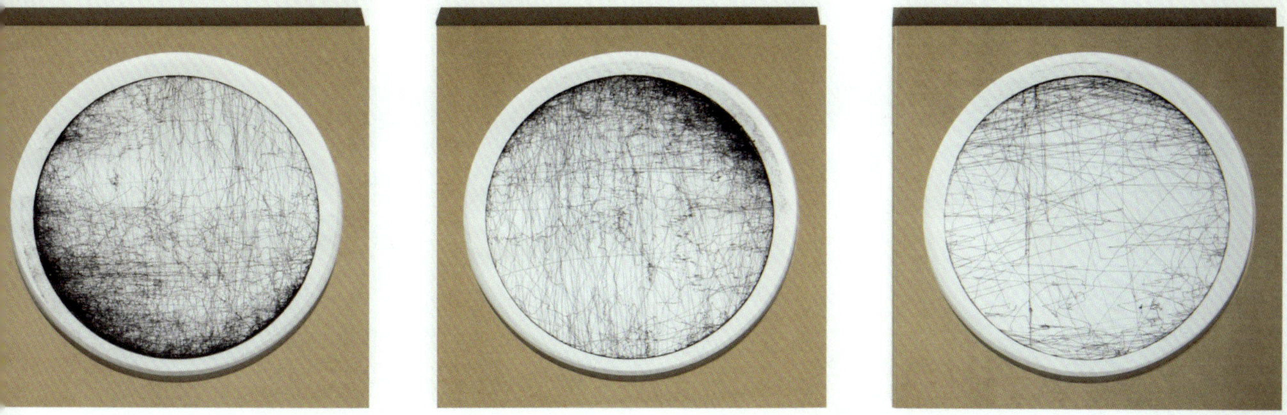

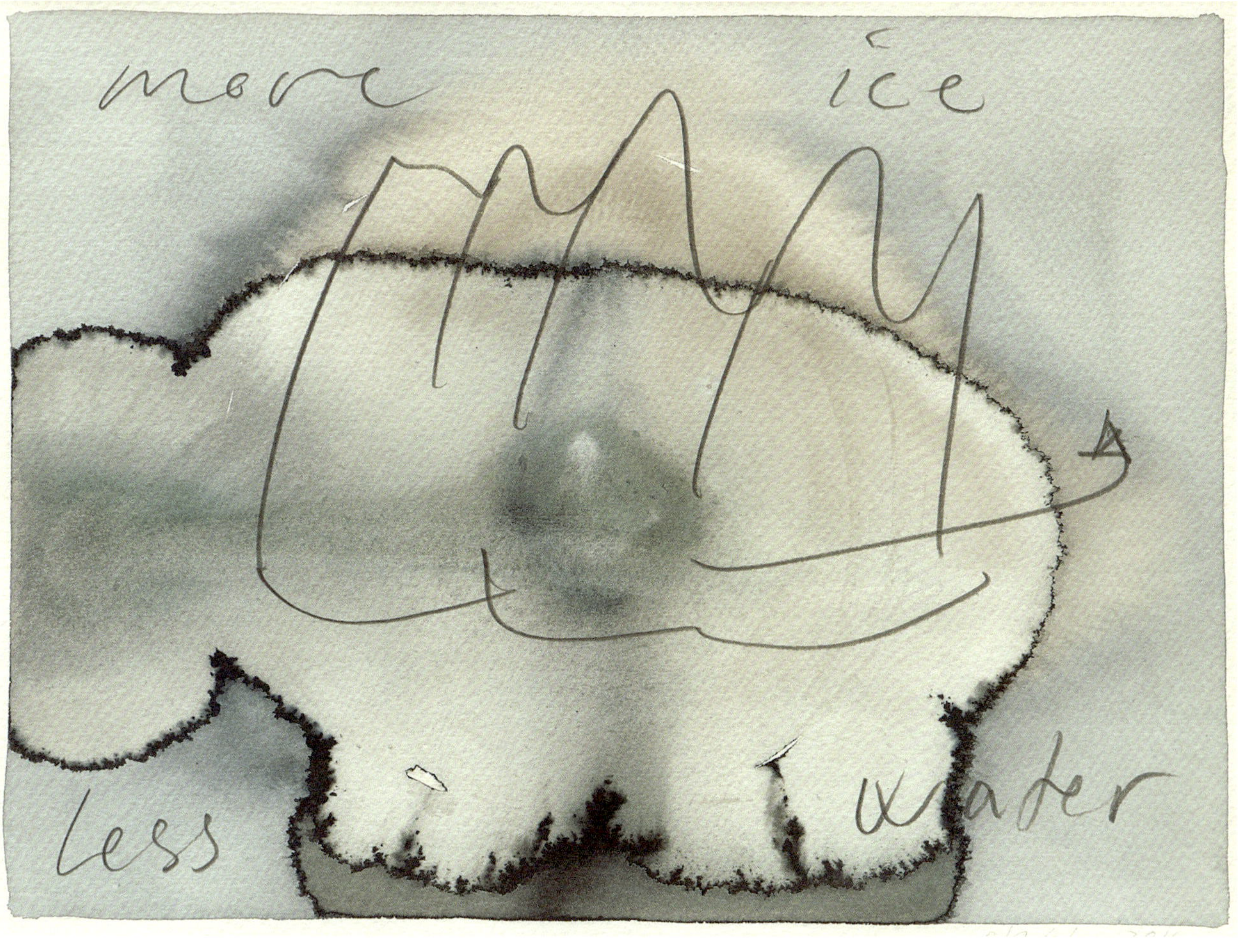

力と思いやりの領分（マインドマップ）no. 8
Spheres of power and care (mind map) no. 8
2016

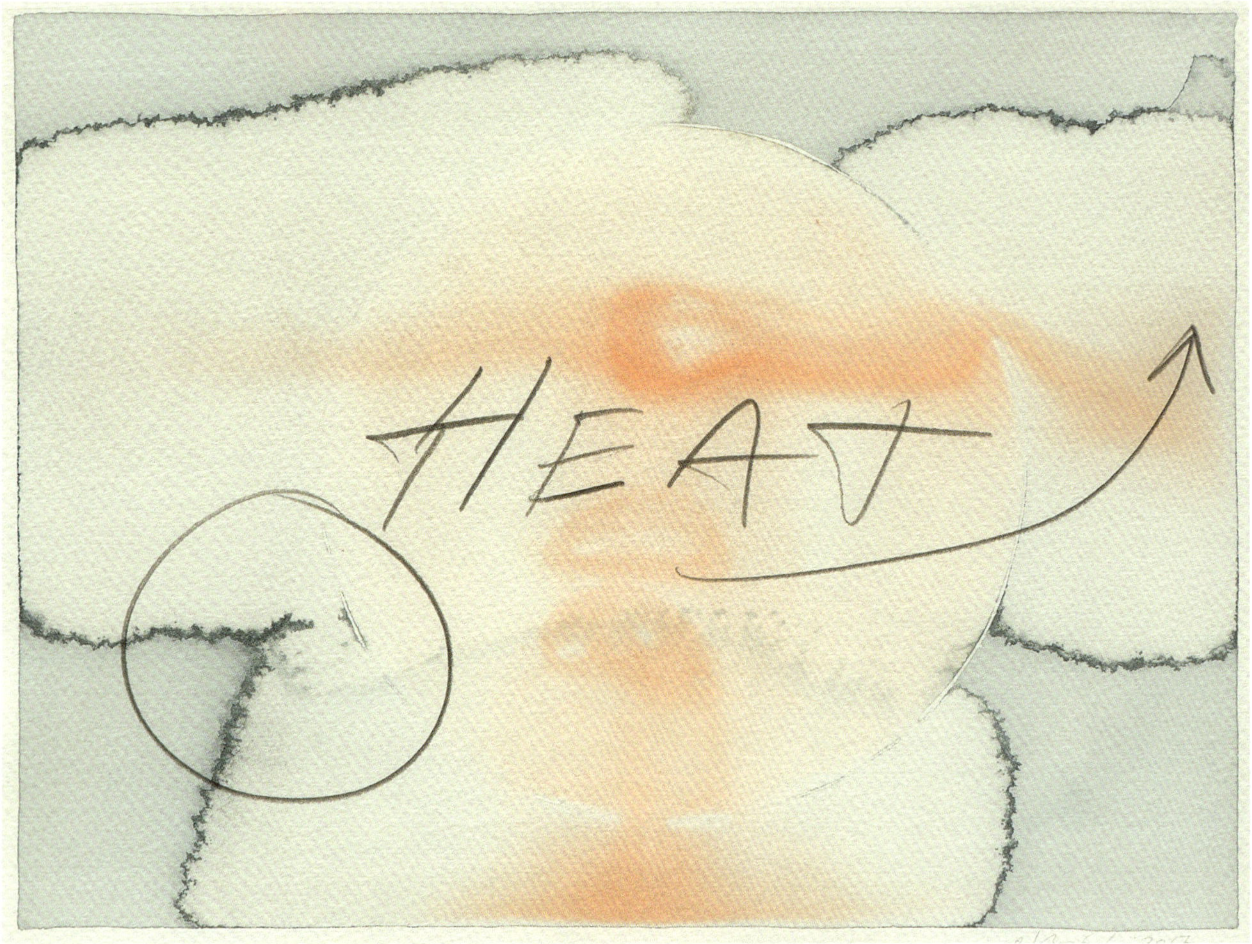

力と思いやりの領分（マインドマップ）no. 5
Spheres of power and care (mind map) no.5
2016

Eliasson often uses sketches to develop his ideas. The drawings here were made on washes of pigment and ink that were co-produced by melting blocks of ice.

エリアソンは自らのアイデアを深め、スタジオのチームと共有するためにドローイングを描く。これらの氷河の氷の水彩画には、私たちを取り巻く地球や環境に対するエリアソンの思考の跡を見ることができる。

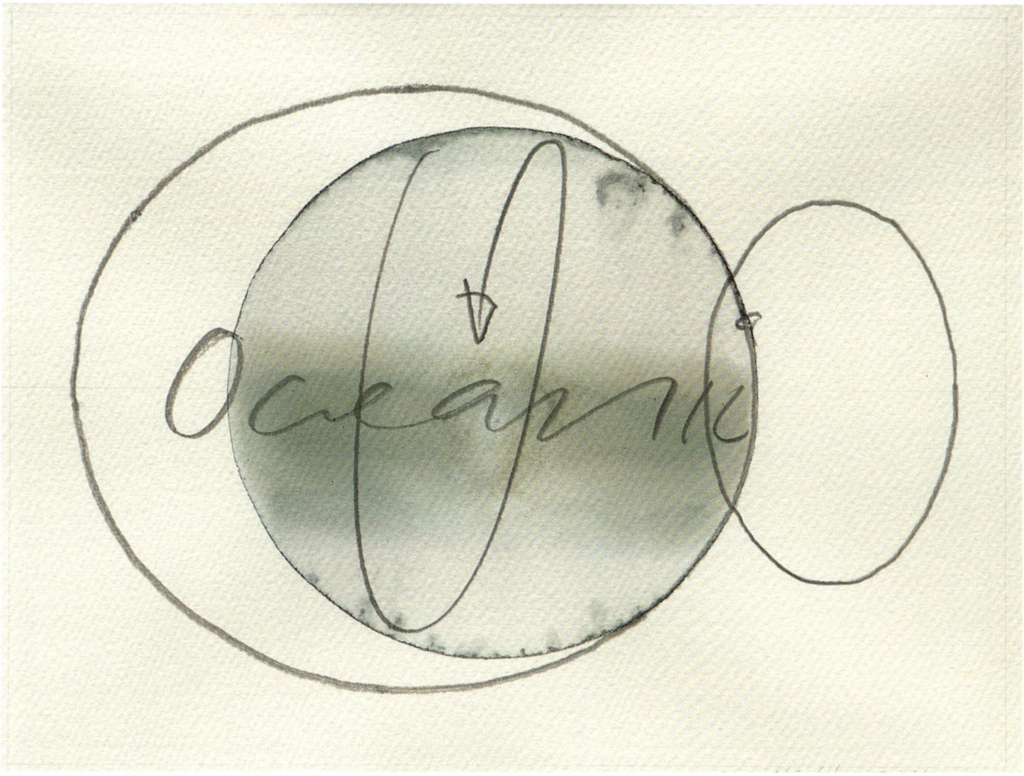

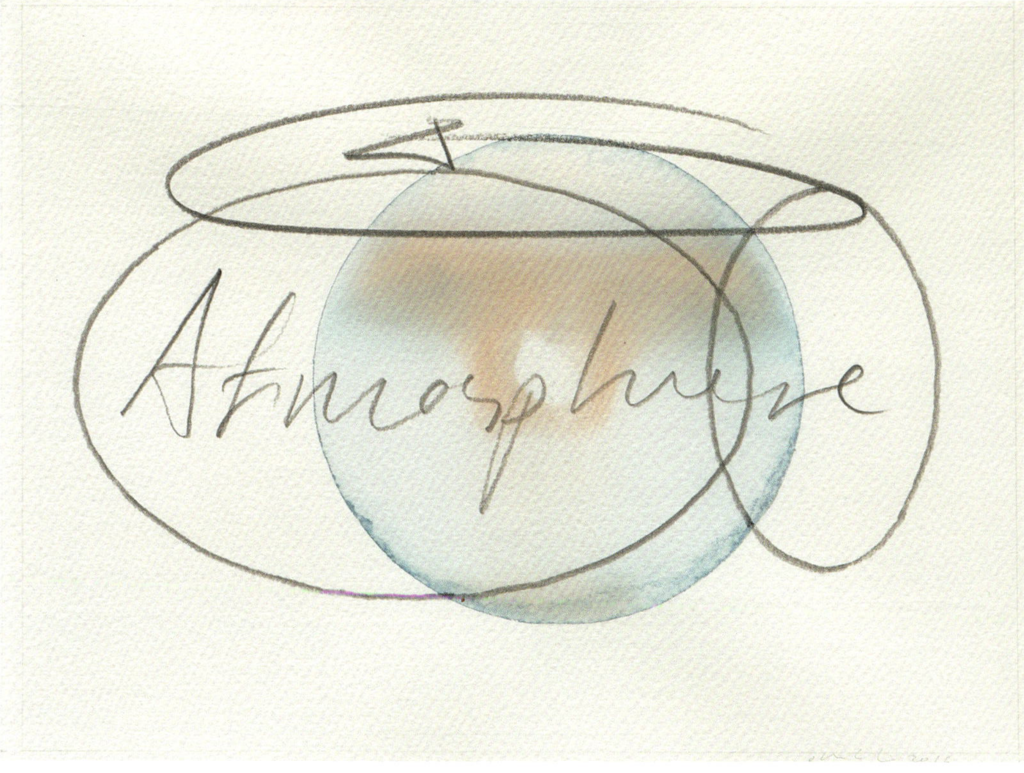

力と思いやりの領分（マインドマップ）no. 10
Spheres of power and care (mind map) no. 10
2016

力と思いやりの領分（マインドマップ）no. 11
Spheres of power and care (mind map) no. 11
2016

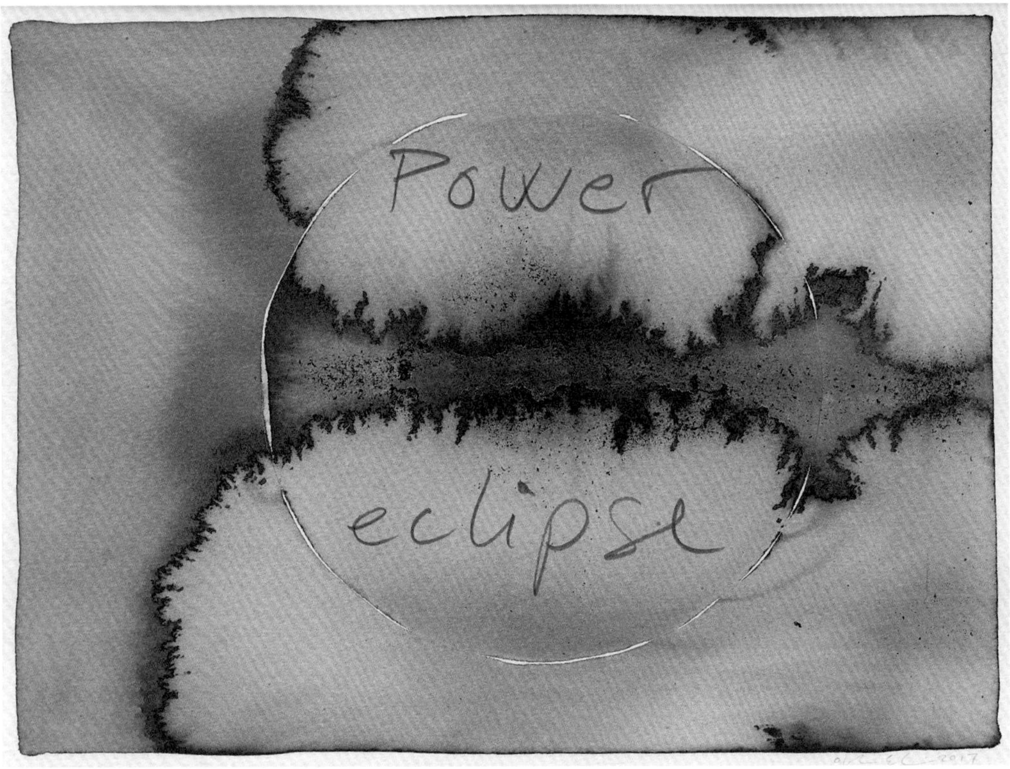

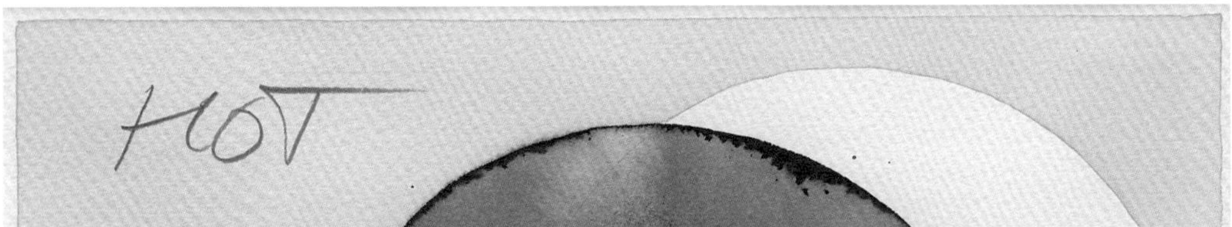

力と思いやりの領分（マインドマップ）no. 2
Spheres of power and care (mind map) no. 2
2016

力と思いやりの領分（マインドマップ）no. 7
Spheres of power and care (mind map) no. 7
2016

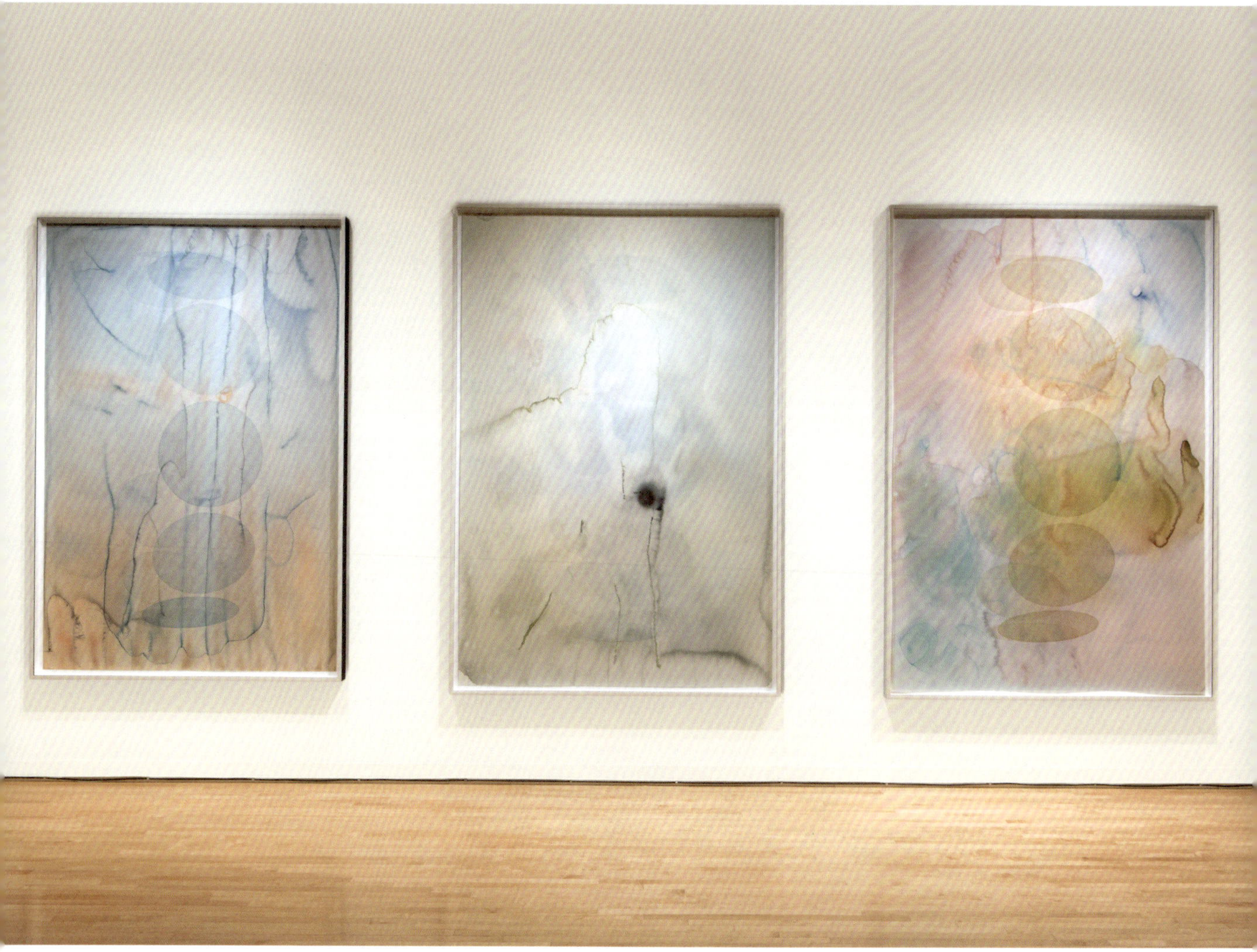

These watercolours were produced using chunks of ancient glacial ice that were fished from the sea off the coast of Greenland. Placed on the surface of the paper, the ice gradually melted and the resulting water displaced the pigment, creating organic swells and fades. Employing chance and natural processes, these watercolours host the spontaneous behaviour of natural phenomena as active co-producers of the artwork.

氷河はアイスランドで多くの時間を過ごしたエリアソンの表現に欠かせないもののひとつである。この3点の水彩画はグリーンランドの氷河の氷で制作された。紙の上で溶けていく氷の水が顔料と混ざり合うことで、豊かな濃淡やにじみが画面全体に広がる。こうした制作の過程には、人間の意志とは無関係に起こる自然現象を共同制作の相手とみなすエリアソンの態度が反映されている。

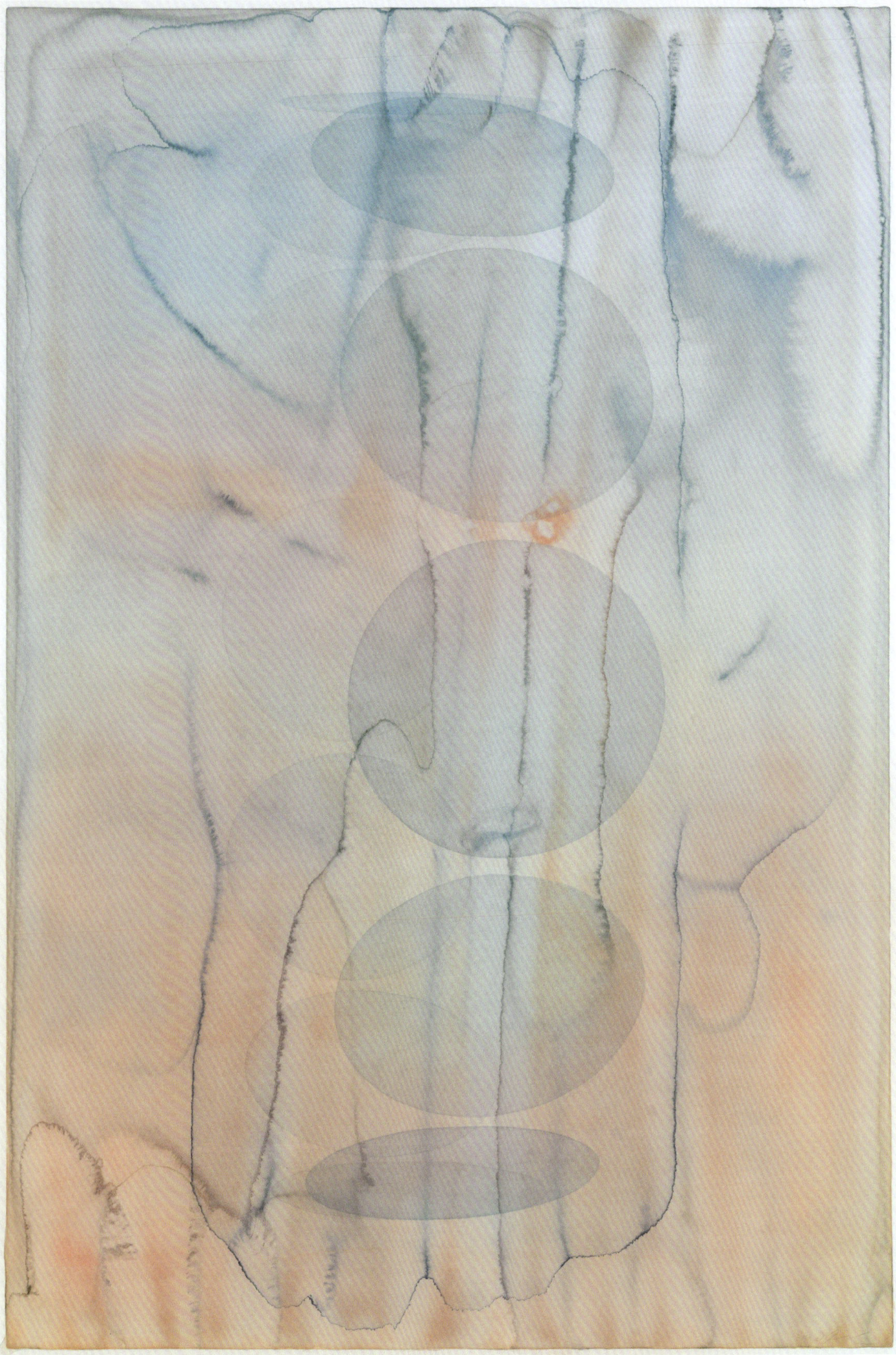

あなたの移ろう氷河の形態学（過去）
Your passing glacial morphology (past)
2019

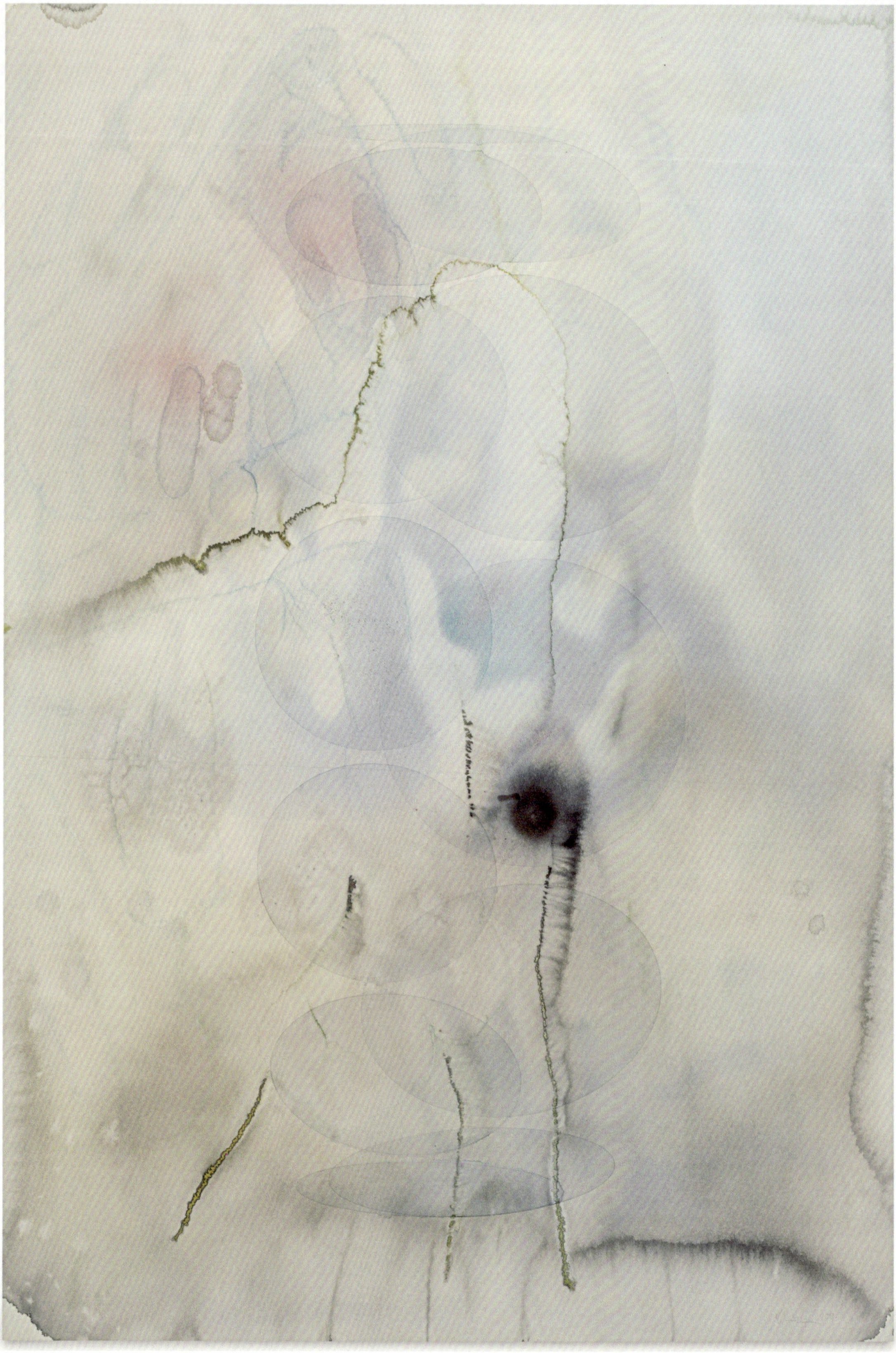

メタンの問題
Methane matter
2019

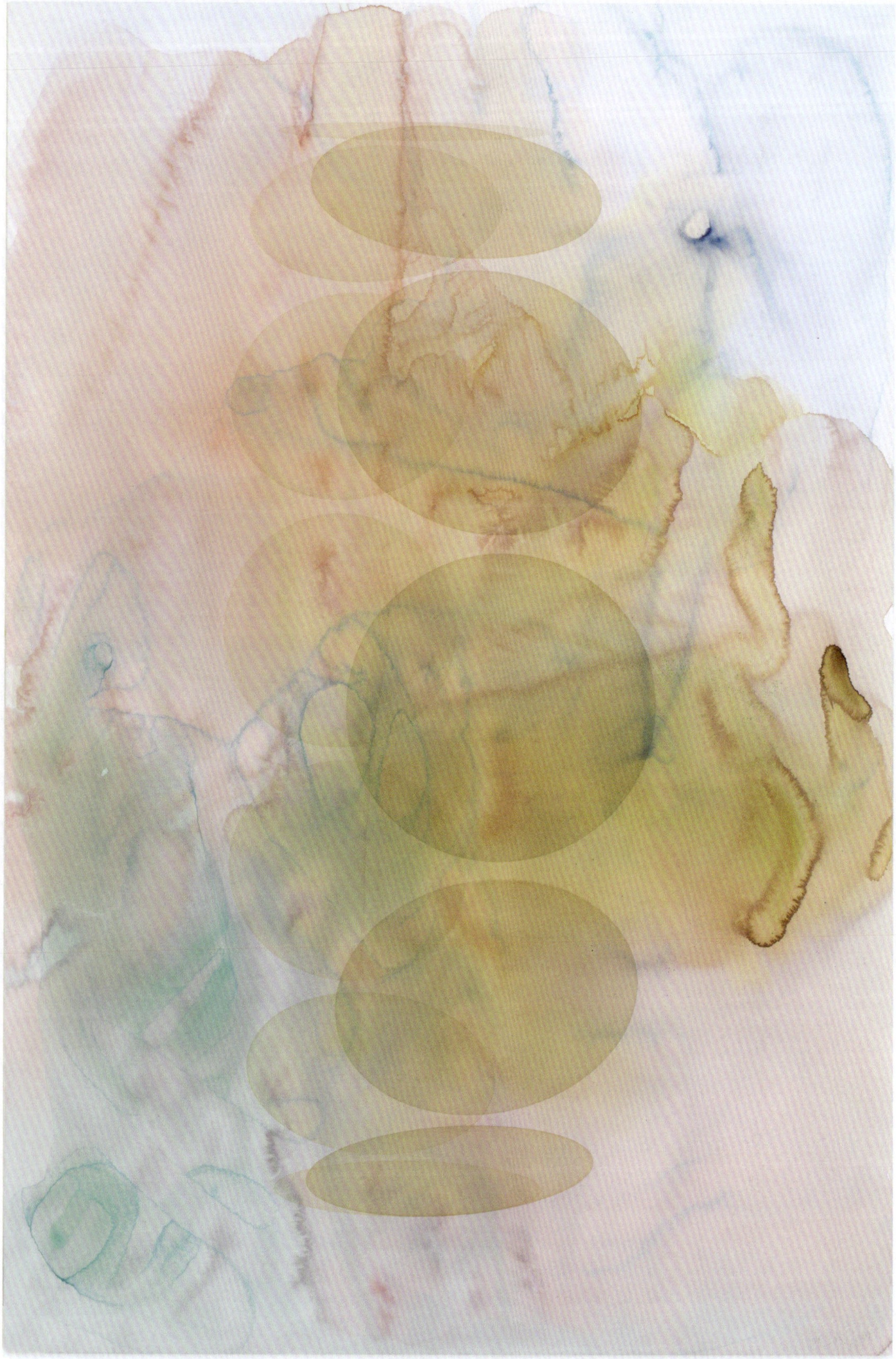

あなたの移ろう氷河の形態学（未来）
Your passing glacial morphology (future)
2019

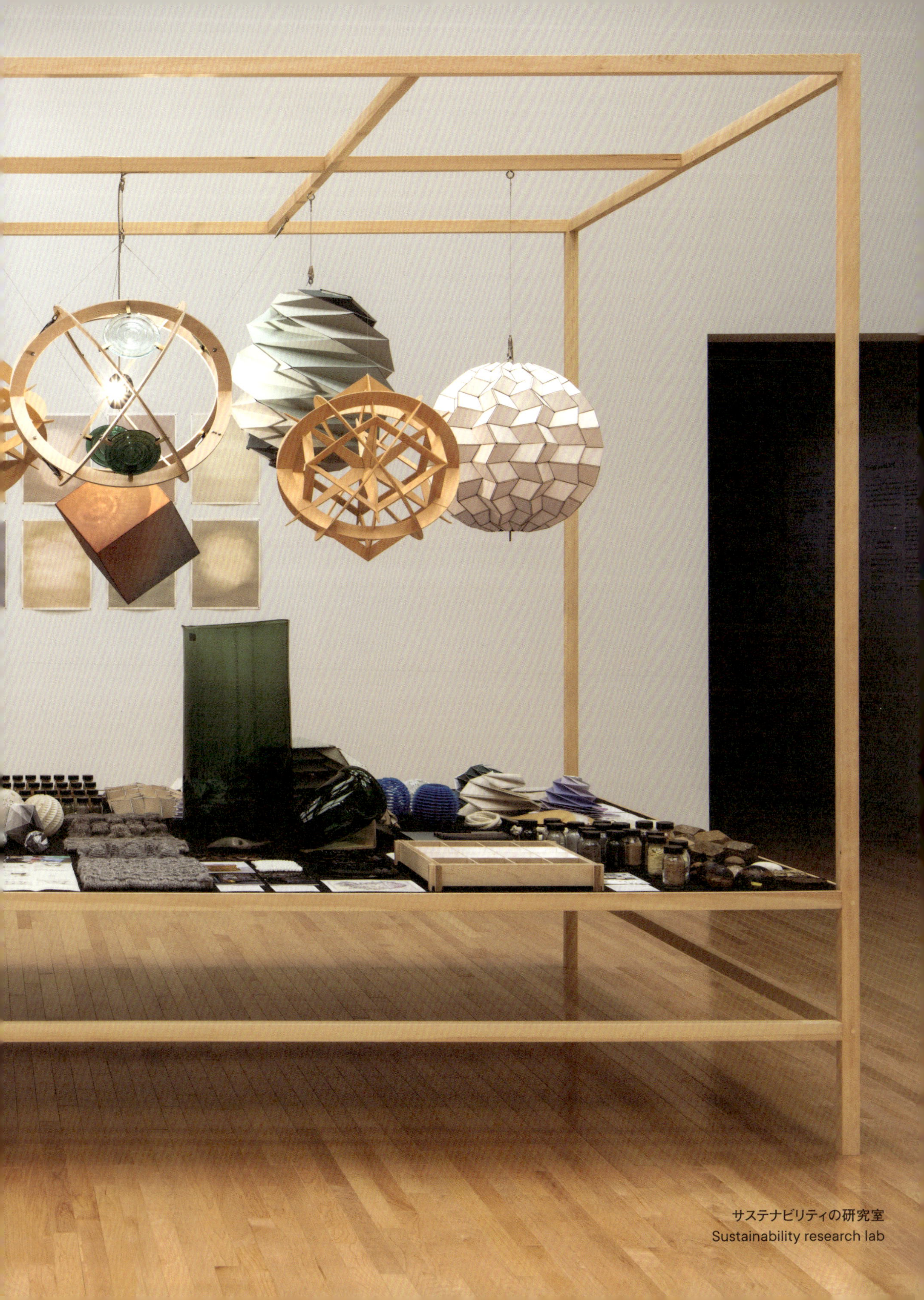

サステナビリティの研究室
Sustainability research lab

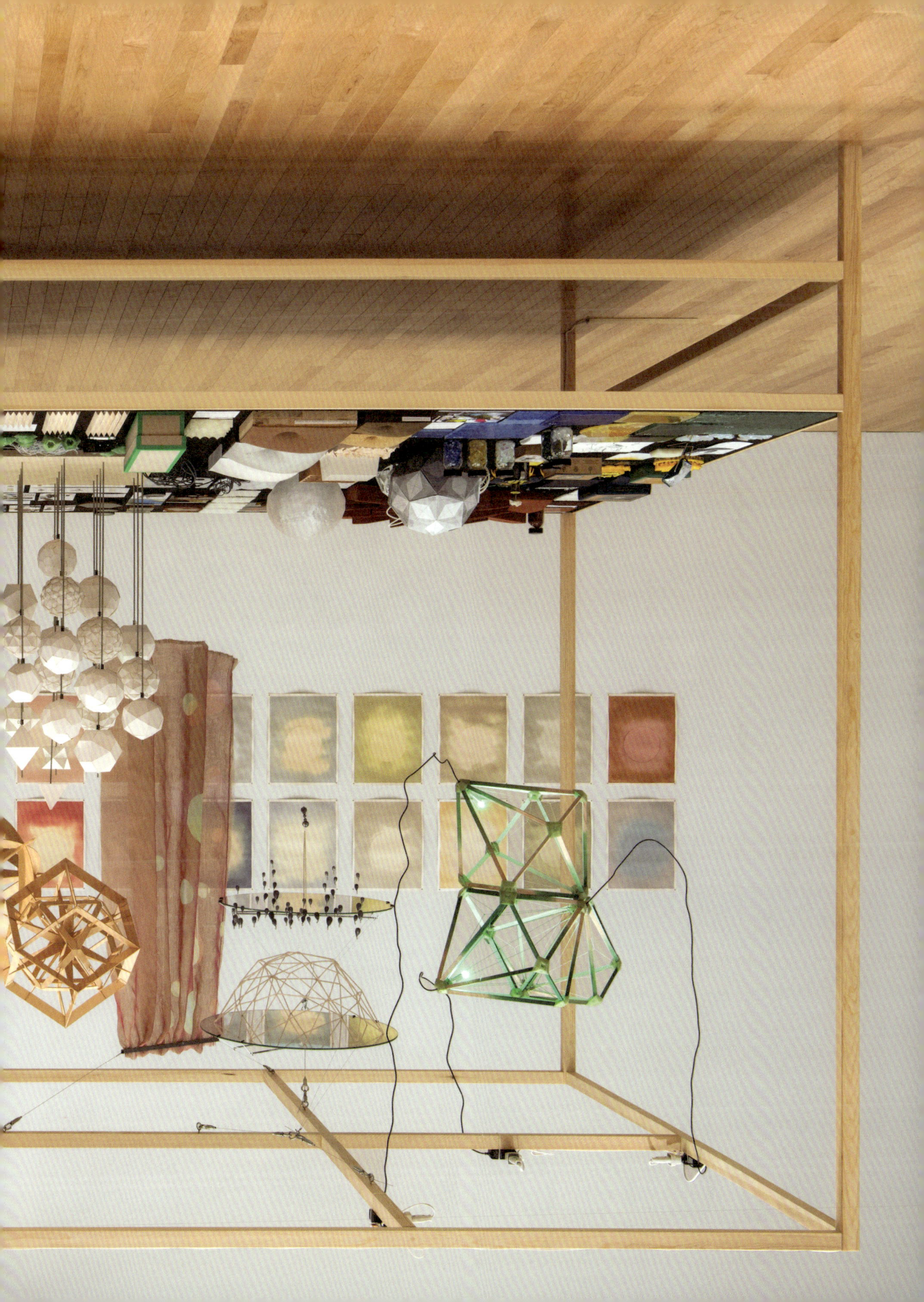

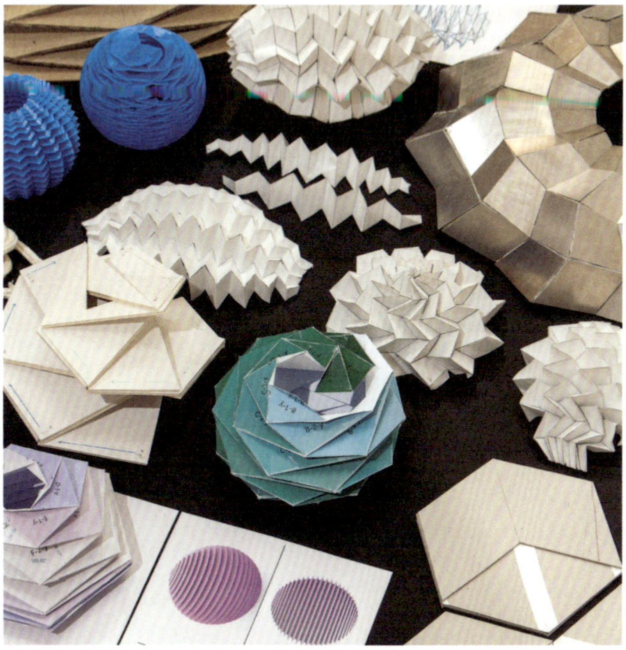

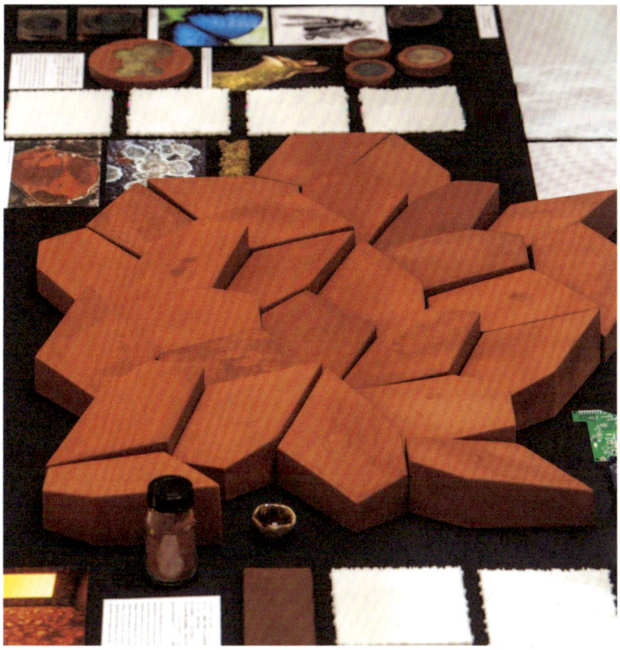

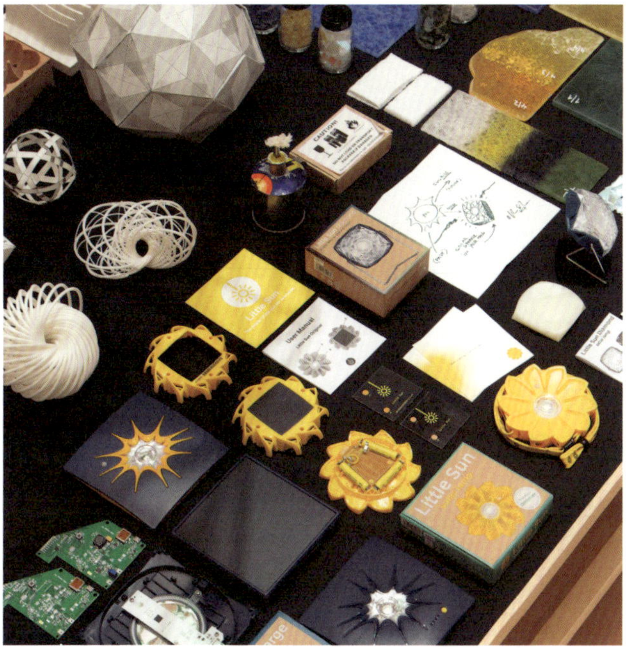

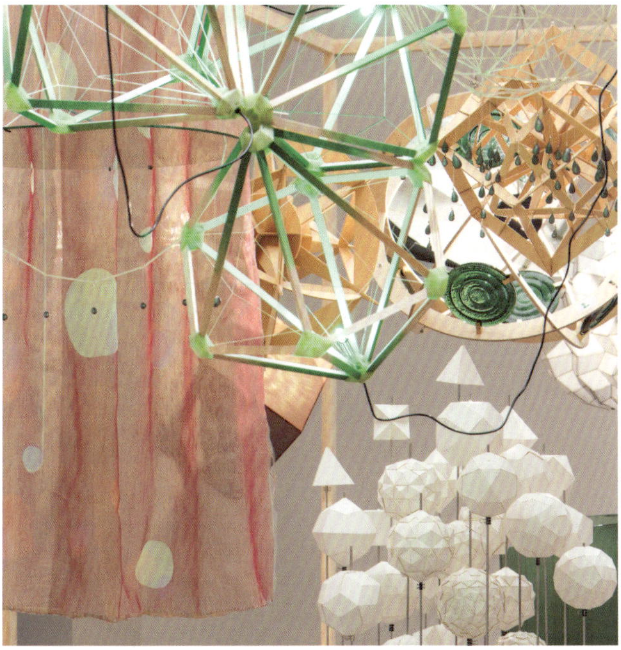

これらの球体の形は効率的な輸送のために折りたたんだり広げることができる。この研究はビルータ・クレスリング、三浦公亮、舘知宏の作品から着想を得て、それをスタジオのチームが球体に応用した。

These spherical forms can be collapsed or unfolded for more efficient transport. This research was inspired by the work of Biruta Kresling, Koryo Miura, and Tomohiro Tachi, which the studio team adapted and further developed to apply to spheres.

エリアソンがエンジニアのフレデリック・オッテセンと共同で開発した携帯式のソーラーライト「リトルサン」(62–67頁を参照)は、電力にアクセスできない地域で灯油ランプの代替品として使われている。クリーンで安価なエネルギーを供給することによって気候変動や健康被害に対する影響を抑えることができる。

Created by Eliasson in collaboration with engineer Frederik Ottesen, Little Sun solar-powered lamps (see pages 62–67) are used to replace kerosene lanterns in areas where people do not have access to electricity. By providing clean and affordable energy, these lamps reduce the negative effects of kerosene use on the climate and individual health.

このタイルは「赤泥」というボーキサイト鉱石をアルミに精製する際に出る有害物質からつくられている。高温で焼成することによって赤泥に含まれる有害なアルカリ成分を除去できる。タイルの形は地衣類の成長構造から着想を得た。スタジオとタイルを共同制作したStudio ThusThat (www.thusthat.com)がこのプロセスを開発した。

The clay in these tiles is made from 'red mud', a toxic material that is produced when refining bauxite ore into aluminium – the firing process used to make the ceramics neutralises the mud's toxic alkalinity. The shapes of these tiles allow them to form a textured pattern that is inspired by the growth structures of lichen. This process was developed by Studio ThusThat (www.thusthat.com), who collaborated with the studio on the making of these tiles.

スタジオはテキスタイル会社のクヴァドラと共同でサステナブルなカーテン生地の製造方法を探究している。この色合いと円形のパターンは3色の薄い布が重なり合うことで生まれる。これは初期のもので、まだサステナブルな素材ではない試作品である。

The studio is exploring ways to produce a sustainable fabric for curtains together with the textile company Kvadrat. A range of colours can be produced by overlapping the thin layers of three colours with circular cut-outs in them. This early prototype is not yet made of sustainable materials.

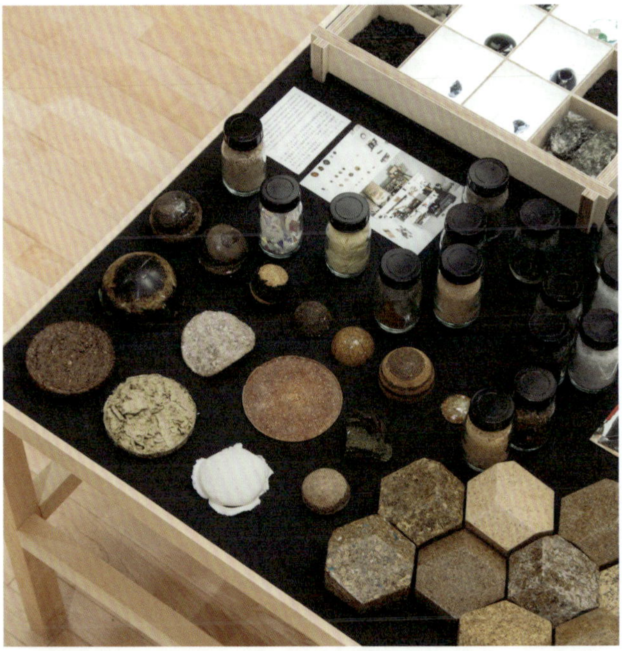

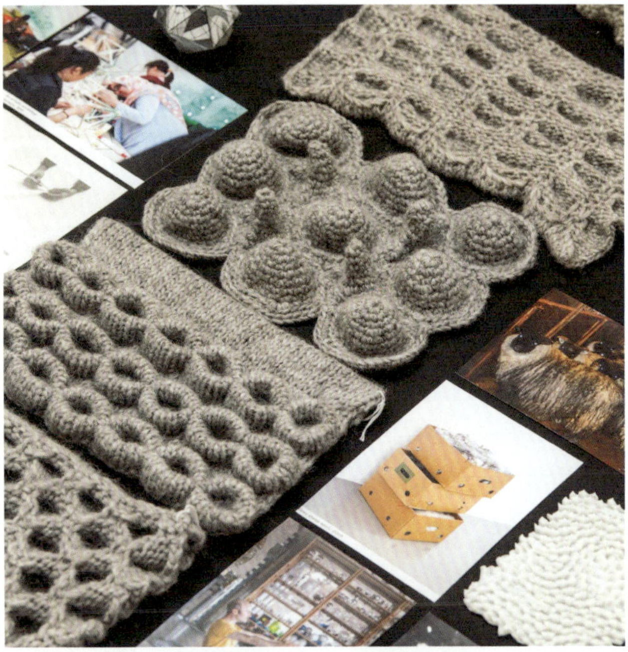

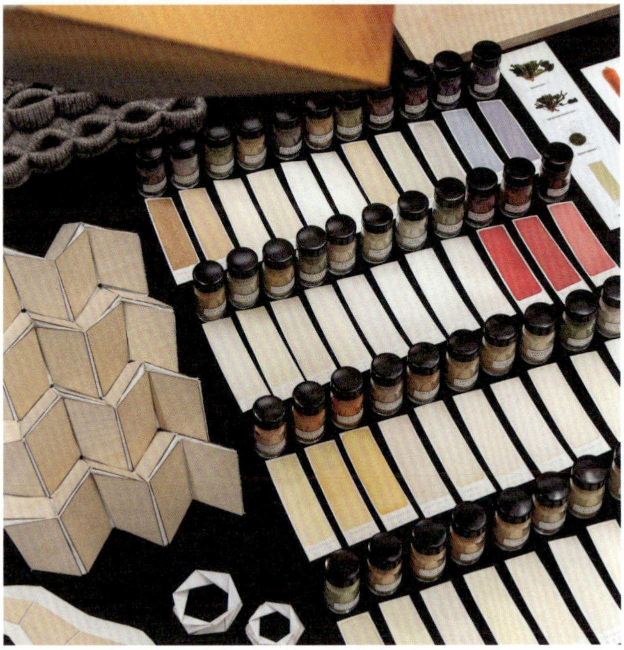

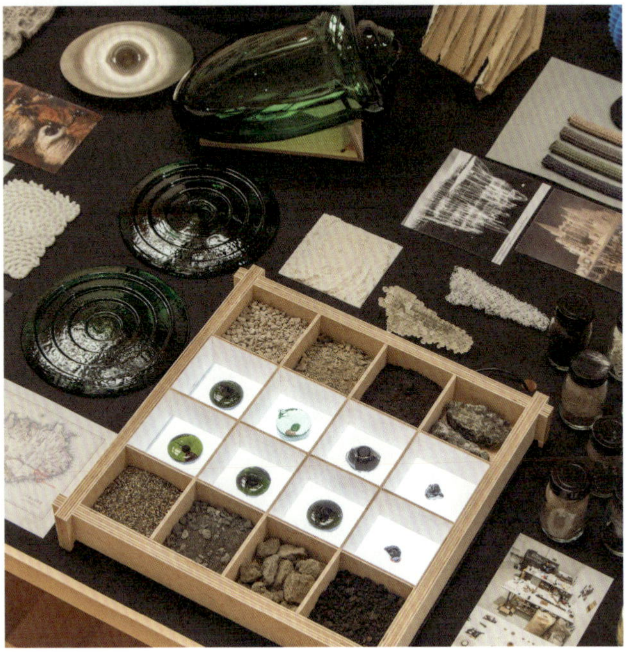

おがくず、3Dプリントの支持構造、真ちゅうの削りくず、ゴム手袋といった作品を制作するときに出る廃棄物は新しい素材につくり替えることができる。作品の制作過程で生まれる副産物に対する態度を再考することで、スタジオのチームはそれらの美しさや潜在的価値を発見するようになった。

Waste resulting from the production of artworks – sawdust, support-structures for 3D printing, brass shavings, latex gloves, etc. – can be made into new materials. By re-thinking its attitude towards these by-products of art-making, the studio team has begun to discover their beauty and potential.

水彩画の顔料はスタジオのキッチンで出た玉ねぎやにんじんの皮といった野菜くずを乾燥、粉砕し、アラビアゴムと混ぜてつくられた。色のバリエーションはスタジオのチームがとった昼食によって異なる。

These watercolour pigments are made from scraps from the studio kitchen – such as onion skins and carrot peels – that have been dried, pulverised, and mixed with gum arabic. The selection of colours depends on what the studio team has been eating for lunch.

この羊毛は《三次元の祈りをささげる者のためのマット》(2014)という作品の習作である。このグレーの毛色はアイスランド羊本来の色であり染めたものではない。伝統的にグレーの原毛は白い羊毛よりも好まれなかった。

These wool samples were created for the artwork *Mat for three-dimensional prayers*, 2014, which is also present in this room. The grey colour of the wool is not dyed, but comes from a herd of naturally grey Icelandic sheep. Traditionally sheep of this colour were less desirable than white sheep.

ハンドメイドのガラスの独特の色合いは、製造の工程で細かく砕いたアイスランドの石をガラスに加えることによって生まれる。鉱物組成が異なるとできあがるガラスの色に違いが出るため、アイスランドの石に関する研究を地質学者と共同でおこなっている。

The unique colouring of these hand-made glass forms comes from ground-up Icelandic stones added to the glass during the fabrication process. The studio is working with a geologist to find stones in Iceland whose mineral composition can yield a range of colours of glass.

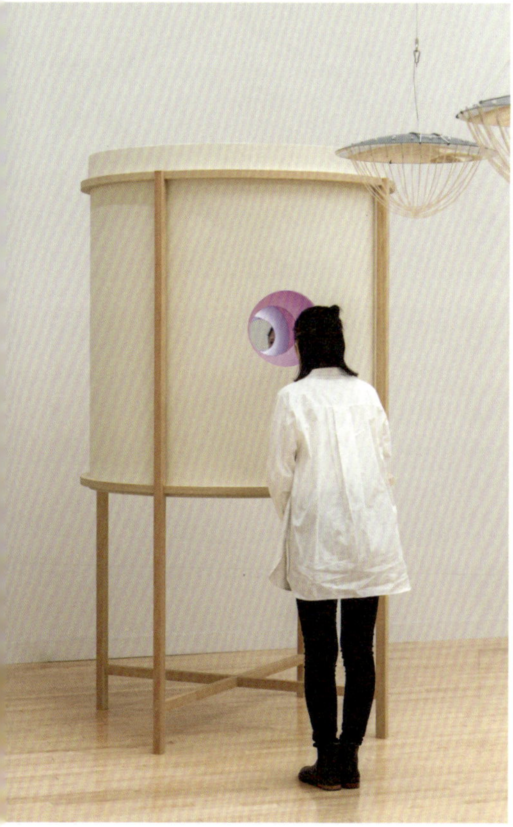

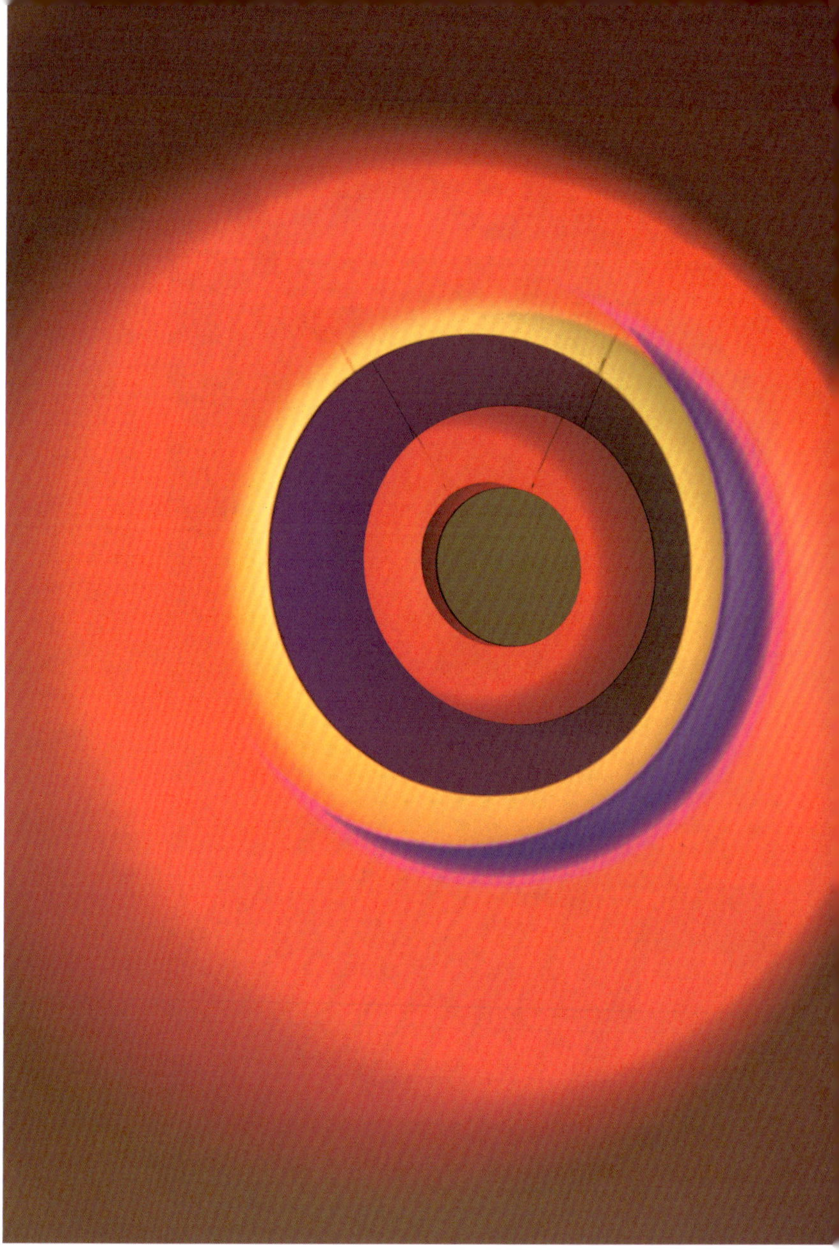

The studio team is researching sustainable new materials from which Eliasson's artworks can be made. This room brings together materials and objects – watercolour pigments made from the kitchen's vegetable scraps, red clay that detoxifies mineral waste from aluminium mining, collapsible forms that would reduce the environmental impact of transport – as well as additional models and experiments.

ベルリンにあるスタジオ・オラファー・エリアソンでは日々さまざまな実験とリサーチがおこなわれている。野菜くずの顔料で描かれた水彩画、作品の制作過程で出るガラスや流木の破片を利用した新たな作品、環境負荷の少ない材料や形状の研究など、エリアソンのスタジオは世界をよりよい場所へと変えていく実践の場でもある。

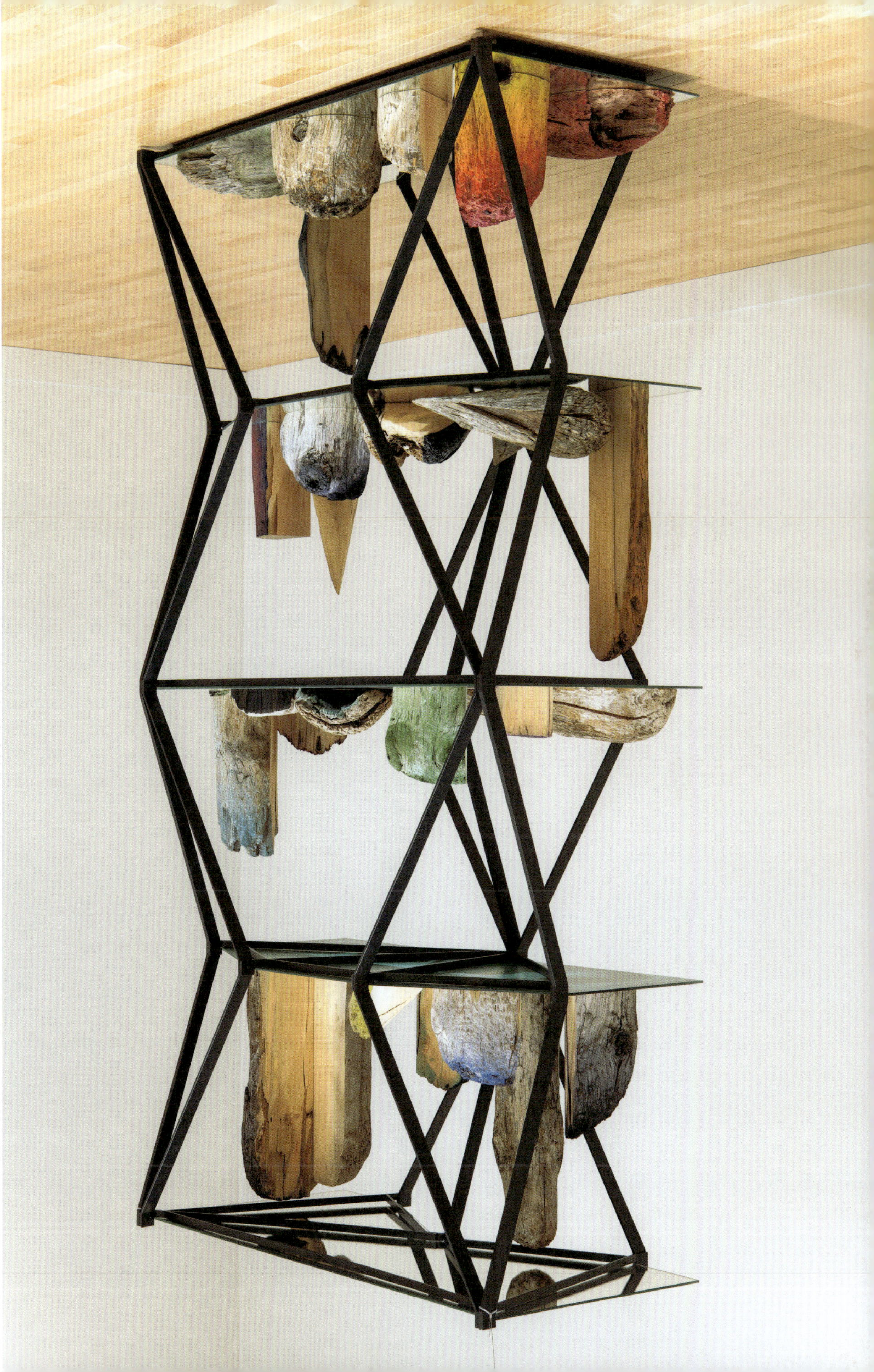

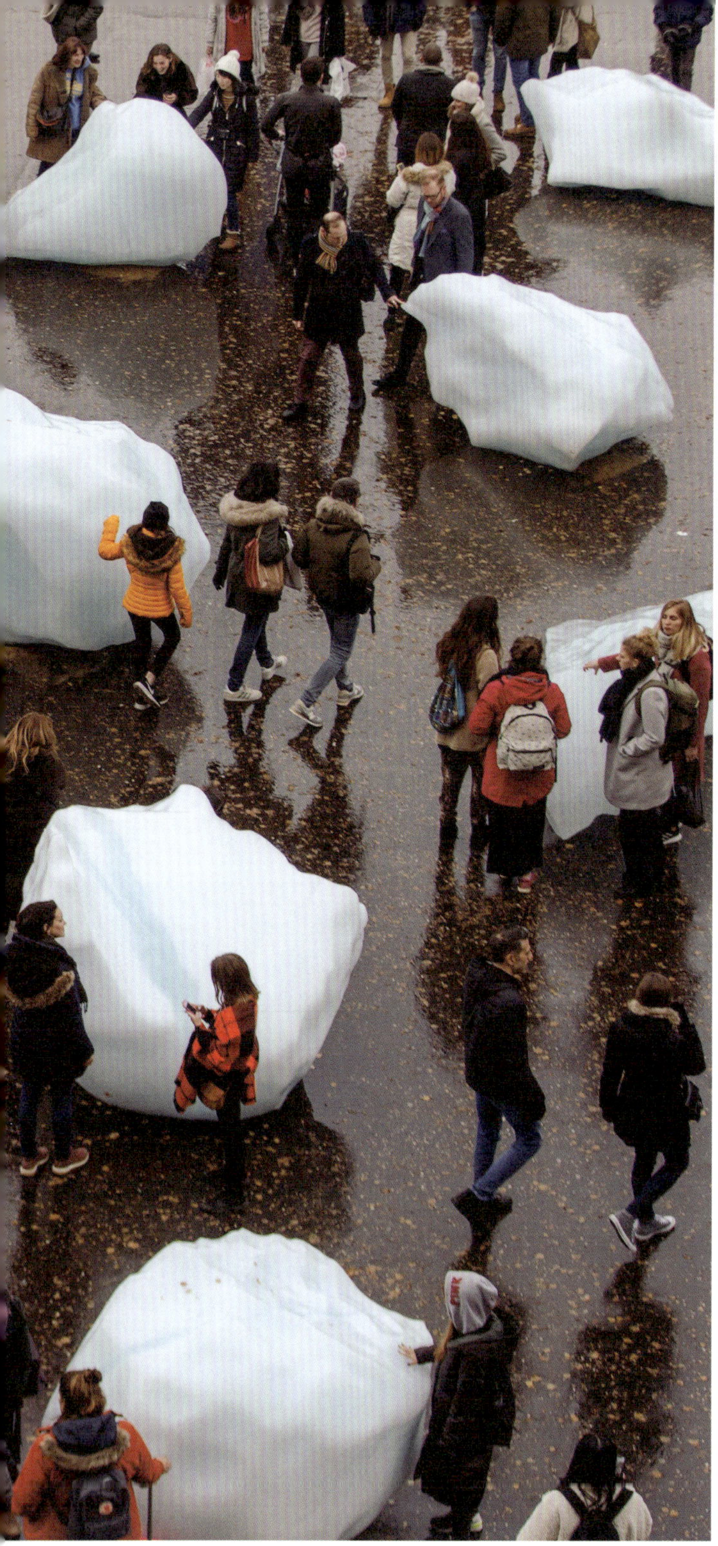

9つのパブリック・プロジェクトの記録写真
Documentation photographs of nine public projects

アイス・ウォッチ
Ice Watch
2014
テート・モダン（ロンドン）での展示風景
Installation view, Tate Modern, London
2018

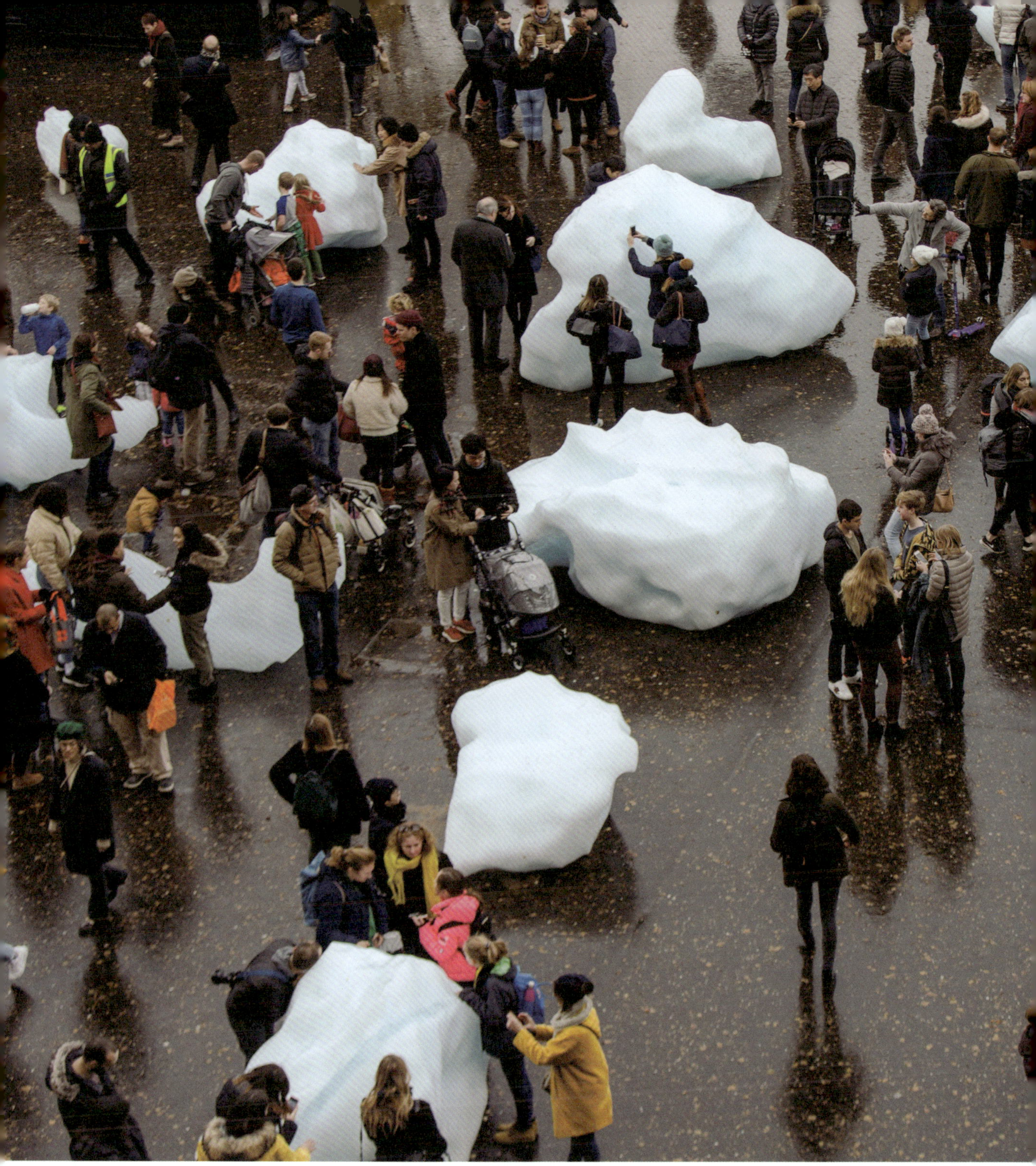

この作品にはエリアソンが公共空間でおこなった９つのプロジェクトが記録されている。プロジェクトに共通しているのは目に見えないものを目の前に現出させることによって人々に気づきをもたらしているという点であろう。たとえば《アイス・ウォッチ》は巨大な氷河の氷を街なかに展示することによって、気候変動を目の前にある現実として実感させるものである。

Eliasson's projects in public space include experiments with mirrors in the streets and parks near his studio; interventions in rivers in major cities and remote wildernesses; unannounced installations that accompanied and extended his exhibitions beyond the walls of the museum or gallery; and *Ice Watch*, which has brought blocks of glacial ice from Greenland to Copenhagen, Paris, and London.

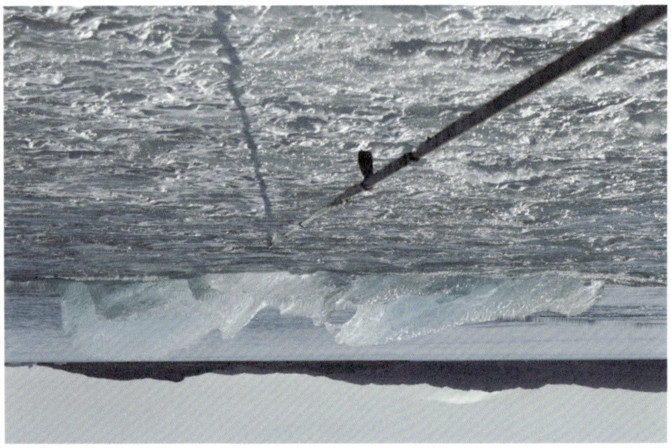

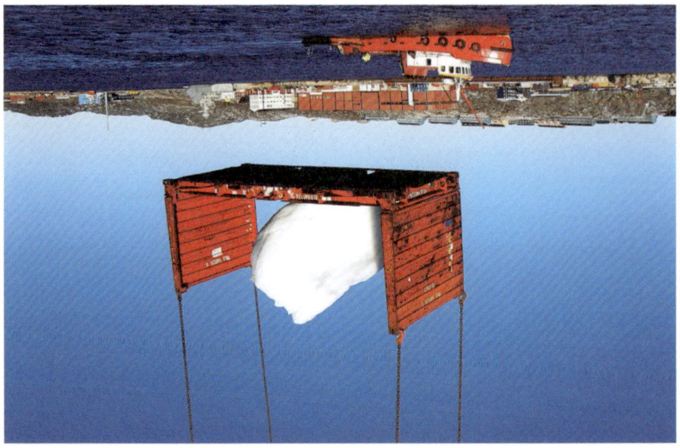

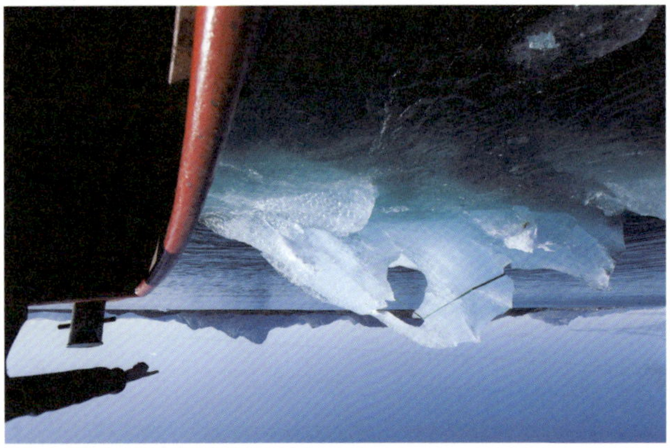

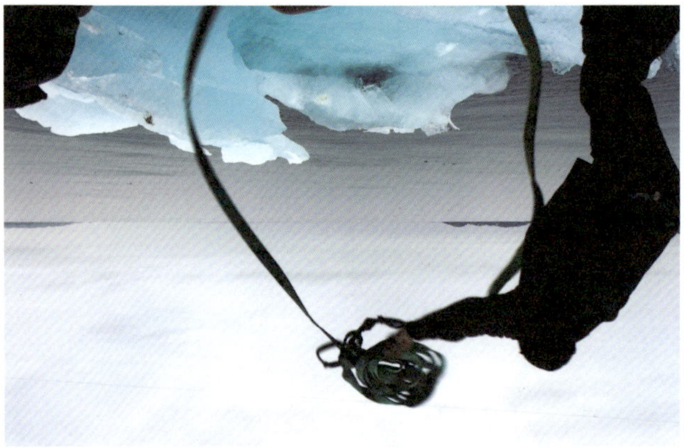

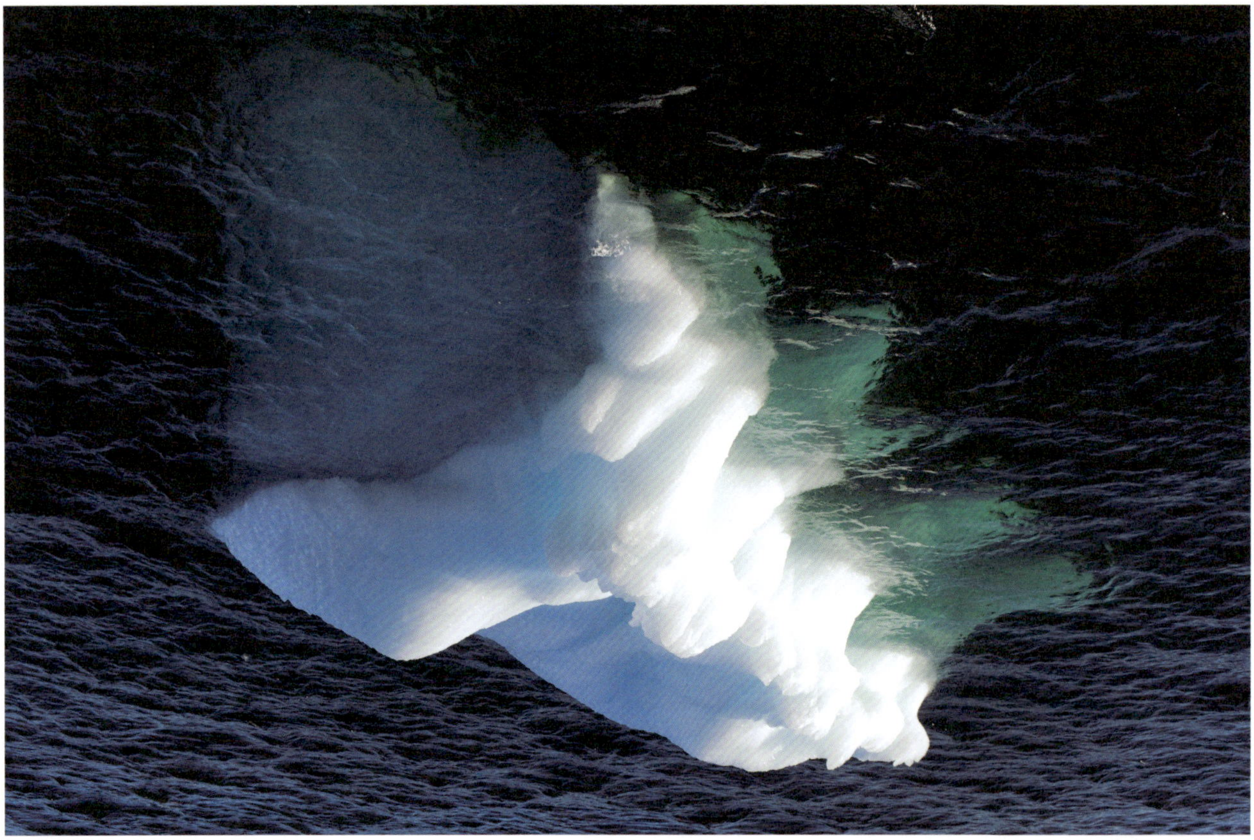

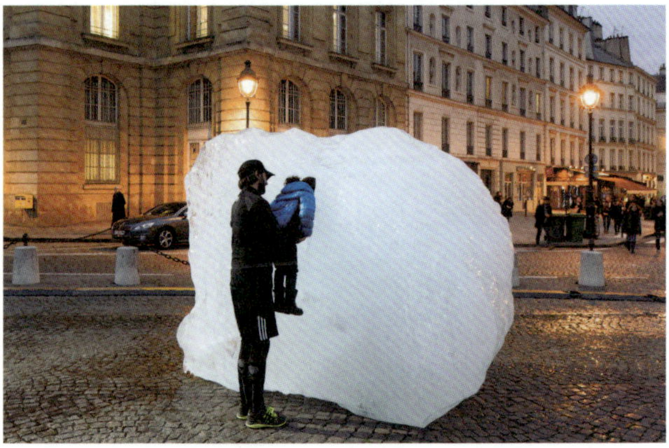

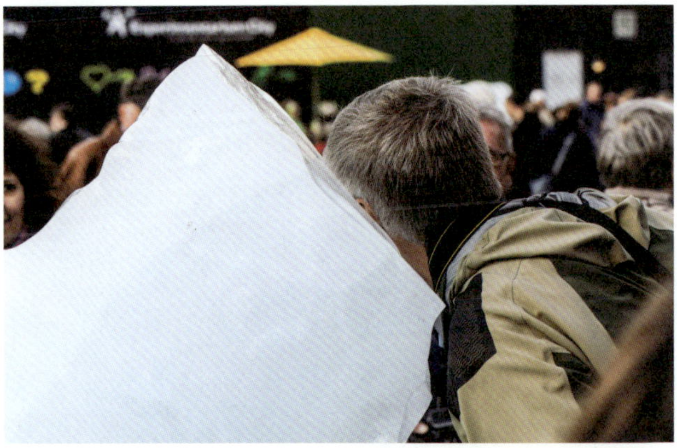

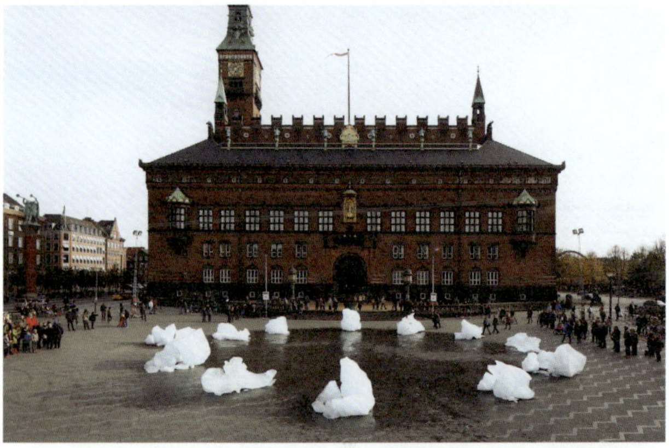

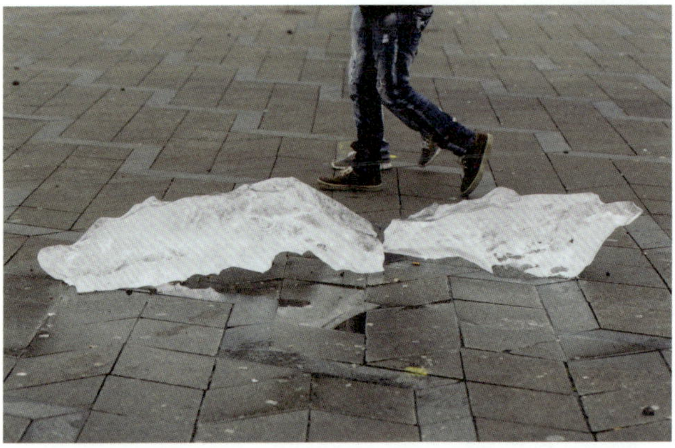

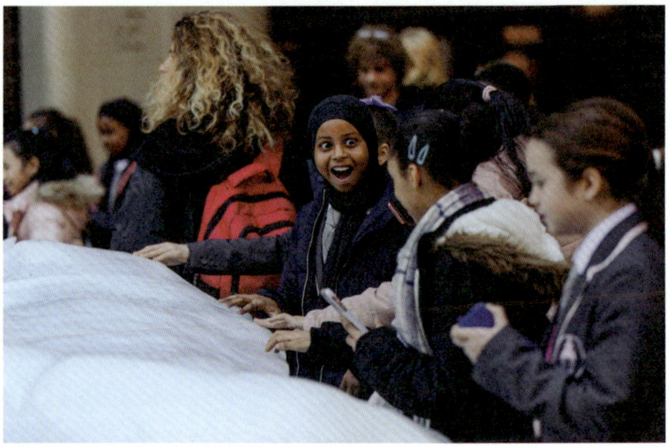

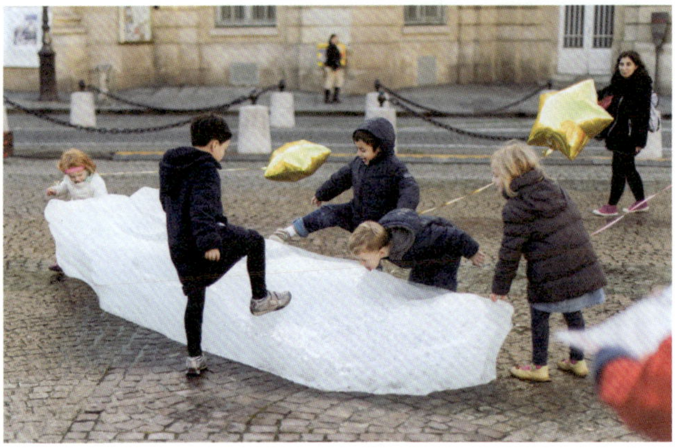

To make *Ice Watch*, Eliasson and geologist Minik Rosing had large pieces of glacial ice, which had broken off from the Greenland ice sheet and fallen into the sea, harvested from the water off the coast of Nuuk. They were then installed in public plazas in the following cities on the occasions of UN initiatives that address climate change:

- Copenhagen, City Hall Square, from 26 to 29 October 2014, for the publication of the UN IPCC's Fifth Assessment Report on Climate Change
- Paris, Place du Panthéon, from 3 to 13 December 2015, during UN Climate Conference COP21 in Paris
- London, Bloomberg European headquarters and at Bankside outside Tate Modern, from 11 December 2018 to 2 January 2019, to coincide with UN Climate Conference COP24 in Katowice, Poland

地質学者のミニック・ロージングとの共同プロジェクト。グリーンランドの氷床から海に溶け落ちた巨大な氷河の氷をヌークの海岸沖で引き揚げ、街なかに展示した。これまでに国連主導の気候変動会議にあわせて３つの都市でおこなわれた。

・コペンハーゲン、市役所広場（2014年10月26–29日）、国連気候変動に関する政府間パネル（IPCC）による第５次評価報告書の発行にあわせて実施
・パリ、パンテオン広場（2015年12月3–13日）、国連気候変動枠組条約第21回締約国会議（COP21）のパリでの開催にあわせて実施
・ロンドン、ブルームバーグのヨーロッパ本部／テムズ川南岸のテート・モダン周辺（2018年12月11日–2019年1月2日）、国連気候変動枠組条約第24回締約国会議（COP24）のポーランド、カトヴィツェでの開催にあわせて実施

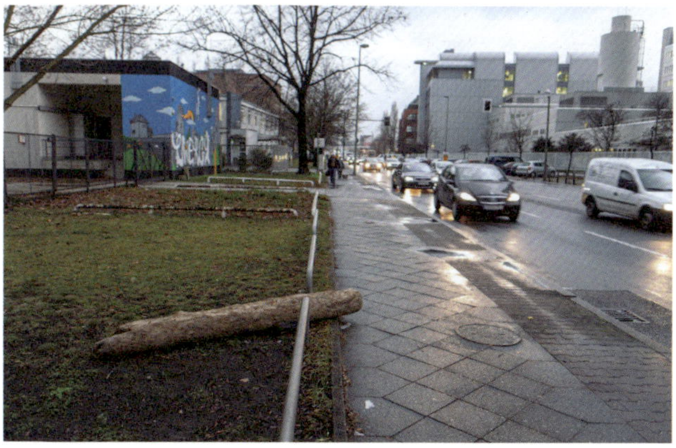

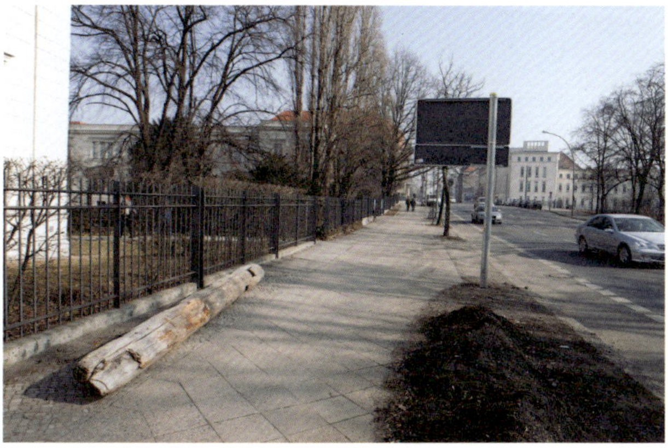

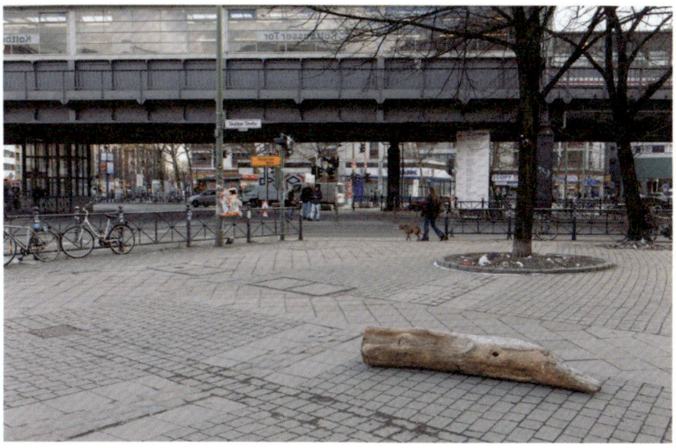

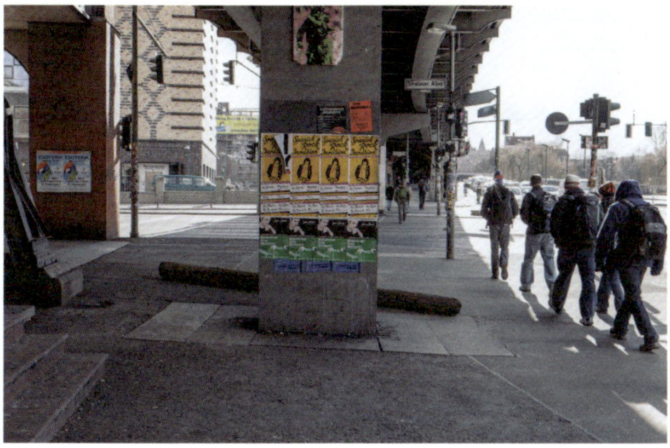

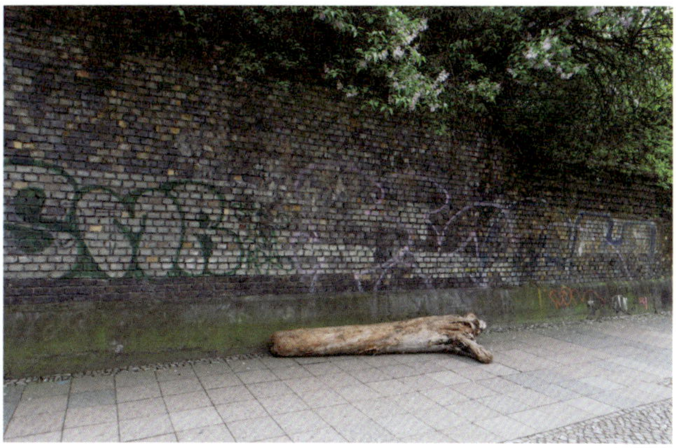

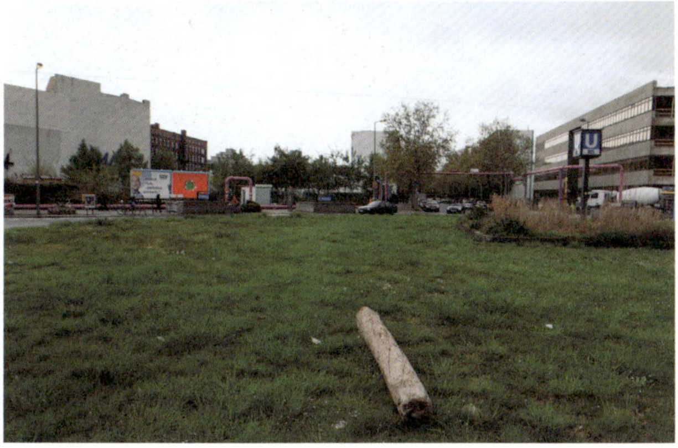

ベルリンの流木
Berliner Treibholz
2009

In 2008 Eliasson collected about fifty large driftwood logs from Iceland's northern shores. Each log had arrived there after a five-years-long journey from Siberia, during which it floated in the sea and was carried by drifting polar ice.
In 2010, as part of his exhibition *Innen Stadt Aussen* (Inner city out) at the Martin-Gropius-Bau, in Berlin, Eliasson and his team clandestinely placed these driftwood logs along public thoroughfares around the city.

2008年、アイスランド北部の海岸で50本の流木を拾った。それらの流木はシベリアから北極圏を超えて、流氷とともに5年もの歳月をかけて海を旅してきたのである。
2010年、ベルリンのマルティン・グロピウス・バウで開催した個展「都市の内側と外側」の一部として、ベルリンの市内各所の道路にひそかに流木が置かれた。

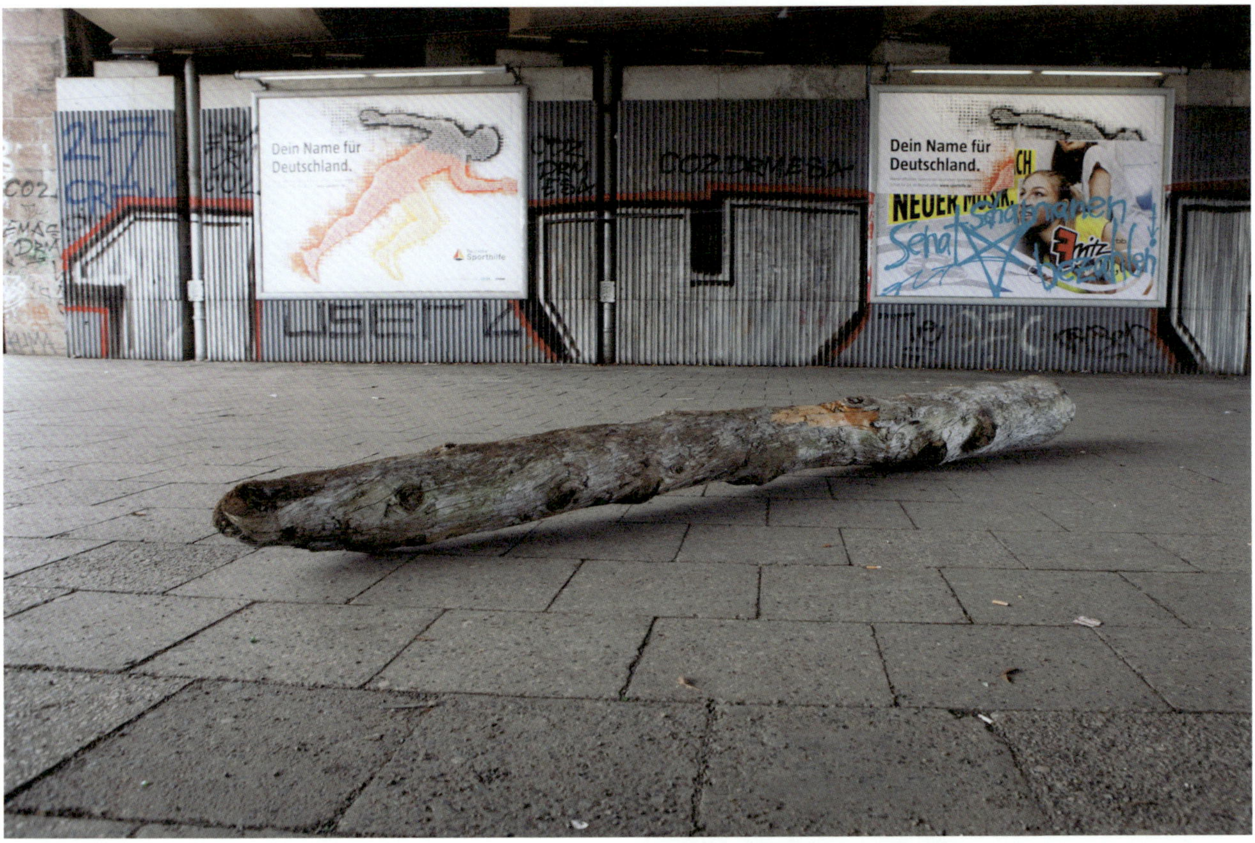
Dein Name für
Deutschland.
Sporthilfe
Dein Name für
Deutschland.
NEUER MUSIK.

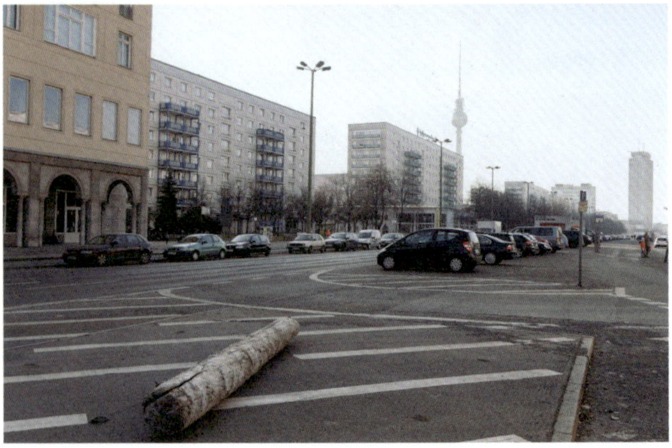

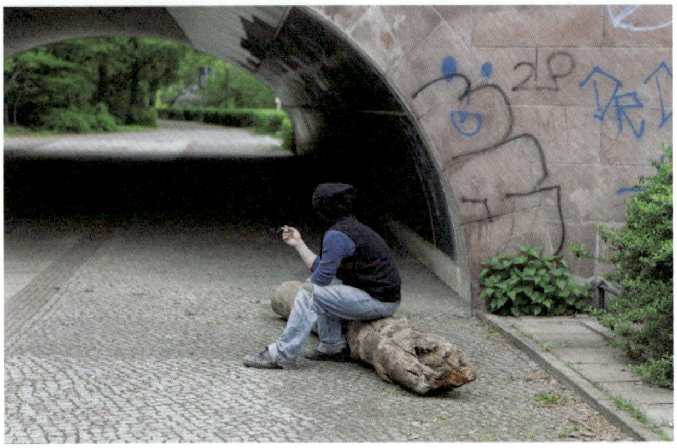

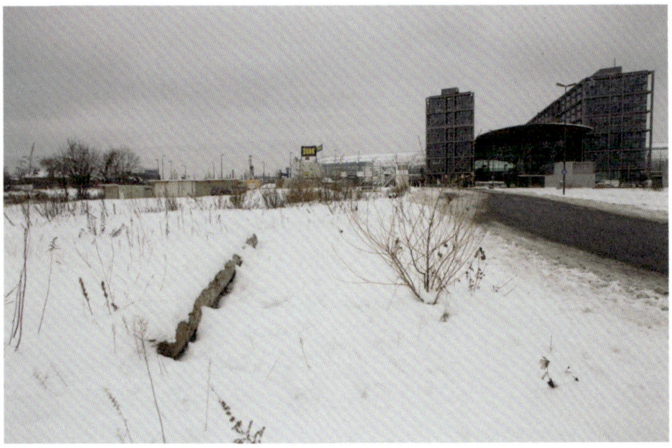

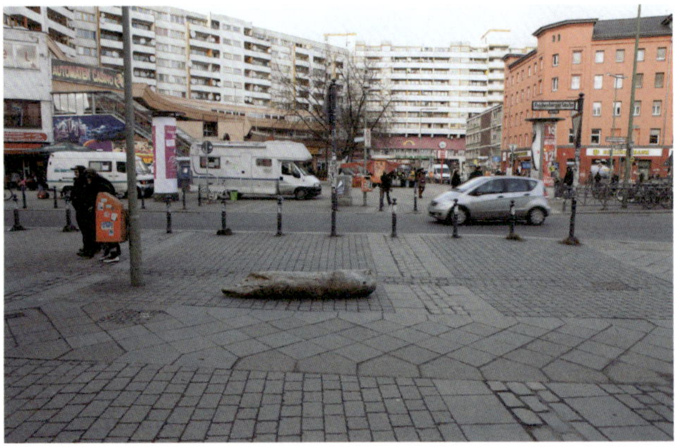

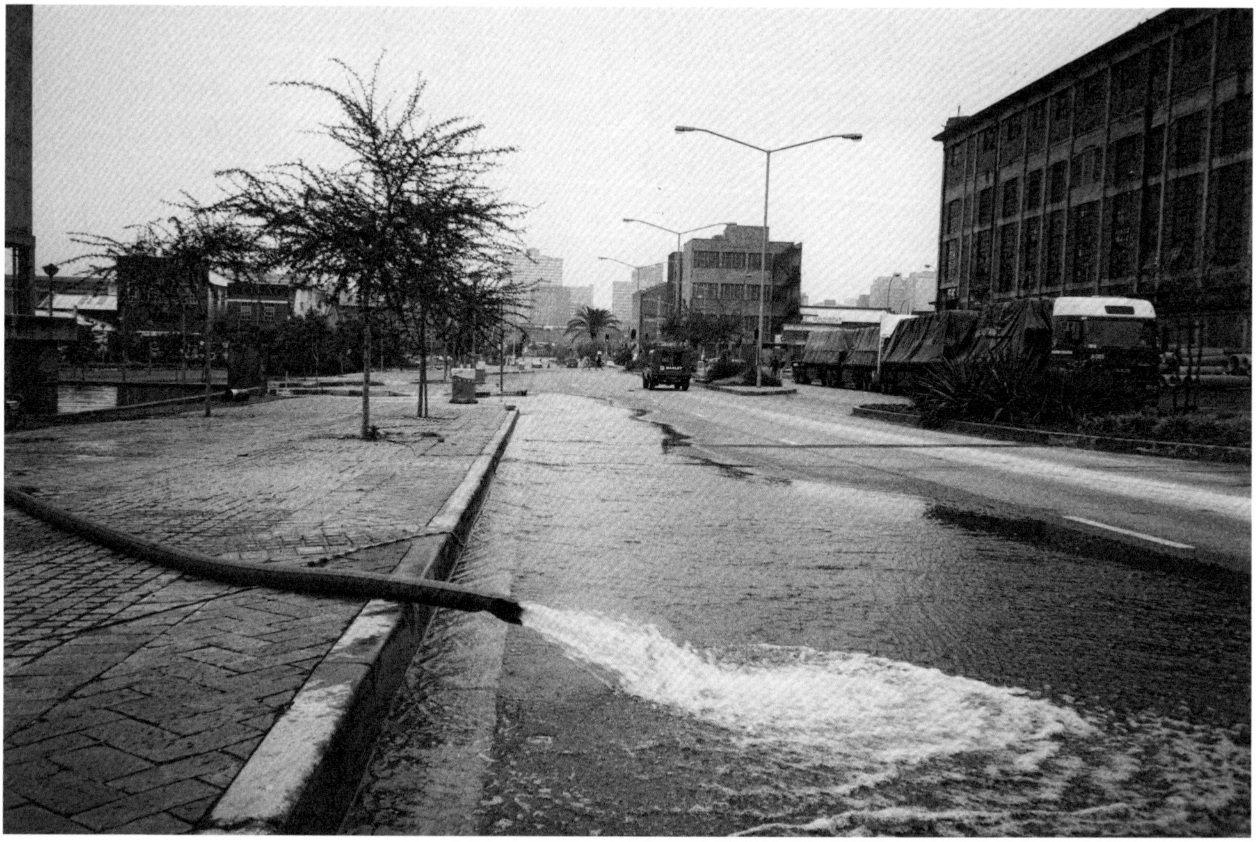

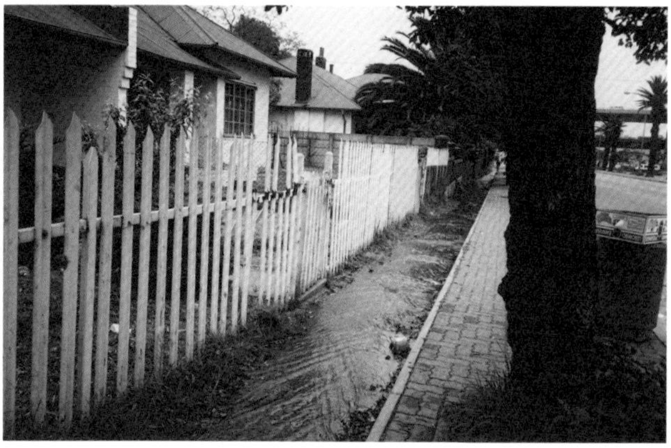

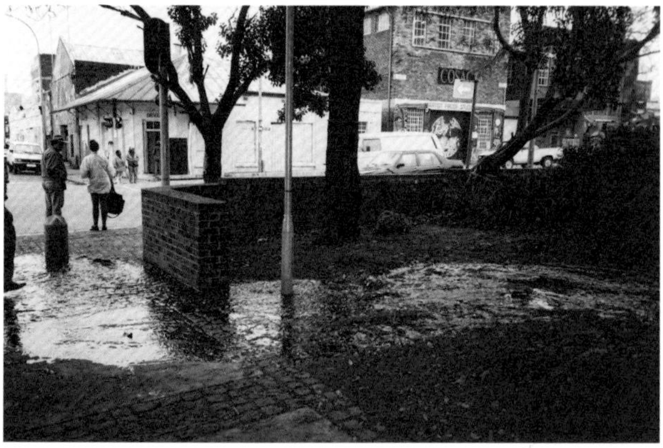

侵食
Erosion
1997

While officially presenting a photographic series in the second Johannesburg Biennial, *Trade Routes: History and Geography*, in 1997, Eliasson also performed an unannounced and unauthorized intervention: he pumped the water out of a small rainwater reservoir next to the exhibition building and let it pour out onto the street, where it formed a narrow stream about 1.5 kilometres long.

1997年、第2回ヨハネスブルク・ビエンナーレ「交易路：歴史と地理」の会期中、展示会場で写真作品を公式に出品しながら、会場の外では非公式の都市への介入を予告もなしにおこなった。それは会場の建物の脇にある小さな貯水プールから水をくみ上げ、道路に氾濫させるというものだった。そして道路は全長約1.5キロメートルの細長く伸びる川となった。

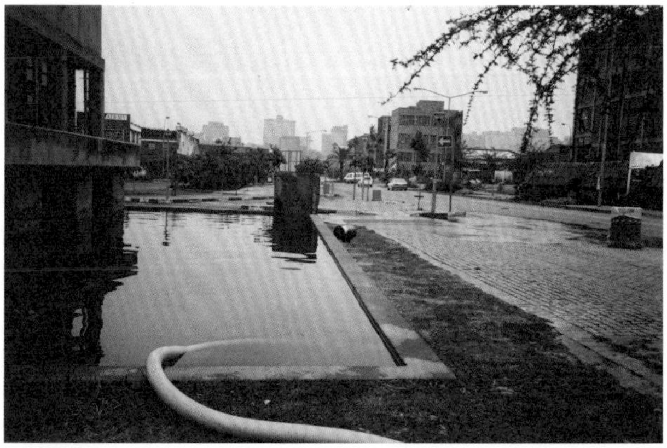
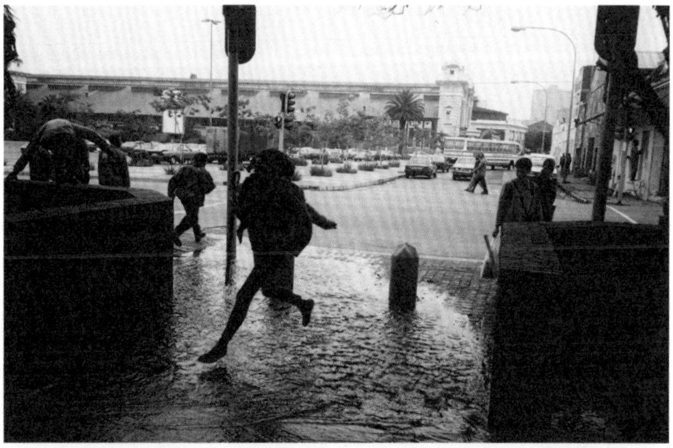
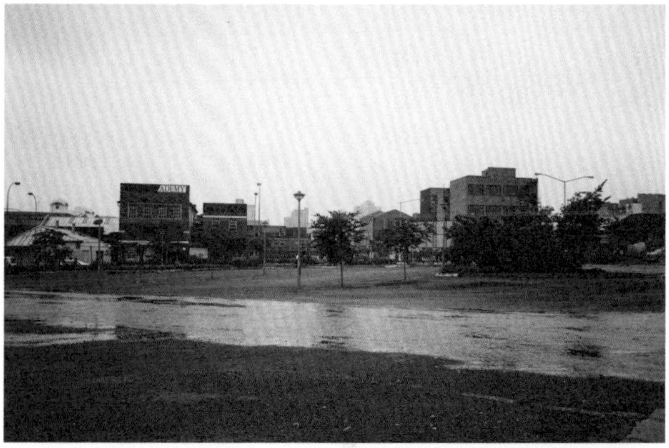
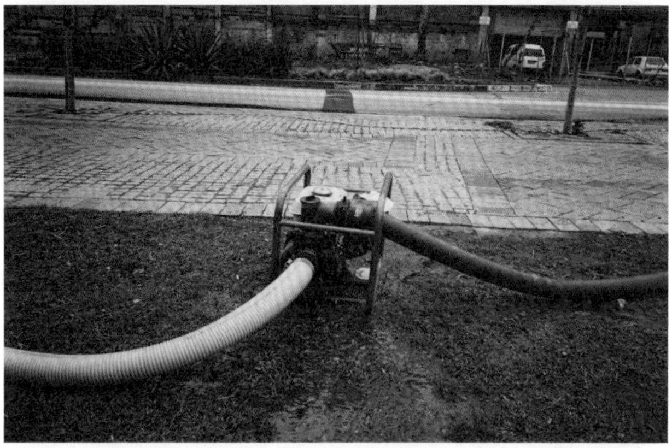
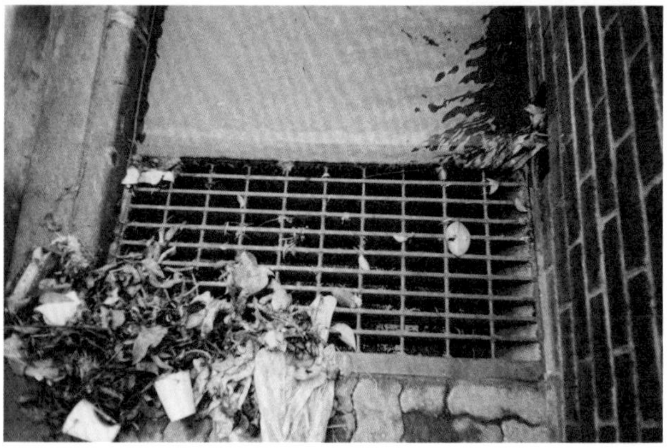
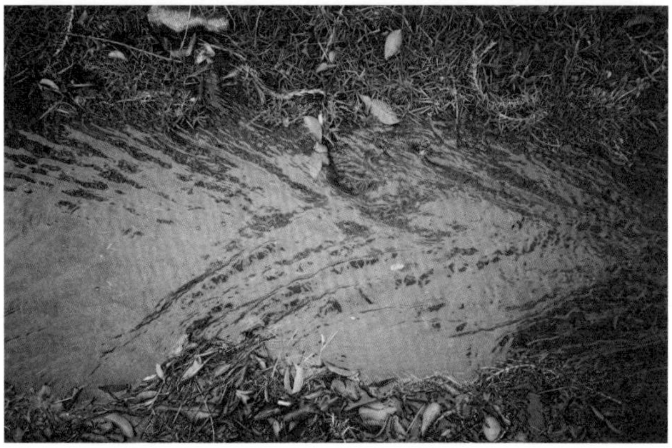
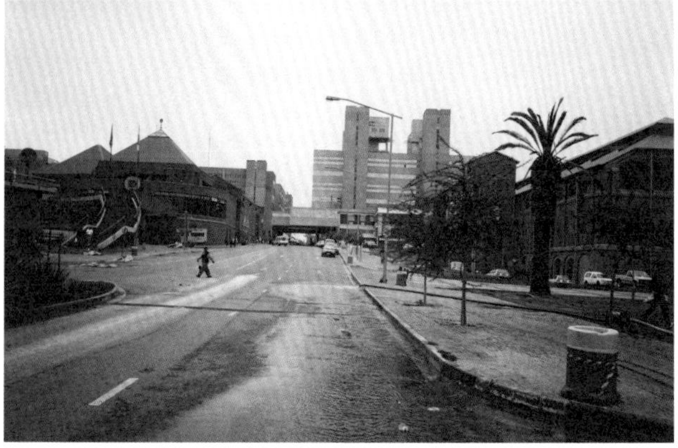
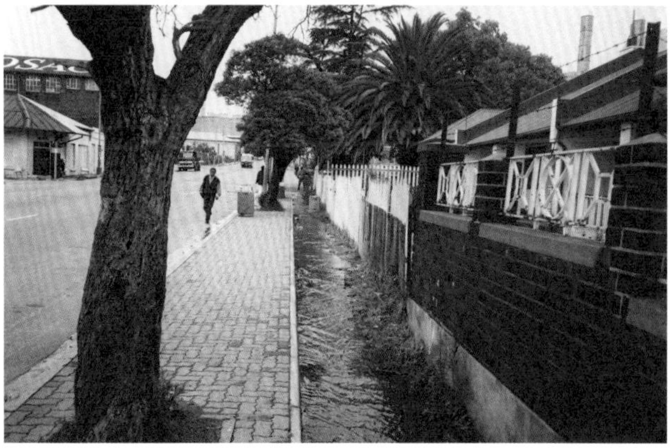

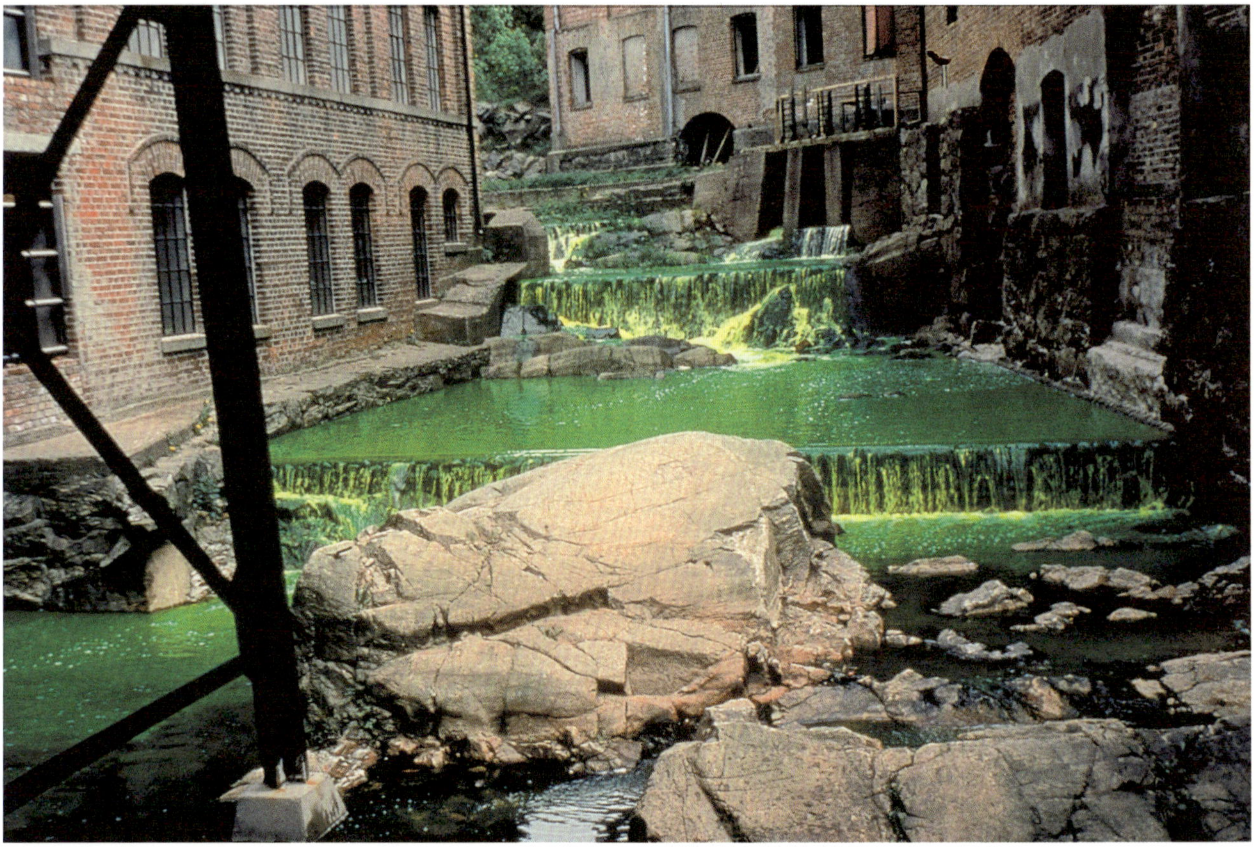

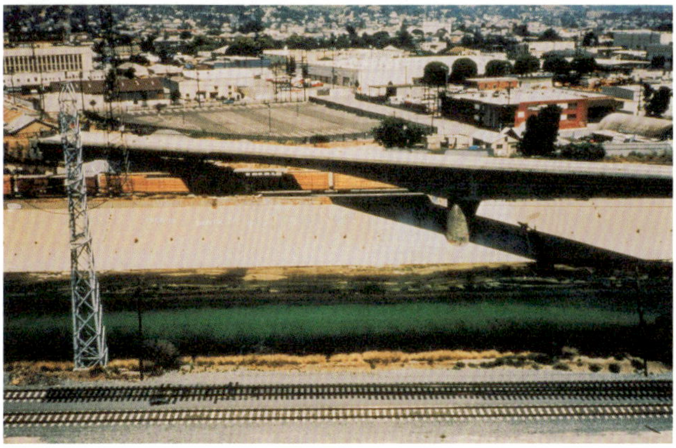

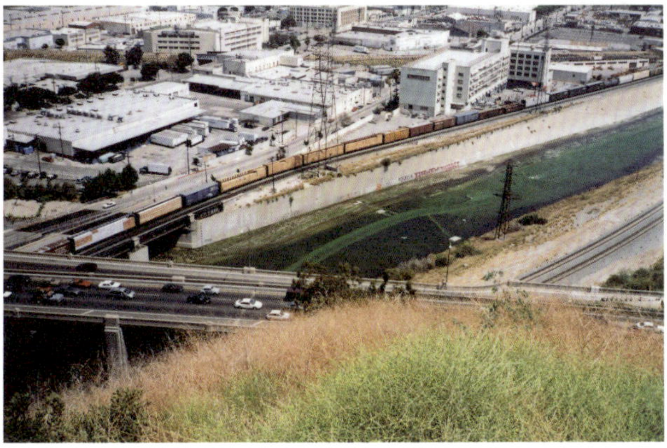

グリーン・リバー
Green river
1998

To make *Green river,* Eliasson poured a non-toxic, water-soluble dye into rivers in both urban and rural settings, turning the rivers green. *Green river* has been carried out in the following cities:

Moss, Norway, 1998 / The Northern Fjallabak Route, Iceland, 1998 / Bremen, Germany, 1998 / Los Angeles, USA, 1999 / Stockholm, Sweden, 2000 / Tokyo, Japan, 2001

無害な水溶性染料を川に流し入れ、川を緑色にした。5つの都市の河川とアイスランドの自然保護区の河川が一時的に緑色の川となった。

モス、ノルウェー、1998年／北フィヤットラバク内陸路、アイスランド、1998年／ブレーメン、ドイツ、1998年／ロサンゼルス、アメリカ合衆国、1999年／ストックホルム、スウェーデン、2000年／東京、日本、2001年

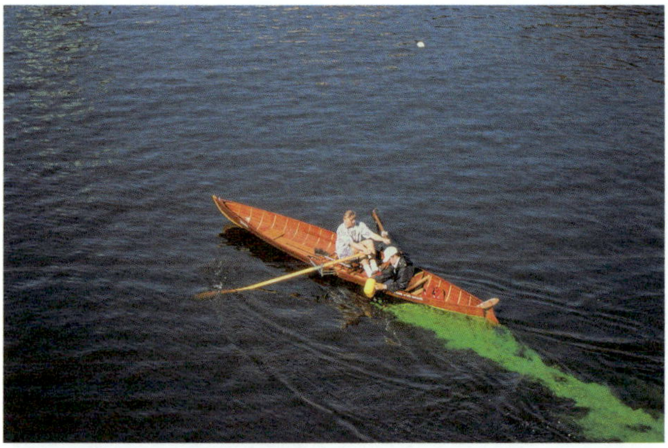
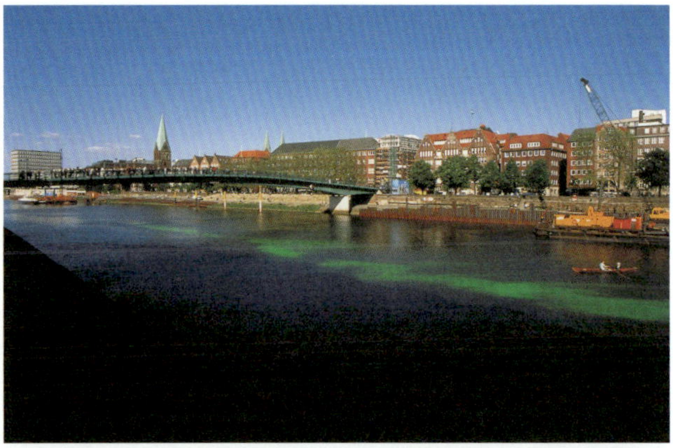
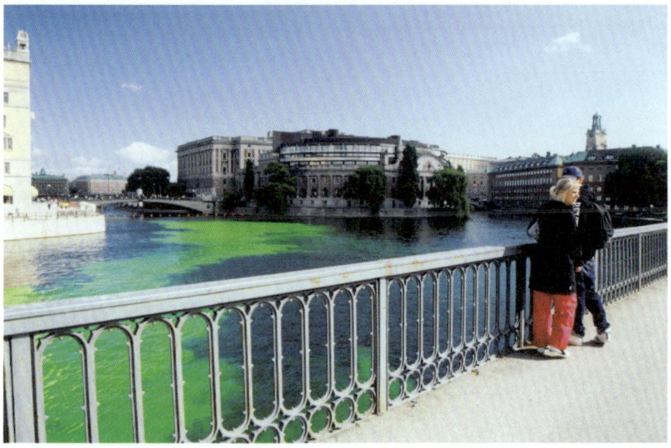
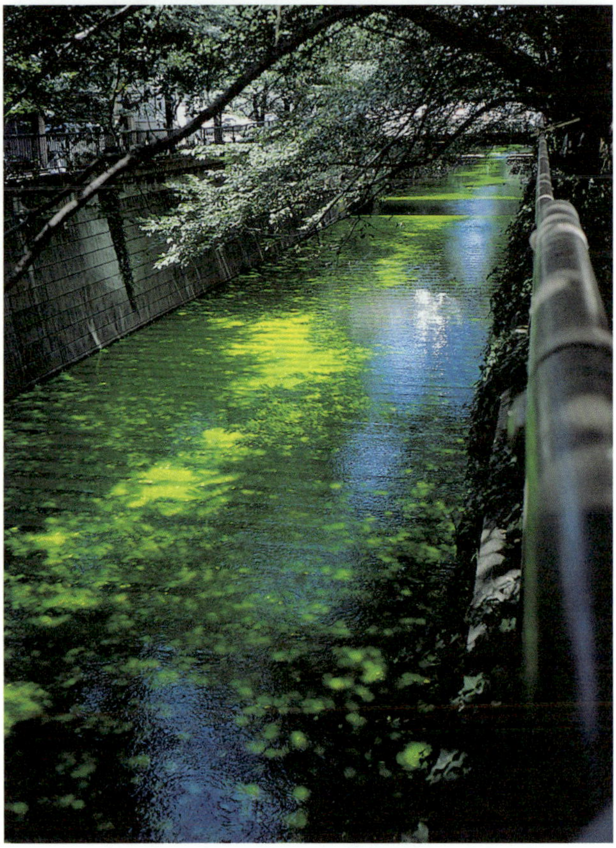
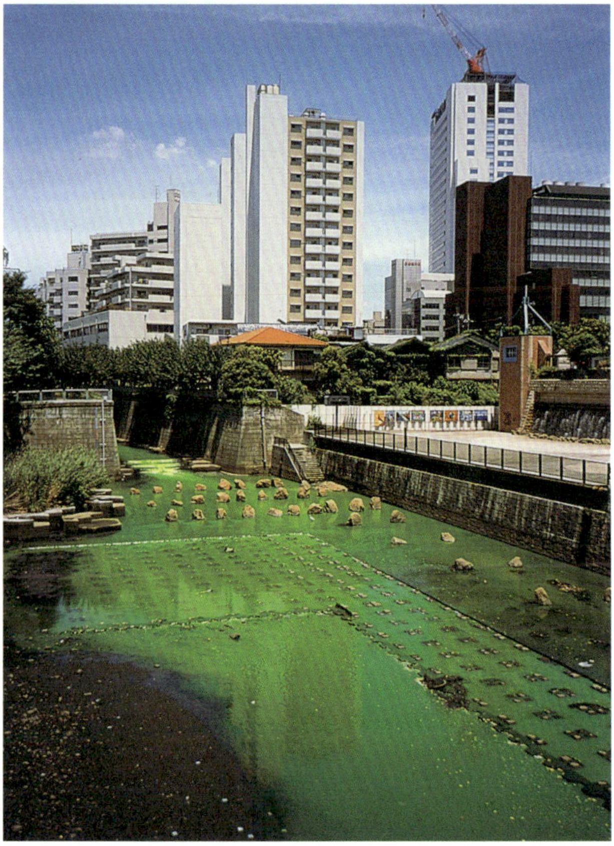
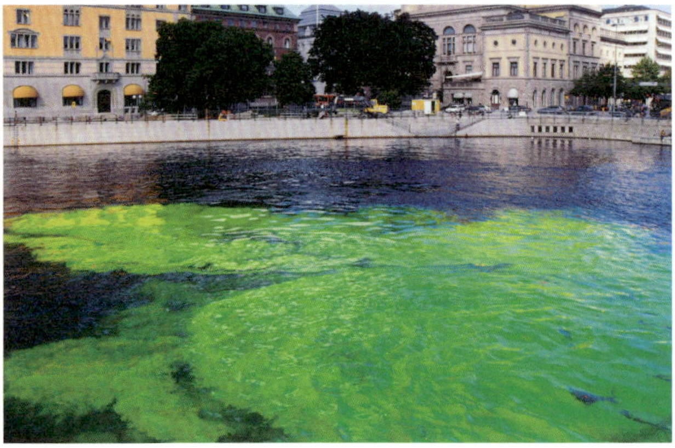

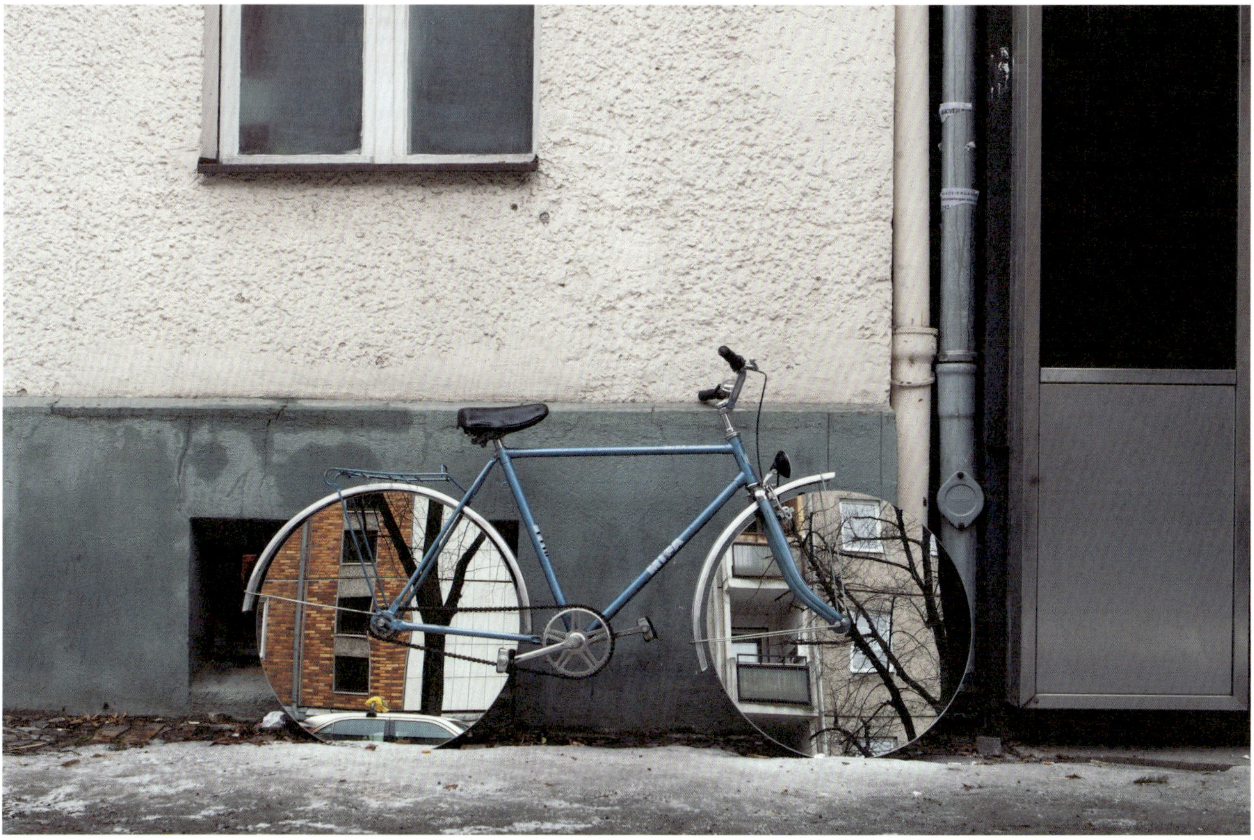

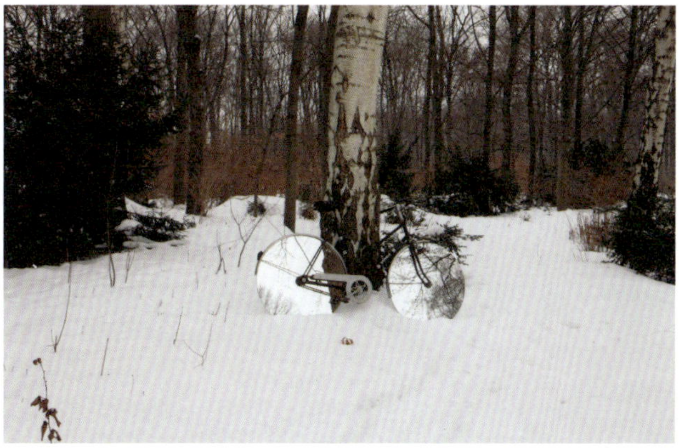

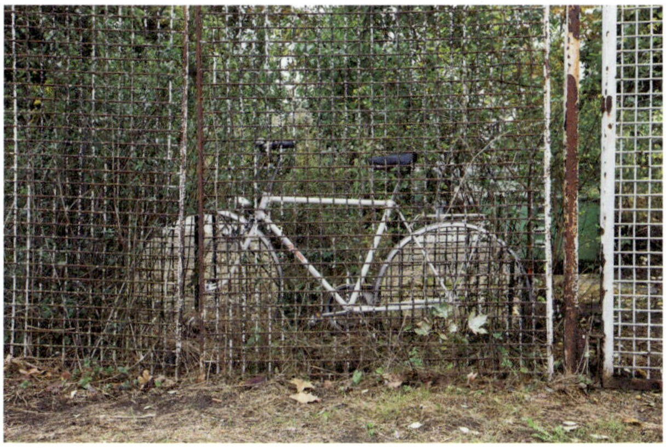

あなたの新しい自転車
Your new bike
2009

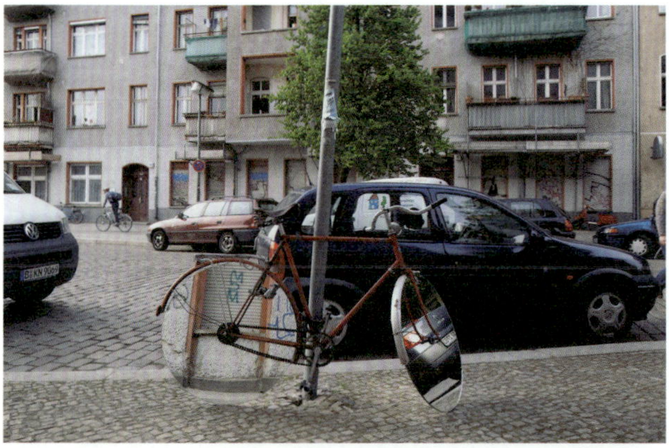

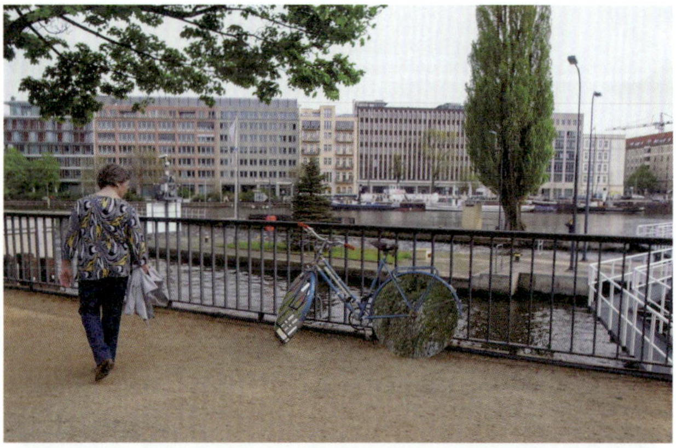

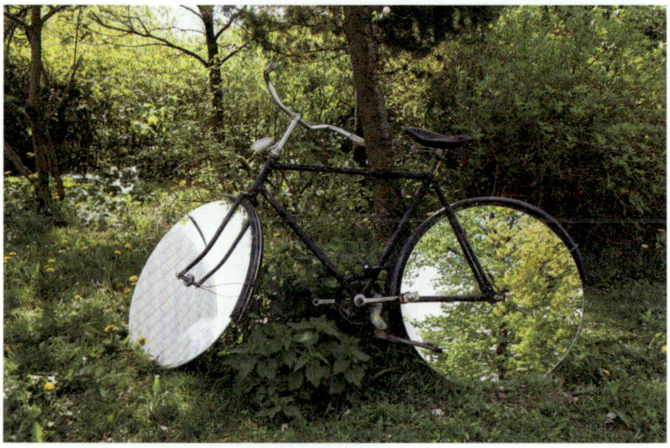

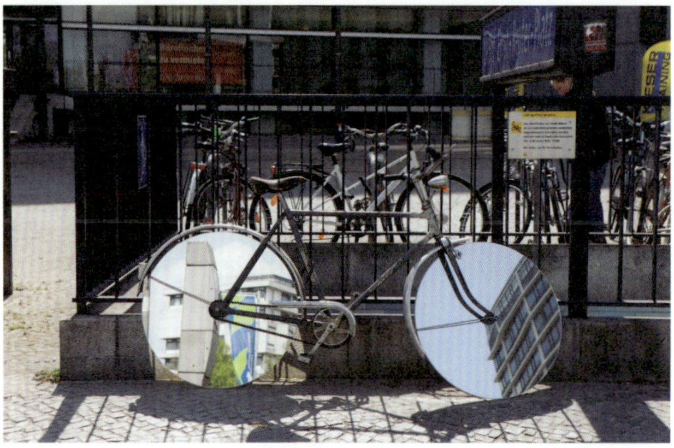

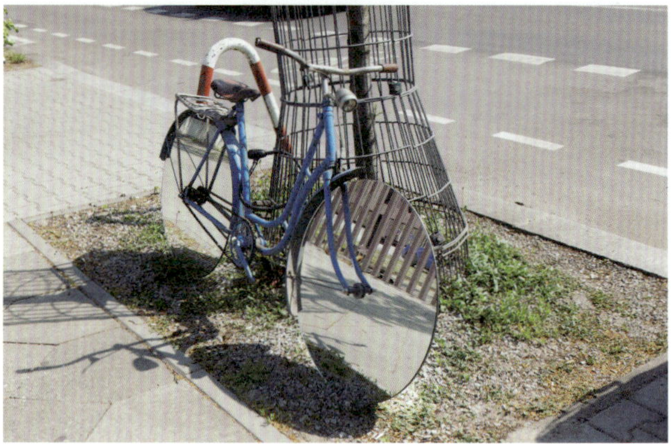

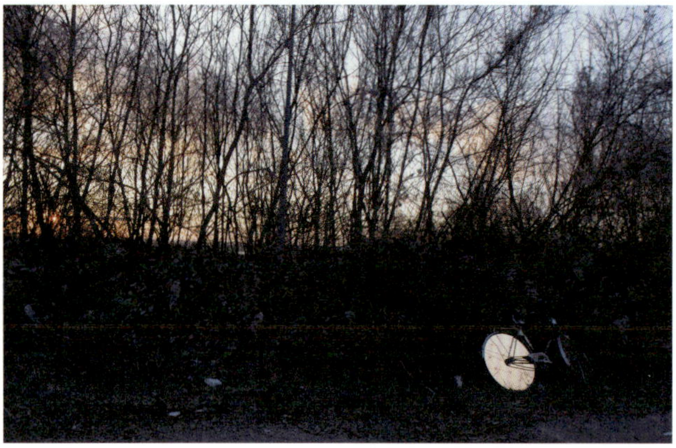

For his exhibition *Innen Stadt Aussen* (Inner city out), at Martin-Gropius-Bau, Berlin, in 2010, Eliasson left twelve bicycles with mirrors for wheels at several locations around the city – without explanation or attribution. He did the project again in 2011 in São Paulo as part of his exhibition there, *Seu corpo da obra* (Your body of work), at SESC Belenzinho, SESC Pompeia, and Pinacoteca do Estado.

2010年、ベルリンのマルティン・グロピウス・バウで開催した個展「都市の内側と外側」のために、12台の車輪が鏡でできた自転車を説明や出処を明らかにしないままベルリンの市内各所に放置した。2011年、サンパウロ州立美術館とセスキ文化センターで開催した個展「あなたの作品」でも再びこのプロジェクトをおこなった。

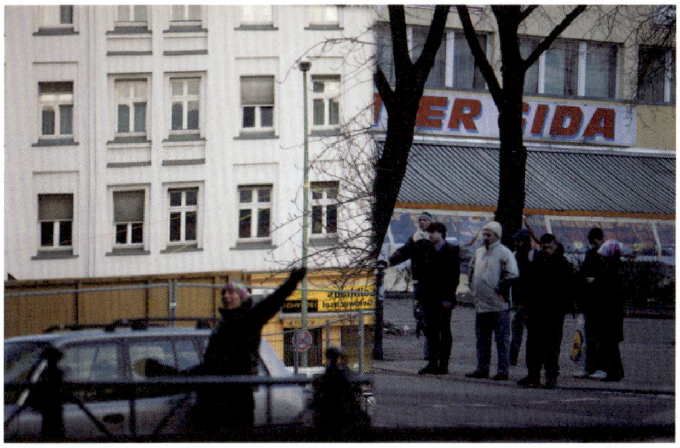

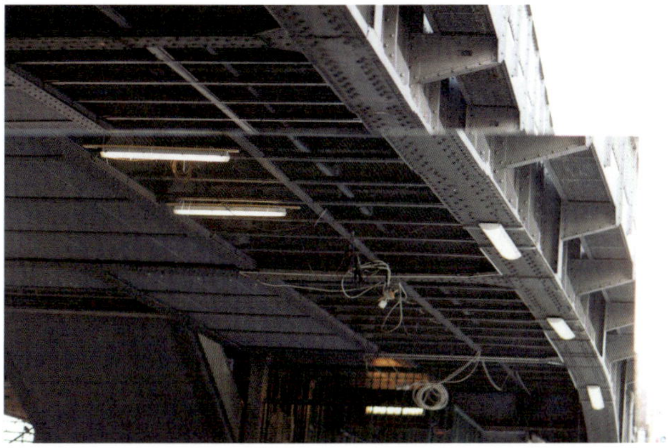

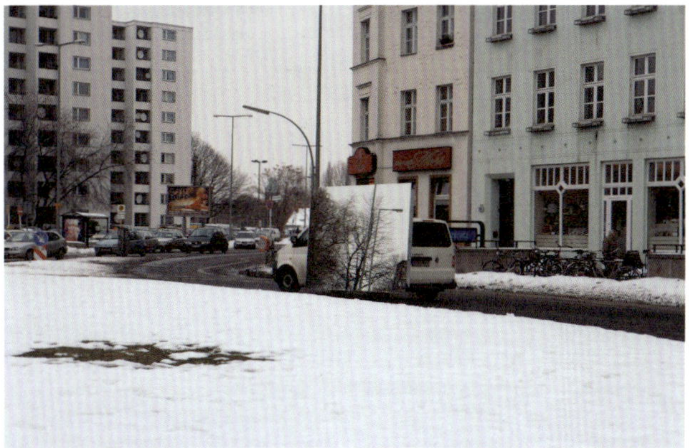

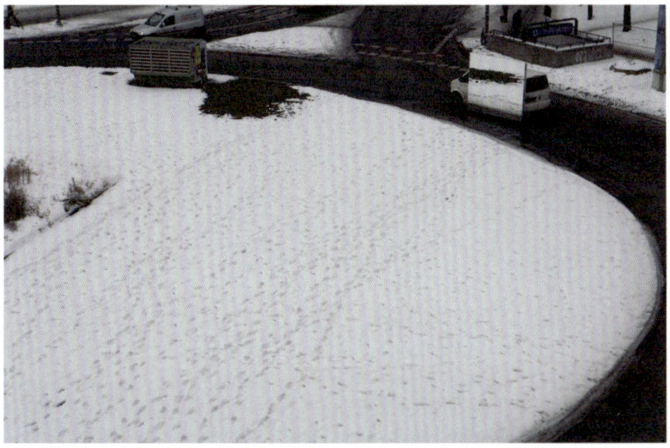

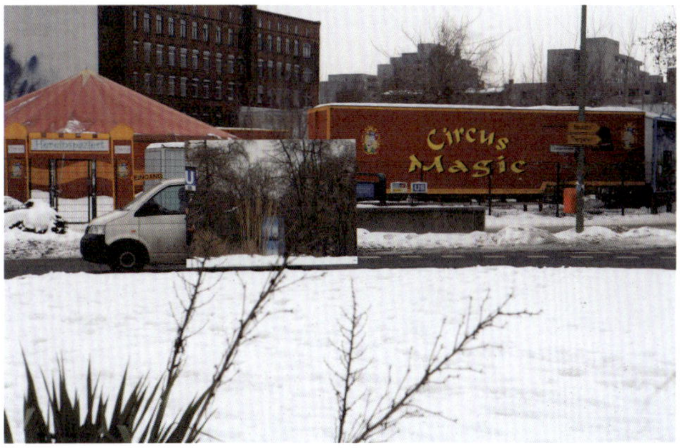

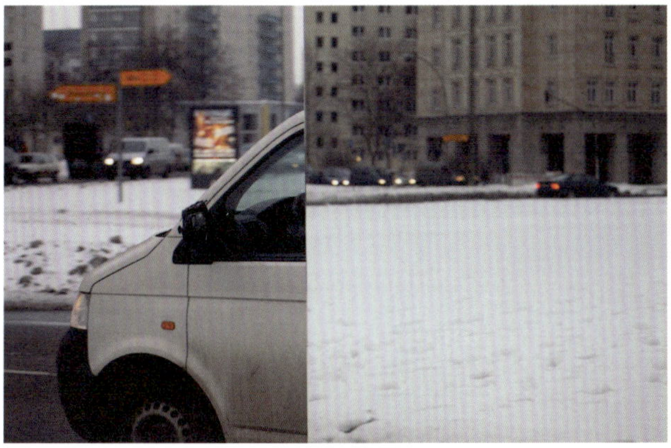

都市の内側と外側
Innen Stadt Aussen
2010

In 2010 Eliasson had a large mirror installed on the side of a van and driven around Berlin. It was filmed as it drove by Kottbusser Tor, Moritzplatz, and Strausberger Platz, and the resulting film was shown in Berlin as part of his exhibition *Innen Stadt Aussen* (Inner city out), at the Martin-Gropius-Bau, in 2010.

2010年、側面に大きな鏡を設置したバンをベルリンで走らせた。コットブッサー・トア、モーリッツプラッツ、シュトラウスベルガー・プラッツを走行した様子が映像に収められ、映像は同年ベルリンのマルティン・グロピウス・バウで開催した個展「都市の内側と外側」で展示された。

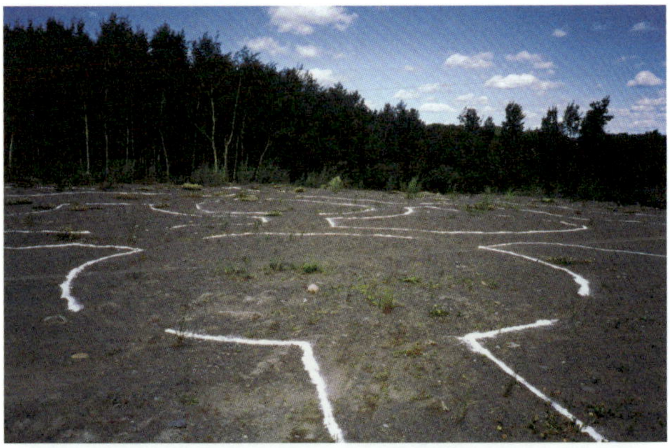

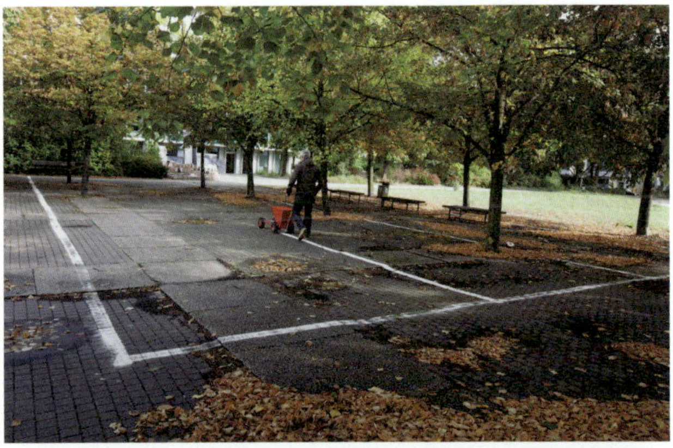

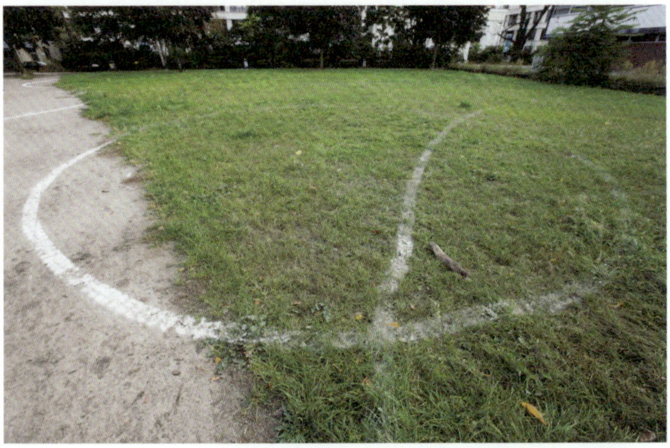

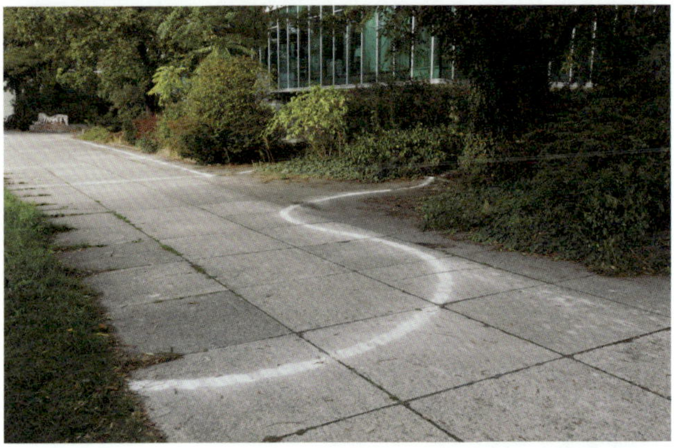

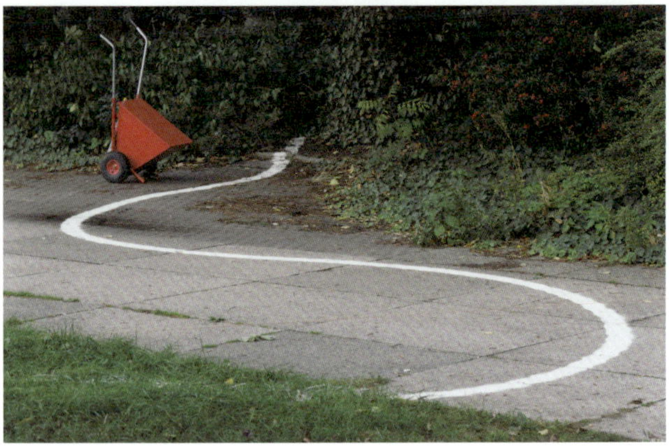

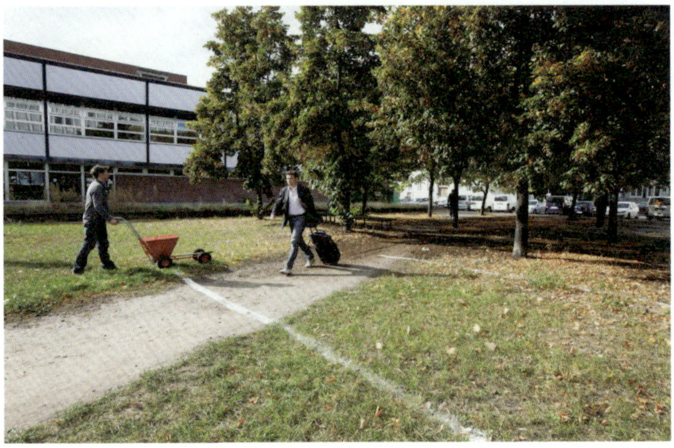

Proposal for a park, 1997
For the third Symposium on Visual Arts, Amos, Quebec, Eliasson painted thick chalk lines on a dirt field to make it into a park.

Non-stop park (Entwurf für einen Park), 2009
As part of a series of public experiments undertaken prior to his exhibition *Innen Stadt Aussen* (Inner city out), at Martin-Gropius-Bau, Berlin, in 2010, Eliasson painted thick chalk lines onto the grass and pathways of Berlin's Reinhardtstrasse Park.

公園のための提案、1997
地面に白線を引いて空き地を公園につくり変えた。ケベック州アモスで開催された第3回視覚芸術シンポジウムで実現した。

動き続ける公園（公園のためのデザイン）、2009
2010年、ベルリンのマルティン・グロピウス・バウで開催した個展「都市の内側と外側」に先立っておこなわれた一連の公開実験のひとつ。ベルリンのラインハルト通りに面した公園の芝生と歩道に白線を引いた。

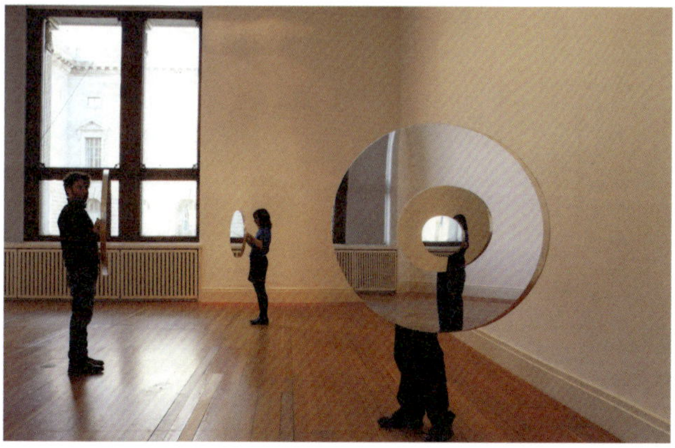

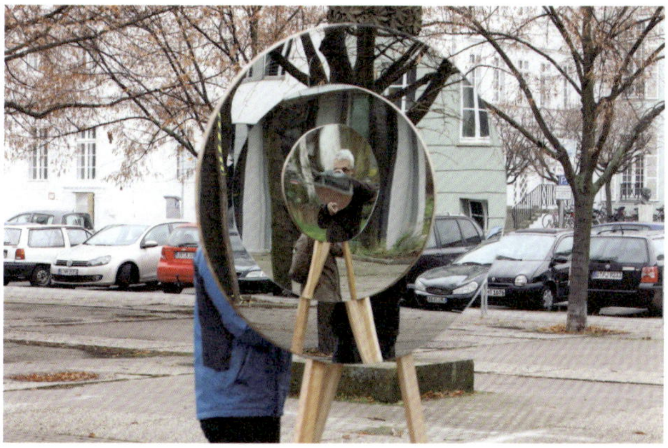

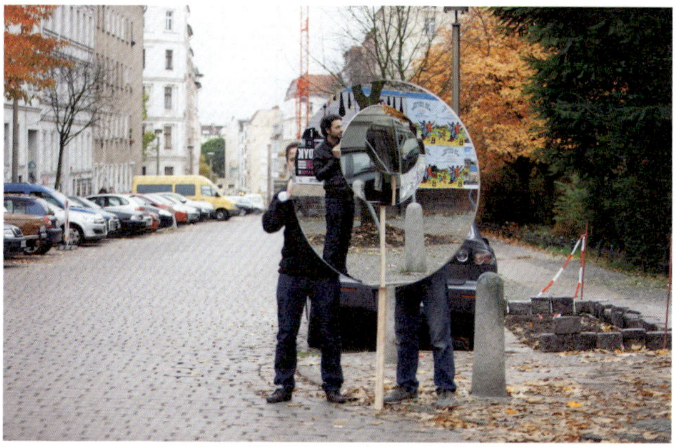

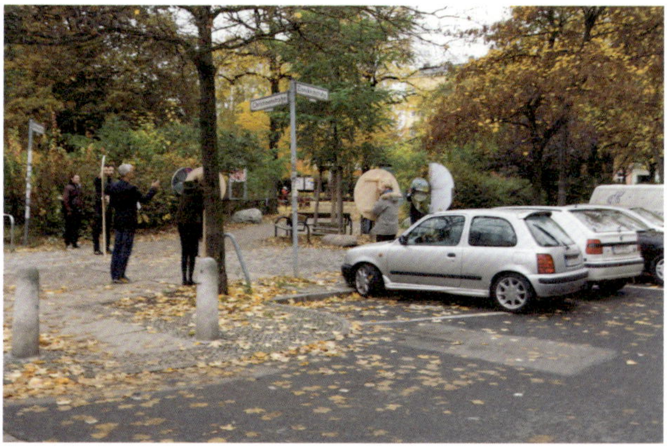

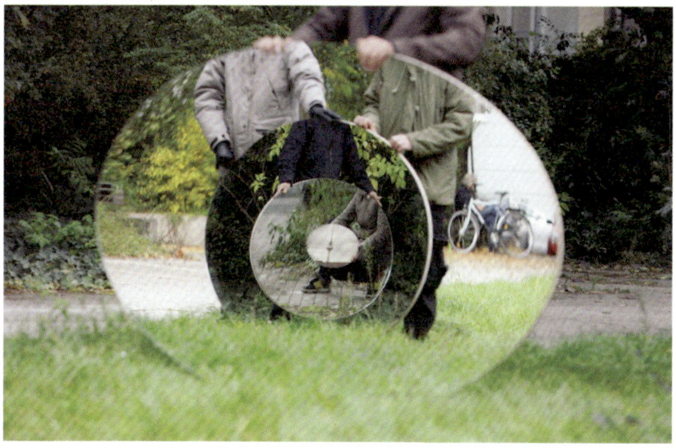

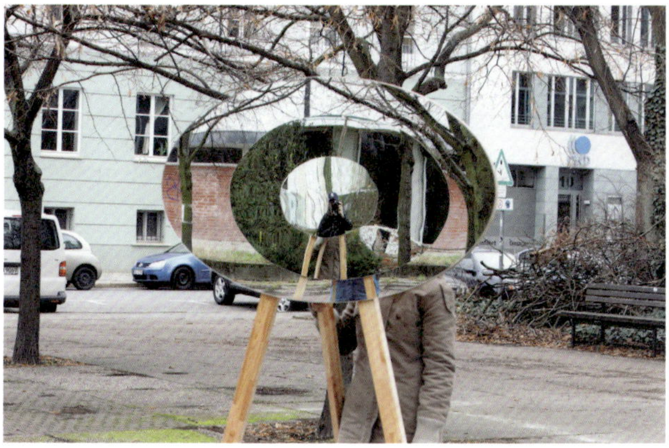

鏡のトンネル
Spiegeltunnel
2009

As part of a series of public experiments undertaken prior to his exhibition *Innen Stadt Aussen* (Inner city out), at Martin-Gropius-Bau, Berlin, in 2010, Eliasson and his team manoeuvred elliptical mirrors until they aligned at just the right angles to create the image, within a single large circular mirror, of a circular tunnel of regressing reflections.

2010年、ベルリンのマルティン・グロピウス・バウで開催した個展「都市の内側と外側」に先立っておこなわれた一連の公開実験のひとつ。いくつかの楕円形の鏡を、大きな円形の鏡に対して直角になるように並べることで、円形の鏡の中に後退していく鏡のトンネルのイメージが現れる。そのイメージが現れるまで鏡の位置を調整していった。

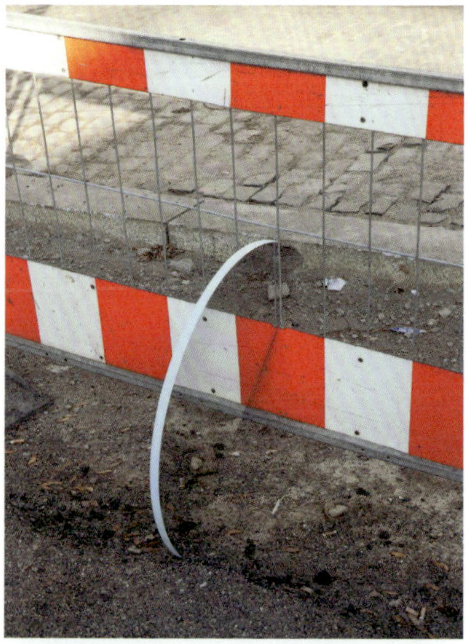
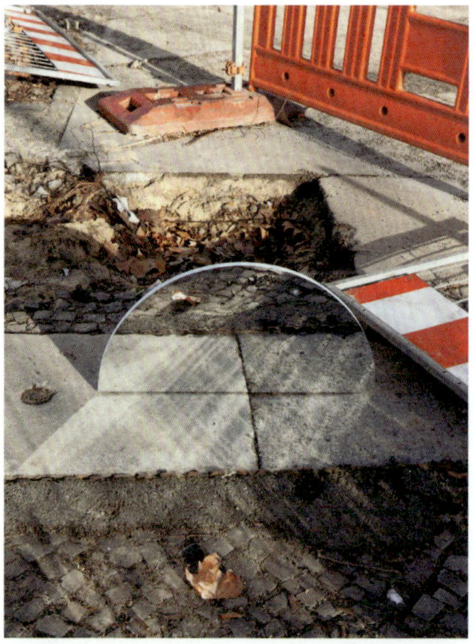
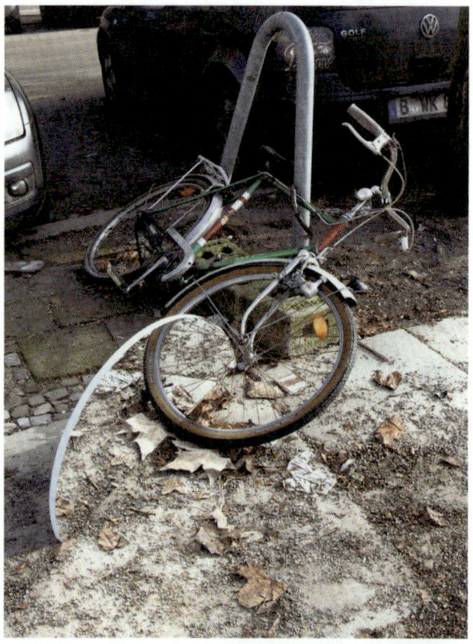
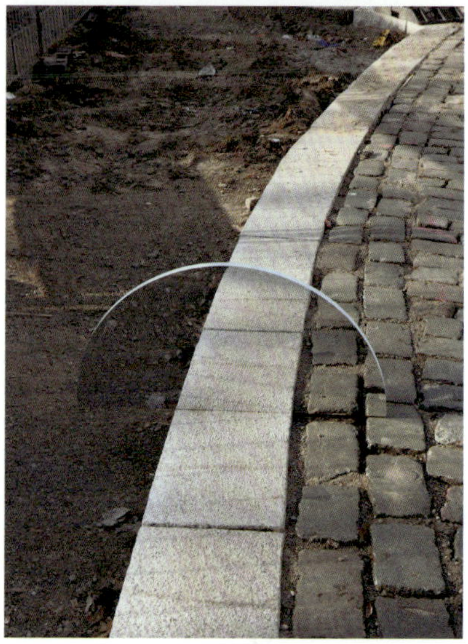
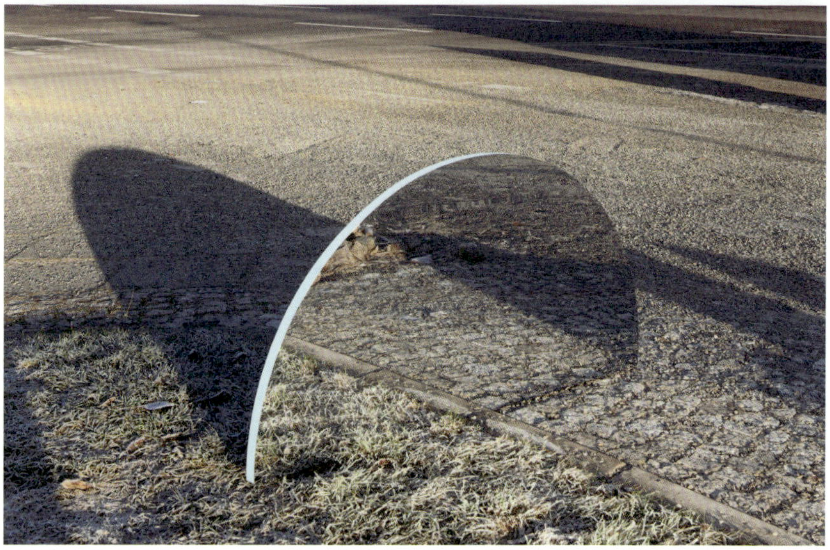
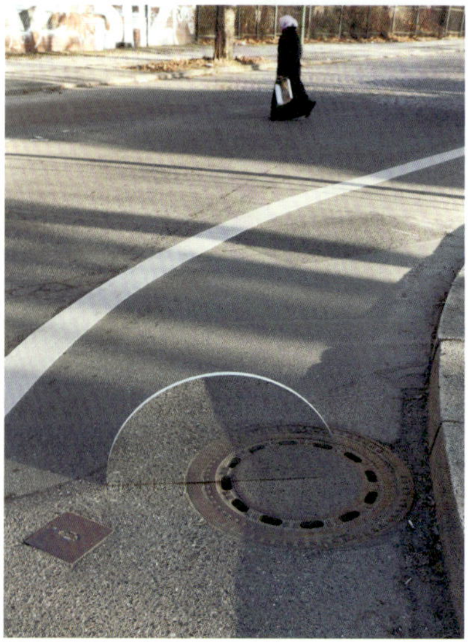

30秒間の鏡
Half-a-minute mirror
2010

2010年、ベルリンのマルティン・グロピウス・バウで開催した個展「都市の内側と外側」に先立っておこなわれた一連の公開実験のひとつ。ベルリンの市内各所に半円形の鏡を置き、その場にあったもの、鏡に映りこんだ世界、その場の環境とのあいだに生じた相互作用が写真に収められた。

As part of a series of public experiments undertaken prior to his exhibition *Innen Stadt Aussen* (Inner city out), at Martin-Gropius-Bau, Berlin, in 2010, Eliasson placed a half-circular mirror in a variety of spots throughout the city and photographed the resulting interplay between object, reflection, and surroundings.

作品解説

スタジオ・オラファー・エリアソン［英語］pp.17–103
楠本愛［日本語］pp.17–89（pp.84–85を除く）

Text

Studio Olafur Eliasson [English] pp.17–103
Ai Kusumoto [Japanese] pp.17–89 (except pp.84–85)

未来に歩いて入っていったら歓迎された——オラファー・エリアソンとティモシー・モートンの対話

I walked into the future and was welcomed: Olafur Eliasson and Timothy Morton in conversation

14名が考えるスタジオ・オラファー・エリアソンのサステナビリティ計画

Fourteen views of Studio Olafur Eliasson's sustainability agenda

未来に歩いて入っていったら歓迎された
——オラファー・エリアソンとティモシー・モートンの対話

哲学者ティモシー・モートンとオラファー・エリアソンの共通の関心は、頭の中のアイデアはどのようにして具体的な形を取るか、ということ——また肝心な点として、気候危機の時代である現在、アイデアが私たちの、そして私たちがともに暮らしている世界の形姿をどのように定めるか、ということだ。モートンは米テキサス州ヒューストン、ライス大学の英文学教授で、オブジェクト指向存在論（Object-Oriented Ontology）の分野でカギとなる思想家の一人である。モートンの仕事はたとえばエコロジー的思考に焦点を合わせている。私たちの生は、この惑星上に存在する他の生命・非生命、人間・非人間の生と深い部分で絡み合っているとする思考のことだ。モートンの造語に〈ハイパーオブジェクト〉がある。全体を把握するのは不可能なほど大きいが、はっきりときわだった諸現象、たとえば地球温暖化を考える一助として編み出された語だ。過去五年間にわたりオラファーとティムは、美術館や文化イベントにともに登壇し——二〇一五年秋にはストックホルム近代美術館、コペンハーゲンＤＯＸ映画祭で、二〇一六年にはソウルのサムスン美術館リウムで——共通の関心や懸案事項をめぐって、たえず新たな会話を紡いできている。

ストックホルム近代美術館
二〇一五年一〇月二日

オラファー｜ティム、『自然なきエコロジー』という本を出されていますが、このタイトルについてちょっと話してもらえますか。

ティム｜実はすごく単純なアイデアなんです。ぼくにとって、非人間存在たち――ウサギとか、川とか、山とか、スプーンなんかのカトラリーでもいいのですが――は、社会空間（ソーシャル）の内側にいるように思える。社会空間の一部を成している。ぼく――こっち側にいる人間存在――と、あっち側の、たとえばホッキョクグマとのあいだに違いはない。つまりそもそも社会空間というのは、一度だって完全に、すみずみまで人間のものだったためしはないんですね。いつだって社会空間には非人間存在たちが入り込んできていた――そうしてこの非人間存在たちがぼくらに対して、いろいろな種類の影響力をもつわけです。オラファーの仕事を見ていて本当にハッとするのは、ぼくらとは違うものたちが、ぼくらに対して影響力をもつのを可能にしている、というところです。非人間存在たちがぼくらに触れてくるのを許そうよ、という呼びかけみたいなものですね。ぼくらはいまこのすごく興味深い美術館にいて、自分は世界より優れていると思って上から目線で見ているような洗練された現代人たちに比べるとちょっとばかりナイーヴ、そんな態度を取ることを自分たちに許している。かつ、こういうナイーヴさにはすごく賢明な部分があるんです。自分が何かに動かされるのを許すという、豊かな質がある。

オラファーの仕事を見ると思い浮かぶ言葉は「運動」です。実はかなり深い哲学的イシューなんですね、この運動という問いは。哲学者の中には、「本当は運動なんか存在しない。運動とは単にモノに対して起きるものであるにすぎない」などと言う人もいますが、運動はぼくらの世界のすごく深い一部なんだという感じがぼくにはします。モノは押されなくても動く――このことは現在、小さなモノを扱った量子力学などの実験から明らかになっているわけです。すごく小さい鏡――といってもまだ目には見えるんですよ、原子サイズではない――を、寒々しい、まわりに何もない場所に持っていったとします。それでも鏡は動くんです。何かが押しているわけではないのに。赤外光を放射するからわかるんです。この鏡は――実際に力学的な意味で押されているわけではないのに――チラチラゆらめいている。ぼくがオラファーの作品から受けるのは、自分が見つめている物体（オブジェクト）が、何というか、生きている、という感じなんです――チラチラゆらめく質がある。

オラファー｜いいですね。さっき「自分が何かに動かされるのをあえて許す」というようなことを言われました。武装解除する、防御的にならない、自分が動かされるのを許す、そういった態度には一定程度、他人や自分に対する信頼が含まれている。たいへんな作業でもありますね——美術館にやってくる、それで、その美術館が歓迎してくれて、生産的な雰囲気なら、作業に取りかかることになります。ここにやってきたのは消費するため、単に食うためだけではない——共同で生産するために来たのであって、共同生産となると、武装解除して、自分が押されるのを許す、そういうことが必要になってきます。

たとえば、みなさんがぼくの《あなたの不確かな影（カラー）》[1]という作品に出会ったとします。部屋に入っていくと、床にちょっと明かりが灯っていて、壁には影が見える。影には何か引き込まれるような質がある——何か色がついていて、見ているとどこかきれいだったり。影が見えるのですが、その影が動くわけです。なのでチェックする、「これ私かな、私の影かな」って。腕を振ったりしてみて、わかるんですね、「そうだ、これ私だ」って。そうすると、何か別のことをしはじめるかもしれない。踊りはじめたり、自分の影と他の人の影を合体させたりしようとするかもしれない。でも自分にそういうことをさせる前に、信頼が基本テーマになっているような質問をいろいろとするかもしれない。「私は一人きりなんだろうか」とか「誰か私を見ている人がいるんだろうか」とか。誰か別の人がもう踊っているのなら、たぶん大丈夫なんだろう、と。もう子どもが遊んでいるのなら、みなさんが遊ぶのも容易になるわけです。

ここで面白いのは、みなさんを動かすのが影だというところです。気がつくと自分が壁の視座に立って動いている。壁と影がみなさんを動かしている。みなさんを押している。だから、みなさんはこのアート作品に関わっていっているわけですけど、作品のほうでもみなさんに関わってきているような感じがする——ひょっとするとその関わり方は、みなさん自身がまだ思考していない思考を言語化してくれるようなものかもしれない。作品が、まだみなさんの意識に到達していなかった感覚に構造をもたらしてくれる、そんなフィーリングをもつかもしれない。みなさんは「あ、このフィーリング知ってる」と言うかもしれない。「これは私だ、これは私の感じ方だ。今ならわかる。このフィーリング、なかなか言葉にできなかったんだけど、この出会いのおかげで、自分が何を感じてるのかわかる」。目の前のアート作品がみなさんの一部分を反映している、と言ってもいい。この反映というアイデアが好きなんです。アート作品が、みなさんのフィーリングをホスティング〔=受け入れて場を提供〕してくれている、というようなね。

ティム｜子どもたちが自分の影と遊ぶという話をしていましたよね。ぼくらは、子どもと呼ばれるこの存在たちに、遊ぶことを許している。もう一つぼくらが子どもたちに許すことがあって、それは、非人間存在たちが生命をもっていると想像してみることです。ウサギが言葉を話せるとか、鳥が階段を歩いて登り降りできるとか。そして、ぼくらの世界にはこういうことがもっと必要なんです——実を言うと、こういう考え方のほうが論理的だとぼくは思うんです。ちなみに、遊ぶのは人間存在だけではないですよね。他の動物も遊ぶし、さっき話した小さな鏡も、ある意味で遊んでいる。飼っているネコがいわゆる甘噛みをする、つまり、じゃれて軽く噛んできたりする。そういうとき、ネコはちょっとふしぎなことを言っているわけです——「これは噛んでるけど噛んでないってこと」と言っている。遊ぶというのは、矛盾するのを自分に許すことも含まれるんです。物体は単なるモノの塊なのではなくて、何かしら摩訶不思議なチカラをもっているかのようなんですね。

オラファー｜遊ぶとき、同時にぼくらは動いてもいる。運動というのは、ぼくらのものの見方が創り出されるときに、他の要素と合わさって本当に大事ですよね。たとえば散歩に出かけると、実はその運動がぼくらの視界を形づくっている。アイスランドでよく夏を過ごすのですが、風景の中を歩いていると、正面に山が二つ見えることがあります。見つめていると、二時間歩けば行けるのか、それとも二日間なのか、わからない。いったん動きはじめれば、片方の山が全然変わらないのが見えるので、歩いていくには丸一日かかるとわかる。最初は全然遠くないと思ったわけですけど。最初は風景のスケールがつかめなかったんですね。歩いて初めてスケールが明らかになった。そうして次に、身体の中にスケールを感じるんです。歩くうちに、片方の山は近くなってきて、もう片方はずっと地平線上にある、ということはつまり、実際には、小さな山が近くにあって遠くに大きな山がある。だから歩くときには、山と風景が身体を取り戻させてくれているかのようなんですね。

ティム｜そうそう！ 何についても言えることなのですが、考えるというのは、フィジカル（具体的・身体的）な行為なんです。誰にだって必ず自分なりの世界というのがある。腕の骨があって、それが脚の骨につながっていて、脚の骨は足の骨につながっていて、足の骨は床の骨につながっていて、床の骨は都市の骨につながっていて、都市の骨は有害ゴミ廃棄場の骨につながっていて、有害ゴミ廃棄場は地政学問題の骨につながっていて、メチャクチャな状況に巻き込まれているわけです。それはわかった、じゃあ自分は何がほしいのか？ 何をつくりたいのか？ オラファーの仕事を見ると、そういうヒラメキをもらうんですよね。ぼくらが何かを決めるとき、その決定は、まわりに何もない真空の中でおこなわれるのではないし、ぼくらはモノを自分の思いどおりあちこち勝手に突きまわしていいわけではない。モノのほうがぼくらを突き動かすという部分も、ちょっとあるんですね。ワインの飲み方はワインしだいで決まる——これこれこういうふうにグラスを手に持って、こういうふうにワインを注いで、こういうふうに空気に触れさせて、と。物体そのものが使い方を指示してくるかのようなんですね、ほとんど。モノと関係を結んでいく。自分ではない一つのモノ、その言い分に耳を傾ける、それが自分に影響するのを許す、そういうかたちで。コーラのボトルはこうやって持つんだ、と。ドアはこうやって持つんだ、と。ヴァイオリンはこうやって弾くんだ、ネコが八つ裂きにされてるみたいな音になったらいけないから、と。ぼくらはモノたちに音程を合わせていくし、モノがぼくらを調律してくることを許す。

オラファー―そういう駆け引き、ひょっとするとぶつかり合いかもしれないけど、その感覚がぼくは好きなんだな。アイデアって、そういうふうに思いつきますよね――ただ座って待っているだけではダメなんでね、つらいけど。アイデアを思いつくって、実はたいへんな仕事なんですね。絵にするのがすごく難しいこともある。単なるフィーリングでしかないからかもしれない、もしかすると。最初のステップは、アイデアの、そういうフィーリングというか感覚を、行為に変えていくこと。アイデアを思いついたとしますね。それを前に動かしていくために、ぼくはこんな問いかけをするかもしれない――「これ、どこから来たんだろう」「あ、腕の中にあるんだ」。次にこう問いかけるかも――「なんで腕の中にあるんだろう」「あ、これこれこういう理由でか」。セラピー的なアプローチですよね――というか、ひょっとすると瞑想のほうが近いかもしれない。呼吸に似ている。「お、腹の中にある。ちょっとぐるぐる動かせる」。次にスケッチを一枚、いや何枚もつくるかもしれない。これをすると、すごく自由になれたりする。次にちゃんとしたドローイングをつくる。それから次に小さい模型。次に、模型を木で試作するかもしれない。大きくしたり、半分のスケールにしたりする。やりながらいろいろと駆け引きしていくと、アイデアがだんだん行為になっていく。最終的には単なる行為ではない――この間ずっと、アイデアは、すでに行為ではあるんですね。〔でもそれに加えて〕アイデアは、出発点からずうっと一つの軌跡をたどっていったわけです。運動なんです。ぼくとしては、創造性というものは、こういった活動が世界にどういう帰結をもたらすか、ということなのではないかと言ってみたい。一つの作品が創造的なのは、それが周囲に対して何かをおこなうからだ、と。おかしな話ですけどね。ぼくらは、作品というのは仕上がってどこかで展示されたら終わり、とすぐ考えてしまうけど、実はまだ作品は旅の途中で、ひとりでに、人々に対して何かをしつづけていくんですね――突き動かしたりとかね、ティムが言ったみたいに。

ティム―すべては行為なんです。ぼくらの仕事は、この事実に対する意識をどんどん許容していくことです。この事実に対する意識が高まれば高まるほど、非暴力が増えて、戦争が減るんですから。

オラファー―それはすばらしいね、ティム。

コペンハーゲンDOX映画祭、デンマーク、コペンハーゲン
二〇一五年一一月一〇日

ティム｜オラファーとぼくとでずっと、地球温暖化について存在している膨大なデータ、膨大な科学的データをぼくらはどうやって手に入れるのかについてたくさん話をしてきているわけですが、問題は、どうやってそういうデータを生きるか、なんですね。

オラファー｜《アイス・ウォッチ》という、ぼくが地質学者のミニック・ロージングとやったアート作品があるんですが、その中の氷のブロックが、ぼくらがすでにデータとして知っていたことを、非常にうまくフィジカルに理解させてくれるんです。このブロックというのは、グリーンランド氷床から海に滑り落ちた巨大な塊です。海から拾い上げて、最初コペンハーゲンに、次にパリに持って行った。[2] 色は青っぽくて、出来てからだいたい一万年で、キシキシいうんです——内側に小さな気泡があって、氷が溶けると小さい破裂音がして、氷の中に封じ込められていた、本当にクリーンな空気を放散するんですね。横に立ってみると、実際すごく生き生きしている。「お、あのすごい氷見て！」なんてみんなが言っているのが聞こえました。それから次に手を当ててみて「冷たい！」と言う。これは面白いところです。というのも、彼らはもちろんこのことを、知的な意味ではすでに知っていたわけです。そうですよね？ 新しい情報は何もない——氷は冷たいものだ、と。でも、知的な意味で知っていたことと、フィジカルに触れたこととのすり合わせが、その瞬間に起きるわけです。自分が知っていたことと、フィジカルにつながるようになる。

それに実際には、ぼくらはいろんなことを知っているんです。データが伝えてくるようなことは全部知っているんですよね。でも身体知、つまり筋肉が知っている事柄、両手が知っている事柄、ぼくらがあらためて考えてみたりしないような事柄——そういう知は全部、説明されないまま放置されているようなところがある。それに、脳知と身体知がもっとうまくつながるようになれば、ぼくらのスキルや能力が——対人関係的(ソーシャル)にも——向上すると思うんです。もちろん、この二つが本当の意味で分離してしまったことは一度もないのですが、ぼくらが住む文化は、脳知のほうを優先する——脳が知っているのならそれで十分、というわけです。新聞で読んだよ——だからもう分かってるよ、と。それに氷って、かなりそのまんまのベタなものでもあるんです。グリーンランドではふつう遠くにあるものを間近から見ると、「あ、氷ってこんななんだ！何となく知ってはいたけど、実際はすごく違う！ すごく違う感じがする！」ってなる。近づいていって抱きついて、「あ、濡れた！抱きついたら濡れるだろうっていうのは知ってたけど、何ていうか、

フィジカルには知らなかった」と。すごく面白いですよね。

ティム｜ぼくらが、世の中に対して物申す——言われた人がすごく反発するような、「皿洗え！」とか、「地球温暖化解決しろ！」とか、その手のことを言う——のはもうやめるにしても、アートはただ単にそういうものにはならないのだとしても、アートはもっとずっと〈耳を傾ける空間〉とか〈音程を合わせていく空間〉に似たものである必要がある。もっと「自分がこの非人間存在と、つねにすでにフィジカルな関係性を結んでいるんだって気がついてた？」と。ぼくはシャツを着てズボンを履いていますよね——〔だから〕非人間存在はそこら中にいるわけです。ぼくの眉毛の中には小さな甲殻類がいる。この微生物叢（マイクロビオーム）というのがまるごと一つあって、ぼくの存在を維持してくれていて、DNAをぼくよりもいっぱいもっているんです。ぼくはすみからすみまで完全にティム・モートンなのではなくて〔他の要素も大量に入り込んでいる〕。実にホッとする、すばらしい話ですよ！　アートは、ぼくらがこういう事実を受け入れて気を楽にしたり、こういう考え方に環境適応したりするのを助けてくれるものであるべきなんです。

オラファー｜氷河の氷はぼくら人間と同じくらい活動的なんだということを考慮に入れると、氷の活動を受容する立場を取ることにもなる——氷のホスピタリティ〔＝こちらを迎え入れてホスティングしようとする性質〕を感じるわけです。

ティム｜こういう種類のホスピタリティというのは、ある種のホスティング空間に似ていて、感情移入が生じるプラットフォームなんだと思います。ある意味で、感情移入というのはそんな大げさな話ではない——誰かを好きになるとき、相手に感情移入しようと努力したりしないですよね？　特別な理由もなく氷の塊を見て「いいな」と思うとき、「さあ感情移入するぞ」なんて自分に言い聞かせる必要ないですよね？　特別な理由もなく「いいな」と思うというのは、すでに感情移入なんです——その氷はすでにこちらの中に入り込んでいて、自分の内側に小さな氷が刻印されているわけです。

オラファー｜アートの視点からすると、空間や現実を共同で創造するというアイデアは、すごくワクワクする——人々を活性化するわけですよね、一定の信頼を共有すること、その信頼を行使することを通じてね。とても美しいと思うんですよ、氷がぼくに触れてくるという事実は。あと、アーティストがアート作品の制作を、観客——「観客」と呼んでおくことにしましょう——の手にゆだねるということ、何が何でも観客を消費者に変えてやろうとするのではなくてね、それは大事なことでもあります。アートは人々を信頼するんです。アートは、「みなさんは本当は強くて、能力があって、自分の手でできるんですよ」と言うわけです。ぼくはそういうのがもっと必要だと思います。

ティム｜親密さというのがあるんですね。ぼくは氷のことを何もかも知っているわけではないし、氷のほうもぼくのことを何もかも知っているわけではないんですけど。ぼくが氷に触れるとき、それはぼくの、人間としての、人間型の触れ方である。それはどうしようもない。ぼくがそのことにじっと思いをめぐらせるとき、そる、聞いている、何かとインタラクションしている、そういう経験をしている瞬間には——全宇宙を征服してやろうなんて企んだりはしていないわけでしょう。

オラファー｜ティム、そういう状況の中で、アート作品はどういうことをしているんだと思う？

ティム｜何かをしているというよりも、もっといろんなことが含まれてきますよね。ぼくらは〈物事をする〉ということを、虚空に飛び込むみたいなふうに考える。でも何かをしているときは、必ずもっと大きなコンテクストの中でしているわけです。たとえば、喋るというのは、実は耳を傾けることですよね。バンドで演奏しているなら、共演している人たちに耳を傾けている——ジャズを演奏しているときはとくに。だから音程合わせの空間というものがあって、「する」行為はそこで生じている。何というか、完全にぼくではないような空間です。©（コピーライト）ティム・モートンというスタンプを押すわけにはちょっといかない。その空間がどこから出てきたのであってもね——ぼくの心の空間かもしれないし、身体の空間かもしれないし、両方の融合かもしれないわけですけど。

現実そのものが、何というか、ふしぎで、暫定的で、仮定法的な質をもっている。ぼくらが今の段階からすでにモノをそういうふうに理解できるといいんですけどね——氷自体がそもそも、ちょっとばかり暫定的だったり仮定法的だったりするんだ、と。完全には氷ではないんですね。最初から最後までずっと氷なわけではない。モノたちは、目に見える姿と完全に同じではない——にもかかわらず、それは、氷にアクセスするための、人間としてのぼくのやり方である、と。氷がぼくに触れているとき、氷のほうも、氷ヴァージョンのぼくみたいなのを、何かしらもっている。それで別にかまわないわけです。まさにそこで、相手の出方を見ながらお互いのまわりをグルグル回るみたいなことが起きる。だからぼくはオラファーの仕事が本当に大好きなんです——現実とは何なのか、それを決める作者としての権利、コピーライトをオープンにしていくことがテーマなわけですよね。氷も現実を決めているし、ぼくも決めているし、何かこう、そこではぼくと氷のあいだに親近性があるような、そういう空間がある。ぼくはこれ、政治的な行為だと思うんです。

オラファー｜もうひとつは、共有する、他の人たちとともに在る、という次元ですね。アートを見るというのはふつう、すごく個人的な活動だと思われている——みんな、美術館でただ一人の人が、孤独に一点の絵を見ているところを想像するわけです。でも、もちろんめったにそういうことは起きない。ほとんどいつでも人に取り巻かれている。混んでいて、行列ができていて、レストランで騒々しくしている人たちがいて……アート作品との出会いは、そのつど複雑な状況である、というのが実情なんです。だから開催場所が、こういうことを全部ホスティングするためにおこなっている努力も非常に関係してくる。

ティム｜公共の空間で、ちょっと内向的になって物を言わないということが、ぼくらにはもっと必要なんですよね。アートの展示室では——どんなものでもいいのですが、とにかく何かを見つめていチーズのブロックは氷のブロックではない。モノたちは完全に、自らがそうであるところのものであるわけです。他の何かに還元することは決してできないんです。かつアートは、単にこのことについて何かを教えてくれるだけではない――このことに対して文字どおり影響するんです。ごくごくストレートな話ですよ。絵の具をちょっと取ってキャンヴァスに載せる。それは一つの行為です。アートをやっているとき、みなさんは何をしているのか？　原因と結果の関係を積極的に壊している。それがみなさんのやっていることなんです。

オラファー――アートというのは、何かについて考えることと、行為――仮に「行為」と言っておきましょう――とのあいだの距離を研究するのにすごくうってつけの場所なんですね。考えること／すること。アイデア／行為。アート作品。小さいスケッチをつくる。メモを取る。最初のスケッチ。二番目のスケッチ。もっと大きいスケッチ。違う色。「うーん、うまくいかない」。模型をつくる。小さい模型、紙の模型。もっと大きい模型を、実物大でつくる。素材をテストする。ティムに電話して、「ティム、この模型で困ってるんだけど」と言う。そうするとキャッチボールになる。行ったり来たり、一歩一歩。すてきなプロセスです。アーティストであること、アイデアを握手や筆触（タッチ）に変えるなんていう贅沢ができるということ、それは本当に自由な気持ちになれます。

ティム――ぼくらが文化の中で抱えている大問題のひとつが、あらゆるものは堅固な実体をもっている、という思い込みです。この想定があらゆるものに影響している。ぼくらの社会空間に最初から組み込まれている――単に頭の中で考えただけのことではない。みなさんはひとつの哲学の中を歩き回っているわけです。哲学を食べている。哲学を飲んでいる。じゃあどうするか。ぼくらがかなり固く信じ込んでいる考えとして一つあるのは、何かが存在するのであれば、その何かは一貫してそこにあり続けるのでなければならない、というものです。でもオラファーとぼくは、実を言うと現実はそういうふうではないんだ、と決めました――そうではなくて現実は、何というか、グラグラした、暫定的な質をもっているんですね。あらゆるものがつねに動いている、突（つつ）かれなくてもね。量子のレベルまで降りていくと、実際モノたちは突かれなくても動いている――それは本当にすごいことです。このことを、説明してわかったつもりになるのではなくて、ただ受け入れたっていいじゃないですか？　アートというのは、ぼくらが実際にこの質を感じとれる場所です。モノたちが何であるのかを、しっかりつかまえたり把握したりすることはできない、そういうフィーリングを本当にもてる場所なんですね。そういう感覚のために、ぼくらが社会の中に取っておいてあるゾーン、それがアートです。かつ、これはとっても貴重です！　単に娯楽を提供したり何かを宣伝したりしようとするのではなくて、アートは、現実について正しい何か、大事な何かを教えてくれているんです。

オラファー――ありがとう、ティム――ぼくは、未来というものはあるんだ、ぼくらはもう未来にいるんだ、と信じるのが好きです。本当に好きなんですね。インスピレーションをくれるから、多様性の包摂（インクルージョン）、行為、参加、共有をホスティングするものだから。

サムスン美術館リウム、韓国、ソウル
二〇一六年九月二八日

は、それが感じ取れるんですね。もしかすると第六感と言ってもいいかもしれない。

ティム―フィジカルな感覚ですよね。哲学もフィジカルな行為なんです。幾何学みたいに。プラトンの学院（アカデメイア）の入口扉の上には、「……でない者がここを入るのは厳禁」というようなことが書いてあった。「……」の部分にはギリシア語の geometricos という単語があって、これは「幾何学に通じている」くらいの意味。どういう意味なのか？〈何かを知っている〉という意味なのか？〈何かについて一つの考え（コンセプト）をもっている〉という意味なのか？ちょっと違うんですね。当時、幾何学は数とは何の関係もなくて、文字どおりには、二つの器具を使って計算をするという意味だったんです。直定規とコンパスです。だからこれはすごくフィジカルで、大地と接しているというのが基本にある考えだったわけです。geo というのが「大地」で、metry は、面白い話ですが、「すたすた行く」とか「歩く」とかを表す言葉から来ている。だから、今でこそモノを測るという意味の言葉ですが、実は geometry はそもそも、むしろ歩きながら瞑想するということだったわけです。

オラファー―ぼくが言いたかったのもそういうフィーリングのことです。ぼくはアイデアを、立っていたり、止まっていたり、座って

オラファー―ティム、今日は来てくれてありがとう。一緒に並んで登壇してもらえるとくつろげます――それからオーディエンスのみなさん、みなさんがいてくださるおかげで、やはりくつろげます。最初に出席でも取ったらいいかもしれませんね。

ティム―出席、取りましょう。くつろぐ――これっていい言葉ですよね。オラファーの作品のまわりを歩くときにぼくが感じるフィーリングがそれです。ヒラメキをもらうと同時に気持ちがスーッと落ち着く。この場に招いてくれてありがとう。みなさんにも、ぼくらのトークを聴きにきてくださったこと、お礼を申し上げたいと思います。ぼくらの希望としては……何が達成できればいいことにしようか？

オラファー―ぼくもちょうどそのことを考えていました。今日の会が成功かどうかは、ここでぼくらが共有している状況しだいで決まるのではないかと思います。ぼくは足で床に触れようとしている。きみは半分くらい床に着いている。

ティム―うん、ぼくは半分くらい着いている。足の一方は空気に触れている。

オラファー―ぼくはすごく直感的に作業することがときどきあります。まだ言語化されてないアイデアができあがってくるときに

いたりするような何かとしては考えないんです。実は、いま生成の過程にある何かなんですね。だからこう言える――「このアイデアは三語で言い表せる」。うち一つは「オープン」かもしれないですね。

ティム｜そう、オープン。これ、ぼくは本気で考えていることなのですが――かつ、あんまりクレイジーに聞こえなければいいなと思うのですが――アートは未来からやってくるものである、かつ、ある意味ではそれ自体が未来である、と。アートというのは、あらかじめ想定できるようないっさいの未来の前に、ある種の未来性に向けて、可能性を開く（オープン）ことである、と。何かこう、オープンなフィーリングがあるわけですよ。オープンというのはすばらしい言葉です。モノたちが存在しているわけですが、そこに〔著作権を特定する〕©スタンプは押してないということだから。いろいろなモノや世界には、いっぱい穴が空いている感じがぼくにはするんですね――いろいろな世界にいっぱい穴が空いているから、ぼくらはお互いにコミュニティと連帯のフィーリングをもてるんだ、と。人間存在どうしだけではなくて、人間存在と非人間存在のあいだでも。

オラファー｜さっき、まだ言語化されてないアイデア――あるアイデアに対して、ぼくらが言語を見つけてやる、その直前の空間――という話をしましたが、あのときぼくが言いたかったのが、そういうオープンな空間のことだったんです。この空間にはぼくたちみんながアクセスできると思います。何かをほとんど意識はしているんだけど、まだ構造――言語など――を与えてない、そういうフィーリングをぼくらがもつ瞬間に注意することが大事だと思います。構造が与えられていないから、まだ生成過程という質や遊びっぽい感覚をもっているような、そんな瞬間ですね。ぼくにとっての作業の出発点になるようなことが、この空間でいろいろと起こります。それに、誰かがやってきてこう言うかもしれない。「あ、このフィーリング、私にもある。私は、自分のフィーリングに構造を与える、言葉を見つけてやる直前だった。あなたのアート作品を見たりティムの話を聴いていたら、私のフィーリングに構造が与えられていた。自分のフィーリングが反映されているなと感じた」。こう言うかもしれない、「というか実際には、見られている感じがした。私のフィーリングがアート作品に、未来に、見られていた」「未来に歩いて入っていったら歓迎された。私でいいんだっていう感じがした。気持ちの面で、私は展覧会に快く迎え入れられた」みたいなね。

ティム｜見られるというのは、全世界で一番すてきなことの一つかもしれない。何かしらトラウマで苦しんでいるときにはね――ぼくらは全員、どこかに何かしらの傷とかトラウマを内側に抱えているとぼくは思うんです。モノたちだってこのトラウマを抱えているかもしれない。どんなものでも何かしらの形や構造をもっているけど、構造そのものが一種の傷とかトラウマなんだと考えることもできるわけですから。だから、オラファーの鏡とか鏡の戯れの使い方、作品が実際にぼくらを見る仕方で――ぼくらは文字どおり、アート作品に見られたと感じるわけです。〈未来に見ら現在という瞬間に関して、すごく否定的な言い方をする哲学者はたくさんいますけど、ぼくはそんな言い方をしたって何の役にも立たないと思う。今あるのとはちょっとだけ違う仕方で何かをする可能性を想像する、いや単に夢見たり妄想したりするだけでもいいのですが、そういう可能性を自分に許す、そのための手立てをぼくらは見つけなくてはならない。オラファーの作品は、それを見つけるのを助ける仕掛けとして一つあるとぼくは思う。オラファーの作品は単に何かを表しているだけではない──実際には、ぼくらの背中を押してくれているんですね。

オラファー──ぼくがティムの書くものに惹きつけられてきた理由として、エコロジカルな共生の必要性を取り上げているということがあります。たとえば、気候をめぐるさまざまな問いをどう取り上げればいいのか？　そうすることの動機、モチベーションは何なのか？　動機はわかっています──ぼくらは解決策がほしいんですね。でもモチベーションのほうはもっとずっと難しい。特定のフィーリングを探しているときに「あ、自分は一人じゃないんだ」と気づいて、モチベーションが見つかることもあるかもしれない。

ティム──「スマイル」のフィーリングというのがあって、それとセットになっている。きみの作品には「スマイル」の質があるよね。今は大量絶滅の時代で、新聞を開くと必ず、何かに関して新しくゾッとするような統計が何かしら出ている。こういう統計は毎日変わるから、常にガンガン降ってくる。ずっとフォローしていくと混乱します。横っ面をバシバシ張られるようなもので。ぼくらには〈まだ……ない〉というのは美しい。

オラファー──〈アート作品は未来から送り込まれている〉というところをもう少し聞きたいんですけど。どういうこと？

ティム──さっききみが言っていた〈まだ……ない〉の話につながるんです。これは実に完璧で、美しくて、壊れやすいフィーリングだと思うし、ぼくらの世界の中では本当に保護してあげる必要がある。ぼくらはすごくさっさとこのフィーリングを削除してしまって、何だか知らないけれども現実的な計画（だと自分が思い込んでいるもの）を続けていく。いま現在、ぼくらはエコロジーへの意識が高まる時代に入りつつあって、じきに人間存在は、計算や政策や倫理や哲学やアートなどなど、あらゆることに非人間存在を含めていかなくてはならなくなります。自分がどこにいるのか、ぼくらにはもうよくわからなくなっていて、これは──自分がどこにいるのかよくわからないというのは──実はすごく重要なフィーリングなんですね。ふしぎですけど、ある場所にいるというのは、本当はそういうことなわけですから。ハードで、堅固で、厳格に境界が定まっていて、とか、本当はそういうことではないんですね。暫定的な、〈まだ……ない〉という質なんです。小さなモノたちをめぐって起きていることにちょっと似ている──量子力学では、小さなモノたちはチラチラゆらめいたり、振動したりしているように見えます。このチラチラゆらめく、振動するという質は、破壊してやろうと思えば実に簡単にできる。だから、この〈まだ……ない〉の質がそれ自体未来なんだという感じがぼくにはします。

ちょっと非暴力が必要なんです。本気でスマイルできるのなら、泣くこともできるとぼくは思います。今現在、そういうことがとても大事だと思います、正真正銘、悲しい心をもてるようになるということは——鬱状態（それならぼくはよく知っていますけど）のフィーリングというのではなくて、ある種軽やかな、やさしい質があって、これが悲しいとしたら、その唯一の理由は、つかまえることができないからなんですね。液体に似ている。物体というのは必ずしもソリッドではないとさっき言っていたけど、物体というのは液体に似ているんじゃないかというのがぼくの考え（アイデア）なんですよね——あんまりつかまえることができない。

オラファー｜モノたちをつかまえることはできないというアイデアはいいですね——モノたちを放っておいてやるというアイデアですよね。ぼくらは放っておいても気にならないのか、それとも、そうすることはある種の失敗と見なされてしまうのか？　子どもがいる人なら、自分の子どもたちを美術館に連れて行くとき、気がついてみるとすごくしつけ志向になっているということがありますよね。ぼくらが育てたいなと思うような探究心旺盛な子どもは、それじゃあできてこないわけなんですけど。《ベンチレーター》[3]というのは、天井からぶら下がっているアート作品で、これを見ると子どもたちはよく、走ったり飛び跳ねたりといった反応をする——ぼくも親なので、心配になってしまうんです！　子どもが走っているからというだけではなくて、子どもを勝手に走りまわらせている、放っておいているのを、他の親たちにどう思われるかなって。でもぼくらの子どもたちが探求してくれるのはありがたいことなんだって、子どもたち自身が感じるべきです。みんなで一緒にそういうふうに決めてしまいましょう。だって、エコロジーに関わるさまざまな問いを将来取り上げていく能力をもっているのは誰なのか？　探究心旺盛な子どもたちですよ！

1　《あなたの不確かな影（カラー）》（2010）は、白い壁に向けて色付きの光を照射するスポットライト五個から構成される。来場者がこの空間に入ると、彼らの影は、それぞれ色の違うシルエットが五つ並ぶというかたちで壁の上に現れる。

2　《アイス・ウォッチ》（2014）は二〇一四年にコペンハーゲンで、二〇一五年にパリで、二〇一八年にロンドンで展示された。詳しくは本カタログ八八–九一頁を参照。

3　《ベンチレーター》（1997）は、付属の電源ケーブルで天井から吊り下げられた扇風機。観客の頭上でぶらんぶらんと派手に揺れる。

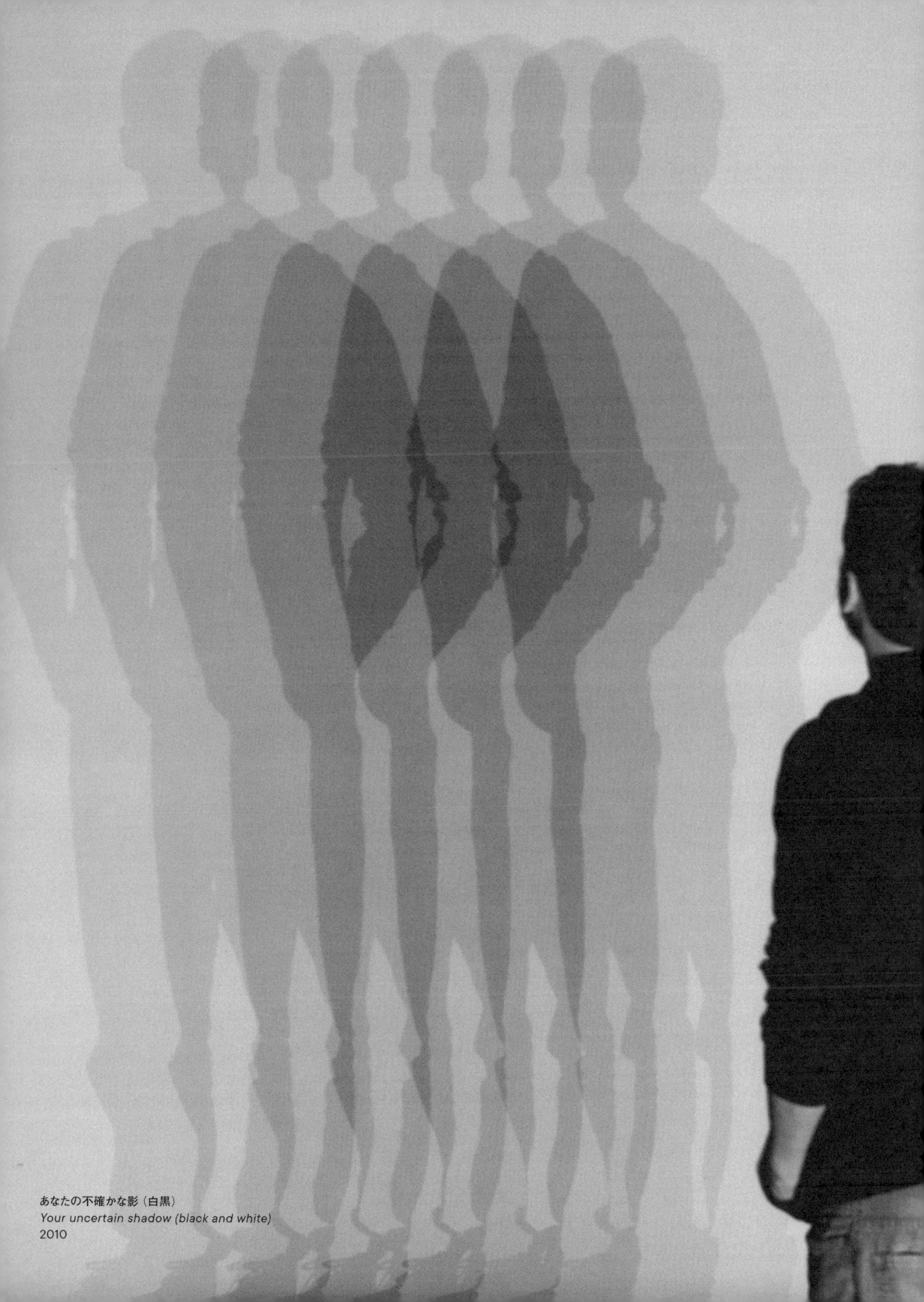

あなたの不確かな影（白黒）
Your uncertain shadow (black and white)
2010

I walked into the future and was welcomed: Olafur Eliasson and Timothy Morton in conversation

Philosopher Timothy Morton and Olafur Eliasson share an interest in how ideas take shape—and crucially, in how they shape us and the world we co-inhabit in an age of climate emergency. Morton is a Professor of English at Rice University in Houston and a key thinker in the field of Object-Oriented Ontology. His work has included a focus on ecological thinking, in the sense of acknowledging that our lives are fundamentally enmeshed with those of the other animate and inanimate, human and non-human beings on this planet. He coined the word *hyperobject* to facilitate thinking about ungraspably large but distinct phenomena like global warming. Over the last five years, Olafur and Tim have spoken together in public at museums and cultural events—at Moderna Museet, Stockholm, and the Copenhagen DOX Film Festival, Copenhagen, in the autumn of 2015 and at the Leeum Samsung Museum of Art, Seoul, in 2016—producing an ever-evolving conversation that orbits around their shared interests and concerns.

Moderna Museet, Stockholm
2 October 2015

Olafur | Tim, could you tell me something about the title of your book *Ecology without Nature*?

Tim | It's a very simple idea, actually. It seems to me that nonhuman beings—like bunny rabbits, rivers and mountains, even spoons and other assorted items of cutlery—are on the inside of social space. They are part of social space. There isn't a difference between me—a human being over here—and, say, a polar bear over there. And this means that social space was never completely, fully, thoroughly human in the first place. It has always been permeated with nonhuman beings—nonhuman beings that have all kinds of influences on us. One thing that really strikes me about your work, Olafur, is that it allows things that aren't us to have an influence on us. It's like an invitation to allow nonhuman beings to touch us. We are in this really interesting art museum now, where we allow ourselves to be a little bit more naive than sophisticated, modern-type people who think they are above the world, looking down on it. And this naiveté has a lot of wisdom. It has a rich quality of allowing ourselves to be moved.

When I look at your work, Olafur, the word that comes up in my mind is 'movement.' It's actually a pretty deep philosophical issue, the question of movement. Some philosophers are like, 'It doesn't really exist; it's just this thing that happens to things,' but I feel that movement is a very deep part of our world. Things move without being pushed—we know this now from quantum-mechanics-type experiments with tiny things. If you get a mirror that is really small—you can still see it, it's not atomic size—and you put it in a cold, isolated place it still moves even though nothing is pushing it. You can tell because it emits infrared light. This mirror—without actually being mechanically pushed—is shimmering. I get this feeling from your work that the object I am looking at is, for want of a better word, sort of alive—it's got this kind of shimmering quality.

Olafur | I love it. You said something like, 'you dare to let yourself be moved.' And to disarm yourself, to be non-defensive, to allow yourself to be moved does include a degree of trust or self-confidence. It's also hard work—you come to a museum and, if the museum presents a productive type of hospitality, you will be put to work. You are not here to consume, just to eat—you are here to co-produce, and co-production requires you to take the stance of disarming yourself and allowing yourself to be pushed.

Let's say you encounter my work *Your uncertain shadow (colour)*,[1] for example: you come into a room with some lights on the floor and you see a shadow on the wall. The shadow has some qualities that could captivate you—it has some colours and it's sort of lovely to look at. So you see the shadow and then the shadow moves. So you check, 'Is this shadow me? Is it my shadow?' You do things like wave your arms and then you see, 'Oh yes, it is actually me.' And so you might start to do other things. You might begin to dance or try merging your shadow with other people's shadows. But before you let yourself do those things, there are a number of trust-based questions you might ask: 'Am I alone?', 'Is anybody looking?' If someone else is already dancing, maybe it's okay. If a child is already playing with their shadow that makes it be easier for you to play too.

What is exciting here is how it is the shadow that makes you move; you find yourself moving from the perspective of the wall. The wall and the shadow are moving you. They're pushing you. So there you are, engaging with this work of art and you feel that the work is also engaging with you—and perhaps that it's doing so in a way that verbalises some of your as-yet unthought thoughts. You might find that the work brings structure to a feeling that had not yet arrived in your consciousness. You might think, 'Oh, I know this feeling.' You might say, 'This is me; this is how I feel; now I know. I was fumbling with this feeling, but now, because of this encounter, I know what I feel.' You could say that the artwork reflected a part of you. I like this idea of reflection. It is as if the artwork hosted your feeling.

Tim | You mentioned how children play with their shadows. We allow these beings called children to play and one of the things we allow them to do is to imagine that nonhuman beings are animated. Bunny rabbits can talk and birds can walk up and down staircases. And we need more of this in our world—in fact, I believe it's actually more logical to think this way. By the way, it's not just human beings that play. Other animals play too and this little mirror I was talking about is also kind of playing. When your cat gives you what is called a nip, a playful bite, the cat is saying something weird—the cat is saying 'this is a bite and this is not a bite at the same time.' Playing involves allowing yourself to be contradictory. It's like how an object is not just a lump of stuff, but also has some mojo to it.

Olafur | When we play we also move, and movement is such an important co-creator of how we see things. If we go for a walk, for example, that movement really shapes our perspective. In Iceland, where I often spend my summers, when you walk in the landscape you sometimes see two mountains in front of you. When you look at them, you wonder whether they are a two-hour or two-day walk away. Once you start to move, you see that one of the mountains is not changing at all so you know that it will take a whole day to go there, even though you'd first thought it wasn't far at all. At first you didn't grasp the scale of the landscape; it was walking that allowed the scale to become apparent. Then you feel it in your body. As you walk, sometimes one mountain gets closer while the other remains on the horizon, which means they're actually a small mountain nearby and a bigger one far away. So when you walk it is as if the mountains and the landscape are actually giving your body to you.

Tim | Yes! Thinking, like everything else, is physical. Thoughts are almost like physical beings. You have to have a world, you know. You have to have an arm bone that's connected to the leg bone and the leg bone's connected to the foot bone and the foot bone's connected to the floor bone and the floor bone's connected to the city bone and the city bone's connected to the toxic waste dump bone and the toxic waste dump bone's connected to the geopolitical problem bone and I'm in a hell of a mess. So now that we know that, what do we want? What do we want to make?

That's the inspiration I get from your work, Olafur. It makes us more conscious of the fact that we don't make decisions in a void and we don't get to push stuff around exactly how we want. Stuff, a little bit, pushes us. How to drink a glass of wine depends on the wine—this is how you hold the glass; this is how you pour the wine; this is how you let it breathe—it's almost like the substance itself is telling you how to use it. You are relating to a thing that isn't you by kind of listening to it, by allowing the thing to affect you. This is how you hold the Coke bottle. This is how you hold the door. This is how you play a violin so it doesn't sound like a cat being torn. We tune to things and we let them tune us.

Olafur | I like this sense of negotiation, or even friction. That's how we get ideas—not by just sitting and waiting, sadly. It's actually hard work to get an idea. Sometimes it's very hard to draw because it's just a feeling, maybe. The first step is how to take that feeling or sense of an idea and turn it into an action. I have an idea and in order to move it ahead I might ask, 'Where did it come from? Where is the idea actually sitting in me?', 'Oh, it's in my arm.' Then I could ask, 'Why is it in my arm?', 'Oh it is because this and that.' It's kind of a therapeutic approach—or maybe it's more like a contemplative approach. Like breathing. 'Oh, it's in my belly and I can move it around a bit.' Then I might make a sketch or maybe many sketches. This can be very liberating. Then I make a proper drawing. And then a little model. Then I might try out the model in wood. I make it bigger, half-scale. As I negotiate along the way, the idea gradually becomes an action. It's not just action at the end—it is action already, all the way along. The idea already had a trajectory from the beginning. A movement. And I would suggest that creativity lies in the consequences this activity has on the world, that, funnily enough, what makes a work creative is what it does to its surroundings. We tend to think a work is done once it is finished and exhibited somewhere, but, in fact, it is still on a journey and it goes on by itself doing things to people—pushing them, as you said.

Tim | Everything is acting. Our job is to allow more and more awareness of that fact, because more and more awareness of that fact equals more nonviolence and less war.

Olafur | That's fantastic, Tim.

Copenhagen DOX Film Festival, Copenhagen, Denmark
10 November 2015

Tim | Olafur and I have been talking a lot about how we have all this data about global warming, all this scientific data, but the question is: how do you *live* that?

Olafur | The blocks of ice in *Ice Watch*, an artwork I did with geologist Minik Rosing, are very good at making us understand physically what we already knew as data. They are huge chunks that fell off the Greenlandic ice sheet into the sea. We fished them out and brought them first to Copenhagen and then to Paris.[2] They are bluish, they are about ten thousand years old, and they are crackling—there are small air bubbles inside, and when the ice melts they make a little pop and emit this really clean air that has been encapsulated within the ice. When you stand by the ice it's actually very lively. I heard people saying, 'Oh, look at this amazing ice!' And then they'd put their hand on it and say, 'It's cold!' Which is interesting, because obviously they already *knew* that intellectually, right? No new information—ice is cold. But a calibration between what they intellectually knew and what they physically touched happened in that moment. They became physically connected with what they knew.

And we do actually know a lot. We know all the things the data tells us. But somatic knowledge, the things that muscles know, the things that hands know, that we don't think about—all of that knowledge is somewhat unaccounted for. And I think we get more skilled and capable—socially also—when we have a better connection between our brain knowledge and our somatic knowledge. Of course they were never really disconnected, but the culture in which we live prioritises brain knowledge—as long as your brain knows something, it's enough. I read it in a paper—been there done that. The ice is also quite literal. Seeing something up close that would normally be far away in Greenland, you go like, 'Oh, this is what the ice looks like! I kind of knew this but it's actually very different! It feels very different!' You go and hug it and then you say, 'Oh, I got wet! I knew that I would get wet if I hugged it, but somehow I didn't know physically.' This is so interesting.

Tim | If we are going to stop trying to tell people stuff—you know, stuff that usually makes people defiant like 'Do the dishes!', 'Solve global warming!', that kind of stuff—if art isn't just going to be like that, then it needs to be about something much more like a kind of listening or tuning space, more about 'Have you noticed that you are always already having a physical relationship with this nonhuman being?' I am wearing a shirt and I am wearing pants—

nonhuman beings are everywhere. There are tiny little crustaceans in my eyebrows. There is this whole microbiome that's keeping me existing, and it has more DNA than I do. I am not completely Tim Morton all the way through, and that is a wonderful relief! Art should help us to relax into or get ourselves acclimatised to that.

Olafur | When you consider that the glacier ice is as active as you yourself are, you also put yourself in a position to receive the activity of the ice—to feel the hospitality of the ice.

Tim | I think that this kind of hospitality, like a kind of hosting-space, is a platform for empathy to happen. In a way, empathy isn't such a big deal—when you're falling in love with somebody, do you have to make yourself empathise with them? When you are appreciating, for no particular reason, a block of ice, do you have to say to yourself, 'Now I will empathise?' To appreciate for no reason is already to empathise—the ice already got inside you and now you have a little ice imprinted there inside you.

Olafur | From the perspective of art, this idea of co-creating space or reality is a very exciting idea—you activate people through exercising a degree of shared trust. It's very beautiful, the fact that the ice touches me. And for an artist to hand over production of the artwork to the—we'll call them the 'viewers'—instead of insisting on turning them into consumers, is important, too. Art trusts people. It says, 'You are actually strong and capable and can do it yourself.' And I think we need more of that.

Tim | There is this intimacy even though I don't know everything about the ice and the ice doesn't know everything about me. When I touch the ice, that's my human, anthropomorphic touch of the ice. And I can't help that. When I speculate about it, that's my human way of accessing the ice. When the ice is touching me, it too has some kind of ice-omorphic version of me. And it's not a big deal. There's a weird diplomatic dance that happens right there. This is why I really love your work, Olafur—it's about releasing copyright control on who gets to decide what reality is. The ice is deciding and I'm deciding and there's this space where we have an affinity for one another. I think that's a political act.

Olafur | Another dimension is that of sharing, of being together with other people. Looking at art is usually thought of as a very individual activity—people imagine a single person looking at a painting, alone in a museum. But, obviously, that seldom happens. You are almost always in crowd; it's busy; there is a line; there are people in the restaurant making noise...the truth is that each encounter with an artwork is a complex situation. So it's also very much about the effort that the setting makes to host all this.

Tim | We need public spaces where we can be a little bit introverted and quiet. In an art gallery—at least in a moment when you're experiencing whatever it is that you are looking at or hearing or interacting with—you are not plotting to dominate the universe.

Olafur | Tell me, Tim, what do you think an artwork is doing in this particular situation?

Tim | It's more inclusive than doing. We think about doing things as a leap into the void. But when you're doing stuff, you're always doing it in some bigger context. It's like how when you speak what you are really doing is listening. If you're playing music in a band you're listening to the people you are playing with—especially if you're playing jazz. So there is some kind of attunement space in which the doing is happening, some space that is not exactly me. I can't really put a Tim Morton copyright stamp on it, wherever it's coming from—my psychic space or the physical space or some kind of fusion of the two.

Reality itself has this kind of strange, tentative, subjunctive quality to it. If only we could see that things were like that already, in fact—that ice is already a little bit tentative or subjunctive. It's not exactly ice: it's not exactly what it is all the way down. Things aren't exactly as they seem—and yet, at the same time, a block of cheese is not a block of ice. Things are exactly what they are. They are not reducible to anything else. And art is not simply telling you something about this—it's literally affecting it. It's perfectly straightforward. You take a piece of paint and you put in on a canvas. That's an action. What are you doing when you are doing art? You are actively messing with cause and effect is what you are doing.

Olafur | Art is a very good place to study the distance between thinking about something and—let's call it 'action.' Thinking; doing. Idea; action. Work of art. You do a little sketch. You make a note. First sketch. Second sketch. Bigger sketch. Different colours. 'Ugh, that doesn't work.' Make a model, a small model, a paper model. Make a bigger model, on a one-to-one scale. Test materials. Call Tim and say, 'Tim, I have a problem with this model.' And then ping-pong; back and forth; step by step. It's a lovely process. And it's so liberating to be an artist and have the luxury of turning an idea into a handshake or a touch.

Tim | One of the big problems we have in our culture is the assumption that everything is solid. It affects everything. It's hardwired into our social space—it's not just an idea in our head. You're walking around in a philosophy. You're eating a philosophy. You're drinking a philosophy. So what are we going to do? One idea that we have quite strongly is that if something exists it must be consistently present. But Olafur and I have decided that's not how reality actually is—instead it has this wavering, tentative quality. Everything is constantly moving, even without being pushed. When you get down to the quantum level things are actually moving without being pushed—and that's really extraordinary. Rather than explain it away, why not just accept it? Art is a place where we can actually sense this quality, a place where we can really feel that we can't hold on to or grasp what things are. Art is the one zone we have reserved in our society for that sensation. And it's very precious! It is telling us something true, something important about reality, rather than just trying to entertain us or promote something.

Olafur | Thank you, Tim—I like believing that there is a future, and that we are already in it. I like this so much because it brings me inspiration, and because it hosts inclusion, action, participation, and sharing.

Leeum Samsung Museum of Art, Seoul, Korea
28 September 2016

Olafur | Thank you for being here, Tim. I feel comfortable on the stage with you at my side—and I also feel comfortable with all of you in the audience being here. Maybe we should start by doing a little presence check with everybody.

Tim | Let's do that presence check, Olafur. Comfortable—that's a good word, isn't it? It's a feeling that I get when I walk around your work. It's a feeling of being both inspired and soothed at the same time. I'm grateful to you for having me here. And I'd like to thank all of you for coming to listen to us talk. I hope we can...what do I hope we can do?

Olafur | I was just wondering that. The success of this depends, I think, on our shared situation here. I'm trying to touch the floor with my feet. You are halfway there.

Tim | Yes, I'm halfway there. One of my feet is touching the air.

Olafur | I sometimes work in a very intuitive way. You can sense when a not-yet-verbalised idea is shaping itself. Maybe I could also call it a gut feeling.

Tim | It is a physical sensation. And philosophy, too, is a physical act. Like geometry. Over the door to Plato's academy was written something like, 'Don't even think about coming in here unless you are,' and then there is a Greek word, *geometricos*, which means sort of 'geometried up.' What does that mean? Does it mean knowing something? Does it mean having a concept of something? No, not exactly. In those days, geometry was nothing to do with numbers at all, it was literally to do with using two instruments to do calculations: a straightedge and a compass. So it was actually very physical, and the idea was to somehow be close to the earth. The word *geo* is 'earth' and *metry*, funnily enough, comes from a word for like 'pacing' or 'walking.' So before geometry turned into a word for measuring things it was really something more like walking meditation.

Olafur | That's the feeling I was talking about. I don't look at an idea as something that's standing or stopped or sitting; it's actually something which is in the process of becoming. So I can say, 'I think this idea could be said using three words.' Maybe one word can be 'open.'

Tim | Open, yes. I truly think—and I hope this doesn't sound too crazy—that art comes from the future and, in a way, that it sort of *is* the future. That art is the opening up of the possibility for a kind of future-ness before any kind of predictable future. There is this open feeling. Open is a great word, because it means that things exist but don't have a copyright stamp on them. I feel like things are perforated and worlds are perforated—and that it's because worlds are perforated we can have a feeling of community and solidarity with one another. Not just among human beings, but also between human beings and nonhuman beings.

Olafur | When I mentioned not-yet-verbalised ideas—the space just before we find language for an idea—I wanted to address that open space. I think we can all access it. It's important to pay attention to those moments where we have a feeling that we are almost conscious of but have not yet given a structure—like language—so there is still an in-process quality or a sense of playfulness to it. A lot of the things that I work on happen in this space. And somebody might come along and say, 'Oh, I have that feeling, too. I was almost at the point of giving my feeling a structure, finding words for it. Now, when I was looking at your work of art or listening to Tim speak, my feeling was given structure. I felt my feeling was reflected.' They might say, 'I actually felt seen. My feeling was seen by the artwork, by the future.' You know, 'I walked into the future and I was welcomed. I felt that I am good enough. I was emotionally welcomed to the exhibition.'

Tim | Being seen might be one of the nicest feelings in the whole world. When you suffer from some kind of trauma—and I think we all, in some way, have some kind of wound or trauma inside us. Even things might have this trauma, because everything has some kind of form or structure and you could think about structure itself as a kind of wound or trauma. So, Olafur, with your use of mirrors and the play of mirrors and the way in which the pieces actually see us—we feel seen, literally, by the artwork. Being seen by the future, that's beautiful.

Olafur | Can you say more, Tim, about this idea that a work of art has been sent from the future? How is that?

Tim | It goes back to this not-yet feeling that you are talking about, Olafur. I think it is a such a perfect, beautiful, fragile feeling and it really needs to be preserved in our world. We are very quick to delete this feeling so that we can get on with whatever we think our practical project is. Right now we are entering an age of ecological awareness when human beings will have to include nonhuman beings in their calculations and policies and ethics and philosophy and art and everything. We don't know exactly where we are anymore, and this is a very important feeling, actually—not knowing exactly where you are—because, in a strange way, that's exactly what being in a place really is. It isn't really this kind of hard, solid, rigidly bounded thing; it's this kind of tentative, not-yet quality. A little bit like what happens with tiny things—in quantum physics, tiny things seem to be shimmering or vibrating. And this shimmering, vibrating quality is so easy to destroy. So I feel like this not-yet quality *is* the future.

Many philosophers talk in a very negative way about the present moment, but I don't think this is helpful at all. We need to find a way to imagine or even just dream or fantasize or allow ourselves the possibility of doing something a little bit different from what we have now. I think your work, Olafur, is a one device that helps us to do that. Your work isn't just representing something—it's actually encouraging us.

Olafur | One of the reasons that I have been drawn to your writing, Tim, is because you address the need for ecological coexistence. How to, for instance, address climate questions? What are the motives, the motivation? We know the motive—we want solutions. But the motivation is much harder. When looking for that particular feeling we might find motivation by realising, 'Oh, I am not alone.'

Tim | It comes with this feeling of 'smile' a little bit. There is a 'smile' quality to your work. We are in an age of mass extinction and every time you open the newspaper there is some horrible new statistic about something. These statistics change every day, so you are constantly being hammered by them. It's confusing to keep up with; it's like being slapped about. We need a little nonviolence. I think that when you can smile for real, then you can cry. I think that's very important right now, learning how to have this genuine heart of sadness—which is not necessarily a feeling of depression (which I know very well) but has a kind of light, tender quality that's sad only because you can't hold onto it. It's more like a liquid. You were talking about how objects are not necessarily solid, and my idea is that they might be more like liquids—you can't really hold on to them.

Olafur | I like this idea of not holding on to things—of letting go. Do we feel comfortable letting go, or is that seen as a kind of failure? Those of us who are parents sometimes find ourselves being very discipline-oriented when we bring our children into museums, even though this doesn't nurture the explorative children we'd like to bring up. When children see an artwork like *Ventilator* [3] swinging from the ceiling, they often respond by running and jumping—and then I, as a parent, get nervous! And not only because they are running, but because the other parents might judge me for letting them run, for letting go. But let's together decide that our children should feel appreciated when they explore, because who is it that will have the capacity to address ecological questions in the future? Explorative children!

1 *Your uncertain shadow (colour)*, 2010, consists of a line of five coloured spotlights directed at a white wall; when visitors enter the space, their shadows appear on the wall as arrays of five silhouettes, each with a different colour.

2 *Ice Watch*, 2014, was presented in Copenhagen in 2014, in Paris in 2015, and in London in 2018. See pages 88–91 for more details.

3 *Ventilator*, 1997, is a fan that is suspended from the ceiling by its own cable; it swings wildly through the space above viewers' heads.

14名が考えるスタジオ・オラファー・エリアソンのサステナビリティ計画

ベルリンで一九九五年に設立されたスタジオ・オラファー・エリアソン（以下、スタジオとする）は、幅広い人材から成るチームを擁している。職人、専門技術者、建築家、アーキヴィスト、美術史家、ウェブ／グラフィックデザイナー、映画作家、料理人、事務担当などだ。彼らの仕事はエリアソンとともにアート作品、プロジェクト、展覧会を開発・制作・設置すること、また実験・アーカイブ化・リサーチ・出版・広報など。以下は、スタジオの活動をもっとサステナブルなものに変える作業に取り組んでいる大勢の人々の中の数名とおこなった会話からの抜粋である。読みやすくなるよう編集を加え、テーマ別に並べかえてスタジオが掲げるサステナビリティ計画の全貌を示してある。

発言者（登場順）

オラファー・エリアソン｜アーティスト
セバスチャン・ベーマン｜スタジオ・オラファー・エリアソン、デザインチーム長、スタジオ・アザー・スペーシズ共同設立者
マルガレート・ルッツ｜デザイン部門、事業開発
ジェフリー（ジェフ）・ガリソン｜リサーチ／広報部門、エディター／コピーライター
ミリアム・トマス｜開発制作チーム長
ローレン・マウラー｜シェフ
ブリッタ・カンペ｜窓口部門、スタジオ・エリアソンでの日常的なサステナビリティへの取り組み担当
ラベア・ヴェルテ｜開発制作チーム、部門コーディネーター
キム・クラソン｜開発制作チーム、管理担当
ケアスティン・パレルモ｜開発制作チーム、プロジェクトマネージャー
カヤナ・ヴァーグナー｜展覧会部門、アート作品コーディネーター
アンナ・エングベリ＝ピーダセン｜リサーチ広報部門長
ヴァーニャ・ザンコ｜オラファーの実務アシスタント
キャロリン・エッゲル｜展覧会部門長、「ときに川は橋となる」展責任者

全体像

オラファー｜一点のアート作品は価値やアイデアを具現している。そこには作者の――たとえばサステナビリティや気候についての――信念が反映されている。アートがテーマとして取り上げることと、アートのつくられ方とはシンクロしていなければいけないとぼくは思う。内容と、アート作品の制作法とを切り離すことはできないというのがぼくの考えだ。アート作品に関して日々さまざまな選択をおこなう際には、ぼくは今言ったような事柄を念頭において作業することが（いつも可能とはかぎらないが）ますます多くなっている。

　ぼくらはみんな地球に対する責任を共有していて、ぼくらのスタジオもその枠の外にいるわけじゃない。小さくてもできることが誰にでも何かしらある。ぼくらみたいな小さめの機関・企業であっても。サッカークラブにだって何かできる。誰にだって。スタジオでやっていることは二つ。プロジェクトや広報を通じて気候危機の意識を高めること、それと、自分たちの運営形態を向上させることに焦点を合わせている。大事な点だけど、ぼくらはまだプロセスの初期段階にいることは言っておかないといけない。倫理的な責任やデータを自分のこととして受け入れると同時に、一つのスタジオとして引き続き存在していきたいという野心もある。うまくバランスを取っていくこと、今言ったような要素がお互いにどういう関係にあるかを見定めることが中心課題だ。

セバスチャン｜たとえば一〇年前には、自分たちのアート作品をもっとサステナブルなやり方でつくる必要があるということは、それほどはっきりしていなかった。当時は、アートのアイデアがある、ぼくら全員がすごくいいと感じる、じゃあ形にしてみよう、というふうに考えていた。自分たち以外の地球にとって、それが実際にはどういう意味があるのかには、あまり関心がなかったんじゃないか。そういった側面は、ぼくらのまわりを取り巻く文化全体の中から自然に出てきた。

　ぼくらは一年半前、この問題について話し合うだけではとにかく十分じゃない、と判断するところまできた。本当に何かを実現しようとするなら、ぼくらのフットプリント〔＝天然資源消費量〕を削減するという仕事を実際にやらなくちゃいけない。自分たちのフットプリントを改善するような計画や試作品を開発して、他の人もツールとして使えるようにするというのがぼくらのアイデアだった。ぼくらはこれを、他のデザイン／プロジェクトとまったく同じように構造化した――基本コンセプトと目標を設定することから始めたんだ。この目標というのは、ぼくらの活動をあらゆる観点から本気で検討することだった。ゴミの管理から始まって、制作の方法、どうやってプロジェクトをプランニングするか、いろいろな国にどれくらい旅行するか、ものを現地にどうやって届けているかというところまで。ぼくらの目標は、プロジェクトのスケジュールや予算を組むだけじゃなくて、自分たちが環境にどういうインパクトを与えるかを計算し評価すること――どこで、何を改善できるかを見きわめること――だ。プロジェクトが与えるインパクトは、ぼくらがそのプロジェクトをそのまま進めていくかどうかの決定に影響する。

　もっとサステナブルになるということのプロセスは、自分にとって快適なゾーンの外に出ること、はっきり言えば現実の世界へと入っていくことを意味する。いろいろと妥協しないといけないが、同時にまた、自分がどこから来てどこへ行くのかも常に明確にしておかなくちゃいけない。こういう種類の葛藤をぼくらは今、たとえば輸送の分野でサステナブルな解決策を実施しようとするときに感じる。自分の倫理的基準をただ持ち込んでもダメだ。違う解決策に対してオープンであること、対話を始めることが必要だ。だから葛藤はすごくポジティヴなものでありうる。

オラファー｜気候をめぐる問いかけのコンテクストをちょっと説明しておいたほうがいいかもしれない。実を言えば、この問いかけはぼくの仕事の中に昔からある。ただし以前のぼくはこの問題に対して、今とは違う考え方、語り方をしていた。

前は、自然というものが存在しているんだ、人間には手の届かない何かがあるんだ、と考えていた。でも、ブルーノ・ラトゥールが言っているとおり「外部はない」、未発見の自然とか天然資源の蓄えなんてない。ここ一〇年くらいでそのことを実感するようになった。なので、今アイスランドの話をするときは、アイスランドの自然じゃなくて風景の話をする。ぼくは何年もアイスランドの風景を写真に撮っている。二〇〇七年、《氷河おう穴のシリーズ》という写真シリーズをやって、表面から溶け出した水が氷に食い込むことで氷河の中にできる深い立坑をドキュメントした。それから《ヨクラ・シリーズ》(2004)があった。アイスランドのヨクラ川が、新しい水力発電所をつくるためにダムで堰き止められる前は元々どう流れていたかをドキュメントする作品。なので、ぼくは自然の消滅や風景、気候に昔からずっと関心をもっているし、何年も前からこういった関心を語る仕方に磨きをかけてきている、と言っていいと思う。

二〇〇三年に《ウェザー・プロジェクト》を創ったとき――テート・モダンに巨大な太陽を設置したんだけど――ぼくにとって気候はまだ作品のテーマではなかった。大気圏や気象系、そして気象状況を〔人工的に〕構築することがテーマだった。ぼくらが社会というコンテクストの中で自分たちをどう組織しているか、どういうふうに天気を共通の参照点として使っているかがテーマだった。今現在このアート作品のことを考えるとき、気候というコンテクストの中で考える人が多い。ぼくとしてもそれは歓迎する。ぼくにとって、あるアート作品の成功を測る尺度の一つは、それが起源から〔違う場所に〕旅する能力をもっているかどうか、ずっと後になってものの考え方や見方が変わっても、引き続き現代的な意味合いをもっているかどうか、だ。

もっと最近では、ミニック・ロージング〔地質学者〕と《アイス・ウォッチ》という公共〔空間への〕大型介入を創った。このプロジェクトに向けてグリーンランドのフィヨルドで氷のブロックを集めたんだけれども、写真ではその美しさはあまり伝わらない。とにかく信じられないくらい美しいんだ！ こういったブロックに触れて、冷たさを感じる――活き活きした青と白の色調を見て、冷たさを感じる――そうすると知覚の中の、実に強力な帯域が活性化する。ミニックとぼくは二人とも科学とデータの価値を熱烈に信じているけれど、多くの場合、単独では行動を駆り立てるほどの力はないという点に関して同意してもいる。有無を言わせない迫力のある物語とか、身体に直接働きかけるような経験とかを使えば、データが違ったふうに感じられることもありうる。

ジェフ｜広報や渉外は《アイス・ウォッチ》の核だった。同時に、そういう露出がきっかけになってソーシャルメディア上では、気候変動への意識を高めるために二酸化炭素を消費するのは賢いことかどうかをめぐって活発なやり取りが生まれた。ぼくらはこのイシューにずばり応答して、こう言うことに決めた――確かにこれ〔＝《アイス・ウォッチ》〕は一定の二酸化炭素を排出しますし、五五トンもの二酸化炭素を消費しました、でも、それならふつうアート作品のそういった側面はどうして話題に上らないのかを話し合おうじゃありませんか、と。

マルガレート｜スタジオでは、気候変動の重大さをようやく掴みはじめたところだと思う。このプロセス全体の中でわたしたちが学んだことの一つ、すぐに思いつくような解決策は、あまりサステナブルではないことが多い、という点がある。自分たちのゴミはどこへ行くのかとか、燃料はどこから来るのかとか、エネルギーはどこから来るのかといったことを調べはじめたんだけれど、サステナブルな解決策に見えて本当はそうじゃないことが時々ある。

ミリアム｜本当に、スタジオで新しく植物が育っていくみたいだった。最初はちょっとたいへんだったし、あまり楽しくなかった。誰にとっても、むしろ重荷みたいなものだった。

でもその後、全員がワクワクしたり楽しく取り組んだりするプロジェクトになった。サステナビリティというトピックや新しい素材から新しいアイデアが生まれてきた。ここにはつくる上でのポテンシャルがたくさんあると思う。確かに制約される面はあるけど、新しい開発、新しいリサーチ、新しい素材を意味してもいる。それに、オラファーにとっては刺激的だった。〔スタジオ・エリアソンでつくられる〕アートに対して影響を与えた。同じ目的に別の素材を使ったというだけのことではなくて、今のわたしたちは新世代のアート作品を開発している。

セバスチャン――スタジオでは、プロジェクトが気候に与えてしまうインパクトの埋め合わせとして自分たちにできる代償措置をいろいろと組織して、そのためのモデルを確立している。

何より第一にぼくらは、スタジオの創造力そのものを利用して、さらにいっそう考えを深め人材を投入しつつ、プロジェクトのインパクトを削減する方法を探していく。もちろんこれにはお金がかかるが、代償措置の一つの形ではある。

第二に、スタジオが広い層に語りかけることができ、高い評価を得ていることを利用して、他の企業やパートナーがよりサステナブルになる手助けをし、彼らの声を外の世界に届けていく。それと同じ広報力を使って、論文を書いたりシンポジウムやカンファレンスに参加したりして、人々をどんどん巻き込んでいく。

第三に、ぼくらはスタジオのインフラストラクチャーがよりサステナブルになるよう改善投資をしていて、たとえば太陽光パネルをスタジオの屋根に取り付けたり、スタジオの前に電気自動車用の充電スタンドを設置したりしている。こういった種類の変化に投資をすると、もちろん見返りもある。一方的にお金を使うだけじゃない。たとえばエネルギーコストにポジティヴな効果がもたらされる。

第四に、ぼくらと考え方が似ている企業や思想家に財政支援を提供する。彼らはサステナブルなプロジェクトを開発中だがまだ初期の段階にあり、自分たちのプロジェクトを市場で売っていくには早すぎて、支援を必要としている。うちのスタジオにとって、自分たちの創造力やオラファーの名前を利用して、この領域で仕事をしている企業や人々を支援するのは大事なことだ。

これからの一〇年でサステナブルなスタジオになっていくためには、ぼくらはアートをつくるやり方、またコミッション・ワークや展覧会をひっくるめた何もかもをつくるやり方を、もっと根本から定義しなおす必要がある。ぼくらが労働時間や努力の面で収入の五パーセントをサステナビリティに費やすようになり、何であれプロジェクトや展覧会を構想しプランニングするやり方全体にサステナビリティが必ず組み込まれるようにしたい。これを実現するためにぼくらは、各部門から一名を選んでサステナビリティ推進活動を統括させ、サステナビリティを専門に担当する立場を新設している。すべての企業が収入の五パーセントを投資したら巨大な額のお金になるし、これを正しく使えば途方もないインパクトを与えて、ごく短時間のうちに状況を改善できる可能性がある。

オラファー――二〇三〇年までに、ぼくらのカーボン・フットプリント〔＝二酸化炭素排出量〕を五〇パーセント削減できるはず。うちみたいな小さい企業にとってはすごい量だ。たぶん、それでも十分ではないだろうけど……。社会の一部であること、気候運動の一部であることはぼくにとって大事なことだし、スタジオもその一部であってほしい。ぼくらが共通の目標をもって、それを目指して全員で奮闘するのでありたい。ミクロな活動だけで十分だなんて幻想はちっとも抱いていないけど、ミクロな活動が十分集まれば、マクロな次元の活動、たとえば二酸化炭素に対する課税を加速することができる。変化を創り出す上では、最終的にはそういうことがカギになっていくだろう。

スタジオの日常の中のミクロな活動

オラファー――前にうちのスタジオで働いていたシェフの一人、〔岩間〕朝子（アーティストでもある）が、ぼくらがまだベルリンのインヴァリーデン通りのスタジオにいたころ、だから二〇〇八年以前のいつだかに、ヴァンダナ・シヴァの本を持ってきた。朝子はシヴァの食物アクティヴィズムや、種、生物多様性、すべてのものが形づくる関係性やネットワークをめぐってシヴァが展開しているラディカルな思想に刺激を受けていた。それでぼくらは、もしこういうことを目標にするのなら、スタジオのキッチンはヴェジタリアンにならないといけないんだと気がついた。そして実際そうなった。次に、わりと最近だけど、実はヴィーガン〔＝卵や乳製品も使わない完全菜食主義〕になった。

スタジオにはすばらしくて腕のいいキッチン・チームがいて、気候を意識した仕事を、うちの他のどの部署よりも長期間にわたって推進してきている。野菜類の仕入元は〈アプフェルトラウム〉といって、ベルリンのすぐ外にあるコミュニティ支援型農園。最近開催したイベントのいくつかでは、キッチン・チームはカーボンニュートラルな〔＝大気中の二酸化炭素を増やさない〕ディナーを考案した。たとえばメアリー・ロビンソンがすばらしい著書『気候の正義（Climate Justice）』を出版したときの記念イベント。わりと最近、「人新世における食物」について報告書が出た。その中で著者たちは〈食物大変革〉をおこなって、増えつづける世界人口のために健康的な食事を実現し、しかも気候変動に応答しようと提唱している。ぼくらのキッチンがすでにそういう方針を採択しているのを誇りに思う。

キッチン・チームはもうちょっと小規模な実験も進めていて、おかげでスタジオの仕事がワクワクするものになっている。たとえば野菜を顔料に変えて、エコロジーが浸透した水彩画の新シリーズをつくるとか。相互接続から成り立つこういったシステムの価値を、ぼくは本気で信じている。

ローレン｜ヴィーガンで植物ベースのキッチンがあるおかげで、わたしたちのカーボン・フットプリントはずいぶん違うものになっている——こんなにたくさんの人が週に四回集まるんだから、なおさら。あと、梱包もある。わたしたちは何でも大きくまとめて、できるだけ生分解可能な梱包で配送してもらうようにしている。一度数値を見てしまうと、頭から離れなくなる。

ヴィーガン料理限定にするのはなかなか難しい。ラブネとかシェーヴルとかのチーズをサラダに足すだけで、すごく簡単においしくなるわけだから。ヴィーガンじゃなくてヴェジタリアンのキッチンにすればずっとずっと楽なんだけど、いつも新しい調理法をディスカッションして、実験して、学んで、植物世界の内部でバランスを取ろうと模索している。

ブリッタ｜去年、スタジオ内で意識が高まったと思う。ペンを買いたいと思ったらこう自問する——わたしこれ、本当に必要なのかな？　それが最初。次に——これ、プラスチック製でなきゃいけないのかな、それとも木製もありかな？　ところが次は——この木材、どこでつくられてるんだろう？　わたしたちはいろいろなアイテムをもっとエコロジカルな代替品で置き換えるようになったから、もちろん同僚たちがやって来て、「このペン、一〇年間使ってたんだけど、なんでもう使っちゃいけないの？」と聞く。だから「うーん、プラスチック製だからね」と答える。するとあっという間にディスカッションが始まる——みんないろいろといいアイデアを出してきて、今よりいっそう深く探っていくことになる。

事務用品は新しい業者から仕入れることにして、リサイクル紙を使うようになった。といってもまだまだ難しい。たとえば図面プリンタの用紙が必要だったのでたくさんリサーチした結果、とうとうリサイクルの図面プリンタ用紙が見つかって買い占めたんだけど、今では使い切ってしまって、もうメーカーでもつくってない。建築家は、図面が灰色っぽくてディテールが見えないのを嫌がるから。なのでさんざんテストをして、いまこの点に関しては振り出しに戻っている。サステナビリティを追求していくとこういうことになる。次の段階、次の段階と調べていって、途中で迷子になってしまうこともありうる。

ローレン—調理したものは捨てない。何も捨てない。午後食べるか、みんなが持って帰るか、次の日か翌々日の食べ物にリサイクルする。たとえばきのうはエチオピア料理にしたけど、これはテーブルによっては、小皿料理に変わってまた出てくることになる。キノコのコンソメをつくってから、調理したキノコを使ってパンに塗るスプレッドをつくった。だから、このことについてわたしたちは本当にいっぱい考えている。

ラベア—アート作品に使ったガラスをリサイクルするのは本当に難しい。ドイツではビンしかリサイクルする仕組みがないから。うちで主に使うのはガラスでできた球体作品と、手吹きのガラス板と、コーティングしたガラス。製品の素材にガラスを使う他の企業に話を聞いて、どうやってリサイクルするのかを勉強しているところ。〔ドイツのガラス製造業者〕〈ランバーツ〉は部品をリサイクルしているけど、明るめのガラスを暗めのガラスに混ぜ込むことしかできないから、暗色のガラスでゴミが出たら捨てるしかない。これはリサイクルも再利用もまったくされてない。

ガラスのリサイクル方法を探しているとき、ガラスを砕いて小さなかけらにし、熱を使って破片を溶かして、建築用の半透明建設資材をつくる企業にたまたま出会った。だから将来は、ガラス製の作品のゴミを別のアート作品制作の素材に使えるかもしれない。

問題は梱包であり、輸送であり、アート作品を取り巻くすべてだ

キム—湿気が付きやすかったり、有害なガスを出したり、酸化してアート作品のまわりで分解してしまったりするような素材は、正直あまり使いたくない。今いろんな素材——とくに、キノコからつくる発泡体——が出てきているけど、大部分はコンセプチュアルで、デザイン・スタジオやアート・スタジオ発で、大量生産向けじゃない。

でも最大一〇〇パーセントまでリサイクル素材でつくった発泡体もある。ただ、これはあまりアーカイヴ向きじゃない。高分子鎖が他より短い、ということは、残念ながら他のよりも早く壊れてしまうから。

ポイントの一つは、こういうものを使う必要をとにかく削減すること。梱包資材を使わない、賢い梱包方法を考え出すこと。まっさきに取り上げる必要のあるイシューがそれだと思う。

セバスチャン—梱包材について考えてみるなら、あれは実際、何のためにあるのか？　作品を固定して、輸送中に傷がつかないよう保証するため。同じことをするには他の方法もある。なのでぼくらは、スプリングをクレートの中にネジではめ込んで、アート作品を固定する仕組みを考えた。作品が到着したらスプリングを外して、別のパッケージに取り付けられる。

ミリアム—アート作品用の素材そのものはそんなに悪くない。アート作品〔のためのもの〕なわけだから、永久に保つようにつくってある。絶対捨てられることがないように。制作方法もそうは変わらない。だけど問題は梱包であり、輸送であり、まわりを取り巻くすべてであり、わたしたちがどうやって作業するかであり、ここ工房でどういう液体を使うか、だ。そっちがむしろ問題なのだ。

わたしたちと緊密に協働している制作パートナーのほぼ全員と話をした。せかしたり、すごく強制したりしなきゃいけないのかと思ったけど、実はパートナーはほぼ全員、もうサステナビリティに取り組んでいることがわかった。彼らが言うには、「スタジオ・オラファー・エリアソンがこういうことを支援しているのは嬉しいし、そういうことなら、ひょっとすると別の素材を使うくらいの柔軟さはこちらにもありますよ。もう一週間待ってください。何かしら届くから」。だから、すごくオープン。

ケアスティン—今わたしたちはあらゆる段階を考え直さないといけないところまで来ていて、ひょっ

とすると自分たちの美学を変えなくちゃいけないのかもしれない。たとえばとてもきれいな大きい表面をつくるときに、完璧な黒じゃなくて少し粗くなるかもしれない。旧式の方法を使って有毒な構成要素を避けるとなると、完璧な黒は難しいから。エコロジカルな色にはそういうパワーがない。これは美学的な問題でもある。

　アート実践の中でわたしたちは、すでにおなじみの、もっと値打ちのある素材に移行したらいいんじゃないかとわたしは思う。というわけで、銅はリサイクルできる。木材一般、硬材はこの先もずっとオーケー。複合木材は違う。だから、こういうすごく純粋で値打ちのある素材を使うべきだとわたしは思う。

オラファー｜ときどきこう聞かれる——アート作品をもっとサステナブルにするためには、あえてアート面で妥協することも辞しませんか？　ぼくにとって答えはノー。ぼくには、自分がいいと思えないアート作品はつくれない。だから気候にとってはよくても、結果としてアート面では悪くなるような決定は下さない。そういう場合にはそもそも作品をつくらないことにしたい。だからぼくは、作品のカーボン・フットプリントに対する配慮と作品の美学のあいだで、主観的な評価にもとづいて釣り合いをとらなくちゃいけない。また、もっとサステナブルな制作方法が見つかるまではつくるのをやめる作品もいくつかはあることになる。

マーガレット｜うちではプロジェクトのサステナビリティを評定するツールを考え出した。プロジェクトが一定の予算の枠内で実現できるかどうかを評定するのとまったく同じ。まだプロジェクト・リーダーの主観的な判断で決まる面が強いけど、現在わたしたちは少なくとも数値を表にまとめて、プロジェクトのカーボン・フットプリントがどれくらいになりそうかを数量化することはやっている。

　二酸化炭素について考えていくと、制作のプランニングにも影響が出る。たとえばわたしたちはシドニーでのコミッション・ワークに取り組んでいるところなんだけど、あまり素材を配送しなくてもすむように、できるだけ作品が設置される場所の近くで制作をする可能性を探っている。世界のどこか別の場所で3Dプリントをすることまで探っている。デザインのプロセスは全部こっちでやって、それからファイルを送ってむこうでプリントしてもらうわけ。同じように、信頼できる企業のネットワークを世界中で築ければと思っている。できあがったプランをただ送れば彼らが制作してくれる、なんてことも考えられる。わたしたちは、重い素材を輸送する必要がほぼなくなるところまで行ければいいなと思っている。

アート作品が移動する

セバスチャン｜ぼくらは契約書に、うちはインスタレーションの重たい部品を航空便で世界中に送ったりはしませんので、と断る条項を入れるようになった。そうすると期日に間に合わなくなる危険もあるわけだけど。これはもちろん大きな決定で、全員がこれを支持しないといけない。クライアントやギャラリーから、うちのチームでプロジェクトを運営している人たちも。

　それに、これはぼくらがプロジェクトを制作したりデザインしたりするやり方に関連していると思う。何かをするときはいつも特別な、新しいやり方を考えないといけない。何かをデザインするという創造プロセスの中でいろいろ努力するのと同じように、ぼくらは配送のときにも努力しなくちゃいけない。そうすれば、プロジェクトをもっとホーリスティックな〔＝世界全体とのつながりに配慮した〕やり方で考えることに近づく。

マルガレート｜配送のときはできるかぎりトラックや鉄道を使う可能性を探るようにしたら、中国で最近やったコミッション・ワーク、ある新しい美術館の建物のために大きなスチールの螺旋を建てるというものだったんだけど、これはトラックで現地に輸送するほうが飛行機に載せるより速いということがわかった。しかもそのほうが速いだけじゃなくて、ずっと安く上がる。飛行機だったら、何しろ巨大なアート作品なので、ドイツを出るときには特定の空港を使わなくちゃいけないし、作品を収容できるだけのスペースがある飛行機の順番待ちをしなくちゃいけないし、北京では現場から遠い特定の空港に到着することになるから。

セバスチャン―航空便じゃなくてトラックとか鉄道で送るという選択をしたせいで何かの到着が遅れることになっても受け入れようという雰囲気が広まりはじめている。もちろんぼくらも作品が時間通りに着いて設置されてほしいとは思っているけど、プランニングが遅れたりややこしくなったりしても、ちゃんとした理由があるかぎりみんな受け入れてくれる。それにはパートナー全員が賛同していないといけない。サステナブルな輸送手段に伴うリスクを受け入れないといけない。環境に関してラディカルな態度を取ると、ある種のリスクを受け入れることになる。

カヤナ―輸送というのは決まった手順(ルーティーン)に頼っている部分がとても多い。「サステナブル」な配送――カッコ付きなのは、もちろんまだ本当の意味ではサステナブルじゃないからなんだけど――に関しては、まだルーティーンがない。習慣を壊す面が強くて、それはわたしたちの側だけじゃなくて、配送業者にとっても〔受け取り手である〕機関にとってもそう。空輸とかについても同じ。何かを始めてみたら、まったく前例がなかったり、あまりなかったり、決まりから外れていたりすることがわかる。最初はみんなあんまり乗り気じゃないんだけど、最初のハードルを何とか三つ乗り越えると、そこからは実はけっこうトントン拍子に行ったりする。

人々が動く

ジェフ―《アイス・ウォッチ》のカーボン・フットプリントのうち一番大きな部分はグリーンランドからロンドンまで氷を輸送したことが原因だったけど、二番目に大きかった要因は、実は打ち合わせや設営や広報目的でロンドンまで乗る飛行機だった。空の旅っていうのは、《アイス・ウォッチ》の総排出量の一六パーセントにしかならないけど、前もって考慮しておけば一番削減できたはずのものだった。カーボン・フットプリントについての報告書でこれを見たときには、やっぱり考え込まされた。

ブリッタ―わたしたちは、自分が乗る飛行機の〔二酸化炭素〕排出量を追跡調査してカーボン・フットプリントがどれくらいなのかを把握したり、どうすれば削減できるかを考えたりするようにしている。驚いたことに〔アイルランドの格安航空会社〕〈ライアンエア〉はカーボン・フットプリントが一番低い会社の一つだけど、飛行機会社を選ぶときはもちろん他にも念頭に置いておかないといけないことがある。ビジネスクラスはたくさんスペースが必要だから、乗るとカーボン・フットプリントがほぼ二倍になる。

次に、飛行機で行く以外の選択肢を探したんだけど、これは場合によってはなかなか波瀾万丈。ヨーロッパ内部なら少なくとも片道は電車で行くようにしていて、排出量はこれで半分になる。ところが、方角によっては電車の乗り継ぎがないことがある。スペインに行こうとするとすごくややこしい。フランスに行って、そこでバスに乗って、また電車に乗るという手がある。だから、本当に実際的なのは何なのか、いまだに旅行する必要のある一企業としてのわたしたちにとって意味があるのは何なのか、いつでも課題を突きつけられる。

二〇一九年には、飛行機に乗ることによるスタジオのカーボン・フットプリントは、二〇一八年の約三分の一だった。もちろん、わたしたちが年間何回くらい、どのくらい遠くまで飛行機に乗らないといけないかについてはたくさんの要因が絡んでいるから、この〔フットプリント減少〕傾向がどれくらい続くか、はっきりしたことはなかなか言えないけど、これからの数年間でどういうふうに発展していくかを見守ろうと思う。

アンナ―わたしの人生は複雑だ。夫と三人の子どもたちと住んでいる国と、働いている国が違う。四年間毎週、飛行機でスタジオに通っていた。火曜はコペンハーゲンからベルリンに、木曜は逆方向に。とくに楽しくはないけど速かった。空港は連続性の感覚を細切れにしてしまいがちだ。バラバラに砕いて、小さくてかなり退屈な行動の連なりにしてしまう。二〇一九年の六月に、飛行機／電車の組み合わせモデルに切り替えてみた。ベルリンに飛行機で行って、コペンハーゲンに電車で戻ってくる。電車に乗っている時間は飛ぶときの二倍で、それなりの代償がともなう。スタジオの同僚たちとも、家族とも、一緒に過ごす時間が少し減った。といっても、仕事をしている時間が減ったわけじゃない――むしろ逆だ。電車はわたしの移動オフィスで、乗っているときの自分はものすごくテキパキしてるなあ、と実感している。外では風景がわたしの横を流れていったりするから、ものを考えるにはなかなかユニークな状態だ。わたしの仕事生活は、無数の考えや情報からできている。こういうものは開発し、テストし、配布し、接続し、修正し、再流通させ……とやっていく必要がある。毎日、反省や決断やミクロな行動がきりなく連続して、わたしはトピックからトピックへと飛び回ることになる。電車に乗ると焦点が固定される。たまに電車に乗っていない週があると、電車が恋しくなってくる。長時間移動するとやっぱり疲れるけど、限定されて、しっかり焦点の合ったあの動くスペースの雰囲気が恋しくなるのだ。スローダウンするように強制されると、意外な利点がある。

ヴァーニャ―始めてからもうしばらくになるが、わたしたちはできるだけオラファーの用務を大陸ごとに一回の出張にまとめて、最小回数の旅行で最大のインパクトを与えられるようにしている。結果として、オラファーが飛行機に乗って過ごす時間が減った。

あと、電気自動車を運転するドライバーの情報を集めるようにしてもいる。これはかなり順調だけど、いつもうまくいくとはかぎらない。小さい街にはそもそも電気自動車がないから。ずっと後になってから、自分たちが実は約五〇〇キロも離れた別の町からわざわざクルマを呼び寄せていたことがわかったりする。何かをするのが実際に正しい判断であるような時と場合を把握するのは本当に時間がかかる。

以前はオラファーのフレキシビリティとか、どこそこの場所に一番速く着く方法とかを優先していた。でも今はサステナビリティを優先している。なので、飛行機よりも電車のほうが時間がかかるとして、その電車が直行便だったら、今は電車を優先する。打ち合わせの時間を交渉したり、開会式の時間を交渉したり、用務を交渉したりして、わたしたちのサステナビリティ計画にとってふさわしい形になるようにする。

デジタルでつながる

ヴァーニャ―近ごろでは、ビデオ会議のおかげでオラファーは、本当に大事な打ち合わせがあって別の大陸に二回出張しなくちゃいけない、というようなことはなくなっている。五年前だったらとうてい考えられなかったような話だ。今スタジオでは、ビデオ会議ができるかぎり快適でプロフェッショナルで自然になるようにいろいろ努力している。ビデオ会議を使うときには、本当に相手が来て打ち合わせしているのとできるだけ近い感じが出るように。ITチームはカメラをセットする位置や、部屋の見え方や、誰がどこに座るかをすごく研究して、〔直接会っておこなう〕打ち合わせの和気あいあいとした感じが本当に感じられるようにしている。

セバスチャン―ビデオ会議はすごく貴重なものだということがわかった。画質が悪くて驚くけど。おかげで、世界中のクライアントと〔直接会っておこなう〕プランニングの打ち合わせをかなり減らせている。これには、絶対に必要でないかぎり、ぼくらは打ち合わせのために旅行しませんから、と広報する意味もある。

今ぼくらは仮想現実の中で打ち合わせをおこなう可能性も掘り下げている。クライアントや建築家が、建築とか制作前のインスタレーションの内部とかを歩きまわったりできるようにするわけだ。実現すれば、プランニングの打ち合わせだけじゃなくて、物理的な建築模型の制作もおおかた不必要になる。

「ときに川は橋となる」展、東京都現代美術館

キャロリン―「ときに川は橋となる」展は、カーボン・フットプリントに常時目を配って、そのインパクトを制作・輸送・移動の面で抑えようとわたしたちが試みた最初の展覧会だ。だから、オラファーとキュレーターの長谷川祐子と会話を重ねる中で、サステナビリティは最初からカギになる主題だった。

全体的にわたしたちは、アートとして強い展覧会をつくりたいと思った。一見すると、サステナブルな仕方で展覧会をしようとすることで、オラファーのアートはすごく自由を制限されたみたいに思える。でも、あらゆる段階を考え直さなければいけなくなったことはオラファーにとって本当に刺激的で、いろいろと新しいアイデアにつながった。

最初に解決しなければいけない課題が、どうやって日本に作品を届けるかであることははっきりしていた。だから「ときに川は橋となる」展は、輸送に対する新しいアプローチを開発するための先行実験プロジェクトになった。まず個々のアート作品をサステナブルなやり方で配送する最良の解決策をリサーチしたわたしたちは、空ではなくて陸・海路でヨーロッパから日本へと作品を送ることに決めた。アート作品はトラックでベルリンからハンブルクに移動し、そこからさらに鉄道で、ポーランド・マワセヴィチェ貨物港駅を経由してロシア・ザバイカリスク、中国・太倉港へ、そこで日本行きの船に積み込まれた。次にこの旅は展覧会の一部になった。各輸送箱には特別に考案されたドローイング・マシンが付属していて、道中の鉄道や船の動きを円形の用紙に記録し、これが展覧会の中で陳列されている。

カヤナ―保険はわたしたちが直面した最初のハードルのひとつだった。〔東京都現代〕美術館と配送業者が、自分たちでは保険をかけられないと言ったからだ。リスクが大きすぎるから、と。それはそうだろう。より時間がかかるし、乗り換えも多くなるから損傷のリスクが増える。クレートを何度も何度も積み込んだり積み降ろしたりすることになる。自分たちで方法を見つけて、自分たちで作品に保険をかけて、ふだんなら配送業者か〔展覧会開催〕機関が決めてくれることを自分たちで決めなければいけなかった。今回は自分たちの手で築き上げていかなければいけなかった――言ってみれば仕組みとか、制度とか、構成要素とか。

といっても、いったん軌道に乗ってからはそれほどたいへんじゃなかった。まったく実行可能だった。

キャロリン―〔出展する〕アート作品のセレクションということで言うと、わたしたちは本気でカーボン・フットプリントを考慮する――すでに〔東京の〕近くにある作品を見つけてきて配送距離を抑える――ようになっていて、また今現在は作品セレクションを改訂したり変更したりしているところだ。オラファーはたえず最適化をおこなっていて、このため変更点がたくさん出てくるから。とはいえ、部品によっては直前に配送しなければいけなくなるという事実があり、これに対処する必要があるので、やり方を見つけなければいけないだろう。ひょっとすると、自分たちでスーツケースに入れて持ってくるのもありかもしれない。いずれにしても、ふだんに比べればずっと少ない。

あとオラファーは、リサイクルしたり再利用し

たりした素材——たとえば、彼が何年もかけてアイスランドの海辺で拾い集めて、たくさんのアート作品で使っている流木——を使ったアート作品を選んだ。あと、この展覧会用に構想した特別ディスプレイもあって、スタジオが取り組んでいる、革新的でサステナブルな素材についての現在進行形のリサーチを紹介している。

ケアスティン｜〔今回の展覧会の一部である〕素材ラボというアイデアは、テキスタイル会社〈クヴァドラ〉と一緒に取り組んでいるあるプロジェクトが出発点だった。わたしたちは力を合わせてすごくサステナブルなカーテンをつくりたいと思った。現在では、他にもいくつか外部の企業と組んで仕事を進めている。それに、スタジオ内だけでもいろんなことをやっている——たとえば食料ゴミからつくった顔料とか。

あと、美学的な面でもサステナビリティの面でも合格と思える素材がいくつか見つかった。〔今回の展覧会の〕素材を集めたテーブルは、アート作品に使える素材だけを見せるということで考えたものだったから。たとえば、アルミを生産すると残る小片（スラグ）からつくった赤いタイル。アルミが一トン必要なら、ああいうアルカリ度の高い素材を一・五トン生産するわけだけど、これは有毒で、処分するときは特別な方法でしないといけない。ところが〈Studio ThusThat〉〔タイルの共同制作会社〕の人たちが、窯でテラコッタみたいに焼けばアルカリ成分が消えることを発見した。安定して、しっかりくっつく。オラファーには、タイルで何かのファサードを覆うアイデアがあったので、生のテラコッタとか何かしらレンガに似た素材とかを使うかわりに、このゴミ素材を使うこともできる。これをホーリスティックな仕方でやっていくのはとてもややこしいけど、わたしたちは今それをやってみている。

キャロリン｜〔今回の展覧会では〕テーマの上でサステナビリティとつながっているという理由で選ばれた作品が多い。つまりオラファーの自然に対するアプローチや、気候をめぐる問いかけを表している作品ということ。たとえば《太陽の中心への探査》はサステナブルなエネルギーを組み入れている。美術館の中庭に太陽光パネルを設置して、作品を照らすライトと、作品を回転させつづけるモーターに直接電量を供給する。「リトルサン」プロジェクトも、クリーンでサステナブルなエネルギーへのアクセスを振興するものなので、展覧会に含められている。言うまでもなくこのプロジェクトは、灯油ではなく太陽光つまりソーラーパワーを使うこと、また重要な点として、オルタナティヴ・エネルギーへの意識を高めることがテーマになっている。《溶ける氷河のシリーズ 1999/2019》（2019）は、一九九九年にオラファーがアイスランドの氷河を撮った航空写真数十点と、去年〔＝二〇一九年〕の夏——二〇年後——に彼が同じ氷河を、だいたい同じ位置から撮ったイメージを組み合わせる。三〇組のイメージからは、地球温暖化が世界に与えつつある劇的なインパクトが明らかになる。

あとオラファーは、トピックと密接に関係しているけど、物理的な意味では美術館に来ていない作品も展覧会に含めたいと考えたので、わたしたちにとっては新しいアプローチをとることになった——以前のアクションや介入のドキュメントをポスターにして紹介したり、そういうアート作品を写真で表すというアイデアだ。こういうアイデアが出てきたのは、オラファーがサステナブルな展覧会を創りたいと考えたからという理由が大きい——それに、わたしたちのカーボン・フットプリントを抑える方法でもある。もちろんわたしたちはすごく全身没入型（イマーシヴ）の作品も引き続きつくっている。

新しいエネルギー

カヤナ｜わたしたちのメインの配送パートナー企業〈ハーゼンカンプ〉に、「こういうリクエストって多いんですか」と聞いてみた。そしたら、こんなこと頼むのはわたしたちが初めてだと言うので、本当にショックだった。ハーゼンカンプが言うには、「うちでは、コレクターや〔美術館などの〕機関に対して彼らが持っている作品の扱い方を指図したりできないけど、実はあなたたちにはできる」と。スタジオであるわたしたちにはそれができる。「この展覧会をやりたいなら、配送には二ヵ月みておかないといけません。わたしたちは航空便は使わないので」と言っていい。でも、すぐに移行して、一度に何もかもやるわけにもいかない。だからわたしたちは始動したばかりで、こちら側からできるかぎりプッシュするようにしている。でもわたしたちだけで決められることでもない。

キャロリン―東京都現代美術館の展覧会は、わたしたちにとって転機だった。本当にすごく努力したし、すごくディスカッションを重ねたし、今回たくさんやったリサーチを長期的に、アートに使いつづけていくことができる。企業が、彼らの考え方に共感して賛同するクライアントもいるんだということを理解するようになったわけだから。空輸はやめてしまおうというのがわたしたちの意図。だから今度は、どうすればそれが可能なのか、本気で考えないといけない。それこそが未来なのだ。

セバスチャン―「何でこんなことしたいんですか、単に象徴的だから?」とか聞かれることがある。これはコンセプトだとか、適切な行動というよりはむしろ思想だとか、「何でまたコンセプトなんかのために、クライアントとの関係を危うくするんですか?」と言われる。でもぼくらの感覚ではむしろ、自分たちの仕事が将来どうなっていくべきかを示そうと思ってやっている。ぼくはこれを、さまざまな試行を重ねながら新しい世界へと、本当にワクワクするような新世界へと踏み出していくことだと考えている。

そしてぼくはこういう関心、こういうワクワクを、ぼくらと共同作業をする人たちにも届ける必要があると思う。いったん理解したら、彼らも自分たちの立場を、少なくともある程度考えなおす能力をもっていると思う。これは義務でもないし、ハードルでもないし、障害物でもないんだということを感じとるから――これは新しいエネルギーであって、自分は未来へと進んでいく何かに参加しているんだというフィーリングを与えてくれる。今、あちこちで森が火事になったり、人々が深刻な行動を取ったりしなくちゃいけなくて、社会の見通しはかなり暗いけど、それを乗り越えさせてくれる。くよくよ心配している状態から、適切で現実味のある行動をとることへ。人々を動かし、人々にエネルギーを与えるのはそれだとぼくは思う。

Fourteen views of Studio Olafur Eliasson's sustainability agenda

Studio Olafur Eliasson, founded in Berlin in 1995, comprises a diverse team of craftspeople, specialised technicians, architects, archivists, art historians, web and graphic designers, film-makers, cooks, and administrators. They work with Eliasson to develop, produce, and install artworks, projects, and exhibitions, as well as on experimentation, archiving, research, publishing, and communications. The excerpts presented here are from conversations with some of the many people working on making the studio's activities more sustainable. They have been edited for clarity and arranged thematically to give a broad view of the studio's sustainability agenda.

Speakers (in order of appearance)

Olafur Eliasson, artist
Sebastian Behmann, heads the design team at Studio Olafur Eliasson and is co-founder of Studio Other Spaces
Geoffrey Garrison, editor and copywriter in the research and communications department
Margaret Lutz, business development in the design department
Myriam Thomas, heads the development and production team
Lauren Maurer, chef
Britta Kampe, works in the front office and on upgrading the studio's day-to-day sustainability measures
Rabea Welte, department coordinator in the development and production team
Kim Kraczon, conservator in the development and production team
Kerstin Palermo, project manager in the development and production team
Kajana Wagner, artwork coordinator in the exhibitions department
Anna Engberg-Pedersen, heads the research and communications department
Vanja Zanko, Olafur's executive assistant
Caroline Eggel, heads the exhibitions department, responsible for *Sometimes the river is the bridge*

The Big Picture

OLAFUR | A work of art embodies a set of values and ideas. It reflects the artist's convictions—about sustainability and the climate, for instance—and I think there has to be synchronicity between what art is about and how art is made. I don't believe that we can separate the content from how an artwork is produced. It's not always possible, but I increasingly work with this in mind when making everyday choices regarding the artworks.

My studio does not stand outside the shared responsibility that we have towards the planet. Everyone can do a little, including smaller institutions or companies like us. Football clubs can do something. Everyone. At the studio we are doing two things: raising awareness of the climate crisis through projects and communication, and we are focused on improving our own operations. It's important to say that we're still early in the process. We embrace ethical responsibility and data, as well as the ambition to continue to exist as a studio. It is about navigation, about defining the relationships between these components.

SEBASTIAN | The need to produce our artworks in a more sustainable way wasn't that clear, let's say, ten years ago. Back then, there was an artistic idea that we all felt was great, and we thought, let's put it out there. And what it actually meant for the rest of the planet was, I would say, less of interest to us. That aspect naturally developed out of the broader culture we were surrounded by.

A year and a half ago, we came to the point where we decided it was just not enough to only talk about the subject. We actually have to do the work of reducing our footprint to really achieve anything. The idea was to work on a kind of blueprint or a prototype for improving our footprint, which others could use as a tool as well. And we structured this as we structure any design project—we started with a base concept and a goal. And the goal was to really look into all the aspects of what we do, from waste management to how we produce to the way we do our planning for projects, how much we travel to different countries and how we get things there. Our goal is to plan not only time schedules and the budget of a project but also to calculate and evaluate our environmental impact—to see where and what we can improve. The impact of a project affects our decision to go ahead with it or not.

This process of becoming more sustainable means getting out of your comfort zone and going into, let's call it, the real world. And you have to make compromises, but you also have to always make clear where you are coming from, where you are going. And that kind of friction is something that we feel now in implementing sustainable solutions in transport, for instance. We cannot come with our ethical standards alone. We have to be highly open for other solutions and start a dialogue. So the friction can be very positive.

OLAFUR | Maybe I should give some context to the climate question because it's actually not new within my work, although I used to think and speak about it in different terms. I used to think that nature exists, that there's something beyond human reach. But as Bruno Latour has said: 'there's no outside,' no undiscovered nature or reservoir of resources. And I've come to realise this over the last decade. So when I talk about Iceland today, I talk about its landscapes, not its nature. I've been photographing landscapes in Iceland for years. In 2007 I made a series of photos, called *The glacier mill series*, in which I documented these deep shafts that form in the glaciers when the melt water from the surface of the glacier bores down into the ice. And there was the *Jokla series* (2004), which documents the original path of the river Jokla in Iceland before it was dammed to create a new hydroelectric power plant. So you could say that my interests in the disappearance of nature, in landscapes, and in the climate have existed for long and I have been refining the way that I talk about these interests over the years.

In 2003, when I created *The weather project*—the big sun that I installed at Tate Modern—it wasn't yet about the climate for me. It was about atmospheres and weather systems and about a constructed weather situation. It was about how we organise ourselves in social contexts and how we use the weather as a shared point of reference. Today, when people think about this artwork, they often think of it within the context of the climate. And I welcome that. One measure of an artwork's success for me is when it has the capacity to travel from its origin and maintain relevance at a much later time, when thinking and outlooks have changed.

More recently I created a large-scale public intervention called *Ice Watch* with Minik Rosing, who's a geologist. Photos don't really convey the beauty of the ice blocks that we harvested from fjords in Greenland for this project. They're just *incredibly* beautiful! To touch a block like that, to see the vivid blue and white tones, feel the cold—that activates such a strong register of perceptions. Minik and I both believe vehemently in science and data, but also agree that they often cannot spur action on their own; a compelling narrative or a direct, visceral experience can make the data felt in a different way.

GEOFF | Communication and outreach were central to *Ice Watch*. At the same time, the exposure gave rise to a vibrant conversation on social media about the wisdom of consuming CO_2 in order to raise awareness of climate change. And we decided to engage with this issue directly by saying, Yes, this has a carbon footprint, it consumed 55 tonnes of CO_2, and let's talk about why we do not usually talk about this side of an artwork.

MARGARET | At the studio, I think, we are just starting to grasp the magnitude of the climate challenge. The one thing we learned in this whole process is that the obvious solution is often not the most sustainable. When we started looking into the details of where our trash goes or where fuel comes from and where energy comes from, sometimes what looks like a sustainable solution is not.

MYRIAM | It's really like a new growing plant here in the studio. In the beginning, it was a little bit hard and there was not so much fun in it. It was more like a burden for everyone.

And then there was this moment when it turned into a project everyone was excited about and happy to work on. The sustainability topic and the new materials created new ideas. I think there is a lot of creative potential here. It's a limitation, but it also means new developments, new research, new materials. Also for Olafur it was inspiring. It influenced the art. It wasn't that we just use another material for the same purpose, but we develop a new generation of artworks now.

SEBASTIAN | We've set up a model for organising the types of compensation we can do to balance a project's climate impact:

First of all, we use the creativity of the studio itself, investing more thinking and manpower to find ways to reduce the impact of a project. That, of course, costs money, but it is a form of compensation.

Second, we use the reach and reputation of the studio to help other companies and partners become more sustainable and get their voice out in the world. In this communication capacity, we also work on articles, take part in symposiums and conferences to bring more and more people on board.

Third, we are investing in infrastructural improvements to the studio to become more sustainable, installing, for example, solar panels on the studio roof, combined with a charging station for electric cars in front of the studio. Investing in these kinds of changes also has a return, of course; it's not just money you spend. It has a positive effect on your energy costs, for example.

And the fourth is to provide economic support to like-minded companies or thinkers who are in the early stages of developing sustainable projects that might not yet be suitable for markets but need support. It is important for us as a studio to use our creativity and Olafur's name to support companies and people working in this field.

To become a sustainable studio in the next ten years, we need to be more radical in redefining the way we do art and the way we do commissions, exhibitions, the whole thing. I would like to see us devote five per cent of our income to sustainability, in terms of work hours and effort, making sure that it is part of the overall way of conceiving and planning any project or exhibition. To make this happen we have chosen one person from each department to oversee the sustainability push and have created a position at the studio devoted to sustainability. If every company invested five per cent of their income, that would be a huge amount of money that, properly spent, could have an enormous impact in a very short time to improve the situation.

OLAFUR | We should be able to cut fifty per cent of our carbon emissions by 2030. That's a lot for a small operation like ours, although probably not enough... It's important to me to be a part of society, a part of the climate movement, and I want the studio to be a part of that. I want us to have some common goals that we are all striving towards. I have no illusions about micro-actions being enough, but with enough micro-actions we can accelerate actions at the macro-level, such as a tax on carbon, which will ultimately be key in creating change.

Micro-actions in Everyday Studio Life

OLAFUR | One of our former chefs, Asako (who's also an artist), brought in a book by Vandana Shiva while we were still at the old studio in Invalidenstrasse, sometime before 2008. She was inspired by Shiva's food activism and her radical thoughts on seeds, biodiversity, and the relationships and networks of all things. And we realised that if this were to be our target, the kitchen would have to become vegetarian. And it did. And then, not long ago, it actually became vegan.

We have a great and dedicated kitchen team at the studio, who have championed climate-conscious work for longer than any other part of the studio. Their produce is delivered from Apfeltraum, a community-supported-agriculture farm just outside Berlin. For some of the events that we have held in recent years, the kitchen team put together carbon-neutral dinners, like the launch of Mary Robinson's great book *Climate Justice*. There was a report not long ago about 'Food in the Anthropocene,' in which the authors advocate a Great Food Transformation to achieve healthy diets for the growing world population and respond to climate change. I am proud that our kitchen has already adopted this.

They are also involved in smaller experiments that bring excitement to the studio work, such as turning vegetables into pigments for a new series of ecologically infused watercolours. I really believe in these larger systems of interconnectivity.

LAUREN | Having a vegan, plant-based kitchen makes a big difference to our carbon footprint—especially when we are this many people, four times a week. And then there's the packaging. We are trying to get everything delivered in bigger packages, also biodegradable when possible. Once you see the numbers, you can't really get it out of your mind.

It is a challenge for us to cook only vegan meals, because it's so easy to add a labneh or some chèvre to a salad to make it tasty. It's really a lot easier to have a vegetarian rather than a vegan kitchen, but we're constantly discussing, experimenting, and learning new techniques, finding balance within the plant world.

BRITTA | I think awareness in the studio has grown over the last year. If you want to buy a pen, you ask: OK, do I need it? That's the first thing. And then: does it need to be plastic or can it be wood? But then, where is the wood being produced? We started to replace items with ecological alternatives and, of course, colleagues come and say, 'OK, I used to have this pen for ten years, why can't I have it anymore?' And you say, 'Yeah, well, it's plastic.' And then you're all of a sudden in a discussion—and people have good ideas to even dive deeper into things.

We found a new supplier for the office supplies and have started using recycled paper. This is still a challenge, however. We needed, for example, plotter paper, and after a lot of research, we finally found recycled plotter paper and bought all they had, but now we have used it all and it's not being produced anymore, because architects don't want to have greyish plots where they can't see the details. So we tested a lot and now we're back to zero on that. This is what looking into sustainability leads you to: you look at the next step and the next step and you can get lost in it.

LAUREN | We don't throw anything away that we have cooked. Nothing. It's either eaten in the afternoons or people take it home or we recycle it in the next day's food, or two days later, like the Ethiopian food we had yesterday, it will come out again in little dishes for some of the tables. We made a mushroom consommé and then used the mushrooms that we had cooked to make a spread for the bread. So we are really thinking about that a lot.

RABEA | Recycling the glass we use for artworks is really difficult because the normal recycling system in Germany is only for bottles. There are no recycling processes for other things made of glass. We mostly use glass spheres and hand-blown glass sheets and coated glass. We are talking to other companies who use glass as a production material, to learn how they recycle it. Lamberts recycles parts, but it's only possible to mix brighter glass in with darker glass, so if they produce dark glass waste, they just have to throw it away. It's not being recycled or reused in any way.

In searching for a way to recycle glass, we came across a company who reuse glass by breaking it into small pieces and using heat to fuse the shards into a semi-transparent construction material for architecture. So maybe it's possible to use the glass sphere waste as a production material for artworks in the future.

It's the Packing, It's the Transport, It's Everything Around the Artworks

KIM | We don't really want materials in packaging that attract moisture and release harmful gases or become acidic and disintegrate around the artworks. A lot of these nascent materials—especially the foam made from mushrooms—a lot of it is conceptual, coming out of design studios and art studios, and it's not meant for mass consumption.

But there are foams that are made out of up to 100% recycled material, although they are slightly less archival, because the polymer chains are shorter, which means they will break down quicker, unfortunately.

One of the main points is to just reduce the need for it: come up with clever packing solutions that don't involve packing materials; I think that is the foremost issue that needs to be addressed.

SEBASTIAN | If you think about packing material, what is it actually for? To hold the work in place to make sure it does not get damaged in transport. And there are other ways of doing this. So we've come up with a system of springs that can be screwed into the crate to hold the artwork in place. Once the work has arrived, you can take the spring system out of the package and install it in another.

MYRIAM | The material for the artworks itself is not so bad. As it is an artwork, it is made to last forever, so it will never be thrown away. And the way it's produced, it's something we wouldn't change so much. But it's the packing, it's the transport, it's everything around it, it's how we work, what liquids we use here in the workshop. It's more this.

We talked to nearly all of our production partners who we are working closely with. We thought we would have to push and really force them to change, but it turns out nearly everyone working with us is already working on sustainability. They said, 'We are happy Studio Olafur Eliasson is supporting this and also flexible enough to maybe then use other materials, wait a week longer until something is delivered.' So, very open.

KERSTIN | We are now at the point where we have to rethink every step, and maybe we have to change our aesthetics. Instead of having, for example, a very beautiful, large surface that is perfectly black it will maybe be a bit more rough, because it's very difficult to achieve this using old-school methods, without any toxic components. Ecological colours don't have this power and this is an aesthetic question also.

I think in our art practice, we might move to the more valuable materials we know already. So copper you can recycle. Wood in general, hardwood, will always be OK. The composites of wood are not. So I think we should go to these very pure and valuable materials.

OLAFUR | A question that I sometimes get is: Would you compromise artistically to make a work of art more sustainable? And for me the answer is, no, I cannot make an artwork that I don't consider good, so I wouldn't make a good decision for the climate that leads to a bad artistic outcome. I'd rather in that case not make the work at all. So based on a subjective evaluation, I have to balance considerations of the work's carbon footprint and its aesthetics. This also means that there are groups of works that I will stop making until more sustainable production methods have been found.

MARGARET | We've come up with a tool for assessing the sustainability of a project, just as we assess whether it can be realised within a certain budget. It's still quite up to the subjective judgement of the project leader, but we now at least have the numbers in a table to quantify the project's potential carbon footprint.

Thinking about carbon also affects the planning of fabrication. For example, we are working on a commission in Sydney, and in order not to have to ship so many materials we are looking into the possibility of producing as much as possible close to where the work will be installed. We are even looking into 3D-printing something in other parts of the world, so that all the design process happens here and then we send the file to have it printed there. Similarly, we would like to build up a network of trusted companies around the world, so that we could conceivably just send a completed plan to them to fabricate. We really would almost never have to transport heavy materials at all.

Artworks on the Move

SEBASTIAN | We have begun inserting clauses into our contracts saying that we will not fly heavy installation parts around the world even though this could mean that we might not meet deadlines. And of course this is a big decision that everyone has to support, starting with the clients and the galleries and also the people running the projects in our teams.

And I think this is related to the way we produce and design projects. There are no standardised products in the art world. We always have to think of special, new ways of doing something, so that the same effort we make in the creative process of designing something we also have to put into the shipping of it. This brings us closer to a more holistic way of thinking about a project.

MARGARET | In shipping, we have started looking into the possibility of using trucks and trains, whenever possible, and it turns out that for a recent commission in China, a large steel spiral built for a new museum building, transporting it there by truck is faster than putting it on a plane. And not only is it faster, but it's a lot cheaper, because with a plane, it's such a big artwork, it would have to leave Germany from a certain airport, and we would have to wait for a plane with enough space for the artwork, and then it would arrive in Beijing at a certain airport that is not close to the site.

SEBASTIAN | We're beginning to see more acceptance today if something does not arrive on time because we chose to send it by truck or train rather than by air. Of course, we want the work to get there and be installed on time, but people are willing to accept some delay and complication in planning as long as it is for a good reason. All partners have to be on board with this. They have to accept the risks of sustainable transport options. Being radical on the environment means accepting certain risks.

KAJANA | A lot of transport is based on routine. And I think for 'sustainable' shipping—in quotation marks because it is not really sustainable still, of course—there are no routines for that yet. It has a lot to do with breaking a habit, on our side as well as on the side of the shippers and the institutions. It's the same for flying and things like that. You start something and you see that it hasn't been done before or not so many times or it's not the norm. And people are, in the beginning, just not so into it, and then you just push through the first three hurdles, and then it actually comes together quite easily.

People on the Move

GEOFF | While the lion's share of the carbon footprint for *Ice Watch* resulted from transporting the ice from Greenland to London, the second largest factor was actually air travel to London for meetings and for installation and communications purposes. Flying, although it was only responsible for sixteen per cent of the work's total emissions, was the one thing we could have most reduced had we taken this into consideration beforehand. Seeing this in the carbon footprint report was certainly food for thought.

BRITTA | We've started tracking the emissions of our flights to get an idea of what our carbon footprint is and considering how we can reduce it. Surprisingly, Ryanair is one of the companies with the lowest CO_2 footprint, but of course there are other things to keep in mind when you choose an airline. Flying business class almost doubles the CO_2 footprint because of the space that it needs.

And then we tried to find alternatives to going by plane and this is kind of adventurous sometimes. Now, we always try if it's within Europe to at least go one way by train, and this halves the emissions. Although it turns out that in some directions, there are no train connections. If you want to go to Spain, it's very complicated. You can go to France and then take the bus and then go by train again. So it's always a challenge of what is really practical, what makes sense for us as a company that still needs to travel.

In 2019 the studio's carbon footprint from flying was almost a third of what it was in 2018. Of course there are a lot of factors that play into how often we need to fly every year and how far, so it's hard to be sure how long this trend will hold, but we will see how this develops over the next few years.

ANNA | My life is complex. I live with my husband and three kids in one country and work in another. For four years I commuted to the studio every week by plane, travelling from Copenhagen to Berlin on Tuesdays and back on Thursdays. It wasn't particularly enjoyable but it was fast. Airports tend to shatter your feeling of continuity; it is broken up, reduced to strings of small and quite boring actions. In June 2019 I switched to a combined plane/train model, where I fly to Berlin and then return to Copenhagen on the train. The train ride is more than twice as long as flying, which has costs: I get to be a bit less with my colleagues in the studio and a bit less with my family. I don't get to work less, though—on the contrary. The train is my mobile office and I've come to realise that I am incredibly efficient there. It creates a rather unique condition for thinking, what with the landscape flowing past me outside. My work life consists of a myriad of thoughts, pieces of information, etc., that have to be developed, tested, distributed, connected, revised, recirculated... My everyday has me jumping from topic to topic in endless sequences of reflections, decision-making, and micro-actions. The train actually consolidates my focus. In the rare weeks where I cannot go by train, I have come to miss it. Not the fatigue that comes with a long transit, but the atmosphere of that contained, focused, moving space. Being forced to be slow has surprising benefits.

VANJA | For some time now we have been gathering Olafur's obligations on one continent into a single trip whenever possible so that Olafur can actually travel the least possible to have the biggest impact. As a result, he spends less time flying.

We've also been trying to gather information about drivers who use electric cars. And this is going quite well, although it doesn't always work, because in smaller cities, there are simply no electric cars. What sometimes happens is we find out much later that the car had to come from another city which is around 500 kilometres away. And it really takes time to understand when it's actually a good decision to do this or not.

In the past, we prioritised Olafur's flexibility and the fastest way to reach a certain place. But now, we are prioritising sustainability. So if he takes a little bit longer with a train than with a plane, and if it's a direct train, now we prioritise the train. We negotiate meeting times, we negotiate opening times, we negotiate obligations according to whatever we think fits better into our sustainability agenda.

Connecting Digitally

VANJA | Recently, video conferencing has resulted in Olafur avoiding two trips to other continents for really big meetings that five years ago would have seemed unavoidable. There is this big effort now to make our video conferences as comfortable, professional, and natural as possible, so when people use video conferencing, the feeling should be the closest to having somebody personally in the meeting. The IT team is working a lot on where to set up a camera, how the room looks, who is sitting where, to really have this cosy feeling of a meeting.

SEBASTIAN | The video conferences turned out to be a very valuable thing, although it has a very bad image, surprisingly. We have saved significantly on the planning meetings we have with clients around the world. It's also about communicating to everybody that we are not traveling for meetings unless it is absolutely necessary.

Now we are also exploring the possibility of carrying out meetings in virtual reality, allowing clients and architects to move through the architecture or installation before it is produced. This will make planning meetings for the most part unnecessary as well as the production of physical architectural models.

Sometimes the river is the bridge at MOT, Tokyo

CAROLINE | *Sometimes the river is the bridge* is the first exhibition for which we have kept a constant eye on the carbon footprint and attempted to reduce its impact in terms of production, transport, and travel. So, from the beginning, sustainability was a key subject in the conversations we had with Olafur and the curator, Yuko Hasegawa.

In general, we wanted to make a very artistically strong show. At first glance, the aspiration to do an exhibition sustainably really restricted Olafur's artistic freedom. But then he had to reconsider every step, which really inspired him and led to new ideas.

It was clear that the first challenge would be to get the works to Japan, so *Sometimes the river is the bridge* became a pilot project for developing a new approach to transport. Having researched the best possible solutions for sustainably shipping the individual works of art, we decided to send works from Europe to Japan by land and sea rather than air. The artworks travelled from Berlin by truck to Hamburg and then on by train via the cargo port station in Malaszewicze, Poland, to Zabaykalsk, Russia, and to the port of Taicang, China, where they were loaded onto a ship to Japan. This journey then became part of the exhibition: each crate was accompanied by a specially devised drawing machine that recorded the movements of the train and the ship along the way on circular sheets of paper that are on display in the exhibition.

KAJANA | Insurance was one of the first hurdles we encountered, because the museum and the shipping company said we are not going to insure this; this is too risky. And it makes sense. There is more risk of damage because it takes a longer time and you have more vehicle changes. It's a lot of loading and unloading of crates. We had to find our own way, we had to insure the works ourselves, we had to make decisions that normally the shipper or the institutions would make. Normally it's all being built for us and we just take it. And this time we had to build it ourselves: the system and order of things and the ingredients, so to speak.

Once it was on track, though, it was not so hard. It was totally feasible.

CAROLINE | When it comes to the selection of artworks, we started really to take the carbon footprint into account—looking for works that were already located nearby to reduce shipping distances—and also now in editing or changing the selection of works, because Olafur is continually optimising and this leads to a lot of changes. We have to face the fact that in the end we will have to ship some parts on short notice, though, so we will have to find ways to do this. Maybe we can bring them ourselves in our suitcases. We have to be inventive there. In any case, it's a lot less than usual.

Olafur also chose artworks that use recycled or repurposed materials—such as driftwood that he scavenged from seashores in Iceland over the years and has used in numerous artworks. There's also a special display that we conceived for the exhibition, which presents ongoing research that the studio is engaged in into innovative and sustainable materials.

KERSTIN | The materials lab idea began with a project we have been working on with the textile company Kvadrat. We wanted to make a very sustainable curtain together. Now we are working with a few other external companies. We also do a lot in-house—for example, the pigments made from food waste.

And then we found a few materials which worked for us in terms of both aesthetics and sustainability, because the idea of the material workshop was that we only show materials we can use for artworks. For example, the red tiles which come from residue left over from aluminium production. If you want to have one ton of aluminium, you produce one and a half tons of this highly alkaline material, which is toxic and has to be specially disposed of. But the guys from Studio ThusThat found out if they burn it like terracotta in the oven, then the alkalinity disappears. It becomes stable, fixed together. Olafur has a few facade tile ideas, so instead of using fresh terracotta or any other brick-like material, we could use this waste material instead. It's very complex to do this holistically, but we're trying.

CAROLINE | Many of the artworks were chosen for their thematic connection to sustainability, works which represent Olafur's approach to nature or questions about the climate. *The exploration of the centre of the sun*, for example, incorporates sustainable energy: a solar panel placed in the museum's courtyard directly powers the light that illuminates the work and the motor that keeps it turning. The Little Sun project is also featured in the exhibition because it promotes access to clean, sustainable energy. This is, of course, about using sunlight or solar power instead of kerosene, and importantly about raising awareness of alternative energy. And *The glacier melt series 1999/2019,* 2019, brings together aerial photographs Olafur took in 1999 of several dozen glaciers in Iceland with images he took last summer—twenty years later—of the same glaciers from roughly the same position. The thirty pairs of images reveal the dramatic impact that global warming is having on the world.

Olafur also wanted to include in the exhibition experimental works and research that are relevant to the topic but not physically present in the museum, and for us this led to a new approach—the idea of presenting documentation of older actions and interventions on posters, representing these artworks in photography. It was an idea that was very much due to the fact that he wanted to create a sustainable show—it is also a way of reducing our carbon footprint. Of course we still put together a number of very immersive works as well.

New Energy

KAJANA | I asked Hasenkamp, our main shipping partner, 'Do you get a lot of requests like this?' And then they said that we actually were the first ones to ask, which I found really shocking. And Hasenkamp said, 'We can't tell the collectors and institutions how to do their work, but actually you can.' We, as the studio, can. We can say, 'If you want this exhibition, we have to calculate two months for shipping because we are not going to fly it.' But you cannot transition immediately to doing everything at once. So we're getting started and from our side, we are pushing as much as we can. But it's not in our hands alone.

CAROLINE | The MOT exhibition was a tipping point for us. We really made a lot of effort, we had a lot of discussions, and we can continue to use all this research in the long-term, artistically. Because now the companies understand that they have clients who are willing to go with them, who are on board. It is our intention to stop shipping by air. So now we really have to figure out how. This is the future.

SEBASTIAN | People ask, 'Why do you want to do this, because it's only symbolic?' They say it's a concept, it's a thought more than proper action, and they say, 'Why do you want to risk the relationship to the client for a concept?' Whereas we feel this is much more about showing what the future of our work needs to be. I consider this to be a step into a new world, into a really exciting new world by trying different things.

And I think we need to bring this interest, this excitement, to our collaborators, and once they understand, I think they are also able to rethink their position, to some extent at least, because they feel it's not an obligation or a hurdle or an obstacle—it's a new energy that makes you feel you are part of something that is moving forward, that transcends this quite depressing view that society has at the moment about burning forests and the serious actions people have to take. And from being in a state of worrying to taking proper and realistic action, I think that is something that moves people and that gives energy to people.

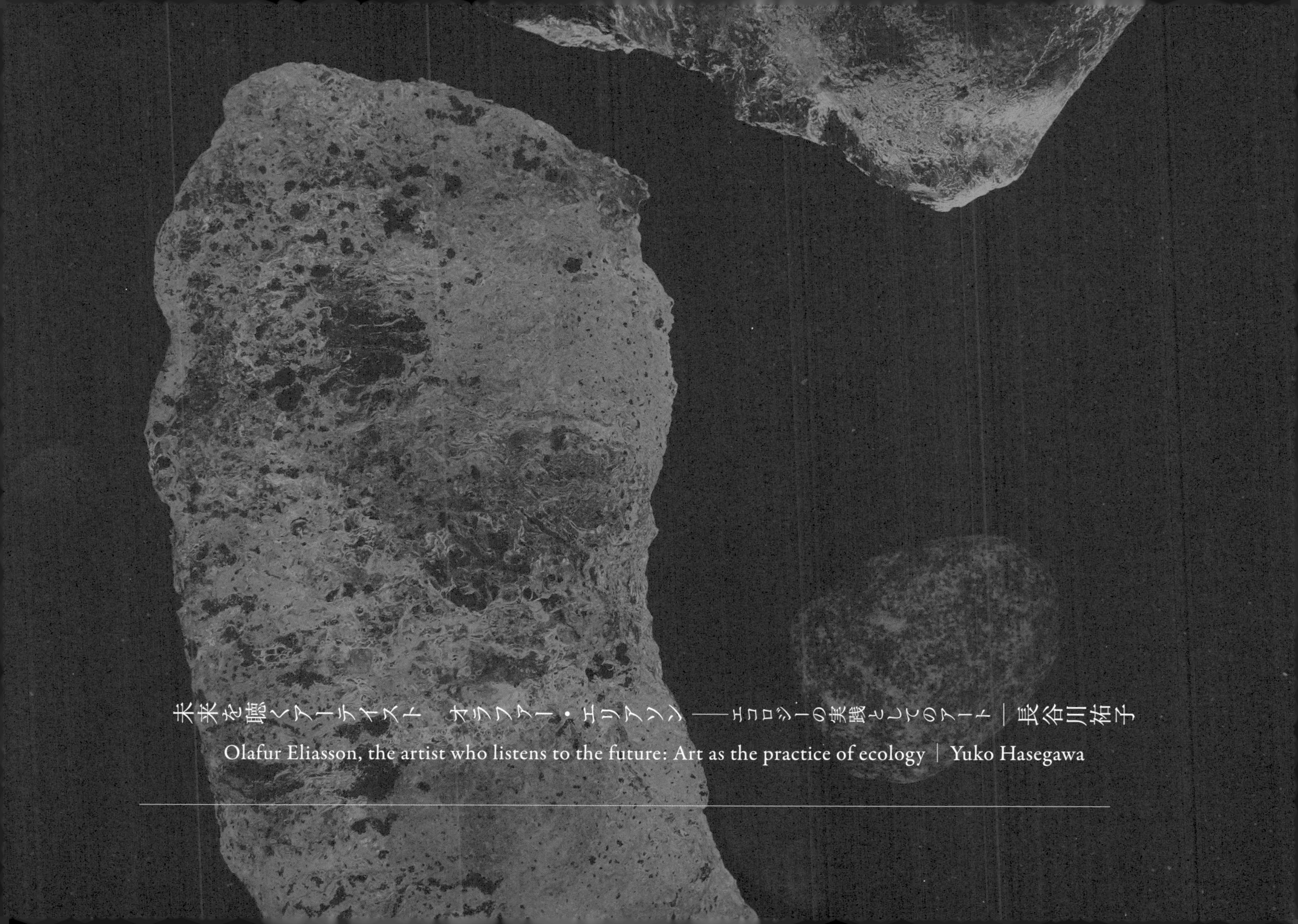

未来を聴くアーティスト　オラファー・エリアソン——エコロジーの実践としてのアート｜長谷川祐子

Olafur Eliasson, the artist who listens to the future: Art as the practice of ecology | Yuko Hasegawa

未来を聴くアーティスト　オラファー・エリアソン

——エコロジーの実践としてのアート

長谷川祐子

調和の感覚とはむしろ不確かさの感覚だと思っている
——オラファー・エリアソン

はじめに

オラファー・エリアソンは、一九九三年以降、霧や夕日、雨などの気象や、水、氷、光などの不定形でとらえがたい物質や事象に形を与え、作品化してきた。彼が登場した一九九〇年代前半は、ピエール・ユイグ、リアム・ギリック、ピピロッティ・リストなど多くの作家が一斉に日常生活やポップカルチャーからテーマや表現媒体を流用し、観客との間に新しいコミュニケーションを求めていった時期である。彼らは、日常体験を流用、あるいは「レディメイド」化し、新しいリアル／環境として提案することを試みた。[1]周囲を取り巻く空間、オブジェ、情報（イメージ、テキスト）などの環境が私たちとどのようにかかわるのか。これらの環境を感じとる新しい感覚によって、内-外の相互作用だけでなく、私たちの中に内省作用を促すというイントラアクション（intra-action）はすでにここから始まっていたと言える。[2]

この作家たちに共通するのは領域横断、メディウムの横断的な探究心と態度である。この一連の作家たちの表現動向のなかで、自然環境あるいはその要素を、レディメイド化、流用したのがエリアソンであった。アイスランド系デンマーク人の彼は、幼い頃よりアイスランドの大自然に親しんできた。エリアソンはアートを、多様なものを受け入れ、それらの間に相互作用と科学反応を起こさせる寛容で自由な関係性のスペースと考えている。彼はその可能性を試みるために、広範なメディア、方法――建築、プロダクトや環境も含めたデザイン、映像、パフォーマンスなど――を用いる。またその関心とリサーチは地質学、地球物理学、光学、生物学、知覚心理学などの科学分野や哲学への学問研究分野におよび、専門家との協働もおこなっている。技術者や調査員、建築家などを含む一二〇人を超えるスタッフをかかえる彼のスタジオ「スタジオ・オラファー・エリアソン」はそれらの活動の中心となっている。

ここで自然環境という言葉について、我々は検証する必要がある。一九五〇年代からグレート・アクセラレーションと呼ばれるように、急速な産業化、開発によって人間が自然とかかわり、これを変えてしまったために、すでに人間‐自然という二項対立は成立しなくなってしまった。これを説明する「人新世」という地質学に由来する概念は、今、政治、経済、文化的なすべての領域で語られている。エリアソンが自然環境の大きな変化に対して、サステナビリティを目的として意識的な活動をはじめたのは二〇〇〇年代からである。「アートが環境変化に対して何ができるのか」というメディアの質問に対して、彼は常に同じことを答えてきた。アートは解決案を提示しない、アートにできるのは人々に気づきを促すことだけだ、そして問題解決にむけた個々人の小さなアクションの意義を信じさせることだ、と。

一九九〇年代のアートは、社会環境の情報化と多様化に対して、人々の個人的な体験や記憶、身体を、その変化にむけて内省を促すことで、修正的に繋げ、調整しようとするものだった。これに対して、グローバル資本主義下の政治的社会的危機が表面化した二〇〇〇年以降は、大きな衝突と断絶に直面した精神と身体のサヴァイヴァル、持続可能性への模索にシフトした。「調整」ではなく「リセット」「オルタナティヴ」が求められるようになったのである。エリアソンはこの状況の変化に対して最も知的で実践的な反応をしたアーティストの一人なのである。

1
主観的、内なるものの共有から集合的な社会的心理の形成にむけて

非物質的で不定形のもの、動き（時間）に対するエリアソンの関心は、自身のブレイクダンサーとしての体験をはじめとして、身体／知覚を核として主観と客観、意識と物体を融合する現象学や、ベルグソンの主観的な時間論、芸術の脱物質化の傾向を論じたルーシー・リッパードの著作、*Six Years: The Dematerialization of the Art Object from 1966 to 1972*などを通して構築された。[3] 見る主体／見られる対象というモデルから、鑑賞者の身体の位相への重視と、脱物質化は並行して起こっていった。

エリアソンにとって、出現させる（appear）有形のものたちは何かを表象することを目的としていない。彼は人々の視線

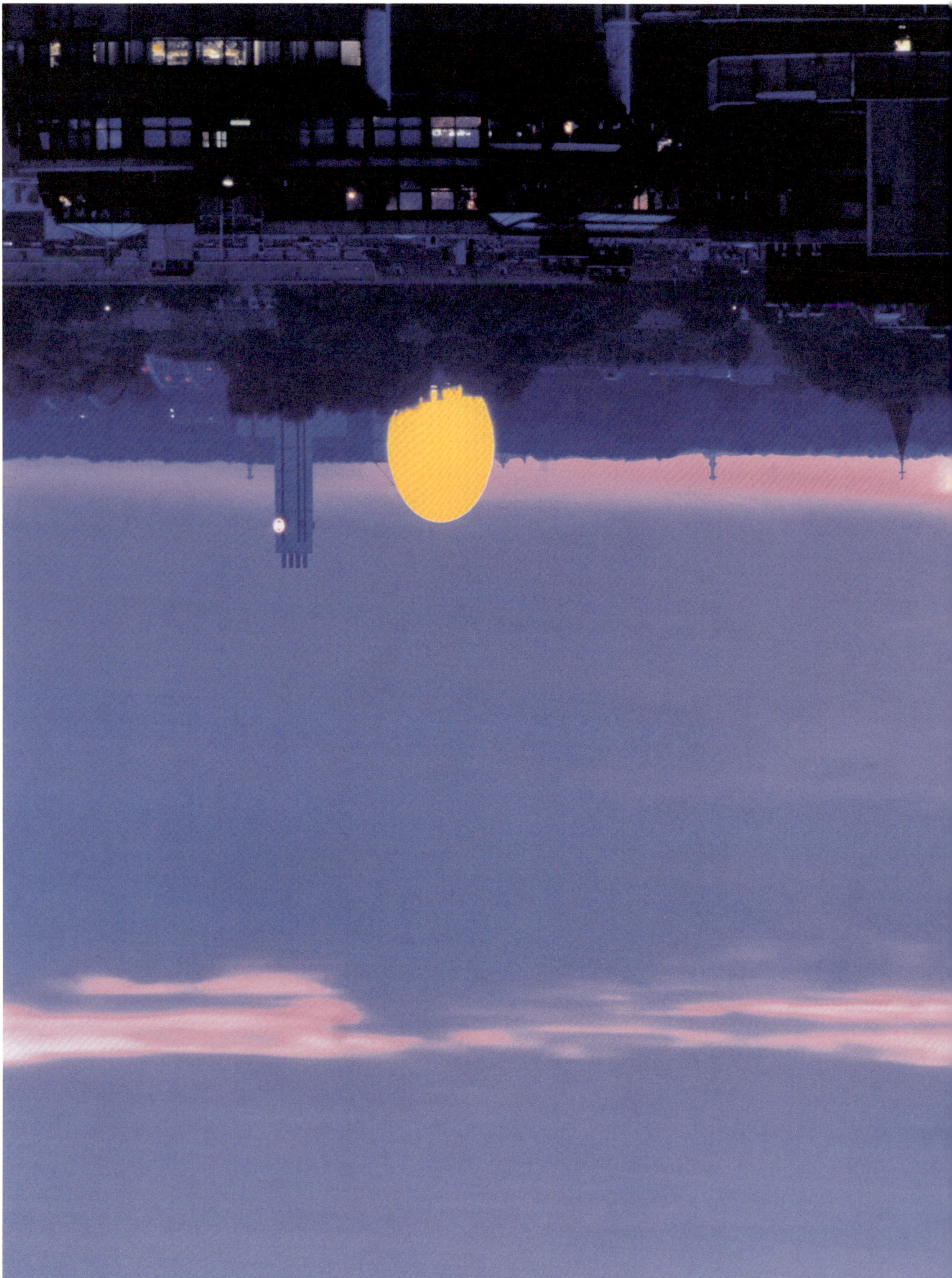

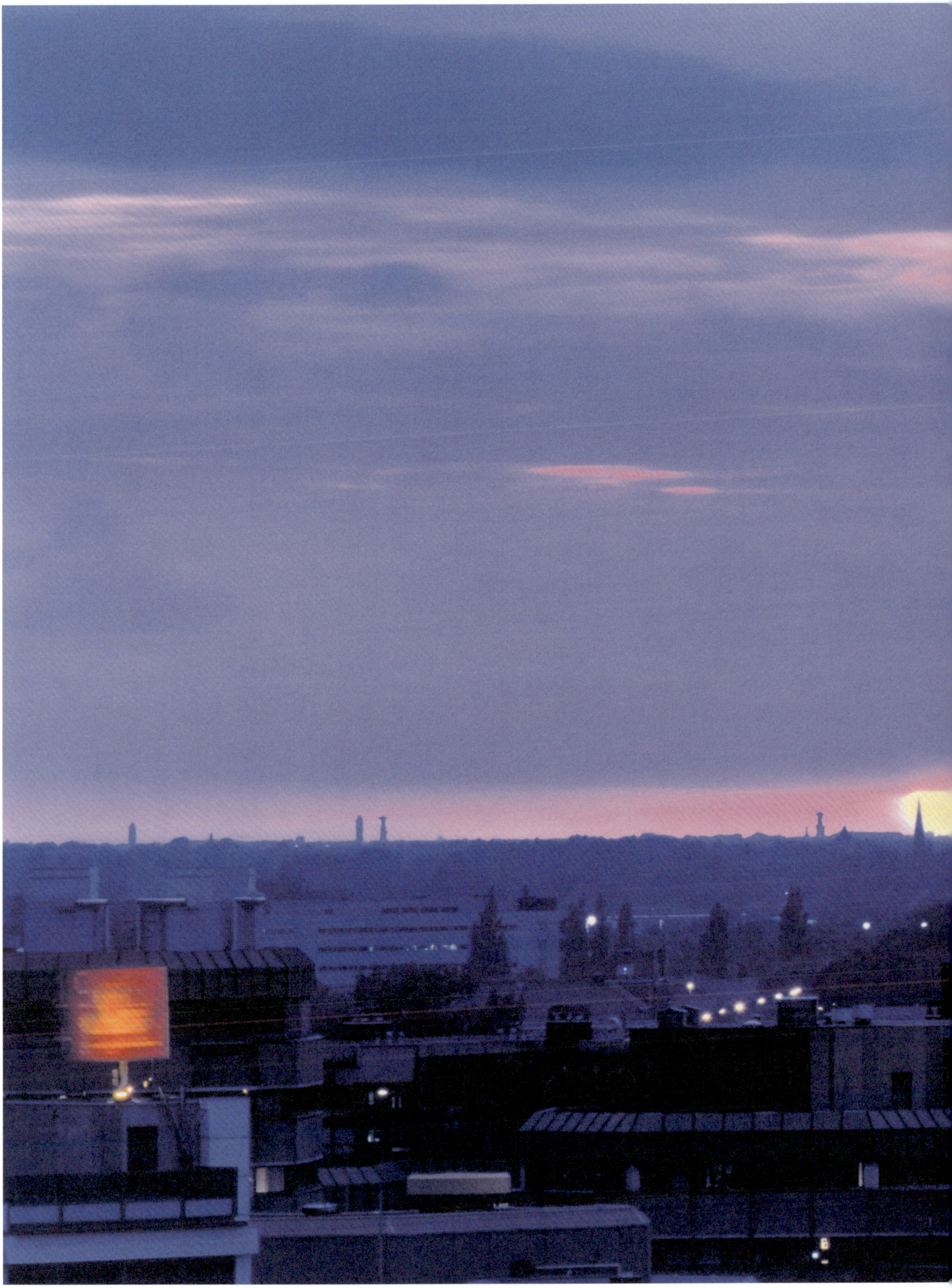

《二つの夕陽》1999、ユトレヒト（オランダ）｜ *Double sunset*, 1999, Utrecht

（gaze）にとって馴染みのあるもの、ないがゆえに不確かさや驚きをはらんでいるもの、を混合させて作品をつくる。つまり、過去の経験から認識できるものを入り口としてできるだけ遠くまで人々の想像力をつれていこうとするのである。それは滝であったり川であったり、水たまりにあたった光が、近くの壁に反射して生じるゆらゆらと動く波紋であったりする。

ゲシュタルトは動きによって絶えず崩されてしまう。作品を観客が目（知性）で見るのではなく、身体で感じること（feeling）と、作品として確かな「存在」を両立させることの矛盾に満ちた課題。エリアソンは、水の流れ→光→ストロボ、そして波／波紋へと方法を変えていった。波は次々とレゾナンスし、生じる波紋によって形を変える。今目の前にあるものと、その前にあったもの（過去）と次にくるもの（未来）の形象は記憶の中にしかとどめておくことができない。波は客観として外部に存在するというより知覚によって主観的に内部に生成されていく。

本展の新作《ときに川は橋となる》（2020）は、波紋の生じる様を複数のスポットライトで照らし出し、リフレクションをシークエンスとして見せ、現象として感じられるものにした。円環状のスクリーン。その真下に置かれ、ゆっくりと揺れ動く水盤に、一二個の光源から投射された光が一二のリフレクションとしてスクリーンに映り込む。直前の波の動きが、直後のリフレクションの形に影響の連鎖を与え続ける。そのパターンはいくつかある。約一五秒の水盤の動きによる波紋の余韻が約一分の続いたあとの約二〇秒の静止——。そのリズムを繰り返しつつ、取り巻く光は絶え間なく変わっていく。円形の波紋が少しずつ崩れて、ゆらぎが一気にバーストするといった劇的変化をとげるものや、ゆらゆらとしたクラゲや扇のようなものもある。波のフィールド（Field of waves）の真ん中に立つと、夢殿ならぬ月の神殿（moon temple）の中で、私たちは惑星間を移動するような浮遊感を味わう。

そこでは瞬間瞬間の「現れ appearance」の連続が時間を形成している。私たちは波紋の動きによって「時間」に見つめられるのだ。エリアソンは長い間波と振動に関心をもってきた。本作は日本庭園にある複数の水のデザインとありようが彼の着想源となったという。「ゆく川の流れはたえずして、しかももとの水にあらず」と鴨長明の方丈記の一説にあるように、水の流れへの視線を通して、移ろいゆく時間性を認識する主観と客観の止揚は日本の思想や美学に根付くものである。本作品は水の記憶と詩学、ポリティクスを含むシンフォニックなものである。そして波というこのうえなく主観的、内的なリフレクションを追求する現象学的な知覚体験を、その複雑さと精度をたもちながらパブリックスペースの規模で人々が共有できるものにした、エリアソンにとってはマイルストーンとなる作品といえよう。

《ときに川は橋となる》で示されるように、エリアソンはたえずテクニカルな方法論や素材を実験的に組み合わせることで新たな視覚効果を探求している。

見る者が環境を探索することで意味を受け取ることのできる、アフォーダンスをもつ作品づくりを、知覚と身体の実験、試行錯誤をへながら実践する。[4] それは明示された目的／意味でなく、不確かさ、解読できない複雑さに観客にたどりついてもらうためである。たとえば《おそれてる？》(2004) では、展示室の中央の天井から吊り下げられた三つのガラスの円盤が、異なるスピードでゆっくりと動く。これらのガラス盤にはある一色の光を透過させ、その補色の光を反射させる特性をもつフィルター（ダイクロイック・フィルター）が使われている。あるガラス盤を透過した光は赤とシアンに分割される。シアンは展示室の壁に投影され、赤は隣接するガラス盤に反射してさらに黄色とマゼンタに分割されて別の壁に現れ、それらが青と緑の光を反射する。一枚のガラス盤の位置や角度が変わることで、無限のプロジェクションの変化が起こる。この原理を用いた分光測定は、ものの性質（成分）を外部から調べることにも用いられている。物質の性質を精査する道具をエリアソンはこともなげに作品に応用する。また《太陽の中心への探査》(2017) は、一二の菱形と二〇の三角形を組み合わせた非対称の複合多面体である。鑑賞者はその周りを歩くことで複数の異なる形状を見ることができる。構造体のフレームには《おそれてる?》で使ったものと同種のフィルターガラス板がはめ込まれ、アームに付けられたライトの光が中を回転しており、部屋全体に銀河のように輝くリフレクションを投射する。別の位相の空間を出現させる多様な鏡の用い方などシンプルな材料を使いながら、知覚体験を大きく変容させるのだ。

それだけでなくエリアソンは、鑑賞者を作品との出会いに導くためのインストラクションを工夫する。彼が開発した鑑賞のための携帯端末向けのアプリは彼自身のパフォーマンスによっていかに深く作品と出会うかが説明されており、教材としても優れている。

エリアソンは観客を作品空間に招き入れ、体験を通してどのように感じるかを発見し、そしてそれが意味の生産に繋がるように提案をするのだ。ノルトライン＝ヴェストファーレン州立美術館で開催された「カンディンスキー、マレーヴィッチ、モンドリアン——無限、白の深淵」展の来館者に彼がガイドとして話す映像《あなたの展覧会ガイド》(2014) は、いくつかの段階を進むようになっている [fig.1]。まず最初は、次第に一つの作品を見る時間を増やす〈time 時間〉、次に、〈focus 集中〉と周辺全体を感じるパノラミックな意識の両方をもつ〈panoramic awareness パノラミックな意識〉、周囲の人の感じているものを自分のものとして共感するために彼らをみる〈empathy 共感〉、呼吸というミクロの動きと身体の大きな動きを同時に意識する〈movement 動き〉、鏡に映る自分を他者と見るように、作品の中に自身の延長を見て、もう一つの自身とともに次の作品を見る〈Your other self あなたの中にいるもう一人の自分〉。この other self は「私の身体は見るものであると同時に見えるもの」（現象学）から着想されている。ゆえに私が「作品」を見ていると同時に「作品」も私を見ていると感じるのである。エリアソンの現象学の応用は、ときに非常に禅の実践過程に近い。それらは、より深い体験へのアプローチを人々に促すものである。

2
共感に浸された空間

アプリの中でも語っているが、エリアソンはよく共同作業という言葉を使う。《あなたのオレンジ色の残像が現れる》(2000)、《あなたに今起きていること、起きたこと、これから起きること》(2020) など作品のタイトルに「あなたの－your」が頻出するように、あなたの中で起こった出来事という個人的でユニークな体験であることを強調する。作品が成立するのはあなたと私（作品／作家）の共同作業であるとする。各自固有の知覚体験によって作品が成立することを意味している。《ビューティー》(1993) は背の高さ（目の位置）によって出現する位置が異なる。「あなたによって存在する、あなたにしか見えない虹」なのである。

霧は共感を引き起こすのに使われる [fig.2]。自分とまわりをとりまくものが溶け合う、まさにアンビエント（曖昧な）空間をつくりだす。光の色が霧とともに、その中を移動する人々の身体に沿って混ざり合うインスタレーション作品は、その典型的な例である。

この「あなたの－your」は環境哲学者であるティモシー・モートンのいう「あなた」と「私」のまわりを取り巻く環境とつながる。モートンは『自然なきエコロジー』で自然を「自然環境」として客体化せず、動物やモノなど含めた他の要素すべてを、「私」を「取り巻くもの」と考え、「私」も「あなた」もそこに含まれると考える。彼は共存の条件を、共通の価値観といった内面的な領域ではなく、環境の共有に見ていこうとする。[5] 環境の共有は、社会学政治学では「ともにある」という形で論じられている。[6] そしてこれはエリアソンの目指す、作品を通して生まれる共感に浸された空間の共有に繋がるといえる。

モートンは最初音楽からアートにアプローチを始めたが、「アーティストは、物事がどうなっていくのかへと感度を合わせていき、未来を聴く」として彼らが現実をより深く徹底的に感覚するからこそ、未来について考えられると述べる。[7] 彼が支持する「オブジェクト指向存在論（Object-Oriented Ontology）」は、オブジェクトそのものを究極の存在とみなし構成素材や用途に還元しないという理論であり、感覚論を超えることを強調する立場である。とらえがたい現象を物質化させて目にみえる、触れられるかたちにする。エリアソンは個人の主観内の作用を超えた、これを取り巻く環境の作用に関心を広げつつあ

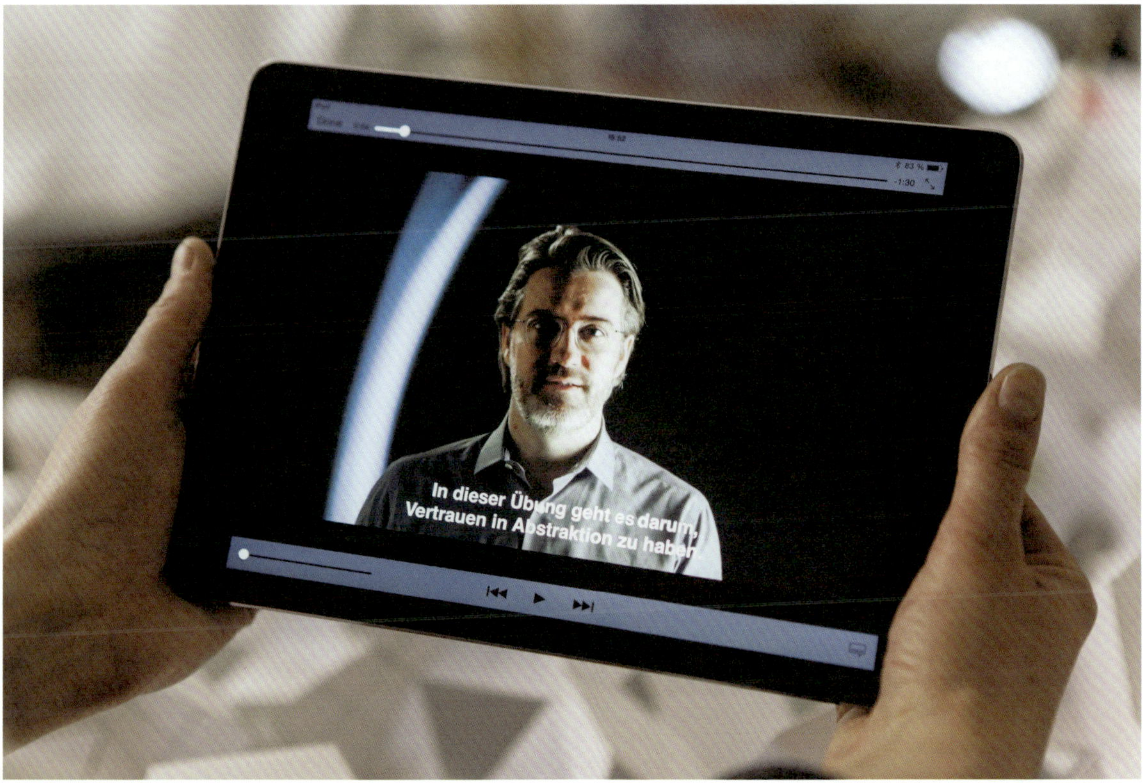

fig. 1 《あなたの展覧会ガイド》2014、iOSおよびアンドロイド向けアプリ｜ *Your exhibition guide*, 2014, Application for iOS and Android

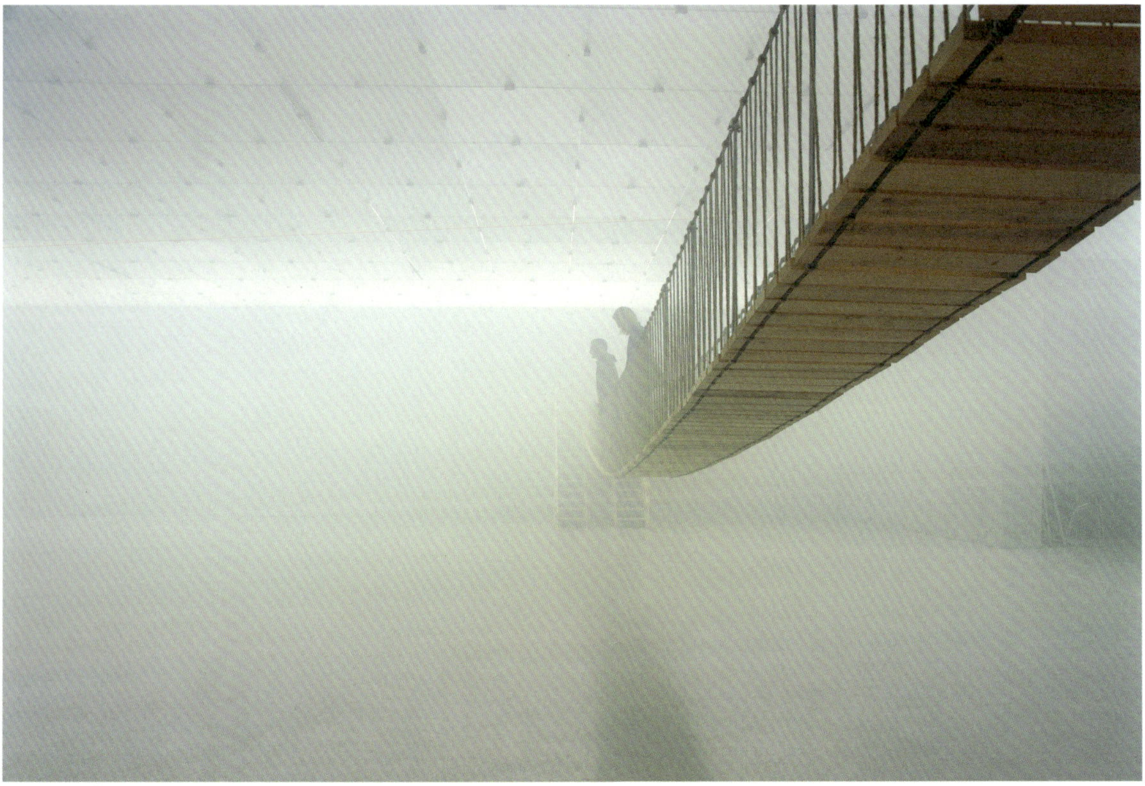

fig. 2 オラファー・エリアソン+ギュンター・フォクト《とりもたれた動き》2001、ブレゲンツ美術館（オーストリア）｜ Olafur Eliasson and Günther Vogt, *The mediated motion*, 2001, Kunsthaus Bregenz, Austria

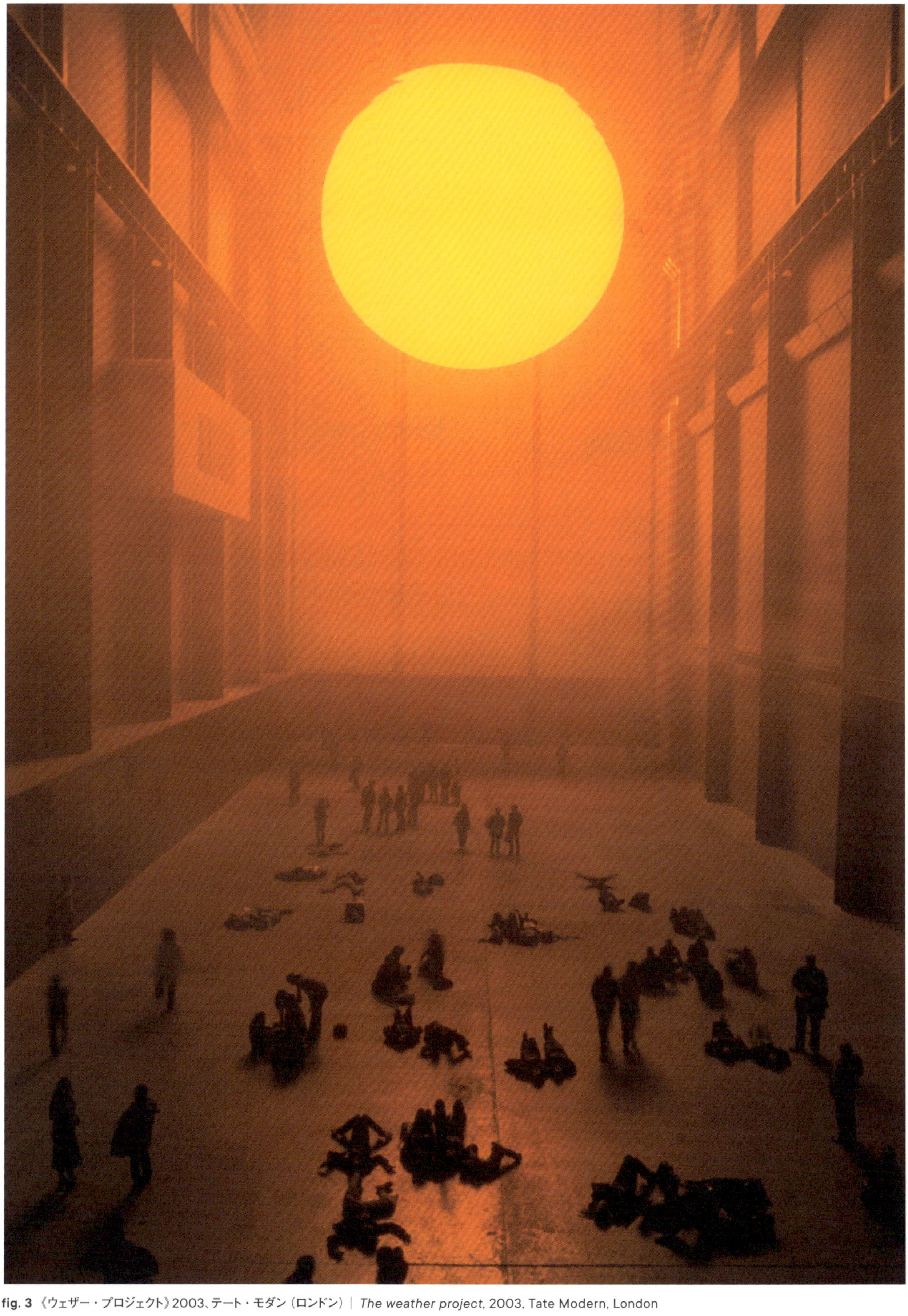

fig. 3 《ウェザー・プロジェクト》2003、テート・モダン（ロンドン）｜ *The weather project*, 2003, Tate Modern, London

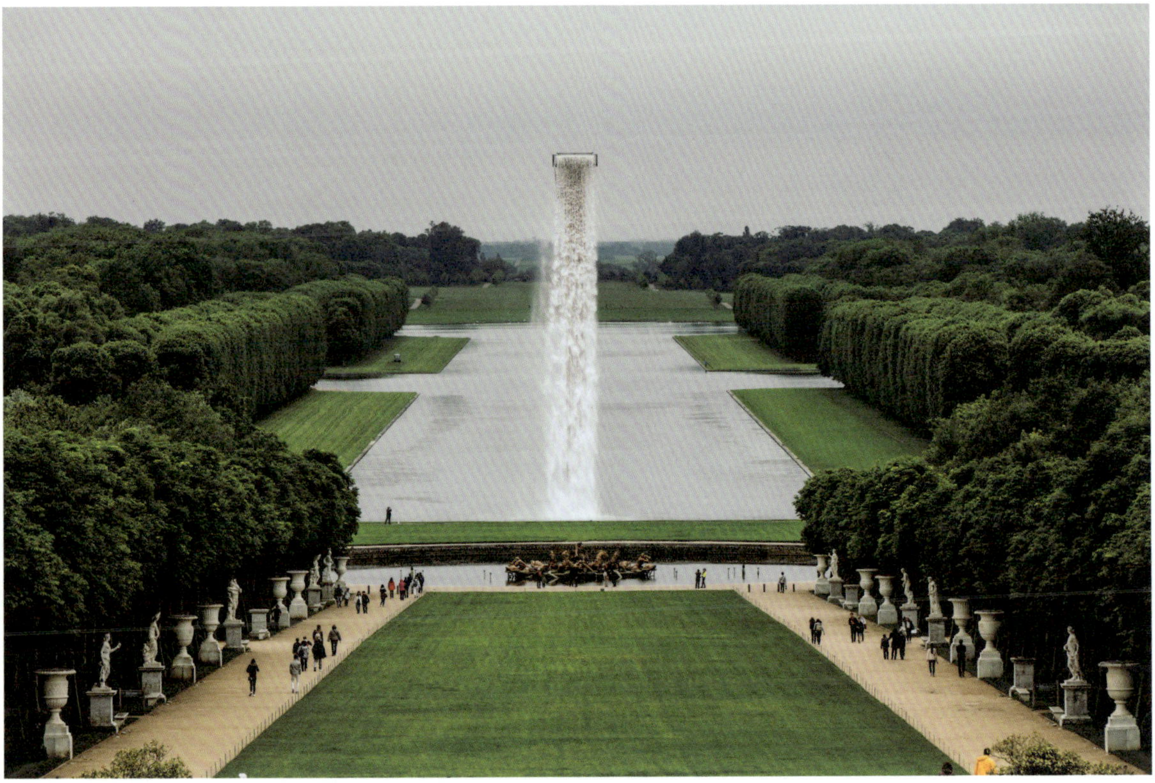

fig. 4 《滝》2016、ヴェルサイユ｜*Waterfall*, 2016, Palace of Versailles

り、モートンや彼の理論との出会いは、その意識をより環境や共有空間に向けるきっかけとなった。

私が対象に対して感じていることだけでなく、他者がその対象に対して感じていることを感じとり、共鳴したとき、それは共感（empathy）となる。それは繋がり（connectiveness）という意識を強化する。ミシェル・クーはエリアソンの作品が引き出す共感は、同じ（sameness）、似ている（mimesis）といったものとは異なり、多様で深刻な状況の中でたえず変わっていく関係、という差異の中でとらえられる、という。[8]

本書のエリアソンとモートンの対話をみていると、それぞれが、気づき（awareness）、共有する（sharing）、もてなす（host）、感じ（feeling）、動き（movement）などの概念の重要性について共有しながら、エリアソンはこれをモノや装置、つくりだされた現象を通して体感させることに、モートンはさまざまな思想や哲学や彼自身の観察を一体化させ、総合的な思考を物質にさわるように体験させようとしているかに見える。

この二人に共通するものは「ゆるやかさ」「くつろぎ」の感覚である。両者とも観客、参加者に洗練された知識の持ち主（アートについてのリテラシー）であることを求めない。二人にはあたかも大きなウォーターベッドの上で弾みながら会話をしているようなリズムがある。エリアソンのつくりだす共感の場もこのような面があるのではないだろうか。それはトラスト、信頼のマットレスでもある。

この共感に浸された場を、エリアソンは、二〇〇三年につくりだしている。テート・モダンのタービンホールを使った《ウェザー・プロジェクト》(2003)であり、これは、天気という事象に対して人々が多くの関心を共有していることがアイデア源となった［fig.3］。トンネルなどに使われている、世界をモノトーンにしてしまう黄色の光を使う。ものたちが色を奪われたとき、人々はそれらに従来と異なった注意を向ける。一つの閉じられた環境をつくることでそこで人々の新しいコミュニケーションや発想がうかぶのではないか。鏡を効果的に用いて空間を拡大し、個人や小さな集まりがそこに分散しつつ、同じ場を共有している状況を、天井の鏡が自分と他者を含めて映し出している。そこには太陽の光の下で「ともにある」という共感の空間が実現されている。

エリアソンは、物質をメタ化、象徴化しない。彼はこれを「脱権威化」と呼ぶ。

「光そのものに関心があるのではなく、自分がやろうとしていることに対して使いやすそうなので選んだまでです」と語る[9]。なぜそれをやるのかが重要で、「どのように」で素材探しが始まる。つくりこまれたデザインの庭園や自然の中の美しい滝に対して、金属パイプで組み上げられた足場、ドライな産業構造物から怒涛のように流れる水を見るという経験は何か［fig.4］。ただ膨大な量の水が音をたてて落下しているという現象から、人々は、落下の「速度」、水の「動き」、落下する水の「ボリューム」などに気づくのである。また「霧」は、人々の知覚や意識の内外の境界を曖昧にし、人々と空間を繋げ一体化させる媒体として有効なのである。

3 システムをつくる――新しい芸術家のモデル

観客の心理に影響を与えることから、「オルタナティヴ」にむけての「応用された行動」へ移る過程で、エリアソンの実践のスタイルも変化していった。

テート・モダンのカタログの中でマーク・ゴドフリーは、エリアソンは新しいタイプのアーティストであることをアクティビスト（リトルサン［fig.5］、緑のランプシェード［fig.6］、アイス・ウォッチングなど）、建築家（フィヨルドハウス［fig.7］とその周辺の環境計画）、舞台デザイナー［fig.8］、国連やテッド、ダボス会議におけるアートの社会的役割や意味の演説など、多岐にわたる活動をあげて説明している[10]。彼は「もっとアーティストはいろいろなことができる」と述べている[11]。エリアソンは、それまでは現象学や認知心理学に関心をもっていたが、二〇〇五年くらいを境に主体性や内省にあまりにオブセッシブになりすぎた現象学的アプローチに疑念をもち、パブリックスペースや建築、都市計画やランドスケープデザインに関心を増大させるように

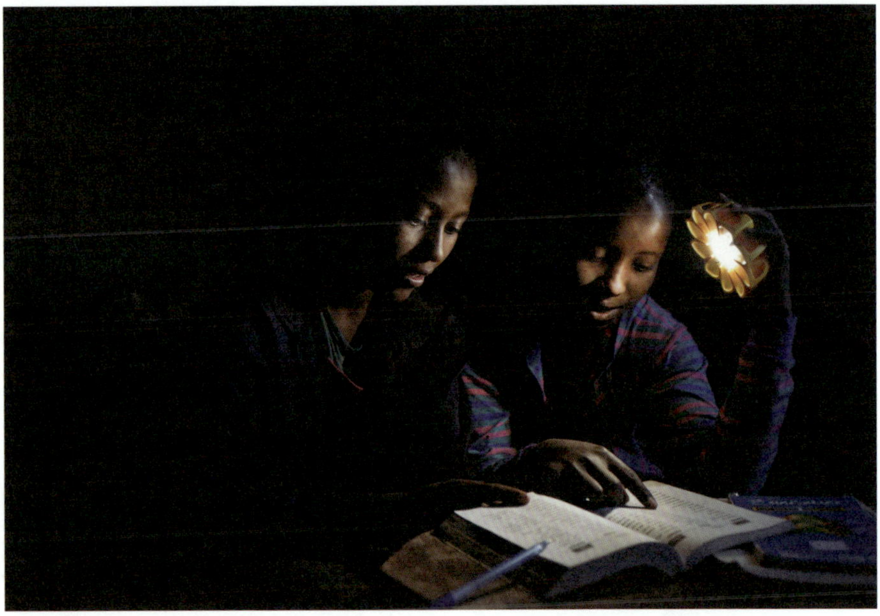

fig. 5「リトルサン」2012、アディスアベバ
Little Sun, 2012, Addis Ababa

エリアソンが携帯式のソーラーライト「リトルサン」は電力にアクセスできない地域で灯油ランプの代替品として使われている。昼間の数時間の光をためるだけで夜じゅう使用できる。価格を先進国とそれ以外の地域で変えている。世界の12億人の人々が電気にアクセスできない状態にあることへの応答である。

Created by Eliasson in collaboration with engineer Frederik Ottesen, Little Sun solar-powered lamps are used to replace kerosene lanterns in areas where people do not have access to electricity. By providing clean and affordable energy, these lamps reduce the negative effects of kerosene use on the climate and individual health.

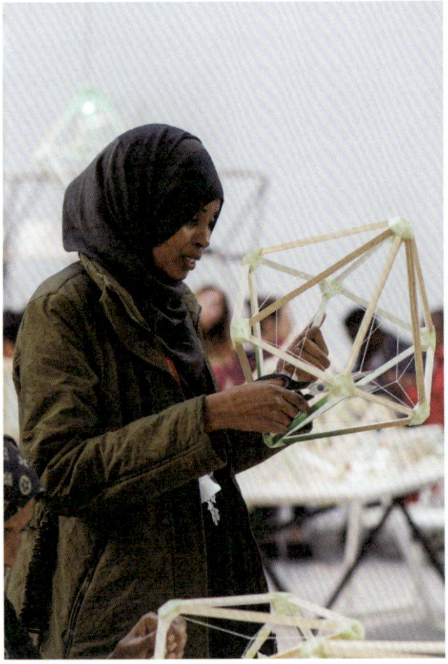

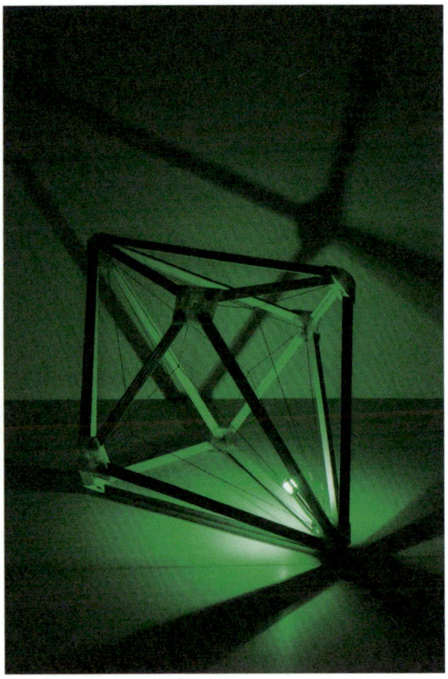

fig. 6《グリーンライト－アーティスティック・ワークショップ》2016、ティッセン＝ボルネミッサ現代美術館との共同開催、第57回ヴェネツィア・ビエンナーレ「VIVA ARTE VIVA」2017年
Green light – An artistic workshop, 2016, in collaboration with Thyssen-Bornemisza Art Contemporary, 57th International Art Exibition of La Biennale di Venezia VIVA ARTE VIVA, 2017

ウィーンの財団TBA21とともに、難民のためにエリアソンが企画した《グリーンライト－アーティスティック・ワークショップ》(2016)プロジェクト(greenlightworkshop.org)。多角形のライト《グリーンライト》は、接合部分はヨーグルトの容器を再利用し3Dプリンターでつくり、糸はAnudandoが製造するビニール袋のリサイクル品を使うなど環境に配慮している。楽しみながら自分のライトをつくり、皆で組み合わせられるようになっている。

Green light – An artistic workshop, 2016 (greenlightworkshop.org) is a project co-organized by Eliasson and TBA21, a foundation based in Vienna. The 3D-printed joints are made from recycled yoghurt cups; the wood is sustainably sourced; the thread is manufactured by Anudando from recycled plastic bags. This environmentally friendly work provides workshop participants with an opportunity to get to know one another by making lamps together. Sales of the lamps raised money for organisations that support refugees.

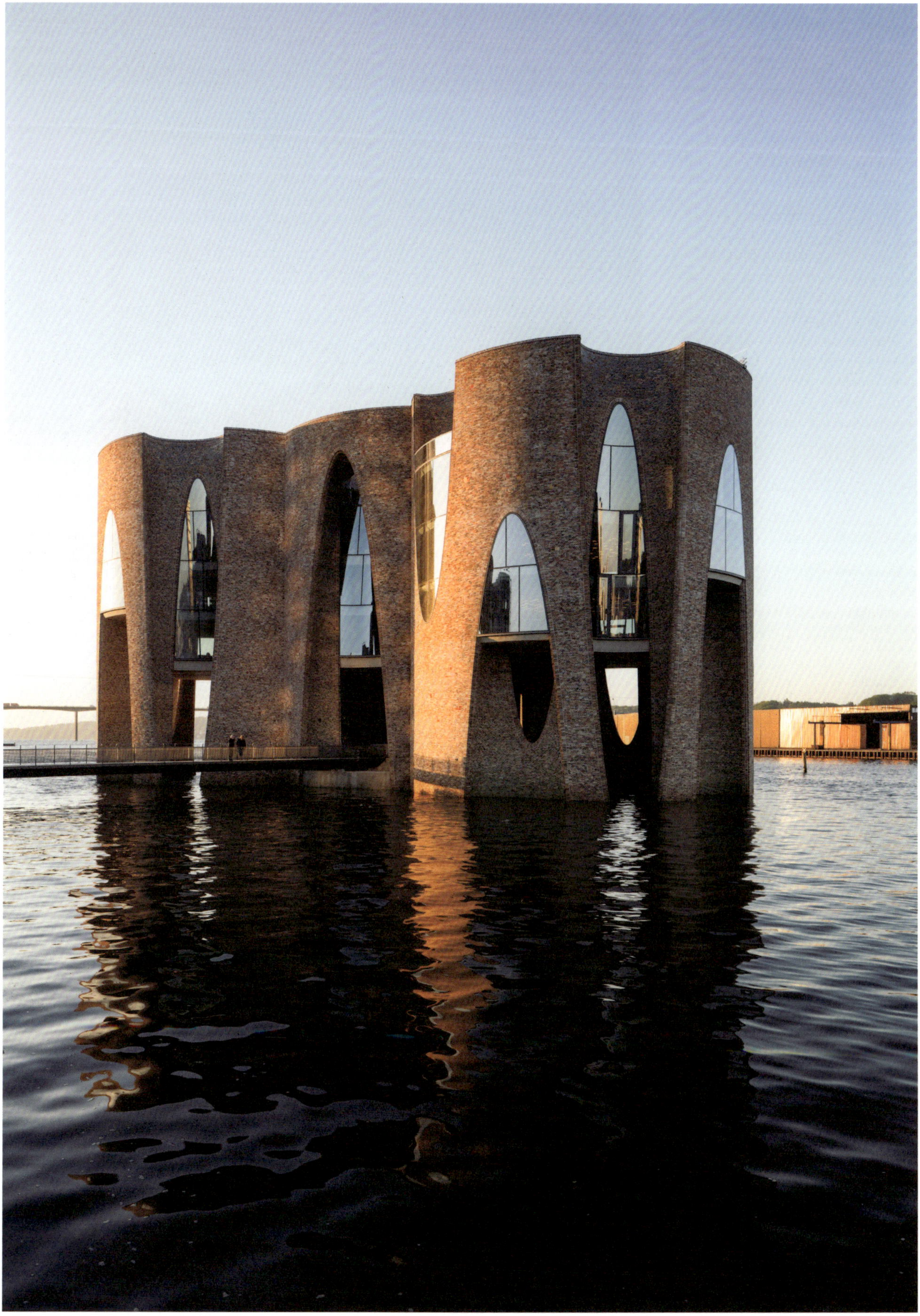

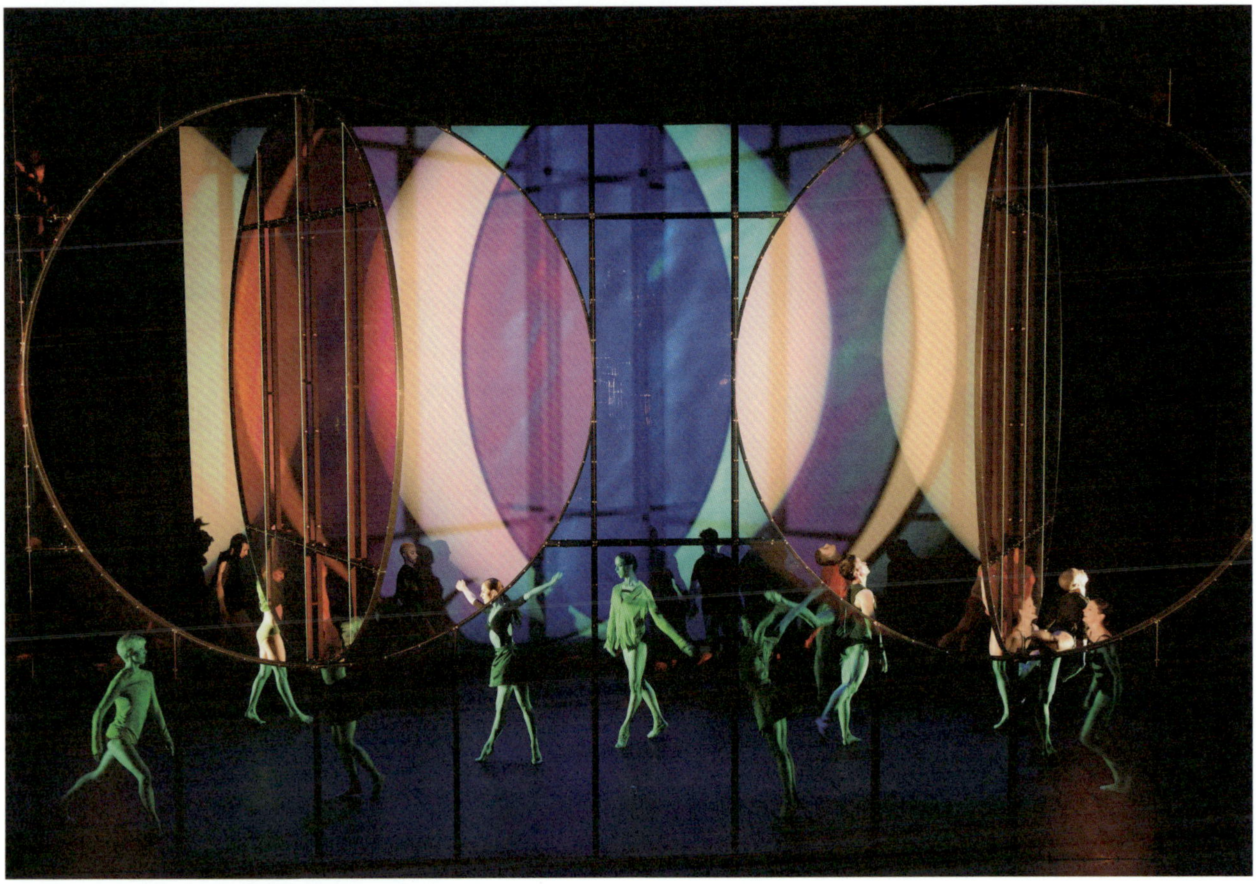

fig. 8 《ツリー・オブ・コーズ》2015、参加：ウェイン・マクレガー、オラファー・エリアソン、ジェイミーXX、ウェイン・マクレガー・カンパニーおよびパリ・オペラ座バレエのダンサー、オペラハウス、マンチェスター
Tree of Codes, 2015, by Wayne McGregor, Olafur Eliasson and Jamie xx with dancers from Company Wayne McGregor and Paris Opera Ballet, Opera House, Manchester

エリアソンは現代バレーの舞台と照明デザインをおこなった。ダンサーの身体と合わせて、次々に多様に変化する光のパフォーマンスが展開された。

Eliasson developed the visual concept for the contemporary ballet *Tree of Codes*, choreographed by Wayne McGregor and with music composed by Jamie xx. His stage design uses intricate sets of reflective, transparent, and refractive surfaces and coloured light to create a dynamic, ever-evolving, complexly layered space in which the dancers are multiplied and overlap, and within which reflections of the audience also appear.

fig. 7 オラファー・エリアソン＋セバスチャン・ベーマン、スタジオ・オラファー・エリアソン「フィヨルドハウス」2009–2018、ヴァイレ（デンマーク）
Olafur Eliasson and Sebastian Behmann with Studio Olafur Eliasson, Fjordenhus
2009–2018, Vejle, Denmark

建築家のセバスチャン・ベーマンとともにエリアソンが初めて建物全体を手がけた「フィヨルドハウス」はデンマークの港湾都市ヴァイレの海の上に建っている。4つの円柱で構成された建物の高さは約28メートル、外壁と内壁はさまざまな形や色のレンガでできており、建物内に置かれた家具や照明もエリアソンと彼のスタジオによってデザインされている。

Fjordenhus (Fjord House) in Vejle is the first building designed entirely by Eliasson and architect Sebastian Behmann. Commissioned by Kirk Kapital, the building brings together years of the studio's research in diverse fields – urban space, light conditions, nature, physical movement, how we use our senses – into one project. Fjordenhus melds artistic and architectural vision, incorporating site-specific artworks with specially designed furniture and lighting.

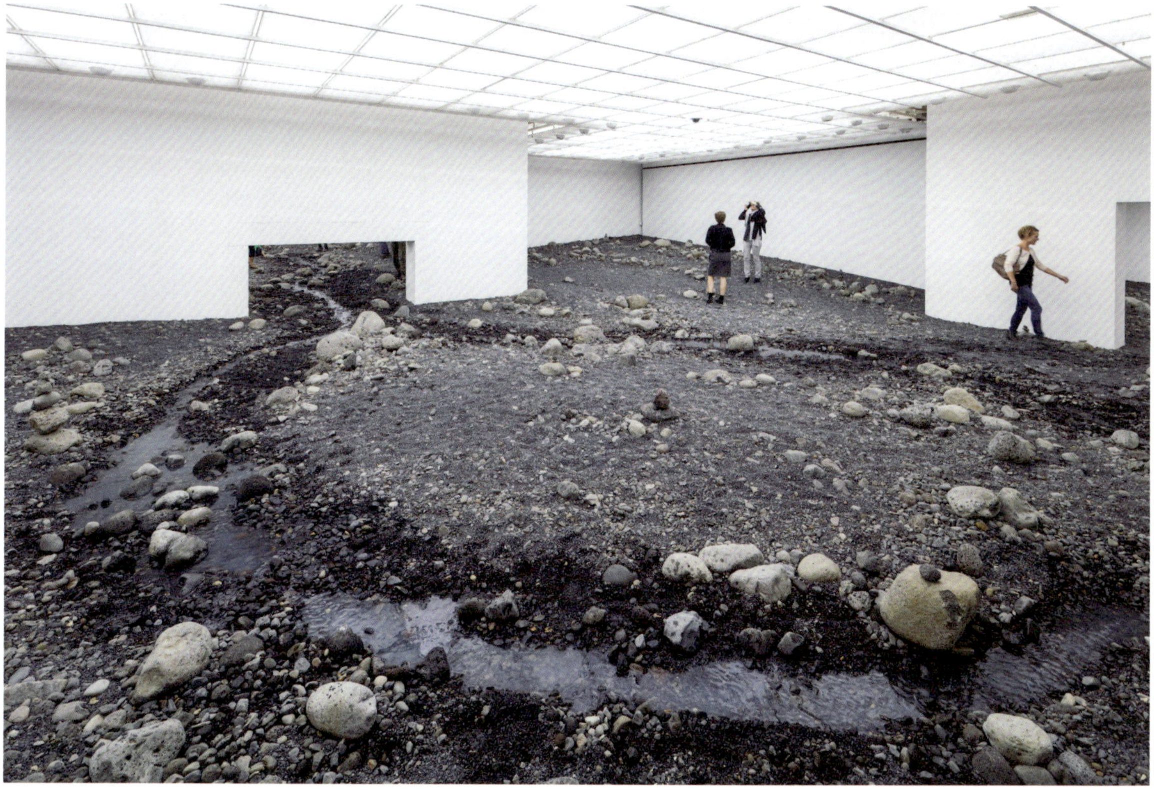

fig. 9《リバーベッド》2014、ルイジアナ近代美術館、フムレバク（デンマーク） *Riverbed*, 2014, Louisiana Museum of Modern Art, Humlebaek, Denmark

なった。その新しい展開は、世界が人新世や、「関係性」を科学的心理的に検証すべき「新たなエコロジー」の時代に突入したことと連動している。科学人類学者のブルーノ・ラトゥールが提唱した人間と非人間が相互作用してつくりだす「アクターネットワーク理論」や、哲学者のグレアム・ハーマンによる「オブジェクト指向存在論」などが、人間中心主義を脱中心化、脱権威化していく動向はエリアソンを惹きつけた。物理的空間を生きているものととらえた文化地理学者のドリーン・マッシー、物の政治的エコロジーについて論じた政治学者のジェーン・ベネットなど政治社会につながる新唯物論の展開がそこにはあった。ベネットは『振動する物質（Vibrant Matter）』において、人間活動の周辺にある「振動する物質性（vibrant materiality）」を明確にすることで「政治的な出来事の分析」が変わると述べる[12]。エリアソンは自らの関心について「それは現象学の内向性に対する批判としての新唯物論への関心の移行というよりは、その中間にあるような立ち位置というべきだろう[13]」と述べている。従来の現象学で、たとえばメルロ＝ポンティがセザンヌの絵画について「振動する」という言葉を使ったとしても、そこにはジェーン・ベネットの『振動する物質』に書かれたような強い社会論や集団で共有できる同義性はないとする[14]。

感じ取ることが行動につながる——共感とその場にあるものをホストする、アートは信頼を基盤としている。それは単純な調和の空間ではない。エリアソンは、シャンタル・ムフが語る政治性の回復──正の多様性（plurality）の中から生まれる敵対性、その基盤となる「信頼（trust）」の議論[15]に対して強い関心をもっている。その「信頼」とは何か、彼はアートを通じて検証しようとしている。

ラトゥールは、非人間のアクター（他に作用をおよぼしうる存在）として、ある川を例にとる。川は氾濫し、流れをかえる、その川の変化は、その領域に作用し、国境の境界設定や人々の生活に影響を与える。彼は川に無害の緑の染料を撒いて、川を緑色にした《グリーン・リバー》（1998-2001）、水管を渠水構に突っ込み溢れ出した水が小さな川ならぬ一・五キロにもおよぶ小さな川をつくった《侵食》（1997）[fig.9]。緑色は川・水の流れに明らかな形を与え、私たちが日常意識していなかったものが、一つの作用体として出現する。溢れた水は勝手に川となり、都市の中に別の風景をつくる。これらは、アクターとみることができ、エリアソン作品がすでに、このラトゥール的な思考の転換を胚胎していたことを示している。

今アーティストとして最も関心があるのは「システムをつくること[16]」であるとエリアソンは言う。この展覧会のコンセプトをエコロジーとサステナビリティにしようと作家とキュレーターとで決めたとき、それはオルタナティヴを提案することを意味していた。エコロジーやサステナビリティに関する表象（イメージ）やプロパガンダ、実践記録の証拠をみせる展覧会ではなく、意識の変化やシステムの変革への提案を含む展覧会である。

まず私たちは、輸送を減らし、地産地消とするため、日本で新作をつくることを構想した。空輸による二酸化炭素排出量を減らすため、最小限に切り詰めた作品を輸送するにあたっては列車と船で輸送することとした。ベルリンを出てハンブルグまでは車、そこから列車でポーランド、マワシェビチェ村、ザバイエカリエ地方、ロシアを経由して中国蘇州の太倉市まで運び、そこから船に積みかえて東京まで運んだ。各クレートにはドローイングマシンが設置されており、紙の淵にセットされているボールペンが列車の振動で機械の手によって自動的に紙の上にドローイングを書いていくようになっている。それはあたかも地震計がアクターとなって描画したようだ。クレートを開けたとき、この一二個のドローイングは時間の記憶を実にさまざまな形で刻印していた。タイトル《クリティカルゾーンの記憶（ドイツ－ポーランド－ロシア－中国－日本）》（2020）の「クリティカルゾーン」は地質学用語で、岩盤と樹冠の最上部との間の地球の薄い層を指し、生命システムを支えている層を意味している。これに加えて、空輸を基本とする美術館の展覧会輸送システムに対する批評としての意味も含んでいる。実際デリケートなドローイング作品と他の美術作品を、列車と船で輸送することに対して、保険をかけてくれる会社がないなど、多くの困難がともなった。

また展示のために必要な電力の一部はソーラーパネルによっ

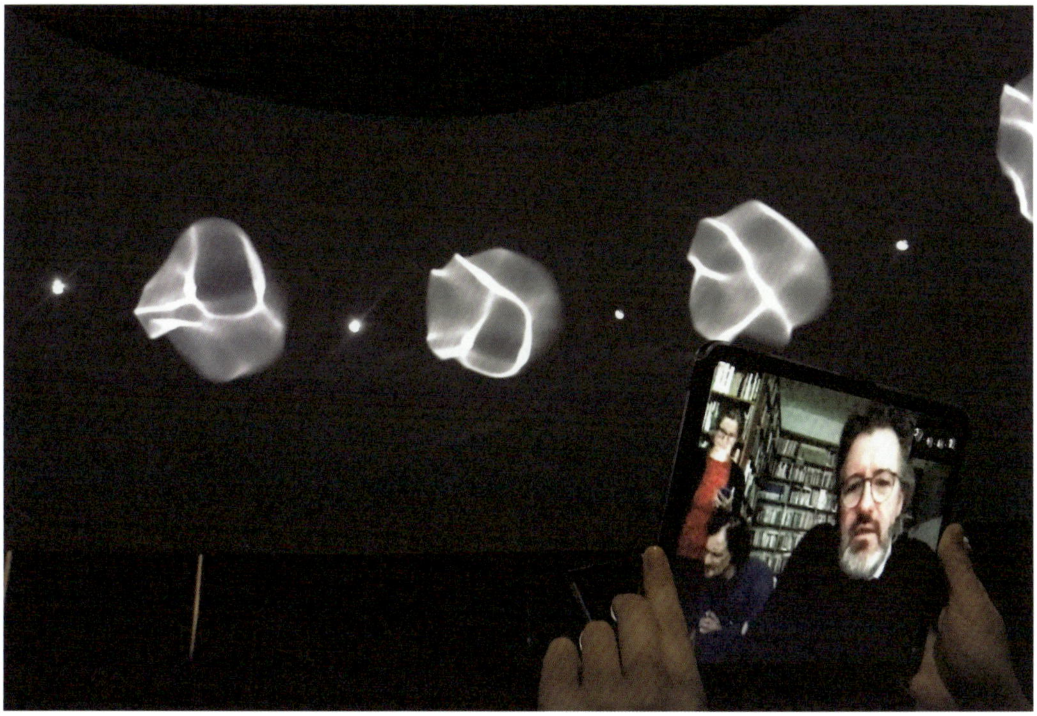

fig.10 展示室で「ときに川は橋となる」の制作途中の光景。スカイプでスタジオとエリアソンをつないだ。iPadのスクリーン上で指示をだすエリアソン。 The exhibition team at the museum used Skype and an iPad to bring Eliasson and his team from his studio in Berlin directly into the museum's galleries to guide the installation process.

てエネルギー供給し、小さなソーラーパネルを装着した携帯ライト、「リトルサン」は、その輝かしい光量を活用して観客が空中にドローイングを描く参加型の作品《サンライト・グラフィティ》(2012)となった。そしてサステナビリティに向かって素材やデザインの開発、実験をしたものを展示する「サステナビリティの研究室」では、スタジオのキッチンからでた野菜クズから作った顔料をはじめとして、スタジオやスタジオと協働する外部企業による、さまざまなテストやプロジェクトが公開された。例えば赤泥と呼ばれる有害物質を、有害なアルカリ成分を高温焼成によって無害化してつくったタイル(Studio ThusThatによって製造)、環境への負荷が少ないバクテリアによる色の製造(Hoekmine B.V.によって開発)などのマテリアルが所狭しと展示された。

アイスランドの氷河が温暖化で溶ける様を二〇年をへだてて撮影した二枚を並べて展示した《溶ける氷河のシリーズ 1999/2019》(2019)、アイスランドのビーチに流れ着き、溶けないでそこに春までとどまる流氷の小さな塊を現場でスキャンして3Dプリンタで造形した「氷の研究室」、それらは将来作品化される素材となる。これらが視覚的な形をつくりだすことで、人々が、ミクロ、マクロの変化を観察し、感じ、思考し、共有することを可能にしている。感じることがアクションに繋がる、展覧会タイトル「ときに川は橋となる」は、オルタナティヴの思考を詩的にあらわしたものである。対立するもの、問題に対して、オルタナティヴな素材や方法を通し、状況に対して絶えず交渉し、ぶつかり、止揚していく複雑で有機的な過程の連続は、そのものがエコロジーとして記述される。

エピローグ

二〇二〇年初頭からの世界的なコロナウイルス感染状況により作家とそのチームは展示来日できなくなった。作家不在の展示室で美術館の展示チームはスカイプなどを駆使して遠隔コミュニケーションによって設置をおこなった [fig.10]。この場・空間でしか感じ取れない何か（アンビエンス）は、私たちの間にどこまで共有されたのだろうか。世界じゅうで、人々がふれあい集まり、共感をホストする場所がすべて失われつつある中で、この東京の一点の場では、再人間化（re-humanization）のためのエンジンが起動していた。エリアソンはすぐにヴィデオグラファーを手配し、（その時点では）公開の日を決められない展示をSNSやウェブをとおして最高の映像でみせられるように計画した。結果起こったこれらの予測できない「現象」は、「ときに川は橋となる」展にかかわる美術館の諸活動の要素をエージェンシーとして、または「展覧会のふるまい」自身が一種の「アクター」となり、サステナビリティを押し出す行為をしたとはいえないだろうか？[17]

輸送、制作、展示などに関わるシステムが、新たな、そしてオルタナティヴとして試行された。エリアソンと東京側のスタッフすべてにとって本展示がもっとも先鋭的であるのはこの点といえるだろう。

それはすべてのシステムのうちのほんの一部にすぎないかもしれない。だが、資本主義やネオリベラリズムによって脱人間化してしまった、そして人間や非人間を含むすべてのモノのバランスを崩してしまった現在において、このことは確実に希望の一つといえるのではないだろうか。

アーティストは未来をつくるのではなく、未来を聴き、それをホストするための準備をするのである。

［注］

1 例えば、ピピロッティ・リストはテレビが我々の生活の一つの環境、友人になっていることを前提として、新しい形のPVをつくり、それを空間の中に多様な形で分散、環境化した。それにより、私たちを取り巻く映像と私たちの心理や知覚の分かちがたい関係を再認識させた。リアム・ギリックはスペキュラティヴなパブリックスペースをデザインするための、さまざまな彫刻的、デザイン的もしくは建築的介入をおこない、パブリックドメインを心理的な環境に変容させた。

2 Karen Barad, *Meeting The Universe Halfway: Quantum Physics and The Entanglement of Matter and Meaning*, Duke University Press, 2007の中で、バラッドは「相互作用 interaction」とは先立つ分離、分断、すなわち個体というものを前提としていると批判し、「イントラ-アクション intra-action」という語を導入する。これは、分断を前提とせず、そもそも「もつれあって」いる存在しているという相互的構成を前提においている。

3 Lucy R. Lippard, *Six Years: The Dematerialization of the Art Object*

from 1966 to 1972; a Cross-Reference Book of Information on Some Esthetic Boundaries: Consisting of a bibliography into which are inserted a fragmented text, art works, documents, interviews, and symposia, arranged chronologically and focused on so-called conceptual or information or idea art with mentions of such vaguely designed areas as minimal, antiform, systems, earth, or process art, occurring now in the Americas, Europe, England, Australia, and Asia (with occasional political overtones)*, Oakland: University of California Press, 1997.*

4 例えば、J・ギブソン『生態学的視覚論』古崎敬訳、サイエンス社、一九八六年、一三七－一四〇頁などを参照。環境のアフォーダンスとは、環境が動物に提供するものを包括的に指している。それゆえ、アフォーダンスは環境の事実であり、同様に動物の行動の事実であるため、主観的特性でも客観的特性でもない。

5 Timothy Morton, *Ecology without Nature: Rethinking Environmental Aesthetics*, Cambridge, MA: Harvard University Press, 2007, p. 9.（ティモシー・モートン『自然なきエコロジー――来たるべき環境哲学に向けて』篠原雅武訳、以文社、二〇一八年、一八頁）、Timothy Morton, *The Ecological Thought*, Cambridge, MA: Harvard University Press, 2012, p. 4. を参照。

6 例えば、George Herbert Mead, *Mind, Self and Society from the Standpoint of a Social Behaviorist*, Chicago: Chicago University Press, 1934（G・H・ミード『精神・自我・社会』〈デューイ＝ミード著作集〉、河村望訳、人間の科学新社、二〇一七年）や Erving Goffman, *Behavior in Public Places: Notes on the Social Organization of Gatherings*, New York: The Free Press, 1963（アーヴィング・ゴッフマン『集まりの構造――新しい日常行動論を求めて』〈ゴッフマンの社会学４〉丸木恵祐・本名信行訳、一九八〇年、誠信書房）を参照。

7 DAZED, Bjork's letters with Timothy Morton 04/24, https://www.dazeddigital.com/music/gallery/20196/3/bjork-s-letters-with-timothy-morton（最終閲覧二〇二〇年三月二三日）

8 Michelle Kuo, "More Than a Feeling," *Olafur Eliasson: Experience*, London: Phaidon Press, 2018, p. 16.

9 ART iT「インタビュー オラファー・エリアソン」、二〇一〇年一二月二六日。https://www.art-it.asia/u/admin_interviews/alkyuvtilzb4opsn25mg（最終閲覧二〇二〇年三月一四日）

10 *Olafur Eliasson: In Real Life (exhibition book)*, edited by Mark Godfrey, London: Tate Publishing, 2019, pp. 10–29.

11 *Ibid.*, p. 22. Olafur Eliasson, 'The Experience Machine–The Artist Interview Himself 1995/2015' in Christiane Maria Schneider and Christian Boros (eds.), *Olafur Eliasson: Boros Collection, exb. Cat., Berlin: Boros Collection*, 2015, p. 57.より。

12 Jane Bennett, *Vibrant Matter: A Political Ecology of Things*, Durham, NC: Duke University Press, 2009, p. viii.

13 オラファー・エリアソン、筆者による電話インタビュー、ベルリン－東京間、二〇二〇年三月一八日。

14 メルロ＝ポンティは『眼と精神』（みすず書房、一九九七年、二六八頁）の中で、セザンヌの絵についてこう述べている。「セザンヌの書こうとしていた「世界の瞬間」、それはずっと以前に過ぎ去ったものではあるが、かれの画布はわれわれにこの瞬間を投げかけ続けている。そして彼のサント・ヴィクトワールの嶺は、世界のどこにでも現れ、繰り返し現れて来よう」。エリアソンは、この表現のヴァイブレーションの感覚をベネットのヴァイブレントの政治性（Fennett, Vibrant Matter）と比較している。

15 シャンタル・ムフ『政治的なものについて――闘技的民主主義と多元主義的グローバル秩序の構築』酒井隆史監訳、篠原雅武訳、明石書店、二〇〇八年などを参照。

16 エリアソン、筆者によるインタビュー、同上。

17 ラトゥールらによるアクターネットワーク理論（ANT）では、あらゆるものがアクターとして認められる。ゆえに、そのネットワークの要素であるエージェンシーもアクターであり、そのネットワークすらもアクターとみなされる。以下の資料を参照。久保明教『ブルーノ・ラトゥールの取説』月曜社、二〇一九年、ブリュノ・ラトゥール『社会的なものを組み直す――アクターネットワーク理論入門』伊藤嘉高訳、法政大学出版局、二〇一九年。

Olafur Eliasson, the artist who listens to the future: Art as the practice of ecology

Yuko Hasegawa

For me, the sensation of harmony may also include uncertainty, chaos.

——Olafur Eliasson

Introduction

Since 1993, Olafur Eliasson has given a palpable shape to meteorological phenomena such as fog, mist, and rain, as well as substances and occurrences with an indeterminate form that are elusive and hard to grasp, such as water, ice, and light, turning these things into works of art. During the early 1990s, when Eliasson launched his artistic career, many artists including Pierre Huyghe, Liam Gillick, and Pipilotti Rist were appropriating themes and artistic media from everyday life and pop culture at all once, in an effort to foster new forms of communication with their audiences. By appropriating everyday experience or treating it as a kind of readymade, these artists attempted to present the realm of this experience as a new environment or reality.[1]

How do we relate to the spaces, objects, and information (images, texts) that surround us? Thanks to a new sensibility and a cognition attuned to these environments, a kind of 'intra-action' (Karen Barad) that evokes in us not only a reciprocal function between inside and outside, but also an introspective function within ourselves, has already emerged from these artists.[2] What unites them is a spirit of inquiry and an attitude that is cross-disciplinary and cross-medium. Faced with the artistic movements represented by these artists, Eliasson appropriated the natural environment and its constituent elements and turned them into readymades. Eliasson, a Danish artist of Icelandic origin, cultivated an intimate relationship to the sprawling nature of Iceland from a young age. To him, the domain of art is a free, tolerant space of relationships that incorporates a wide variety of elements, hosting and encouraging interaction and chemical reactions between them. In order to experiment with these possibilities, Eliasson deploys a wide range of media and approaches—including architecture, product and environmental design, film and video, and performance. The scope of his interests extends to fields of academic research related to scientific fields like geology, geophysics, optics, biology, and perceptual psychology, as well as philosophy. His studio, Studio Olafur Eliasson, lies at the centre of these activities, encompassing a staff of more than 120 technicians, researchers, architects, and other experts.

It seems imperative to verify what exactly is meant here by the term 'natural environment.' The 'great acceleration' is said to have started in the 1950s. With rapid industrialization and development, humans have become excessively involved in nature, thereby altering it: as a result, the binary opposition between human society and nature is no longer valid. The notion of the Anthropocene, which explains this shift and can be traced back to geology, is now being debated in all sorts of fields, from the political and economic to the cultural. It was in the 2000s that Eliasson began intentionally steering his practice towards the objective of sustainability, in response to dramatic shifts in the natural environment. When the media asked him what art could do in the face of environmental change, he always gave the same answer. Art offers no solutions: it can only encourage awareness in people, or to make them believe in the significance of their own small, individual actions (directed at solving the problem).

The art of the 1990s sought to build and make adjustments to connections between individual human experiences, memories, and bodies; it encouraged critical self-reflection in response to the increasing informatization and diversification of the social environment. In contrast, the period since the year 2000, when political and social crises came to a head under global capitalism, has seen a shift towards a search for spiritual and physical survival and sustainability in the face of major conflicts and ruptures. What is demanded of us is not a process of modulation, but a total resetting, or viable alternatives. Eliasson is one of the artists who has responded to this situation in the most astute, intellectual, and practical fashion, as the proposition itself has shifted.

1
From the sharing of a subjective, inner world towards the formation of a collective social psyche

Eliasson's interest in immaterial things with an indeterminate form and movement (time) was cultivated by his own personal experience as a breakdancer, a phenomenology centred on the body and perception that fused the subjective with the objective and consciousness with the object, Henri Bergson's subjective theory of time, and Lucy Lippard's *Six Years: The Dematerialization of the Art Object from 1966 to 1972*[3], which traced various movements surrounding the dematerialization of art. Emerging in parallel to this model of the seeing subject and the object being seen was an increased emphasis on the position of the viewer's own body, and the process of dematerialization.

For Eliasson, the objective is not for the tangible objects that 'appear' to represent something or other. He creates works of art by combining objects familiar to the human gaze with those that are not: as such, they entail a degree of uncertainty or surprise. In other words, by taking his starting point from recognizable past experiences, Eliasson seeks to take our imaginations to places that are as distant as possible. These places might be a waterfall, a river, or the blurry ripples formed by the light that strikes a puddle and gets reflected off a nearby wall.

The *Gestalt* continued to collapse as a result of these movements. The task at hand was replete with contradictions: if the audience did not view the work of art with their eyes (intellect), was it possible to interpret it with one's body as a feeling, while also validating it as a work of art with a definite 'existence'? Eliasson shifted his approach, from flows of water to light to strobe lighting, and then to waves and ripples. Waves continuously shift in form thanks to resonance and ripples. The form of what lies before you now, what lay there before (the past), and what comes after (the future) can only be fixed in one's memory. Waves take on a subjective, interior presence thanks to our perception, rather than existing as an objective, external phenomenon.

For *Sometimes the river is the bridge* (2020), a new work on display at this exhibition, multiple projectors are used to project ripple patterns, while their reflections are shown in sequences, allowing viewers to apprehend them as a phenomenon. A large, ring-shaped screen is hung in the cavernous space of the atrium, which has a height of twenty metres. Light from twelve sources is projected onto a basin of gently swaying water in the centre of this space, and reflected onto a screen that encircles the area. A continuous chain reaction occurs in which the wave movements from a few seconds prior exert an influence on the reflections in the present. Although the shapes of the wave reflections obey several patterns, they exhibit a diversity of changes while repeating a steady rhythmic pattern of movement and stillness. The shapes of these rings of waves fall away bit by bit: some burst forth all at once in a dramatic transformation, while others transform more gradually into something resembling a jellyfish or a fan. Standing in the middle of the field of waves, one has the impression of being subject to a kind of planetary, floating sensation, in some sort of moon temple.

A continuous series of 'appearances' from one moment to the next creates time. We are being gazed at by 'time' through the movements of these ripples. Eliasson has long been fascinated by waves and vibrations. According to him, the multiple designs and forms associated with water in a Japanese garden inspired this work. Similar to the sentiment expressed in the opening sentence of Kamo no Chōmei's *Hōjōki* (The Ten-Foot-Square Hut)—'the current of the flowing river does not cease, and yet the water is not the same water as before'—a subjective awareness of the transience of time and the sublation of one's objectivity, attained by observing how water flows, are notions that are rooted in Japanese thinking and aesthetics. This work by Eliasson is a symphonic whole that encompasses the memory of water, poetics, and politics. For the artist himself, it is also a milestone in terms of how it allows people to share, on the scale of a public space, a phenomenological perceptual experience that seeks out the subjective, interior reflection par excellence represented by waves, all the while preserving its complexity and precision.

As this work demonstrates, Eliasson constantly seeks to create new visual effects through experimental combinations of technical methods and materials.

Eliasson creates works of art with certain affordances[4]—in the sense of viewers acquiring meaning through the exploration of environments—through experiments related to perception or the body, and a process of trial and error. All of this is not for the sake of some articulated objective or meaning, but in order to enable viewers to arrive at a state of uncertainty, or a complexity that cannot be deciphered.

In *Who is afraid* (2004), for example, three slowly rotating glass discs are suspended in the middle of the gallery, each of which moves at a different speed thanks to motors. These glass discs use dichroic filters, which allow light of one colour to pass through while reflecting the remaining light, which appears as the complementary colour. When light strikes one of these slowly rotating (dichroic mirror) filters, it is diffracted into red and cyan light. The cyan light shines onto the gallery wall, while the red light reflects onto the adjacent disks. These cause yellow and magenta light to appear on the wall; the light they reflect is blue and green. Shifts in the position and angle of the three discs produce infinite variations in these projections. The spectrometry that relies on this principle is also used to ascertain the nature (composition) of things from the outside. Eliasson casually applies these tools that are used to scrutinize the nature of material in his artworks. *The exploration of the centre of the sun* (2017), meanwhile, combines a rhombic dodecahedron (a polyhedron with twelve rhombic faces) with an icosahedron (which has twenty triangular faces). The result is a complex, not-quite symmetrical polyhedron that allows the viewer to move around the work and see multiple shapes and forms. The structural frame is fitted with panes of filter glass like those used in the glass discs of *Who is afraid*. Light from the LEDs mounted on a slowly rotating armature suspended within the work's core produces a galaxy-like array of shifting stars in a variety of colours throughout the entire space of the exhibition.

Eliasson takes great pains over the instructions that are crafted to guide the viewer through the experience of his exhibitions. The application software for appreciation that he creates through his own performances are remarkably effective as teaching materials that explain how we might enter into a profound encounter with the artwork.

He also offers suggestions that invite us to discover how to feel something thoroughly—and thereby to produce meaning. *Your exhibition guide* (2014), a video in which Eliasson speaks as a guide for those visiting the exhibition *Kandinsky, Malevich, Mondrian: The Infinite White Abyss*, at the Kunstsammlung Nordrhein-Westfalen, works on several levels. [fig. 1] At first, it gradually increases the time spent viewing a single work of art. Next, it possesses both focus and a panoramic awareness that permits one to feel the entirety of one's surroundings, to look at those around you in order to empathize with their feelings just as if they were your own, to be conscious of both the micro-movements of one's breathing and the larger movements of one's body, and to look at the self reflected in a mirror as an other. You see an extension of yourself in the artwork, before looking at the next work together with 'your other self.' This 'other self' is inspired by the phenomenological notion that 'my body is one that sees, while also being something that can be seen.' Accordingly, at the same time that I am looking at the artwork, I feel as if the artwork is looking at me.

Eliasson's applications of phenomenology are sometimes extremely close to the practices of Zen; they encourage people to cultivate an approach to experience that allows them to feel deeply.

2
A space of empathy

Eliasson often uses the term 'co-production.' Similar to how the word 'your' frequently appears in the titles of works like *Your orange afterimage exposed* (2000) or *Your happening, has happened, will happen* (2020), he emphasizes the fact that these events that happen within you are in fact individual, unique experiences. The work of art comes into being through a collaborative effort between 'you' and 'I' (the artwork/artist): in other words, through the singular perceptual experiences specific to each person. The position at which *Beauty* (1993) makes itself visible depends on one's height (the position of one's eyes): a rainbow that exists because of you, that only you can see, as it were.

Fog is deployed in order to elicit a sense of empathy. [fig. 2] The things that surround you melt into each other, creating an ambient (ambivalent) space. The classic example here is of an artwork where the colour of the light merges and coalesces with the fog in accordance with the bodies of the people moving through it.

This notion of 'your' is connected with environmental philosopher Timothy Morton's assertion that 'ecology has to do with you and me.' He considers all other elements including animals and things as that which 'surrounds' me, without objectifying nature as a 'natural environment' within the context of *Ecology without Nature*. Morton seeks to locate the conditions for coexistence in the sharing of this environment, rather than some interior domain based on shared or common value systems.[5] In the fields of sociology or politics, the sharing of this environment is discussed in terms of 'being with.' In a certain sense, this notion is linked to the sharing of a space of empathy that emerges as a result of the artwork—which Eliasson strives to co-produce.[6]

Morton first approached art by way of music. For him, artists perceived reality more deeply and thoroughly: because they 'listened to the future by modulating their sensitivity to how things and events would end up,' these artists were able to think about the future.[7] The term 'object-oriented ontology' (OOO), strongly advocated by Morton, is a theory that views the object as a form of ultimate existence without reducing it to a constituent material or use: it represents a position that emphasizes the process of transcending sensualism. Eliasson, who takes ephemeral phenomena and gives them a material form that can be seen or touched, has extended the scope of his interest to the operations of an environment that transcends the functions of individual subjectivity. His encounter with Morton and his theory was the impetus that prompted a shift in his consciousness towards the environment and shared spaces.

When my feelings toward a given object are shared with

others and resonate with them, this creates a sense of empathy, and strengthens our awareness of this 'connectiveness.' Michelle Kuo argues that the empathy that Eliasson's work elicits is not one of sameness or mimesis: rather, it 'poses empathy in terms of difference: the multiplicious and constantly changing relationships between vastly disparate phenomena.' [8]

While the dialogue between Eliasson and Morton in this catalogue seems to indicate that both of them have a shared understanding of the importance of qualities like 'awareness', 'sharing', 'hosting', 'movement', and 'feeling', Eliasson seeks to make us experience these qualities through objects, devices, and phenomena that have been contrived or created. Morton, on the other hand, integrates his own observations with various schools of thinking and philosophy, striving to elicit in us the experience of a comprehensive form of thinking that is akin to having a physical encounter with a material presence.

What Eliasson and Morton share in common is a certain sensation of 'looseness' or 'relaxation'. Neither of them demands that their audiences possess a refined intellect, or literacy with regard to art. There is a certain rhythm in both of them that approximates the feeling of having a conversation while bouncing and jumping atop a huge waterbed. This is something that can also be found in the spaces of empathy that Eliasson creates—a mat (bed) of trust, as it were.

In 2003, Eliasson created just this sort of space of empathy: his *Weather project* in the Turbine Hall of the Tate Modern. [fig. 3] The idea for this work came from a desire to see how much of a sense of empathy could be shared by people in relation to a meteorological phenomenon. When the yellow light—of the sort used in tunnels, it turns the world monotone—deprived objects of their hue, people paid a kind of attention that was different from that of their conventional encounters with objects. The act of creating a single, closed environment caused a new form of human communication and expression to emerge. The space was expanded through the effective use of mirrors; individuals and small gatherings were dispersed throughout, while the mirrored ceiling enabled this first-hand experience of one's own likeness 'existing together' with everything in a situation that also encompassed the other, with which it was shared.

Eliasson does not transform material into something self-referential or into a symbol. He refers to this phenomenon as a 'deauthorization.'

In an ART iT interview (February 16, 2010)[9], Eliasson goes so far as to say that 'it is not that I am interested in light as such. I chose light because it seemed easy to work with, in relation to what I was trying to accomplish.' What is important here is the question of why he chose to do what he did. The search for his materials begins with this 'how.' What does it mean to watch a raging cascade of water fall from a scaffold constructed out of metal piping, this most banal of industrial structures, rather than a painstakingly contrived garden or a beautiful waterfall in the midst of nature?[fig. 4] Faced with the noise made by this monumental volume of water as it flows downwards, humans become aware of the speed of this falling movement, the movement of this water, and the volume of this falling water. Fog, on the other hand, blurs the boundary between what lies within and outside the realm of human perception and consciousness: it is an effective medium for connecting humans and spaces, and integrating them with each other. In Eliasson's work, light is deployed in order to make something *else* appear. These 'appearances' foster or elicit a relationship to you, becoming a kind of event or physical encounter that occurs within your reach.

3
Creating systems: a new model for artists

As he has shifted from influencing the psychology of the audience towards a form of 'applied activity' aimed at creating 'alternatives', the style of Eliasson's practice has also evolved.

In the Tate Modern catalogue, Mark Godfrey explains how Eliasson represents a new type of artist[10], by making reference to the wide scope of his activity as an activist (Little Sun [fig. 5], *Green light* lanterns [fig. 6], *Ice Watch*), architect (Fjordenhus [fig. 7] and his planning of the surrounding environment), stage designer [fig. 8], and speaker on the social function and meaning of art at the United Nations, TED, and the World Economic Forum in Davos. Eliasson insists that 'artists are capable of doing many other things.'[11] Although he was previously interested in phenomenology and perceptual psychology, it was around 2005 that Eliasson began to harbour doubts about an exceedingly obsessive phenomenological approach to the notion of subjectivity and introspection. Accordingly, he went on to expand the scope of his interests to public space, architecture, urban planning, and landscape design. This new development coincides with how the world has now entered the age of the Anthropocene, as well as a 'new ecology' that seeks to affirm and validate the notion of relationality from a scientific and psychological perspective. Eliasson finds himself attracted to movements that seek to decentralize or deauthorize the concept of anthropocentrism, including actor-networks created by mutual interactions between humans and non-humans as proposed by the scientific anthropologist Bruno Latour, and an object-oriented ontology that views the object as a form of ultimate existence without reducing it to a constituent material or use. The evolution of a new materialism connected to politics and society can also be seen here, whether in the work of Latour, the cultural geographer Doreen Massey, who understood physical space as a living thing, or political theorist Jane Bennett, who argued for a political ecology of things. In *Vibrant Matter*, Bennett argues that our 'analysis of political events' will shift as a result of clarifying the nature of the 'vibrant materiality' that surrounds human activity.[12] 'I think it's quite important not to present the new materialism as the opposite of phenomenology,' notes Eliasson, 'and I might say that my thinking lies somewhere between the two.'[13] In terms of conventional phenomenology, even if Maurice Merleau-Ponty refers to Cézanne's paintings as 'vibrating,' this usage is not synonymous with the capacity to share a strong sense of social theory and collectivity, as seen in Bennett's use of the phrase 'vibrant matter.'[14]

What we feel is connected to how we act. Art, which serves as a host for empathy and everything in that space, is built on a foundation of trust. This is not simply a space of harmony.

Eliasson is deeply interested in Chantal Mouffe's argument about the recovery of the political, the antagonism that arises from true 'plurality', and the sense of 'trust' that serves as a foundation for both.[15] It is through art that Eliasson seeks to examine what the nature of this 'trust' might be.

Latour gives the example of a river as a non-human actor—that is, an existence that can act, or exert an effect, on something else. A river overflows and changes direction: these shifts operate on that domain, exerting an influence on how national boundaries are determined and the lives of people. This notion calls to mind Eliasson's early work, such as *Green river* (1998–2001), in which a non-toxic green dye is released into a river in order to turn it green, or *Erosion* (1997), where water pipes were plunged into a reservoir, thereby turning the water that flowed out into a narrow stream that ran for some 1.5km. [fig. 9] The green hue gives the river and the water a clear and definite form: that which had escaped our everyday consciousness now appears as an acting body. The overflowing water arbitrarily turns into a river, creating another landscape within the city. This phenomenon can be seen as an actor, and suggests that these early works already prefigured a shift towards Latour's mode of thinking.

As an artist, Eliasson says that he is currently most interested in 'creating systems.'[16] When both artist and curator decided to base this exhibition on the theme of ecology and sustainability, it was with a view towards proposing alternatives. This is not an exhibition that seeks to display representations (images) and propaganda related to ecology and sustainability, or evidence of documented practices. It is an exhibition that proposes a shift in consciousness, and the reform of systems.

Firstly, we decided to create new works in Japan in order to reduce the need for transportation, and to encourage the process of local production and consumption. In a bid to reduce carbon dioxide emissions from air shipments, works of art to be shipped to Japan were kept to a bare minimum, and transported by train or ship. The journey from Berlin to Hamburg was made by truck. From there, the artworks were transported by train to the city of Taicang in Suzhou, China, via the village of Małaszewicze in Poland and Zabaykalsk in Russia. From Taicang the cargo was then loaded onto a ship and transported to Tokyo. A drawing machine was installed in each crate: a ballpoint pen was attached to the edge of a sheet of paper so that a drawing would be automatically generated by this mechanical arm as a result of the rattling and rolling movements of the train—almost as if a seismograph had become an actor and created this drawing. When the crates were opened, these twelve drawings had actually inscribed the memory of the time elapsed in various ways. The 'critical zone' in the title *Memories from the critical zone (Germany–Poland–Russia–China–Japan, nos. 1–12)* is a geological term that refers to the thin layer of the earth between bedrock and the top of the tree canopy that supports living systems, in addition to functioning as a critique of the transportation systems that serve exhibitions at art museums, which are basically reliant on air shipments. This decision was accompanied by numerous difficulties, including the lack of companies willing to insure the transport of delicate drawings and other artworks by train or ship.

Some of the electricity required for the exhibition is supplied by solar panels. The portable Little Sun lights, each equipped with a small solar panel of their own, turned into an interactive work of art—*Sunlight graffiti* (2012)—in which visitors can create drawings in mid-air using this brilliant light. In the Sustainability Research Lab, where the results of developing and experimenting with materials and designs with a view to sustainability are on display, one can see pigments made from vegetable scraps taken from the studio kitchen, as well as various tests and projects by the studio and outside companies working with the studio, like bricks (manufactured by Studio ThusThat) made by using high temperature firing to render a hazardous substance called red mud and harmful alkaline constituents harmless and colours made using bacteria (being developed by Hoekmine B.V.), that will have a minimal impact on the environment.

Ice Lab was created by using a 3D printer to make three-dimensional representations of onsite scans of small pieces of drift ice that have washed up on Iceland's beaches and stayed there through the spring without melting, which may form a basis for future artworks, exhibited alongside two photographs from *The glacier melt series 1999/2019* (2019), taken twenty years apart, that show how Iceland's glaciers are melting due to global warming. This work creates visual forms that allow one to observe, feel, and think about changes at both a micro and macro level, and share them with others. The exhibition title, *Sometimes the river is the bridge*, which suggests that feeling is connected to action, is a poetic expression of an alternative mode of thinking where the flowing water in a river can sometimes function as a bridge that connects people. Through the use of alternative materials and approaches, this continuous series of complex, organic processes that negotiate endlessly with a given situation, running up against it or coming to a halt, in response to confrontations and problems, is depicted here as an ecology.

Epilogue

Due to the global spread of the coronavirus in early 2020, Eliasson and his team were unable to come to Japan for this exhibition. In the absence of the artist, the museum's exhibition team used Skype and other tools in the galleries to communicate remotely and carry out the installation work. [fig. 10] To what extent was this 'ambience,' which can only be felt in person, able to be shared? At a moment when the spaces around the world that allow people to come together and interact, serving as hosts for empathy, were being closed, this single location in Tokyo was like an engine that had come to life in the service of a process of re-humanization. Eliasson quickly arranged for a videographer and formulated a plan to be able to show top-quality footage of this exhibition—the opening date of which had not yet been decided at the time—on the internet and social media. By relying on the museum's various activities as a form of agency, or treating 'institutional behaviour' itself as a kind of 'actor', it might be argued that the unpredictable 'phenomena' that ultimately came to pass worked to create a certain sustainability. **17** Systems related to transport, production, and exhibition were trialled as new alternatives. For both Eliasson and all of us in Tokyo, this aspect of the exhibition is perhaps what is most progressive and forward-looking.

Perhaps these represent only a small minority of all systems.

At a time when capitalism and neoliberalism have resulted in a thorough dehumanization, and the balance between things, both human and non-human, has been thrown off balance, however, surely this initiative represents a kind of unassailable hope.

Artists do not create the future. They listen to it and make preparations to host it.

Notes

1. Pipilotti Rist, for example, began from the premise that television had become an environment, or even a friend, in the context of our lives, creating a new point of view, dispersing it within space in various forms, and transforming it into an environment onto itself. In doing so, Rist prompted a renewed consciousness of the images that surround us, as well as the inseparable relationships that govern our psychological and perceptual faculties. Liam Gillick stages a variety of sculptural, design-related, or architectural interventions that seek to design speculative kinds of public space, transforming the public domain into psychological environments.
2. In her book *Meeting The Universe Halfway: Quantum Physics and The Entanglement of Matter and Meaning* (Duke University Press, 2007), Karen Barad critiques the way in which the term 'interaction' presumes a prior state of separation or division based on the notion of an individual, and suggests the term 'intra-action' instead. 'Intra-action' does not presume a separation: rather, it is predicated on a state of mutual, reciprocal organization among entities that are 'entangled' with each other.
3. Lucy R. Lippard, *Six Years: The Dematerialization of the Art Object from 1966 to 1972; a Cross-Reference Book of Information on Some Esthetic Boundaries: Consisting of a bibliography into which are inserted a fragmented text, art works, documents, interviews, and symposia, arranged chronologically and focused on so-called conceptual or information or idea art with mentions of such vaguely designed areas as minimal, antiform, systems, earth, or process art, occurring now in the Americas, Europe, England, Australia, and Asia (with occasional political overtones)*, Oakland: University of California Press, 1997.
4. See, for example, J. Gibson, *The Ecological Approach to Visual Perception*, London: Routledge Press, 2014. Environmental affordance is a comprehensive term that refers to everything that the environment provides to animals. Accordingly, as affordance represents a reality to both the environment and the actions and behaviour of animals, it is neither a subjective nor an objective property.
5. See, Timothy Morton, *Ecology without Nature: Rethinking Environmental Aesthetics*, Cambridge, MA: Harvard University Press, 2007, p. 9.; Timothy Morton, *The Ecological Thought*, Cambridge, MA: Harvard University Press, 2012, p. 4.
6. See, for example, George Herbert Mead, *Mind, Self and Society from the Standpoint of a Social Behaviorist* (Chicago: Chicago University Press, 1934); Erving Goffman, *Behavior in Public Places: Notes on the Social Organization of Gatherings* (New York: The Free Press, 1963).
7. DAZED, 'Bjork's letters with Timothy Morton 04/24', (last viewed March 22, 2020) https://www.dazedigital.com/music/gallery/20196/3/bjork-s-letters-with-timothy-morton
8. Michelle Kuo, "More Than a Feeling", *Olafur Eliasson : Experience*, London: Phaidon Press, 2018, p. 16.
9. ART iT asia, interview (last viewed March 14, 2020) https://www.art-it.asia/u/admin_interviews/alkyuvtilzb4opsn25mg
10. *Olafur Eliasson: In Real Life (exhibition book)*, Mark Godfrey (eds.), London: Tate Publishing, 2019, pp. 10–29.
11. *Ibid.*, p. 22. Quoted from Olafur Eliasson, 'The Experience Machine–The Artist Interview Himself 1995/2015' in Christiane Maria Schneider and Christian Boros (eds.), *Olafur Eliasson: Boros Collection*,

exh. cat., Berlin: Boros Collection, 2015, p. 57.

12. Jane Bennett, *Vibrant Matter: A Political Ecology of Things*, Durham, NC: Duke University Press, 2009, p. viii.

13. Olafur Eliasson interviewed by Yuko Hasegawa via WhatsApp between Berlin and Tokyo March 18, 2020.

14. In *Eye and Mind*, Merleau-Ponty describes the paintings of Cézanne as follows: 'The 'world's instant' that Cézanne wanted to paint, an instant long since passed away, is still hurled toward us by his paintings. His Mont Sainte-Victoire is made and remade from one end of the world to the other.' Eliasson compares the sensation of this 'vibration' with the social nature of the 'vibrant,' in terms of what Bennett calls 'vibrant matter.'

15. See, for example, Chantal Mouffe, *On The Political,* London: Routledge Press, 2005.

16. Olafur Eliasson interviewed by Yuko Hasegawa via WhatsApp between Berlin and Tokyo March 18, 2020.

17. Latour's actor-network theory (ANT) recognizes all things as actors. Accordingly, the agency that constitutes one element of that network is also an actor, while that network itself is also construed as an actor. For further reading on this topic, see Akinori Kubo, *A Bruno Latour Manual*, Getsuyosha, 2019, and Bruno Latour, *Reassembling the Social: An Introduction to Actor-Network-Theory*, Oxford University Press, 2005.

[Translated by Darryl Wee]

謝辞
Acknowledgments

本展覧会の開催にあたりご協力いただきました下記の方々、ならびにここにお名前を記すことができなかった方々に深い感謝の意を表します。（順不同、敬称略）

We would like to express our deepest gratitude to the following people and organizations as well as to the many others, too numerous to mention, who provided us with their generous assistance in organizing this exhibition.

オラファー・エリアソン　Olafur Eliasson
スタジオ・オラファー・エリアソン　Studio Olafur Eliasson

neugerriemschneider, Berlin
Tanya Bonakdar Gallery, New York/Los Angeles

伊藤東凌　Toryo Ito
上村梨乃　Rino Uemura
内田洋子　Yoko Uchida
大林剛郎　Takeo Obayashi
大林ミカ　Mika Obayashi
加藤賢策　Kensaku Kato
桑島祥　Sho Kuwajima
小柳敦子　Atsuko Koyanagi
佐野誠　Makoto Sano
渋谷清道　Kiyomichi Shibuya
鈴木秀生　Hideo Suzuki
田中仁　Hitoshi Tanaka
寺岡環　Tamaki Teraoka
中根史郎　Shiro Nakane
野口有紀　Yuki Noguchi
原俊夫　Toshio Hara
藤本幸三　Kozo Fujimoto
藤本美紗子　Misako Fujimoto
薮崎今日子　Kyoko Yabusaki
Tim Neuger
Burkhard Riemschneider
Tanya Bonakdar
PKM Gallery, Seoul
i8 Gallery, Reykjavik
Timothy Morton
Gunther Vogt and Vogt Landscape Architects
Francesca Astesani
Anders Byriel
Njusja de Gier

Artist's acknowledgments

The making of *Sometimes the river is the bridge* has been a collective journey. Making an exhibition always means paving new ways of working. I am, first of all, incredibly grateful to Yuko Hasegawa for her long-standing collaboration: she has championed the idea of realizing a comprehensive exhibition of my work in Japan for years and was instrumental in turning this idea into a reality, together with Ai Kusumoto. Thanks go to the full team at the Museum of Contemporary Art Tokyo for inviting me and hosting this exhibition.

Working closely with Yuko and everyone at MOT team Caroline Eggel and, with her, my studio's exhibitions team, have nurtured and developed the curatorial vision for this show from the beginning – my thanks go to them all. I would also like to express my thanks to Anna Engberg-Pedersen, Myriam Thomas, Anja Gerstmann, and Sebastian Behmann and their respective teams at my studio. Also thank you to Daniel Massey for developing the *Sunlight graffiti* for MOT together with the studio team.

In Japan, I am privileged to have an extended family of friends, including Atsuko Koyanagi; Kazuyo Sejima and Ryue Nishizawa of SANAA; Akiko Miki and Aki Hoashi of the Yokohama Triennale; Soichiro Fukutake of Benesse Corporation; and Yuka and Kentaro Shimura of SHIMURAbros. Their continuing friendship means much to me. I would also like to express thanks to my gallerists Tim Neuger and Burkhard Riemschneider at neugerriemschneider in Berlin and Tanya Bonakdar at Tanya Bonakdar Gallery in New York and Los Angeles, with whom I've worked for so many years, as well as to Gallery Koyanagi in Tokyo, i8 Gallery in Reykjavik, and PKM Gallery in Seoul.

The publication accompanying this exhibition groups dialogues with my friend Timothy Morton, whose thinking continues to inspire me, alongside an insightful curatorial essay by Yuko Hasegawa, and a text outlining my studio's thinking and continued efforts towards more sustainable ways of making art. Thanks are also due to designer Kensaku Kato and translator Gaku Kondo for finding shape and words for this catalogue.

In my venture of decreasing the carbon footprint of this exhibition, I have worked with specialists in transport and art handling in both Berlin and Tokyo, including Hasenkamp and Super Factory – to them I would like to extend my thanks.

My sincere thanks go to Anders Byriel, Njusja de Gier, and Misako Fujimoto of Kvadrat as well as to Yuko Noguchi and Patricia E. Harris of Bloomberg for their support of Sometimes the river is the bridge.

Finally, I would like to express heartfelt thanks to my family and the people closest to me.

As always, I would like to extend deepfelt thanks to my entire studio team – their skills and expertise make exhibitions such as these possible:
Benjamin Albrecht, Jessica Alcázar, Andrew Amondson, Stefano Arrighi, Nathan Baker, Soetje Marie Beermann, Sebastian Behmann, Aleksandra Bielas, Florian Bielefeldt, Thomas Blumtritt-Hanisch, Marco Antonio Bocardo Fuentes, Patricia Bondesson Kavanagh, Ornruja Fame Boonyasit, Christine Bopp, Peter Bosch, Sylvain Brugier, Ruben Bygvraa, Michelle Chen, Catriona Collins, Odey Curbelo, Sarah Davies, Heide Deigert, Erzë Dinarama, Taylor Dover, Jesper Dyrehauge, Caroline Eggel, Victoria Eliasdóttir, Tegan Emerson, Anna Engberg-Pedersen, Martin Enoch, Sophie Erlund, Laura Freiling, María del Pilar García Ayensa, Geoffrey Garrison, Timothy Gasbarro, Lauren Gemmo, Matthias Gerber, Anja Gerstmann, Celina Gonzalez Sueyro, Millicent Green, Elisabeth Greinecker, Jessica Groome, Franziska Harnisch, Frank Haugwitz, Dorothea Hendrichs, Friedrich Herz, Phil Höhn, Nina Hoffmann, Florian Hollunder, Erik Huber, Jörg Hugo, Jöran Imholze, Brita Jaichner, Thordur Jörundsson, Biljana Joksimović-Große, Philipp Käfer, Roger Kaiser, Olga Kalina, Britta Kampe, Judith Karla, Marcus Knupp, Kristina Köper, Vera Kox, Kimberly Kraczon, Camilla Kragelund, Anna Kreutzträger, Jakob Kukula, Susanne Kunkel, Camilla Storgaard Larsen, Ilja Leda, Sharron Ping-Jen Lee, Luca Longagnani, Lars Lubnau, Margaret Lutz, Riccardo Mariano, Lauren Maurer, Patsy McCartan, Elizabeth McTernan, Jan Mennicke, Andreas Meyer, Niël Meyer, Eva Maria Mikkelsen, Daniel Mock, Nora Mandray, Minh-Tu Nguyen, Anders Hellsten Nissen, Jasper Nöllner, Marie-Charlotte Nouza, Reinhard Ostendorf, Kerstin Palermo, Marc Pätzold, Seth Pick, Jan Plater-Zyberk, Roża Plater- Zyberk, Kathryn Politis, Matteo Rapini, Phillip C. Reiner, Petra Rickhof, Sharman Riegger, Elena Rocabert, Bettina Roeder, Andreas Roscher, Imogen Ruthven-Taggart, Al Mohamad Aboud Said, Victoria Sándor, Fabian Schäfer, Dominic Schneider, Dayoung Shin, Salome Sommer, Vajra Spook, Alcuin Stevenson, Hannah Rose Stewart, Ramona Taterra, Caspar Teichgräber, Myriam Thomas, Stefanie Toch, Montse Torredà Martí, Christian Uchtmann, Kajana Wagner, Michael Waldrep, Jill Wambach, Melissa Weigel, Johann Weismann, Rabea Welte, Christina Werner, Pascal Wiemer, Matt Willard, Roberto Winter, Brigitta Witt, Timo Wuchner, Nora Wulff, Aleksandra Zajko-Kusmierczuk, Vanja Žanko, Alexander Zerning and Ariana Zilliacus.

展覧会「ときに川は橋となる」は多くの人々との旅だった。展覧会の制作はどんなときも新たな作品制作につながる道を切り開いてくれる。はじめに、長年にわたり協働してきた長谷川祐子さんに心からの感謝の念を捧げたい。長谷川さんは私の大規模な個展を日本で実現するという構想を何年間も抱き続けて、楠本愛さんとともにその構想の実現に力を尽くしてくださった。日本で個展を開催していただいた東京都現代美術館のチーム一同に謝意を表したい。

この展覧会の企画構想は長谷川さん、日本側の展覧会チーム、スタジオのCaroline Eggelと展覧会チームと協力しながら組み立てていった。改めて御礼申し上げたい。また、スタジオのAnna Engberg-Pedersen、Myriam Thomas、Anja Gerstmann、Sebastian Behmannとそれぞれのチーム、ならびにMOTヴァージョンの《サンライト・グラフィティ》をスタジオのチームと共同開発したDaniel Masseyに感謝したい。

ギャラリー小柳の小柳敦子さん、SANAAの妹島和世さんと西沢立衛さん、横浜トリエンナーレの三木あき子さんと帆足亜紀さん、ベネッセコーポレーションの福武總一郎さん、シムラユカさんとケンタロウさんをはじめとする日本の友人たちとの親交は私にとってかけがえのないものである。また、長年仕事をしてきたギャラリーのneugerriemschneider（Tim Neuger、Burkhard Riemschneider）、Tanya Bonakdar Gallery（Tanya Bonakdar）、ギャラリー小柳、i8 Gallery（Börkur Arnarson）、PMK Gallery（Park Kyung-mee）に心からの謝意を表したい。

展覧会にあわせて刊行されるカタログには、いつもインスピレーションを与えてくれる友人Timothy Mortonとの対話、長谷川さんの洞察に満ちた論考、スタジオによるサステナブルな作品制作に向けた取り組みと考えを概説したテキストが収められた。このカタログに形を与えてくれたデザイナーの加藤賢策さんと言葉を与えてくれた翻訳家の近藤学さんにも感謝したい。

この展覧会にかかる二酸化炭素排出量を削減するという私の試みは、ハーゼンカンプ、スーパー・ファクトリーなど、ベルリンと東京双方の輸送会社と作品取扱の専門家たちによる助力で実現できた。みなさんに感謝の意を伝えたい。

また、展覧会への格別の支援に対して、ブルームバーグの野口有紀さんとPatricia E. Harris、KvadratのAnders Byriel、Njusja de Gier、藤本美紗子さんに深く御礼申し上げたい。

最後に、私の家族と親しい友人たちに心から感謝したい。

そして、いつものことだが、スタジオのチーム全員に感謝の気持ちを伝えたい。この展覧会は彼らの技術と専門知識によって今ここにある。

黒澤浩美「オラファー・エリアソン――あなたが出会うとき」『Я（アール）：金沢21世紀美術館研究紀要』5号、2013年、70–73頁

大森俊克「オラファー・エリアソンの『光』」（「コンテンポラリー・ファインアート」第16回）『美術手帖』67巻1023号、2015年7月号、98–115頁

中島恭子「オラファー・エリアソンの『リトルサン』」『AXIS』187号、2017年6月号、78–83頁

「Artist Interview オラファー・エリアソン――ヒエラルキーのない、思考と実践をつなぐ場」伊東豊子（聞き手）『美術手帖』69巻1055号、2017年7月号（特集：アートフェスティバルを楽しもう!）、36–39頁

Web

IKUKO KOHNO「オラファー・エリアソン『影の光』」TOKYO ART BEAT、2006年1月18日
http://www.tokyoartbeat.com/tablog/entries.ja/2006/01/post_28.html

Yoshitaka Futakawa「オラファー・エリアソン『ニューヨーク・ウォーターフォールズ』」SHIFT、2008年7月9日
http://www.shift.jp.org/ja/archives/2008/07/nyc_waterfalls.html

「インタビュー オラファー・エリアソン」ART iT、2010年2月26日
https://www.art-it.asia/u/admin_interviews/alkyuvtilzb4opsn25mg

中村幸「オラファー・エリアソン――あなたが出会うとき（4）インタビュー」donner le mot、2010年5月15日
http://donnerlemot.com/2010/05/15000711.html

「犬島『家プロジェクト』I邸『Self-loop』――オラファー・エリアソン インタビュー」ベネッセアートサイト直島、2016年12月14日
http://benesse-artsite.jp/story/20161214-749.html

「オラファー・エリアソン インタビュー」RIMOWA、2018年11月27日
https://www.rimowa.com/jp/ja/stories/article-olafur.html

後藤美波「IKEA×現代美術作家オラファー・エリアソンがコラボ。太陽光の利用を促進」CINRA.NET、2019年6月7日
https://www.cinra.net/column/201906-olafureliassonikea

映画「オラファー・エリアソン 視覚と知覚」公式サイト
http://ficka.jp/olafur/

佐々木俊尚「オラファー・エリアソン　視覚と知覚」（佐々木俊尚コラム：ドキュメンタリーの時代）映画.com、2017年8月3日
https://eiga.com/news/20170803/17/

主要日本語参考文献
Selected bibliography
Resources on Olafur Eliasson available in Japanese.

書籍

『オラファー・エリアソン　あなたの差異と反復／Olafur Eliasson: Your difference & repetition』CCAアーティスツ・ブック・シリーズ、現代美術センターCCA北九州、2001年

「オラファー・エリアソン　私たちに共通しているのはみんな違うということだけ（2000年2月21日–3月10日）」『CCA project 05. 1997–03. 2007』三宅暁子編、現代美術センターCCA北九州、2007年、100–103頁、104–107頁

西沢立衛、オラファー・エリアソン「現代美術の視点から美術館概念を再構築する」西沢立衛『美術館をめぐる対話』集英社新書、集英社、2010年、147–180頁

スタジオ・オラファー・エリアソン『スタジオ・オラファー・エリアソン キッチン』水原文・定木大介訳、碓井美樹編、美術出版社、2018年

展覧会図録

『Daiwa Radiator Factory Viewing Room vol. 1』糸井恵・鈴木美和訳、大和ラヂエーター製作所、2006年、48–49頁

『オラファー・エリアソン　きみの参画がもたらすもの――きみのリアリティの相対性について』原美術館、2007年（原美術館およびボイマンス・ファン・ブーニンヘン美術館とマルモ美術館で開催されたオラファー・エリアソンの3つの個展を機に制作されたカタログ *Olafur Eliasson: Your Engagement has Consequences: On the Relativity of Your Reality*, Baden: Lars Müller Publishers, 2006のサプリメントとして出版）

『Space for your future――アートとデザインの遺伝子を組み替える』東京都現代美術館監修、INAX出版、2007年

『万華鏡の視覚――ティッセン・ボルネミッサ現代美術財団コレクションより』森美術館、2009年

Olafur Eliasson : your chance encounter, Baden: Lars Müller Publishers, 2010（金沢21世紀美術館での個展「オラファー・エリアソン あなたが出会うとき」にあわせ出版）

『ゼロ年代のベルリン――わたしたちに許された特別な場所』東京都現代美術館、2011年

『シンプルなかたち――美はどこからくるのか』森美術館、平凡社、2015年

『ヨコハマトリエンナーレ2017――島と星座とガラパゴス』横浜トリエンナーレ組織委員会監修、青幻舎、2017年

逐次刊行物

三木あき子「Valuable 10 オラファー・エリアソン」『美術手帖』52巻782号、2000年1月号（特集：ミレニアム・スペシャル VERY NEW ART 2000）、13–16頁

「Artist Interview オラファー・エリアソン――パブリック・テロリズム」神谷幸江（聞き手）『美術手帖』52巻787号、2000年5月号、139–148頁

市原研太郎「アーティスト オラファー・エリアソン――認識論的変更を迫る現代美術」『美術手帖』58巻876号、2006年2月号、123–130頁

「art news オラファー・エリアソン――静かな光の使い手」『芸術新潮』57巻3号（通号675）、2006年3月号、138–142頁

「Space for your future展」内「オラファー・エリアソン《四連のサンクッカー・ランプ》」『美術手帖』59巻902号、2007年12月号（特集：現代アート展の仕掛け人 キュレーターという仕事）、57頁

「若手注目のエリアソンとは？――知覚を揺さぶる実験空間の大規模展覧会、日本で開催」『日経アーキテクチュア』第912号、2009年11月号、60–65頁

「ARTIST INTERVIEW オラファー・エリアソン」中山英之（聞き手）『美術手帖』62巻934号、2010年3月号、145–159頁

2007–10	- *Take your time: Olafur Eliasson*, San Francisco Museum of Modern Art, CA, USA. Travels to The Museum of Modern Art, New York, and P.S.1 Contemporary Art Center, Queens, NY, USA; Dallas Museum of Art, Texas, USA; Museum of Contemporary Art, Chicago; Museum of Contemporary Art, Sydney, Australia.
2008	- Moves his studio to a former brewery in Prenzlauer Berg, Berlin. - *The New York City Waterfalls*, commissioned by Public Art Fund, New York, NY, USA.
2009	- As a professor at the Berlin University of the Arts, founds and runs the Institute for Spatial Experiments (Institut für Raumexperimente) until 2014. - *Olafur Eliasson: Your chance encounter*, 21st Century Museum of Contemporary Art, Kanazawa, Japan.
2010	- *Olafur Eliasson: Innen Stadt Aussen*, Martin-Gropius-Bau, Berlin, Germany.
2011	- *Façades of The Harpa Reykjavik Concert Hall and Conference Centre*, commissioned by Eignarhaldsfélagið Portus Ltd., design by Henning Larsen Architects, Reykjavik, Iceland. - *Your rainbow panorama*, permanent installation, commissioned by ARoS Aarhus Kunstmuseum, Denmark.
2012	- Founds the social business Little Sun with engineer Frederik Ottesen.
2014	Founds Studio Other Spaces with architect Sebastian Behmann. - *Ice Watch* brings melting brings of ice from Greenland to Copenhagen in 2014, to Paris in 2015, and to London in 2018, in collaboration with geologist Minik Rosing.
2015	- Participates in the establishment of a new global museum: Museum for the United Nations—UN Live.
2016	- *Green light—An artistic workshop*, created in collaboration with TBA21 (Thyssen-Bornemisza Art Contemporary), offers a response to the challenges of mass displacement and migration. Originally hosted by TBA21 in Vienna in 2016, the project was part of Viva Arte Viva, the 57th International Art Exhibition—La Biennale di Venezia, in 2017, and Yokohama Triennale, Yokohama Museum of Art, Japan 2017.
2019	- *Olafur Eliasson: In real life*, Tate Modern, London, UK. Travels to Guggenheim Bilbao, Spain. -Named as Goodwill Ambassador for climate action and the Sustainable Development Goals (SDGs) by the United Nations Development Programme (UNDP).
2020	- *Olafur Eliasson: Sometimes the river is the bridge*, Museum of Contemporary Art Tokyo, Japan.

Selected chronology

Based on documents provided by Studio Olafur Eliasson, this selected chronology was compiled and edited by Museum of Contemporary Art Tokyo.

1967	- Born in Copenhagen, Denmark; his mother a dressmaker, his father an artist and cook.
1970s	- Spends time with his father in Iceland during weekends and summer holidays, while living with his mother in Copenhagen.
1982	- Holds his first solo show, exhibiting landscape drawings and gouaches at a small alternative gallery in Copenhagen.
1983–87	- Gets involved with the breakdance scene and forms a breakdance troupe with two of his friends, twice winning the Scandinavian championship.
1989	- Enrolls in the Royal Danish Academy of Fine Arts in Copenhagen. - Travels to Berlin in the early days after the fall of the Wall.
1989–91	- Stays in New York with the support of the academy, where he works as an assistant to Canadian artist Christian Eckhart.
1993	- Stays in Cologne for a year. - *Beauty*, Galerie Lukas & Hoffmann, Cologne, Germany. - Starts making photographic series that document the Icelandic landscape.
1995	- Receives his degree from the academy. - Founds Studio Olafur Eliasson in Berlin, initially located at Rungestrasse, Berlin.
1996	- Starts working with Einar Thorsteinn, an architect and geometrician as well as a former friend of Buckminster Fuller.
1997	- *Erosion*, intervention as part of *Trade Routes: History and Geography* , 2nd Johannesburg Biennial, South Africa.
1998	- *Green river*, intervention in Bremen, Germany, 1998; Moss, Norway, 1998; The Northern Fjallabak Route, Iceland, 1998; Los Angeles, CA, USA, 1999; Stockholm, Sweden, 2000; and Tokyo, Japan, 2001.
1999	- Wins the third Benesse Prize.
2003	- Moves his studio to a former train depot next to the Hamburger Bahnhof in Berlin. - *The blind pavilion*, Danish Pavilion, 50th La Biennale di Venezia, Italy. - *The weather project*, Tate Modern, London, UK.
2005	- *Your light shadow*, Hara Museum of Contemporary Art, Tokyo, Japan.
2007	- *Serpentine Gallery Pavilion 2007*, collaboration with architect Kjetil Thorsen, commissioned by Serpentine Gallery, London, UK.

2007–10年	- 初の大規模回顧展「Take your time: Olafur Eliasson」がサンフランシスコ近代美術館、ニューヨーク近代美術館等を巡回する。
2008年	- ベルリンのプレンツラウアー・ベルクの旧醸造所にスタジオを移転する。 - パブリックアート・プロジェクト《ニューヨーク・シティ・ウォーターフォールズ》を実施。
2009年	- ベルリン芸術大学教授として空間実験研究所を設立（2014年まで）。 - 個展「オラファー・エリアソン　あなたが出会うとき」金沢21世紀美術館
2010年	- 個展「オラファー・エリアソン　都市の内側と外側」マルティン・グロピウス・バウ（ベルリン）
2011年	- ヘニング・ラーセンが設計するハルパ・コンサートホール（レイキャビク）のファサードをデザインする。 - デンマークのアロス・オーフス美術館に円形の展望台《あなたの虹のパノラマ》を設置。
2012年	- フレデリック・オッテセンと共同でソーシャルビジネス・プロジェクト「リトルサン」を設立。
2014年	- 建築家のセバスチャン・ベーマンと「スタジオ・アザー・スペーシズ」を共同設立。 - グリーンランドの氷を街なかに展示するプロジェクト《アイス・ウォッチ》をコペンハーゲンで実施。パリ（2015年）、ロンドン（2018年）でも実施。
2015年	- 博物館の新しいモデル「国連博物館（UN Live）」を共同設立。
2016年	- 難民支援を目的としたプロジェクト《グリーンライト—アーティスティック・ワークショップ》をティッセン=ボルネミッサ現代美術館（TBA21）と共同で開催。ヴェネチア（2017年）、横浜（2017年）でも開催。
2019年	- 個展「Olafur Eliasson: In real life」テート・モダン（ロンドン）、グッゲンハイム美術館（ビルバオ） 国連開発計画（UNDP）の気候変動とSDGs親善大使に任命される。
2020年	- 個展「オラファー・エリアソン　ときに川は橋となる」展を開催。

略年譜

本年譜はスタジオ・オラファー・エリアソンから提供された資料をもとに編集したものである。(編集:東京都現代美術館)

1967年	-コペンハーゲンに生まれる。父はアーティストであり料理人、母は洋裁師。
1970年代	-幼少期は母とコペンハーゲンで生活しながら、週末や夏休み中はアイスランドで父親と過ごす。
1982年	-コペンハーゲンの小さな画廊で初個展を開催し、風景画を出品。
1983–87年	-ブレイクダンスをはじめる。1984年、2人の友人とブレイクダンスのチームを結成。チームは4年間活動し、スカンジナビアの大会で大賞を2度獲得。
1989年	-デンマーク王立美術アカデミーに入学。 -ベルリンの壁の崩壊直後のベルリンに滞在する。
1989–91年	-アカデミーの支援でニューヨークに滞在し、カナダ出身のアーティストであるクリスチャン・エッカートのアシスタントとして働く。
1993年	-1年間、ケルンに滞在する。 -個展「ビューティー」ギャラリー・ルーカス&ホフマン(ケルン) -アイスランドの自然を撮影した写真のシリーズの制作を始める。
1995年	-デンマーク王立美術アカデミーの学位を取得する。 -スタジオ・オラファー・エリアソンを設立する。ベルリンのルンゲ通りにスタジオを構える。
1996年	-バックミンスター・フラーの友人であった建築家であり幾何学の専門家のアイナー・トースタインがスタジオに参画。
1997年	-《浸食》を第2回ヨハネスブルク・ビエンナーレで実施。
1998年	-《グリーン・リバー》をブレーメン(ドイツ)で実施。モス、ノルウェー(1998年)、アイスランド(1998年)、ロサンゼルス(1999年)、ストックホルム(2000年)、東京(2001年)でも実施。
1999年	-第3回ベネッセ賞を受賞。
2003年	-ベルリンのハンブルガー・バーンホフのすぐ隣にある旧鉄道車庫にスタジオを移転する。 -個展「ブラインド・パビリオン」第50回ヴェネチア・ビエンナーレ、デンマーク館 -個展「ウェザー・プロジェクト」テート・モダン(ロンドン)
2005年	-個展「オラファー エリアソン 影の光」原美術館(東京)
2007年	-サーペンタイン・ギャラリー・パビリオン(ロンドン)をシェティル・トールセンと共同制作。

凡例
・本カタログ未掲載の出品作品には*印を付した。
・作品情報は、作品名、制作年、技法/素材、サイズ、所蔵/提供、掲載頁の順に記載した。

・*refers to exhibited works that are not published in this catalogue.
・The data on each work are listed in the order of title, year, techniques/materials, size, collection/courtesy and pages.

力と思いやりの領分(マインドマップ)
no. 2, 3, 6, 7, 8, 9, 14
Spheres of power and care (mind map) no. 2, 3, 6, 7, 8, 9, 14
2016
水彩、インディアンインク、鉛筆、紙
Watercolour, Indian ink, and pencil on paper
H 40.3×W 47.5 cm
[no. 8 : p. 74、no. 2, 7 : p. 77、no. 3, 6, 9, 14 : 本カタログ未掲載/not published in this catalogue]

力と思いやりの領分(マインドマップ)
no. 5, 10, 11
Spheres of power and care (mind map) no. 5, 10, 11
2016
水彩、鉛筆、紙
Watercolour and pencil on paper
H 40.3×W 47.5 cm
[pp. 75–76]

あなたの移ろう氷河の形態学(過去)
Your passing glacial morphology (past)
2019
水彩、鉛筆、紙
Watercolour and pencil on paper
H 220×W 146×D 8 cm
[pp. 78–79]

メタンの問題
Methane matter
2019
水彩、インディアンインク、鉛筆、紙
Watercolour, Indian ink, and pencil on paper
H 231.6×W 155×D 8 cm
[pp. 78, 80]

あなたの移ろう氷河の形態学(未来)
Your passing glacial morphology (future)
2019
水彩、鉛筆、紙
Watercolour and pencil on paper
H 233×W 155×D 8 cm
[pp. 78, 81]

サステナビリティの研究室
Sustainability research lab
[pp. 82–87]

9つのパブリック・プロジェクトの記録写真
Documentation photographs of nine public projects
デジタル・プリント
Digital prints
H 61×W 85.5 cm/H 85.5×W 61 cm
Courtesy of the artist
[pp. 88–103]

フィヨルドハウス*
*Fjordenhus**
2018
ヴィデオ
Video
7'55"
Copyright Studio Olafur Eliasson
[p. 164に参考図版掲載/see p. 164 for reference]

所蔵/提供の記載のない作品はすべて、作家、neugerriemschneider(ベルリン)、Tanya Bonakdar Gallery(ニューヨーク/ロサンゼルス)の所蔵/提供である。

Unless otherwise stated, all works courtesy of the artist; neugerriemschneider, Berlin; Tanya Bonakdar Gallery, New York/Los Angeles

出品作品リスト
Works in the exhibition

溶ける氷河のシリーズ 1999/2019
The glacier melt series 1999/2019
2019
Cプリント（30点組）
30 C-prints
H 226.6×W 478 cm
[pp. 8–17]

昼と夜の溶岩
Day and night lava
2018
凹面鏡ガラス、ステンレススチール、溶岩石、LED、モーター、塗料（黒、白）、ワイヤ
Concave mirror glass, stainless steel, lava stone, LED, motor, paint (black, white), wire
H 84.5×W 67×D 62 cm
[pp. 18–21]

氷の研究室
Ice lab
Courtesy of the artist
[pp. 22–27]

ときに川は橋となる
Sometimes the river is the bridge
2020
木、プラスチック、スチール、水、LEDライト、塗料（黒、白）、布、ワイヤ、モーター、コントロールユニット
Wood, plastic, steel, water, LED lights, paint (black, white), fabric, wire, motor, control unit
H 960 cm, ø 12 m
[pp. 28–35]

ビューティー
Beauty
1993
スポットライト、水、ノズル、木、ホース、ポンプ
Spotlight, water, nozzles, wood, hose, pump
サイズ可変
Dimensions variable
[pp. 36–39]

あなたのオレンジ色の残像が現われる
Your orange afterimage exposed
2000
スポットライト、調光器、三脚、カラーフィルター（青）
Spotlight, dimmer, tripod, colour filter (blue)
サイズ可変
Dimensions variable
Courtesy of the artist
[pp. 40–41]

あなたに今起きていること、起きたこと、これから起きること
Your happening, has happened, will happen
2020
ハロゲンランプ、カラーエフェクトフィルターガラス（黄、緑、青）、アルミニウム、変圧器
Halogen lamps, colour-effect filter glass (yellow, green, blue), aluminium, transformers
サイズ可変
Dimensions variable
[pp. 42–47]

おそれてる？
Who is afraid
2004
カラーエフェクトフィルターガラス（赤、黄、青）、モーター、HMIランプ、三脚
Colour-effect filter glass (red, yellow, blue), motor, HMI lamp, tripod
サイズ可変
Dimensions variable
Kunstmuseum Wolfsburg, Germany
[pp. 48–53]

人間を超えたレゾネーター
Beyond-human resonator
2019
プリズムガラスリング、カラーエフェクトフィルターガラス（青）、LED、バラスト、ステンレススチール、真鍮、塗料（白）、ケーブル
Prismatic glass ring, colour-effect filter glass (blue), LEDs, ballast, stainless steel, brass, paint (white), cable
D 95 cm, ø 86.5 cm
[pp. 54–57]

太陽の中心への探査
The exploration of the centre of the sun
2017
ステンレススチール、塗料（黒）、カラーエフェクトフィルターガラス（青、緑）、LED電球、太陽光発電ユニット、モーター
Stainless steel, paint (black), colour-effect filter glass (blue, green), LED bulbs, photovoltaic unit, motor
ø 202 cm
Courtesy of the artist and PKM Gallery, Seoul
[pp. 58–61]

サンライト・グラフィティ
Sunlight graffiti
2012
プロジェクター、スクリーン、リトルサン、ヴィデオカメラ、ソフトウェア、タブレットコンピュータ
Video projector, projection screen, Little Sun solar-powered lamps, RealSense video camera, software, tablet computers
サイズ可変
Dimensions variable
[pp. 62–65]

あなたの光の動き*
*Your light movement**
2012
監督・撮影・編集：トマス・ギスラソン
ダンサー：スティーン・カーナー、キャシー"Qミン"グエン・バン、トニア、ロボズィー
Directed, filmed, and edited by Tomas Gislason
Dancers: Steen Koerner, Cathy "QMinh" Nguyen Van, Toniah, Robozee
5'05"

クリティカルゾーンの記憶（ドイツ–ポーランド–ロシア–中国–日本）no. 1–12
Memories from the critical zone (Germany–Poland–Russia–China–Japan, nos. 1–12)
2020
スチール、木、ボールペン、インク（黒）、紙、プラスチック、ボールベアリング、バネ
Steel, wood, ballpoint pen, ink (black), paper, plastic, ball bearings, springs
nos. 1–6: H 82.8×W 82.8×D 3.8 cm, nos. 7–12: H 57.8×W 57.8×D 3.8 cm
[no. 7：p. 68、no. 10：p. 69、no.1：p.70、no. 2：p. 71、nos. 7–12：pp. 72–73、nos. 3–6：本カタログ未掲載／not published in this catalogue]

Photo credits

Martin Argyroglo: p. 91
Iwan Baan: p. 166
Anders Sune Berg: pp. 16–17, 27, 38–39, 91, 161, 164
Jørgen Chemnitz: p. 90
Olafur Eliasson: pp. 8–15, 26, 27, 94–95, 96, 97, 99, 101–103
Joel Chester Fildes: p. 165
Charlie Forgham-Bailey: pp. 88–89, 91
Kazuo Fukunaga: pp. 4–5, 7, 28–37, 40–53, 58–65, 68–73, 78, 82–87, 105
María del Pilar García Ayensa/Studio Olafur Eliasson: pp. 92–93, 98, 99, 100, 159, 163
Group Greenland: p. 90
Yuko Hasegawa: p.168
Frank Haugwitz/Studio Olafur Eliasson: pp. 1–3, 23–25, 151
Matthias Kolb: pp. 74–77
Kuupik V. Kleist/KVK Consult: p. 90
Steven Sebring: pp. 66–67
Tate Photography (Andrew Dunkley & Marcus Leith): p. 160
Markus Tretter: p. 159
Michael Tsegaye: p. 163
Helmut Wieben: p. 97
Hans Wilschut: pp. 154–155
Jens Ziehe: pp. 19–21, 27, 54–57, 79–81
Damir Žižić: p. 163
Unknown photographer: p.119

[Jacket]
Beauty, 1993; Photo: Anders Sune Berg
Memories from the critical zone (Germany–Poland–Russia–China–Japan, nos. 1–12), 2020, detail;
Photo: Kazuo Fukunaga

[Exhibition]

Olafur Eliasson: Sometimes the river is the bridge

Period

14 March–14 June, 2020

Venue

Museum of Contemporary Art Tokyo

Organized by

Museum of Contemporary Art Tokyo
operated by Tokyo Metropolitan Foundation for History and Culture
The Sankei Shimbun

Supported by

Embassy of Iceland, Japan
Royal Danish Embassy

Sponsored by

Kvadrat
Bloomberg L.P.
JINS HOLDINGS Inc.

Grant from

The Scandinavia-Japan Sasakawa Foundation
Obayashi Foundation

Concept

Olafur Eliasson
Yuko Hasegawa (Museum of Contemporary Art Tokyo)
Caroline Eggel (Studio Olafur Eliasson)

Chief Curator of the Exhibition

Yuko Hasegawa

Curator of the Exhibition

Ai Kusumoto (MOT)

Exhibitions Team (SOE)

Caroline Eggel
Dayoung Shin
Patricia Bondesson Kavanagh
Kajana Wagner

Development and Production Team (SOE)

Myriam Thomas
Kerstin Palermo
Brita Jaichner
Christian Uchtmann
Jöran Imholze

Public Relations

Mihoko Nakajima (MOT)
Catriona Collins (SOE)

Technical Support and Installation

Super Factory

Transport and Installation

Yamato Global Logistics Japan Co., Ltd.
Hasenkamp

Sustainability Research Lab

With research and experiments by Studio Olafur Eliasson and innovative materials by the following partners:
Arte 9 Milano
Hoekmine
Kvadrat
Magna Glaskeramik
Studio ThusThat

［展覧会］
オラファー・エリアソン　ときに川は橋となる

会期
2020年3月14日－6月14日

会場
東京都現代美術館

主催
公益財団法人東京都歴史文化財団 東京都現代美術館
産経新聞社

後援
駐日アイスランド大使館
デンマーク王国大使館

協賛
クヴァドラ
ブルームバーグ L.P.
株式会社ジンズホールディングス

助成
スカンジナビア・ニッポン ササカワ財団
公益財団法人大林財団

構成
オラファー・エリアソン
長谷川祐子（東京都現代美術館）
キャロリン・エッゲル（スタジオ・オラファー・エリアソン）

チーフ・キュレーター
長谷川祐子

キュレーター
楠本愛（東京都現代美術館）

広報
中島三保子（東京都現代美術館）
カトリオナ・コリンズ（スタジオ・オラファー・エリアソン）

テクニカルサポート・展示
スーパー・ファクトリー

輸送・展示
ヤマトグローバルロジスティクスジャパン株式会社
ハーゼンカンプ

Olafur Eliasson: Sometimes the river is the bridge

First Edition: April 25, 2020

Supervised by
Museum of Contemporary Art Tokyo

Authors
Olafur Eliasson
Yuko Hasegawa
Timothy Morton

Translators
Gaku Kondo
Darryl Wee
Ai Kusumoto

Editors
Yuko Hasegawa, Kiyoe Shimbata, Ai Kusumoto (MOT)
Kyoko Yabusaki, Momoko Usuda (Film Art Inc.)

Editorial Team (SOE)
Anna Engberg-Pedersen
Geoffrey Garrison
Biljana Joksimović-Große
Kristina Köper
Kathryn Politis
Vajra Spook

Editorial Assistant
Mio Harada (Intern, MOT), Takahide Yoshida

Designer
Kensaku Kato (LABORATORIES)

Printing and binding
iword Co., Ltd.

Publisher
Tetsuro Uehara

Film Art Inc.
21 Arai Building, 1-20-6, Ebisu-minami, Shibuya-ku, Tokyo 150-0022
Tel: +81-(0)3-5725-2001
Fax: +81-(0)3-5725-2626
http://www.filmart.co.jp

Printed in Japan
ISBN978-3-8459-2000-6 C0070

CARBON OFFSET

Paper
Jacket and belly-band: Graphy CoC Crystal white (FSC-certified paper containing more than 20% waste paper pulp.)
Cover: Yuru-chip Sand (100% waste paper which was invented with chip balls mainly composed of used newspapers and magazines.)
Body: b7 bulky (Paper produced at the Nippon Paper Ishinomaki Factory, which was severely damaged by the Great East Japan Earthquake. This paper helps reconstruction of the damaged area.)
In the making of this catalogue, a total of 1.996 tons of CO_2 emissions related to paper production and paper and book transportation have been offset by using paper certified according to J-Credit Scheme (Domestic CDM).

オラファー・エリアソン　ときに川は橋となる

2020年4月25日　初版発行

監修
東京都現代美術館

執筆
オラファー・エリアソン
長谷川祐子
ティモシー・モートン

翻訳
近藤学
ダリル・ヴィー
楠本愛

編集
長谷川祐子、新畑清恵、楠本愛（東京都現代美術館）
薮崎今日子、臼田桃子（フィルムアート社）

編集補助
原田美緒（東京都現代美術館インターン）、吉田崇英

デザイン
加藤賢策（LABORATORIES）

印刷・製本
株式会社アイワード

発行者
上原哲郎

発行所
株式会社フィルムアート社
〒150-0022 東京都渋谷区恵比寿南1-20-6 第21荒井ビル
Tel: 03-5775-2001
Fax: 03-5725-2626
http://www.filmart.co.jp

Printed in Japan
ISBN978-3-8459-2000-6　C0070

CARBON OFFSET

用紙
カバー・帯：グラフィー CoC クリスタルホワイト（古紙パルプ20%以上配合、FSC® 森林認証紙）
表紙：ゆるチップ すな（新聞古紙・雑誌古紙を主体とするチップボールを元に開発された用紙。古紙配合率100%）
本文：b7 バルキー（東日本大震災で被害を受けた日本製紙石巻工場で開発された復興支援商品）
本カタログは、J-クレジット制度が利用可能な用紙を本文に使用することで、二酸化炭素排出量（1.996トン［発行部数分］）をオフセットしています。